OUR HOUSE

A Tribute to Fenway Park

OUR HOUSE

A Tribute to Fenway Park

CURT SMITH

MP
MASTERS PRESS

NTC/Contemporary Publishing Group

Library of Congress Cataloging-in-Publication Data

Smith, Curt.
      Our house : a tribute to Fenway Park / Curt Smith
         p.   cm.
      Includes bibliographical references (p.) and index.
      ISBN 0-8092-2664-2
        1. Fenway Park (Boston, Mass.)—History 2. Boston Red Sox
(Baseball team)—History.   I. Title.
      GV416.B674S55   1999
      796.357'06'874461—dc21   98-54350
                                                    CIP

Cover design by Nick Panos
Cover illustration (Ted Willliams hitting a home run in the final at bat of his
major league career): Bill Purdom, *Splendid Fenway Finale* (detail), 1993.
Copyright © Bill Purdom.
Interior design by Hespenheide Design
All color lithographs of Fenway Park—by William Feldman, Andy Jurinko,
Bill Purdom, and Bill Williams—are published by and reproduced courtesy of:
Bill Goff Inc.
5 Bridge St., P.O. Box 977
Kent, CT 06757
(800) 321-GOFF, (860) 927-1411; fax: (860) 927-1987

Published by Masters Press
A division of NTC/Contemporary Publishing Group, Inc.
4255 West Touhy Avenue, Lincolnwood (Chicago), Illinois 60646-1975 U.S.A.
Copyright © 1999 by Curt Smith
Printed in the United States of America
International Standard Book Number: 0-8092-2664-2
99 00 01 02 03 RRD 19 18 17 16 15 14 13 12 11 10 9 8 7 6 5 4 3 2 1

For the Kid

Other Books by Curt Smith

CONTENTS

FOREWORD

Old baseball parks evoke both high deeds and low comedy. Some salute a name. Say Ebbets Field, and you think of Jackie Robinson — Kauffman Stadium, George Brett — Sportsman's Park, the Man (Stan Musial) whom former Commissioner Ford Frick, dedicating his statue, called "Baseball's perfect warrior. Here stands baseball's perfect knight."

Even positions invite epitaphs. Third base at Forbes Field meant Pie Traynor; center field in the Bronx, Numbers 5 and 7; right field at Ebbets Field, Carl Furillo playing balls off the wall like Jascha Heifetz played a violin. At Fenway Park, left field meant the Kid, the Splendid Splinter, the greatest hitter who ever lived.

The first big-league game I attended was August 30, 1960 — Ted Williams's forty-second birthday, against the Tigers, at Fenway Park. Eleven years earlier, my parents had watched a Red Sox–Indians game at Fenway on their honeymoon. Now, on a night so hot that, as broadcaster Vin Scully said, "The moon got sunburned," I saw on my father's face why Williams became John Wayne in baseball woolies for a generation of Americans.

Years later, I recalled Number 9 pinch-hitting amid waves of noise. Lofted to deep right field, his drive barely missed the bull pen. I took home a charged puzzlement as to Williams's voltage on the crowd. Only retrospect taught that in his day, or should I say my father's, Teddy Ballgame was the greatest menagerie since the Babe — long-limbed like a pelican, elegant as a stallion, and jittery like a colt — save Ruth and Jackie Robinson, the one athlete of this century who corkscrewed into an epic.

"It's his *presence*, that's the word," Williams explained of 1948–50 Sox manager Joe McCarthy. One need not explain Ted's presence to see why headlines raked his path. At bat, he was quick, loose, and striking — to poet Donald Hall, "coiling on himself like a barber pole turning around." Williams threw tantrums, spit at fans, and reviled the press, but was a dazzling interview — also, a pre-recyling conservationist. Said his friend, broadcaster Curt Gowdy: "Where would you find another like him in a million years?"

"In 1955, there were 77,263,127 male American human beings," wrote authors Brendan C. Boyd and Fred C. Harris. "And every one of them in his heart of hearts would have given two arms, a leg, and his collection of Davy Crockett iron-ons to be Teddy Ballgame." Profane, profound, well-spoken, handsome, Williams became a hero to Woody Hayes, John Updike, Bobby Knight, and George Herbert Walker Bush. I have never known anyone so lionized by men, say, now over fifty.

I first met Williams in 1966, as he and Casey Stengel were inducted at Cooperstown. Revisiting the Glimmerglass, T. Ballgame amazed by upstaging the Ol' Perfessor with an acceptance speech — written, longhand, the night before — that many locals still call the finest talk in the sixty years of the Hall of Fame.

Afterward, autograph seekers besieged the Kid — and true to fashion, he rebelled. "You kids pushing me to sign, I'm not gonna. You ought to learn some manners." His roar eclipsed mere voice, and stunned them into silence. "You know who I'm going to sign? The kids at the outside of the circle who aren't rude," and jostling pens and paper, he pushed his way toward me. Hooked from there to eternity, I have never forgotten the honest outrage of this part-Gibraltar and part-child.

One night in March 1991 I went to a restaurant in Alexandria, Virginia, saw a Cadillac license plate, "BOSOX-9," and waited a half hour to meet the admirer. It recalled for me June 1990, when Williams was rumored to receive (and would have, except for surgery) the Medal of Freedom — America's highest civilian award. Reports of the honor swept the White House like sightings on the anniversary of Elvis's death.

Waiting for Williams finally ended on July 9, 1991, when President Bush saluted him and Joe DiMaggio for their 1941 daybook — DiMag's fifty-six-game hitting streak, the Splinter's grand .406. Marveling at middle-aged West Wing aides turned teeny/Teddy-boppers, one presidential assistant shook his head. "They're like parishioners," he said, "hoping to meet the Pope."

With Ted Williams, one could become excited to almost a ridiculous extent. In 1960, he batted .316 and smashed twenty-nine home runs and, at forty-two, declined to tip his cap. He also exited as only a deity could — with a home run, number 521, in his final time at bat.

"And now Boston knows," wrote Ed Linn, "how England felt when it lost India." Hope that Gibraltar tumbles and, yes, the Rockies crumble before New England loses Fenway Park.

Imagine two strangers marooned on a South Sea isle from Providence, Rhode Island, and Presque Isle, Maine. They differ in age, race, career, and religion. Their common denominator is the Boston Red Sox.

The Red Sox won five of baseball's first fifteen World Series—but none since 1918, the year that the Twenty-sixth Division entered France. (Its moniker was the Yankee Division: who claims the military lacks a sense of humor?) Extremes unite the Olde Towne Team. Ted Williams and Don Buddin. Carl Yastrzemski and Pumpsie Green. Roger Clemens and Bob Stanley. Years that ring like chimes—1946, 1948–49, 1967, 1975, 1977–78, 1986.

"Hell," says ex-manager Don Zimmer, who should know, "the record speaks for itself." No club has mixed more ghosts and giants of the past. Few became more a parish team, or baseball's Old Man of the Sea. From Babe Ruth through Joe Cronin via Billy Rohr to Yaz, the Sox have been defined by their domicile—"New England's nightclub," Curt Gowdy calls it. For generations, going to Fenway Park has meant coming home.

One day in December 1988, I visited then–National League President A. Bartlett Giamatti at his New York office. Admitting to the state of Red Sox fan, I asked whether that bespoke masochism or loyalty. Giamatti sat back and roared his teddy bear of a laugh. "No question," said the longtime resident of Red Sox Nation. "Clearly, it speaks of both." He was right, of course.

In 1948, Giamatti's father took him at age ten hand-in-hand to Fenway for the first time. "As I grew up," he later wrote, "I knew that as a building it was on the level of Mount Olympus, the Pyramid at Giza, the nation's capital, the czar's Winter Palace, and the Louvre—except, of course, that it was better than all those inconsequential places."

If the Red Sox 'r' us, Fenway Park is the Red Sox. Take Texas. Its spiritual core is—what?—Houston or the Alamo. Consider the mid- and deep South. Its crucible might be Stone Mountain or Disney World. In Needham or New Haven, such doubt would be as unlikely as Dick Stuart snaring a ground ball. In the evaluating and rubbing together of the American Century, the Sox have owned a diocese's sensibility. New England's core is its baseball cabaret.

Fenway Park opened—as Jack Paar would say, "I kid you not"—the week that the *Titanic* sank: since 1912, a jut-jawed jewel at the union of Lansdowne and Jersey Streets. John Updike dubbed it "a lyric little bandbox of a park"; Clark Booth, a Boston television anchor, "baseball's basilica." Its lure fuses, among other things, a lyric field design, hand-operated scoreboard, odd quirks, eccentric angles, low fences, schizophrenic wind, slanting shadows, seats up close to the field, and a *nonpareil* view—also, a left-field wall topped by a twenty-three-foot screen. Smiling wryly, the Green Monster muffles pitchers with a blanket of gloom—oft-scarred, star-crossed, and ultimately beloved.

A Dublin ballad says, "Being Irish means laughing at life knowing that in the end, life will break your heart." A *region's* heart will break if the Red Sox leave Fenway. In 1999, hoping to compete in today's luxury-suite, corporate-boxed Klondike of an age, the team vowed to build a larger nearby park. Others point to the friendly confines of born-in-1914 Wrigley Field. The Cubs do not intend to leave its bleachers, real grass, and blaze of color. Why should New England's prosopopoeia?

Forget tomorrow (the Red Sox have often seemed to). More than any park, Fenway stirs the tender ear of memory. To retrieve it, this book recalls how the Red Sox have bound generations from Long Island Sound through northern New Hampshire to the tip of easternmost New Brunswick.

Here is the place where nearby Kenmore Square empties pilgrims by foot, car, and subway. Here are essays by extended members of the Red Sox family: the *Boston Globe's* Marty Nolan; ESPN Television's Peter Gammons; authors Updike, Doris Kearns Goodwin, and Beth Hinchliffe; announcers Ned Martin and current voice Joe Castiglione; the late A. Bartlett Giamatti; and former President George Bush.

Here are photographs of Fenway from a given day—to be precise, July 4, 1998, the Red Sox versus the Chicago White Sox—from before gates open to past their close. Enjoy the wizened fan, wide-eyed doyen, and vendor hawking peanuts. Share batting practice, pepper games, mileposts from the Triangle to the Citgo sign, and groundskeepers tilling the pitching mound for Pedro Martinez — or was it Mel Parnell or Smoky Joe Wood? Here you will see Fenway between and beyond the lines — and why embracing it is as natural as a smile.

Here is the story of Boston baseball — above all, its Xanadu of personality. "We went through the tunnel," Giamatti said of that first game at Fenway Park, "and there was emerald grass and bases whiter than I'd ever seen. It was a coming of age." So it is since China became a republic, Zane Grey published *Riders of the Purple Sage*, and the Sox played their first game at then–24 Jersey Street on April 20, 1912.

"To mention one is to mean the other," 1961–92 radio/TV voice Martin says of Fenway and its proprietor. "Over the years, you remember the ups and downs, but above all the excitement of this boundless, confounded team. Remember them and weep, or laugh, or sing. And wrap yourself in this Red Sox thing."

Is Fenway doomed, or timeless? Either way, it turns us toward baseball like a heliotrope turns toward the sun. Call it passé, or sacrosanct. Call it baseball's Bali Ha'i. Its name is Fenway Park. Above all, call it ours.

ACKNOWLEDGMENTS

Like baseball, the Red Sox hearth is a peculiarly American institution. Many people helped bring its essence to *Our House: A Tribute to Fenway Park*.

A number of writers were most helpful—notably, David Chase, Leo Egan, Peter Gammons, Jim Mandelaro, Marty Nolan, Scott Pitoniak, Rob Rains, and Bill Schulz. Many broadcasters contributed facts and recollections: I especially want to thank Joe Castiglione, Ken Coleman, Curt Gowdy, Ned Martin, Sean McDonough, Dick Stockton, and the late Jim Woods.

Shakespeare wrote in *Love's Labour Lost* of "the heavenly rhetoric of thine eye." Fenway's eye is evinced by the photos of Bill Polo, Cindy Loo, and Beth Hinchliffe. The lithographs of Bill Goff Inc. and artists William Feldman, Andy Jurinko, Bill Purdom, and Bill Williams show a park chockablock with charm.

I am also grateful to Red Sox vice president of public affairs Dick Bresciani; vice president of broadcasting and technology Jim Healy; publications manager Debra Matson; director of communications and baseball information Kevin Shea; and customer relations manager Ann Marie C. Starzyk.

Ken Samelson, a Mets fan who, like me, will never forget 1986, edited this manuscript with insight and care. Bob Orlando transcribed taped stories. My wife, Sarah, and literary agent, Bobbe Siegel, came to learn why Red Sox Nation is a state of place, and hope—and Fenway a cube of the Nation's mind.

As always, the Baseball Hall of Fame in Cooperstown provided surpassing help. I am particularly thankful to former president Donald

Marr Jr.; vice president Frank Simeo; John Ralph, director of communication and programs; librarian Jim Gates; senior researchers Bruce Markusen and Scot Mondore; researcher Jill Renwick; Pat Kelly, director of the photo collection; and Helen Stiles, of the technical services department—and pleased that the Hall will receive a portion of the proceeds from this book.

Willa Cather wrote, "A book is made with one's own flesh and blood of years. It is cremated youth." Reviewing bits and pieces of Fenway's years, the above were generous with their time and aid—and I cannot help but be generous in my gratitude toward them.

OUR HOUSE

A Tribute to Fenway Park

"My house, my house, though thou art small,
thou art to me the Escurial."

—George Herbert

Beginnings
Early Boston Baseball

To many, baseball's classic parks are sport's holy sites—the kindly lights that led. Their age began in 1909, with the opening of Forbes Field and Shibe Park, crested in 1923 at Yankee Stadium, and begot Comiskey Park (1910), League Park ('10), Griffith Stadium ('11), the Polo Grounds ('11), Crosley Field ('12), Navin Field ('12), Ebbets Field ('13), Wrigley Field ('14), Braves Field ('15), and Fenway Park. Looking back, the effect turned heads.

At the time, these idiosyncratic, largely downtown, mainly steel, often reinforced concrete parks seemed the fiercest compulsion in the land. Their birth, however, was indigent, not immaculate. "The most ignored parks in history are sites *before* the Wrigleys and Ebbets Fields!" the late Hall of Fame historian Lee Allen observed of preclassic parks— to be approximate, those built between the Civil War and about 1910. "If we don't *love* them it's because we don't *know* them." Unlike Fenway, they leave little to our imagination—lacking reputation, frame of reference, and fixed sense of place.

The Greeks are said to have invented the first major grandstand for a sporting event. "In fact," said Allen, "their name for a footrace watched by spectators developed into *stadium*." The age near the start of organized major-league ball—May 4, 1871, Hamilton Field, Ft. Wayne, Indiana, before two hundred fans on the Jail House Flats: host Kekiongas 2, Forest City of Cleveland 0—flaunted fewer stadia than fields and parks and bowls. Their Olympus was intimacy; you were right on the field.

Fields like Brooklyn's Union Park and Philadelphia's Jefferson Street Grounds linked insects, cow dung, potholed infields, a single deck, small wooden bleachers, and vast outfield terrain: like admission fees, fences later mixed necessity and afterthought.

"Typically," Allen affirmed, "the parks were built in stages."

"Patchwork jobs?" I asked.

"Absolutely," he said. Each of these less-Yankee-Stadium-than-*State-Farm*-on-parade parks buoyed baseball's rise from footnote to centerpiece. The game as we know it began then, and there.

Boston baseball began, three decades pre-Red Sox, with the Red Stockings, an 1871 charter member of the National Association. Yearly, the Sox test loyalty. From '71 to '75, Harry Wright's Red Stockings rewarded it with pennants. In 1876, the N.A. dissolved into the National League of Professional Baseball Clubs. It buoyed an age in which, as John Connally once said of the Vietnam/student protest/sexual revolution early 1970s, "Everything about it was big!"

In a century, America had turned from wilderness to settlements, agrarian to manufacturing, states' rights to United States. The number of states had leapt from thirteen to thirty-eight; population from 2.5 million to 46 million; area from 889,000 square miles to 3 million. Limits seemed, well, so un-American. "People here are far less raw and provincial than their fathers," said *The Nation* of America at age one hundred. "They have seen more . . . read more . . . mixed more with people of other nationalities, thought more and had to think more . . . spent more for ideas and given more away."

By 1876, almost one in five Americans was foreign-born. Cities exploded in the postwar industrial boom—Boston to nearly 400,000 people; New York, more than 1.9 million—but nearly 80 percent still lived on farms or in towns that relied on agriculture. A land boom hit the Dakotas. Alaska hailed its first major gold strike. The Sioux War sired the defeat of Sitting Bull and Crazy Horse. From 1865 to 1901, total national income quadrupled. America's umbilical cord was railroads— by 1880, 93,262 miles of line. Aptly, Boston's South End Grounds—a.k.a. Boston Baseball, Union Baseball, or Walpole Street Grounds— anchored railroad lines that led to Hartford and Providence. It needed a new tenant, and found it in the National League charter Red Caps.

On April 29, 1876, the Caps uncorked their first game—a 3–2 ten-inning loss to Hartford. A year later, Arthur Soden bought the club: "Common sense," he said, "tells me that baseball is played primarily to make a profit." Later, Red Sox fans knew sportsman/owner Thomas A. Yawkey. Even from afar, he was a friend of ours. Arthur Soden was no Tom Yawkey. Soden owned the future Beaneaters and Braves through 1906. (Boston owned them until '53, one of two NL charter teams continuously active.) The Red Caps won pennants in 1877, '78, and '83. A half century later, politicians chimed, "Prosperity is just around the corner." Soden's led him to expand the site on Tremont Street—his first of six renovations. In 1960, Ted Williams preceded his final game by tarring "the knights of the keyboard." He would have liked how Soden tore out the press box to increase capacity, making writers something to take or leave.

Like Williams, pre-Fenway Boston mixed good, bad and ugly. *Good*, as in the Impossible Dream: the Braves won flags in 1891, '92, '93, '97, and '98. From 1900 to 1909, pitcher Charles (Kid) Nichols won 297 games, including thirty or more seven straight years. South End Grounds II fused a twin-spiraled roof, 6,800-seat grandstand, and Sullivan Tower, beyond the right-field fence, where one could gape for free. "Unlike Soden, they didn't worry about profit," the late Hall of Fame librarian Jack Redding chuckled. "They dared him, 'You raise the wall, and we'll raise the tower.' Soden did, and so did they."

Bad, as in, say, post-July 1978. At Fenway, marijuana often tars the bleachers. On May 15, 1894, fire did, though fans doubted its verity. Scoffing "Play ball!" as Boston hit in the third inning, they recanted as seats began to burn. Some fled through a hole in the center-field fence. The nearby area was less immune than the park. Lost: 13 brick and 164 wooden buildings, $500,000 to $1 million damage, and one thousand families homeless. Wrecked: the Braves' tiara of a park. Revealed: South End Grounds II was valued at more than $75,000, but insured for barely half.

Ugly, as in October 1972, September 1974, or 1986 Game Six: For two months, the 'Eaters played at Dartmouth, or Congress Street, Grounds. (On May 30, 1894, Bobby Lowe whacked a big-league-first four homers in a single game.) They returned to rebuilt South End Grounds III on July 20, and found it downsized with insurance money: suddenly, baseball's Ritz had become sport's Dead-End Kid.

"What irony!" said ex–*Boston Herald* writer Leo Egan of the new Grounds' one deck, puny foul lines, right-field incline, cigar factory beyond the bank, and sheep meadow of a center field. Small and cramped, the Grounds III exuded limits. By contrast, infinite were the 1914 "Miracle Braves." On September 7, they moved to larger Fenway Park, won the pennant, and played the World Series in the Red Sox new steel-and-concrete home.

We will come shortly to the Sox' bandbox plot (and how a trip there today seems akin to touring Lourdes). For now, visit the Braves' first truly big-league household, hard by the tracks of the Boston and Maine.

"For years, the Braves had owned Boston," recalled 1966–74 and 1979–89 Sox broadcaster Ken Coleman, born eight miles from Fenway Park. "After Fenway opened, they struggled as distant number two."

"Their solution," I said, "aped today."

"Yep," he said. "When in trouble, build a park"—which they did in 1915, rooming most of the year at Fenway Park. On August 11, 1914, the Braves closed South End Grounds by tying Cincinnati, 0–0, in thirteen innings. August 18, 1915, augured better things for Boston's baseball diaspora: Boston 4, St. Louis 3, in the first game at Braves Field.

The new den at Commonwealth Avenue, on the former site of the Allston Golf Club, featured a single-deck, covered grandstand behind home plate and along the baselines; uncovered pavilions to the foul side of left and right field; a small right-field bleacher area (the "jury box," as in twelve men); a modest ten-foot wall around the park; and an immodest seating capacity (baseball's largest, forty thousand). Foul lines approached a short taxi ride—402 feet from home plate. Center field paralleled the lot's farthest edge—550 feet away.

"Forget Murderers' Row," said Jack Redding. It took twenty-one games for a batter—the Cardinals' Walt Cruise—to clear Braves Field's concrete wall. In the 1916 World Series, the wanting-to-sell-more-tickets Sox traded Fenway for Boston's now-larger park: three Game Two runs scored in fourteen innings. On May 1, 1920, darkness spun a 1–1 Boston-Brooklyn tie after twenty-six innings. Offense passed "go" only when the '27 Braves installed an interior fence. It is no trick to observe that normally rivals had the edge.

"For years," said Til Ferdenzi, an Ashland, Massachusetts, native and former *New York Journal American* reporter, "the Braves entered April full of hope and found calamity." Six times Boston's 1925–38 Nationals placed seventh or last. In 1935, they won 39, lost 115, and drew barely three thousand per date to their anti-dollhouse of a hearth. Self-abasement draped even future Hall of Famers. Casey Stengel managed four straight (1939–42) seventh-place teams. Rabbit Maranville—to writer Tom Meany, "a midget with the arms and shoulders of a weight lifter"—joined the Braves at age twenty and played twenty-three years and 2,620 games. Boston heightened his boozer's bent. "There is much less drinking now than there was in 1927," Maranville said in 1929. "I know because I quit drinking on May 24, 1927." Despairing, most fans were not as blest.

From 1935 to 1945, the Braves brooked the second division. Then, in 1948, third baseman and '47 MVP Bob Elliott, Tommy Holmes, Eddie Stanky (traded by the Dodgers), and Alvin Dark (Rookie of the Year) fielded and hit effectually; Warren Spahn and Johnny Sain won forty games between them ("Spahn and Sain," the jingle went, "and pray for rain"); and the Braves greeted their first World Series in thirty-four years. In 1951, Holmes replaced Billy Southworth as Boston manager. The next year, drawing so badly that "We were playing to the grounds help," Charlie Grimm succeeded Holmes.

On March 18, 1953, the Braves of Boston since 1876 fled anonymity in the Athens of America to briefly bathe in Wisconsin's love. The '50s Braves rafted down a river of handclapping that overlapped Wisconsin, Upper Michigan, and parts of Minnesota, Illinois, and Iowa. In their first seven years, the ex-Bostons won two pennants, narrowly missed two more, set a National League single-season attendance record, and regularly enjoyed paid admissions in excess of 2 million per year. The Braves sold out night after night. One writer called County Stadium "an insane asylum with bases." In particular, its Golconda crazed Brooklyn owner Walter O'Malley.

The Braves were the first big-league franchise to change cities in half a century; their success led others to follow the wagon train. Homesteaders included O'Malley's Dodgers, the San Francisco Giants, Milwaukee Brewers, Texas Rangers, and *Atlanta* Braves. Today, Nickerson (née Braves) Field, owned by Boston University, waves a sleepy hello to yesterday. Few save the grounds help watch its minor sports on artificial turf at a place that once housed the National League Baseball Club of Boston, Massachusetts.

Memento mori.

2

Yesterday Once More
The Pre-Fenway Sox

It is possible, if picaresque, to trace each major-league team from birth to the present. Take the Orioles. (Sadly, Peter Angelos already has.) Their roots grew from Milwaukee's Lloyd Street Grounds (1900–01) by way of Sportsman's Park in St. Louis (1902–53) to Baltimore's Memorial Stadium (1954–91) and Camden Yards (1992–). Try the Reds on. (Save Marge Schott, one size fits all.) Their genealogy binds Avenue Grounds (1876–77), Bank Street Grounds (1880 and '82–83), League Park (1884–1901), Redland Field (1902–11), Crosley Field (1912–70), and Cinergy Field née Riverfront Stadium (1970–). "How do you get there from here?" actress Shirley MacLaine asked in her biography. If it's good enough for her, well, you get the idea. Continuum counts.

By foil, the Red Sox' road to today is straighter than a Cal Koonce curve. Now: a cachet as civic ministry. "Only two things count in Boston," former U.S. Speaker of the House of Representatives Tip O'Neill said. "Politics and the Red Sox." Then: an early-1900s stab to keep the Braves from gripping the upper hand. In 1889, Rutherford Hayes exclaimed, "If a Napoleon ever became president, he could make the executive almost what he wished to make it." A decade later, William McKinley was president, x-rays were discovered, and what baseball's newest big league wanted was to dent the older National.

In 1901, the minor Western League became the major American and planted outposts in Baltimore, Boston, Cleveland, Detroit, Milwaukee, Philadelphia, St. Louis, and Washington. Ironically, AL President Ban Johnson didn't want a franchise in Boston. He changed his mind on learning that the NL wanted to revive the American Association, make *it* the second major league, and put a team in the Hub. "They were trying to keep the AL out of here," said Lee Allen. "It's amazing what competition will do."

Quickly, Johnson moved his proposed Buffalo franchise to Boston. He found an owner: Charles Somers of coal, lumber, and shipping. Then, a park: Boston's charter Pilgrims (or Puritans, Americans, Plymouth Rocks, Somersets, or reviewing the century, the massively ironic Speed Boys) debuted at a nine-thousand-seat grounds on Huntington Avenue owned by the New Haven Railroad, that had a toolshed in play, popgun right field (280 feet from home plate), other un-Fenway distances (left-center and center field, 440 and 635! feet away), and whose ribbon of reminiscence includes a Cyclone, the Gray Eagle, and first-ever Oktoberfest.

Pilgrims' progress bared early cleavage. Hallo to 1905, '06, '07, and '11's second division. At the other end, '01's Denton True Young—or Cyclone, in deference to his fastball—had league-bests in earned run average (1.62), strikeouts (158), shutouts (five), and wins (33–10). Young knew where the plate was, walking only thirty-seven in 371 innings, and had a bent for precedent. On April 26 and May 8, respectively, he started the Pilgrims' first game (versus Baltimore's "Iron Man" Joe McGinnity: Orioles 10, Boston 6) and the Huntington Avenue inaugural (Pilgrims 10, A's 4). Cy also benefited from Somers's wealth, which gave Boston a deep and abiding leverage.

From Cleveland via St. Louis came Young and catcher Lou Criger. Next, Somers fixed Beaneaters pitcher Bill Dinneen in his crosshairs. "Big Bill" hesitated: "Cy was the best in the game," he later said. "If the new league folded, he still would have been OK, but what about me? I'd have been in trouble." By and by Dinneen joined Hessians like shortstop Fred Parent, second baseman Hobe Ferris, and Beaneaters outfielders Chick Stahl and Buck Freeman at Huntington Avenue. "The triumvirate [the group that owned Boston's NLers] don't like to pay the players much," Stahl mused. Somers, who didn't, did.

"People say money is important today," Jack Redding observed in 1985. "The Red Sox are lucky that it was in the early century, too."

In 1902, the Pilgrams' El Dorado of a cooperative tripled the Braves' attendance. Young tossed a still-Sox record twelve straight victories. Freeman hit in twenty-six consecutive games, and nineteen or more triples for the first of three straight years. A year later, Boston became the capital of baseball. Its player/manager was ex-Beaneaters third baseman Jimmy Collins, who enslaved ground balls like a centurion. He also baptized what became, if not a Beulahland, exactly, a folk-passion symbol of the American Century: the World Series—crowed flacks, "our greatest sports spectacle." From a distance, can we divine the extempore action present at its creation? We can.

In 1903, Somers sold the Pilgrims to Milwaukee lawyer Henry Killilea. His team soon showed that flush, it could be hard. On Opening Day, A's manager Connie Mack started alcoholic Rube Waddell. "Boys," Collins told his players, "the Rube has just come off a tremendous bender. We're going to bunt the hell out of him—run his ass all over the park." The Pilgrims sailed, 9–4, and christened their Mayflower of a team. Patsy Dougherty hit .331. Freeman became the first Pilgrim to hit for the cycle, and clubbed thirteen homers and 104 runs batted in to lead the league. Boston flaunted three twenty-game winners (Young 28–9, Dinneen 21–13, and Tom Hughes 21–7), won its first of twenty straight games versus Washington, and lapped second-place Philadelphia by 14½ games.

Winning runaway pennants, Killilea and Pirates owner Barney Dreyfus prophesied Peggy Lee: "Is that all there is?" Their reply: a best five-of-nine game series to decide the world's champion. "We can beat Pittsburgh no matter how good [Honus] Wagner is," shrilled patrons at Boston's McGreevey's saloon. Its owner's intuitions were in tune. "Enough said," McGreevey said, lifting his arm in certainty. His sobriquet became "Nuff Ced," his saloon the envy of all Boston businessmen. Its fan club—the Royal Rooters—traded taunts, inhaled balls and strikes, and sang for a glad hand and a drink. Often, Young joined them for a rye whiskey called Cascade at the Hotel Putnam on Huntington Avenue.

"Honus, why do you hit so badly," Rooters jeered to the tune of "Tessie" in October 1903. "Take a back seat and sit down. Honus, at bat you look so sadly. Hey, why don't you get out of town." The Rooters were beery, working-class, and slightly déclassé. They especially toasted the '03 Fall Classic, which merited its name. "Young was thought," wrote Grantland Rice of the Sox all-time leader in complete games, wins, and losses, "the greatest of all pitchers." From 1901 to 1904, Cy won 119 games and completed 153. From 1901 to 1908, he won twenty or more sets in six of eight years. Five times, Young pitched 341 or more innings. In 1904 and 1908, he no-hit the A's and Highlanders, respectively. The Pirates were unawed. "Who are they going to beat us with—that farmer?" one jeered. "We chased him out of town. Or Dinneen? He never beat us when he was with the Beaneaters."

Now thirty-six, Cy threw the first-ever Series pitch. The future Red Sox lost three of the first four games—then, in stunning role reversal, turned tomorrow on its head. Before Game Five, Pittsburghers gave McGreevey an umbrella. "You'll need this to ward off our base hits." He replied, "We may make a few of our own, don't you know," and danced on the Boston dugout. The 11–2 Young victory whipsawed the Classic. Wagner hit .222, Dinneen threw three complete games, and Boston won, five sets to three. At age two, the norm of Red Sox baseball was the Hub's sun, moon, and stars.

In 1978, Bucky Dent hoisted a windblown fly ball into Fenway's screen to score three runs and prepare the way for a 5–4 Yankees triumph, winning a playoff for the Eastern Division title. In 1904, the Pilgrims and Highlanders trooped to New York's Hilltop Park between 165th and 168th Streets to decide *that* pennant on the final day. The result inversely foretold Bob Stanley, Rich Gedman, and Mookie Wilson: Jack Chesbro had won forty-one games for New York, but wild-pitched Boston's Lou Criger home with the winning run.

Tip O'Neill laughed in his gravelly, whiskied voice. "And that was just a part of the year," the late Sox fan recalled eight decades later. "Think of what went before." In 1903–04, the Lumiere brothers produced the first photographic plates. The Wright brothers flew successfully. The first trans-Pacific cable was completed. Secured: Panama's independence, presaging the canal. Published: Jack London's *Call of the Wild* and Henry James's *The Ambassadors*. Elected: Theodore Roosevelt, as president, hailing "the strenuous life." TR trust-busted, strike-mediated, and could not abide being pygmy in any way. His sons called him "the old lion"; a British visitor, a mixture "of St. Vitus and St. Paul."

These writhings interested much of Boston. In 1904, *Globe* owner General Charles Taylor bought the Pilgrims for son John. *That* transfixed. On April 19, a Pilgrims Patriots Day doubleheader packed 36,034 into the Huntington Avenue Park. The Beaneaters that day drew 5,667. Among them, Young, Dinneen, and Jesse Tannehill won seventy games. Stahl's twenty-two triples led the league. The Pilgrims won the pennant by 1½ games.

Such a year deserved a coda, and got it with a historic first. To John McGraw, manager of the NL champion Giants, the American League was "bush, a joke. We don't play minor leaguers," said Little Napoleon, refusing to stage the Series. In response, *The Sporting News* pronounced the Pilgrims "world champions by default." Where was "Baseball's Bible" in 1946, '67, '75, and '86?

In time, Soxaphiles became cast as hoping for the best, expecting the worst, their open veins bleeding, and carting history's baggage. Not at pre–Fenway Park. History lay out ahead of them, like a day right behind the rain. In 1907, at nineteen, center fielder Tristram Speaker— "the Gray Eagle"—arrived in Boston from Hubbard, Texas. Like his nation-state, Tris aired everywhere a sense of impatience with limits of any kind.

Speaker brought what he knew as a restless boy to a world beyond his imaginings. He flung throws like an arrow, stung the ball with insolence, and made four unassisted triple plays—a record for an outfielder. Among Tris's untrivia: 3,515 hits, including an all-time best of 793 doubles; a still-league-high thirty-five assists in 1909 and '12; and a .345 lifetime average. He played "a kind of baseball that none of us had ever seen before—throwing and running and hitting at something close to the level of absolute perfection, playing to win but also . . . as if it were a form of punishment for everyone else on the field." Writing of Roberto Clemente, Roger Angell could have meant Speaker, too.

In 1910, Ray Collins and Joe Wood, respectively, twirled 1.62 and 1.68 ERAs. Jake Stahl's ten homers led the league. Longevity became a pillar: earlier, Freeman, Candy LaChance, and Freddy Parent played in 413 or more straight games. Still, hints arose that this franchise might be, uh, a tad more byzantine than most. The early Grounds hosted Bill Cody's Wild West Show. Sniffed "Nuff Ced" McGreevey: "Who's going to play second base, Sitting Bull?" Even the Gray Eagle was not infallible. In 1911, pitcher Ed Karger threw a pitch that the A's Stuffy McGinnis lined to right field. Thinking it a warm-up toss, Speaker failed to chase it. McGinnis completed an inside-the-park home run.

Today, play-by-play ferries past small shops and gas stations and back-yards in Red Sox Nation. Far from Boston, you can drive by front stoops and stop at traffic lights and not miss a pitch. Nearer Fenway, Collins and Dinneen and Speaker buoy the Sox' ex-site at the indoor athletic facility of Northeastern University. Visiting, you sense little of any current niche as baseball's Heartbreak Kids.

A plaque marks the old right-field foul pole—and World Series Exhibit Room, in the Cabot Cage, the 1901–'11 AL age. Nearby, Tufts Medical College looms behind what was once third base. Presaging Jim Lonborg's knee, Jose Santiago's arm, and Butch Hobson's elbow, leave it to the Red Sox to arrange emergency care.

3

Pastures of Plenty
1912–18

I first met Fenway Park over a Montpelier, Vermont, affiliate on the Red Sox Radio Network as my family drove toward Nova Scotia in August 1960. The Townies were hosting New York, and from Albany eastward I heard broadcaster Mel Allen record the early innings on the Home of Champions Network. By Worcester, static blurred his voice. Turning the dial, I found another voice—the Sox' Curt Gowdy, who etched names like Runnels, Casale, Monbouquette, and Tasby and transported me to the coast of Maine.

Thus began my tie to the avatars and asterisks of New England's household team. Was there a better outfield *anywhere* than the 1950s trio of Ted Williams, Jim Piersall, and Jackie Jensen? ("No," agreed the shoe salesman in Nashua, New Hampshire, "but as usual, it's not enough.") Was this the year Tom Brewer and Frank Sullivan untangled the Bosox pitching staff? ("Maybe," cried the Cape Cod vacationer, swizzling his Narragansett, "but who's this Pumpsie Green, and how do we unload him?") Would the Red Sox land a decent stopper, or break .500 away from Fenway? Could skipper Pinky Higgins (or Billy Jurges or Billy Herman) inspire the Boston regulars—or Sox starters challenge the hated Yanks? Would Don Buddin, fielding a ball at shortstop, *ever* manage not to heave it into the box seats beyond first base?

Why did Felix Mantilla greet ground balls like lepers at a bazaar? Could gangling Dick Stuart, jibed a '60s adage, even pick up a hot-dog wrapper without dropping it? Amid grinding teeth, other queries took a swing. When would the Red Sox steal a base? When would the bull pen not self-immolate? Was this the Biblical season when Williams,

Jensen, Billy Goodman, and Frank Malzone—the Bostons sterling heart—got even a shroud of a supporting cast? ("Sure," said Berkshire residents, "the same year Vermont goes Democratic.") What *was* it with these guys? In Calvinist New England, did the Red Sox disprove "life after death," or invert it?

Return with us now to a time pre–Don Schwall and Galen Cisco and Dom DiMaggio and even Babe Ruth. I am here to tell you: Doctors Mishap and Malady did not always pay house calls on New England's baseball public.

The *New York Times*' William Safire once likened Richard Nixon to a layer cake. To know him, the columnist said, you must sample each layer. Ballparks, too, have evolved through stages. The newest: baseball's "old new park" layer, born April 6, 1992, at Camden Yards in Baltimore. Already stale: the oval or circular multipurpose layer—circa 1960–90—first baked at Candlestick Park. Allegedly, its huge stadia would feed many sports; in fact, they satisfied none. By contrast, the delicious 1909–23 steel-and-concrete layer still dominates the platform of current memory. Only three of its fourteen parks remain: Fenway Park, Wrigley Field, and, until the year 2000, Tiger Stadium. Yankee Stadium doesn't count: In 1974–75, it was remade into a grotesquerie.

A writer was once asked what he would take if his house were on fire and he could remove only one thing. He replied: "I would take the *fire*." Wooden pre-Fenway sites lacked an extinguisher. From 1894 to 1896, flames strafed or wrecked National League parks in Baltimore, Boston, Chicago, Louisville, and Philadelphia. In 1911, the Polo Grounds and Washington's National Park became matching pyres. A year later, the Red Sox moved Huntington Avenue's infield grass one mile to the north and west and welcomed their own steel-and-concrete park. First game: April 20, 1912. Pitcher/batter: Boston's Buck O'Brien and New York's Guy Zinn. Score: Sox 7, Highlanders 6. Star: Tris Speaker, driving in the winning run. A crowd of twenty-seven thousand dotted Fenway's grandstand and wooden wings flanking the foul lines beyond the infield.

Even then, baseball was not, as some reminisce, America's glad tidings to Zion. It is not—never was—as winsome as Lassie, pervasive as television's *Gunsmoke*, or resplendent as Rodeo Drive. It is, though, in a unique and treasured way, our richest cultural bequest—older than Broadway; less brooding than Faulkner; less regional than the Grand Ole Opry; more populist than the grand Walt Disney. Its lure bloomed amid Fenway Park's alchemy of look, sound, and feel.

Later, Sox baseball often came to mean sadness, memory, and evenings in the rain. Fenway's entrée was of a different bent—mixing sunshine, pride, and jolt of throw and slide. A fan could now board a trolley and, smacking nonchalance, open a two-story drawer of oaken seats and overhung roof and jigsaw of an outfield fence. From Jamaica via Swampscott through Salem to Newton Center, Fenway spurred a smugness in the Hub's behavior to outsiders and to itself.

"Jesus, it was about time," boomed the Splendid Splinter in 1972. "Finally, a park worthy of the town!" From his view Boston would never wander far away.

There is no mystery to why Fenway corkscrewed into Boston's baseball temple. First, shape: like most early parks, it abutted nearby streets— here, Lansdowne and Jersey—which, in turn, decreed outfield acreage. Watching, you trod a Khyber Pass of nook, intrigue, and cranny.

"I went there as a kid," observed Tip O'Neill, who found it exquisitely second-guessable. "You never knew what would happen—pop-fly homers down the lines, a ball ricocheting off the wall, or bouncing off the [left-field] door. Center field, whoa. A guy could make a circus catch—or fall down and miss an inside-the-park homer. Nothing was uniform. Pal, let me tell ya', that was the miracle of the place."

Jackie Gleason said, "Some people drink to find religion. Some drink to seem sociable. *Me?* I drink to get bagged." Fenway led straight-away hitters to a monastery or distillery. From 1912 to 1929, center field loomed 488 feet from home plate, then fell back to 468 and 389, respectively, in 1930 and '34. Right-center began at 380, and in 1955 increased to 383. Farther right required a deeper indrawing of breath—405 feet— until, as we shall see, 1940's built-for-Number-9 bull pen lopped it to 380. Finally, baseball's deepest center-field corner—a.k.a. the Triangle— 550 feet as of 1922, 593 in 1931–33, and 420 since '34. On the other hand, right and left field—initially, 314 and 324 feet, respectively, now 302 and 310—hit you in the face.

Wall heights wrote like notebooks of variety. At first, center field's wall was eighteen feet, and right-center's nine. From there, the fence ebbed sharply to three feet at the right-field pole. Before 1934, the left-field wall was twenty-five feet high. In front of it, a ten-foot incline— Duffy's Cliff, named for 1910–17 outfielder Duffy Lewis—linked the left-field pole and center-field flagpole. Removed in 1970 from the field of play, the flagpole was five feet in front of the wall in deep left-center. (Six hitters have cleared the field and bleachers to the flagpole's right: Hank Greenberg, May 22, 1937; Jimmie Foxx, August 12, 1937; Bill

Skowron, April 20, 1957; Carl Yastrzemski, May 16, 1970; Bobby Mitchell, September 29, 1973, and Jim Rice, July 18, 1975.)

In 1933, Smead Jolley fell on Duffy's Cliff while chasing a carom off the wall. "You guys taught me how to go up the hill," he told teammates between innings, "but nobody taught me how to come down." By 1936, new owner Tom Yawkey had cut the cliff, painted the wall green, raised the height to thirty-seven feet, built a twenty-three-foot-tall net above it to protect windows on the other side of Lansdowne Street, and installed tin over a framework of two-by-four-foot wooden railroad ties. A ball hitting the ties refracted back toward the infield. Finding tin, it deadened and dropped straight down. The effect was antipodal—like Roger Clemens facing Ike Delock.

The Sox' empyrean linked scarce foul ground, a tier of grandstand flanking it, bleachers tying center field and the right-field pole, and a red-brick facade that meshed with the neighborhood. "It looked like part of the area," recalled the Kid. "From the outside you didn't know Fenway was a park." Inside, emerging from its belly, you spied the Monster, the Siberia of a center garden, and seats so near the field that, observing Number 9, you sensed what he was like. All this ascribed tangible causes to Boston's baseball reawakening. Too, its blue bloodlines, sharing a communion of lore. Fans elbowed their way into Fenway's large-for-its-age capacity, which roved between 1947's 35,500 and '61's 33,357 (current capacity is 33,871. Seats: roof, 2,168; boxes, 13,121; reserved grandstand, 12,075; and bleachers, 6,507). Normally, they espied a place of skylark goings-on.

Bowie Kuhn cheerily conspired with memory. "As commissioner, you're supposed to be objective," baseball's 1969–84 duce confided. "It wasn't much of a secret, though, that I loved Fenway—especially how it made you a participant, not a spectator." In 1912, the Red Sox more than doubled the Yankees' attendance; by 1918, they nearly tripled the crosstown Braves'. Even visitors loved Fenway's stronghold of enthusiasm, its identity spread through unorthodox dwelling on the personal and quaint.

Cramped and urban, Fenway's wonder was evoking a Mayberry of puppies and emerald turf and picket fences and small-town marms—frozen in amber, but fixed and sure. There it was, in downtown Boston, all mythy and sweetly rural. Green Acres was the place to be—as long as the Red Sox won.

For America, 1912 sowed a springtime of possibility. New Mexico and Arizona became states. Color photography blossomed—to George

Eastman, "a mirror with a memory." Once playthings for the wealthy, cars now carted Everyman. In 1900, eight thousand automobiles saw the USA. By 1912, more than 3 million did—up nearly 40,000 percent. Ford and Chevrolet ads appeared by Coca-Cola and Quaker Wheat Berries and Uneeda's boy in a slicker for Nabisco crackers. The Republican Party declared civil war, helping elect Woodrow Wilson. Shy and formal, the former head of Princeton University mixed acerbity, propriety, and a reformer's zeal. "We are not put into this world to sit still and know," Wilson said at his Princeton inauguration. "We are put into it to act."

In 1916, he became the first president to attend the Autumn Occasion. To Wilson's age, sport meant baseball, and baseball meant newspapers. Inning-by-inning scores filled telegraph-office windows. Dailies printed "baseball editions" with partial scores on the front or back page. Bylines blurred Damon Runyon, the Salieri of the short story, and Grantland Rice—"Grannie," the courser of the press box— and Ring Lardner, *le père grand* of "Alibi Ike" in the *Saturday Evening Post*. In the 1910s, their narratives turned to a team in its prime.

From 1912 to 1918, the Boston Red Sox won more games than any other club in baseball. Forget a future curse. Fenway became a pastiche of hits and deeds and recollections. Each decade has moments that KO boredom: 1960, Maz versus the Yankees; 1975, Game Six of the Reds-Sox Oktoberfest; 1988, Kirk Gibson and his dream-stuff autumn; 1996, Jim Leyritz rallying the Bronx Bombers in World Series Game Four. Boston in the '10s reveled in four pennants, four world titles, and Ozymandian ballplayers. Freeze-frame 1912, '15, '16, and '18. In a reverse twist from, say, Bob Bolin or Juan Beniquez, the Wilson Sox threw mellowspeak a curve.

Today's Townies extol continuum. Contrary was 1912's ode to novelty. Boston had new owners, with former outfielder Jim McAleer and American League secretary Bob McKay replacing John Taylor. Moreover, old/new 1905–06 and 1912–13 player/manager Jake Stahl replaced manager Patsy Donovan. Donovan hated obscenity: "Tish, tish," he told players, or "Tut, tut, boys, please don't say those words." (He should have managed in the 1920s, when Sox play was unprintable.) Stahl grasped what 1997-manager Jimy Williams said: "Baseball knows two languages—English and profanity." All sensed how their new park might kick apathy aside to become a kind of splendid arcadia.

For those who recall Walt Dropo, Dick Gernert, Dick Stuart, or Rudy York, it is improbable but true: the 1912 Red Sox won with a trifecta worth living by—pitching, defense, and (*mirabile dictu*) speed. Bill Carrigan caught, helped by rookie Hick Cady. The infield yoked Stahl at first, Steve Yerkes at second, Larry Gardner at third, and shortstop Heinie Wagner. Duffy Lewis, Speaker, and Harry Hooper—to Ruth, "my favorite fly chaser"—formed baseball's best defensive outfield. Later, Yankees general manager Ed Barrow said of Bob Meusel, Earle Combs, and Ruth: "Defensively, I would rate Speaker, Lewis, and Hooper first."

Lewis and Hooper caught everything in their area code and hit over .300 in 1911. Speaker (Cooperstown, 1937) and Hooper (1971) constantly threw runners out at first base and doubled them off second. In 1913, Tris lashed a franchise-high twenty-two triples. From 1909 to 1914, he stole thirty-five or more bases five times. Speaker's Everest was 1912. He averaged .383 (.392 at Fenway), had fifty-three doubles and 222 hits, led the league in home runs with twelve (tied with Frank "Home Run" Baker), and won a Chalmers car as AL MVP.

Carrigan sighed: "He played like a cross between Cobb and Wagner"—a surpassing baseball personality in the flesh. Trading taunts, citing batting averages, or swapping a dozen Yankees tobacco cards for a dog-eared Speaker, New Englanders found baseball composed of sudden, dramatic starts. Other sports were said to exist. Who knew? They seldom made a ripple.

The dictionary defines *fan*, deriving from *fanatic*, as "A person whose extreme zeal, piety, etc. goes beyond what is reasonable." At Fenway, fans hailed the baseball cant of the century's second decade. *Sluggers* like Gardner (with an *eagle-eye*) and a *foot in the bucket hit the dirt* and earned the *horse collar* or shook a *slump* and (after clubbing a *long strike*) *laid it down* or *teed off* in their *groove*. Batted balls like Hooper's became a *blooper, bleeder, banjo hit* or *Baltimore chop, clothesline,* or *Texas leaguer*. Fielders like Lewis, Collins, and Cady made a *boner* or *boot* or *circus catch* or *shoestring catch* or were *handcuffed* at the *hot corner* or *keystone bag* or *second sack* or (who, behind the plate) donned the *tools of ignorance* or (whose talent) voided the *squeeze play* or (whose charity) sired the cry of *butterfingers*. Inept pitchers were a *scatter-arm* who tossed a *rabbit ball* or *gopher ball* or *cripple* (if behind the batter) or *free ticket/Annie Oakley* (if, say, Ernie Shore walked the hitter). Adept, they threw a *high, hard one* (brushing back the hitter) to *fan* or *whiff* or *strike out* or, in a *shutout* by, say, Carl Mays, *whitewash* the hitters so that, bespectacled (a *cyclops*) or not, he could avoid a *Mexican standoff* and, not *crabbing*, become a *meal ticket*, not a *grandstander* or *bush leaguer*, but an *Ace*.

In 1912, fans specially hailed a Kansan-turned-Coloradoan turned palatine on the mound. Baseball is chockablock with single-season art: 1934, Dizzy Dean's thirty victories; '59, Elroy Face's eighteen successive triumphs; 1968, Bob Gibson's 1.12 earned run average; '86, Roger Clemens's 24–4. All were child's play compared with Joe Wood's welcome to history and largesse.

The Philadelphia Athletics began 1912 as three-time defending champion. "I still think my team in 1912 was my best of that era," said manager Connie Mack, "but Wood kept winning those games." Smoky Joe won thirty-four games and lost five, completed thirty-five of thirty-eight starts, struck out 258, and hurled a franchise-high ten shutouts. He also had a 1.91 ERA and winning streaks of eight, nine, and sixteen games.

Wood's Gettysburg was September's clash with Walter Johnson, also possessed of sixteen straight victories. Who needed licensing, marketing, or satellite telegraphy? Joe and the Big Train were a huckster's dream. "Remember Dempsey and Tunney?" Larry Gardner mused years later. "Newspapers ran comparison charts—height, weight, chest size, reach. That's what they did when the Train came to Fenway." Thousands sat on grass beyond the foul poles or behind the outfield ropes. "I remember the trouble they had warming up. Police had to charge in to break up the crowd."

In the sixth inning of a scoreless tie, Speaker hit a ground-rule double into the crowd. Lewis then lofted the ball down the right-field line. Outfielder Doug Moeller couldn't reach it, and Speaker scored: Sox win, 1–0. Later, the Big Train consoled a teary Moeller: "Don't feel badly. I should have struck him out." A reporter asked if he could throw faster than Wood. Johnson gaped as if the man came from an alien orb.

"Can I throw harder than *Joe Wood*?" he said. "Listen, friend, there's no man alive who can throw harder than Smoky Joe Wood." Surely not in 1912.

From 1921 to 1933, the sole Sox pitchers to win twenty or more games were Sam Jones (twenty-three in '21) and Howard Ehmke (twenty in '23). In 1912, on the other hand, Buck O'Brien and Hugh Bedient each took twenty to augment Wood's thirty-four. O'Brien, of Brockton, Massachusetts, chucked the then-legal spitball. Bedient was a rookie from the highlands and rolling greenery of upstate New York. Ray Collins and Charley "Sea Lion" Hall both won fifteen games. Five starters won 101 of the team-record 105. Womping second-place Washington by fourteen sets, the Red Sox literally strong-armed the field.

In 1972, owner Charles O. Finley had his "Swingin' A's Band" play "Sugar in the Morning" each day of the Oakland-Cincinnati World Series. It had nothing, fans of a certain age will tell you, on Boston's Royal Rooters, who, reprising their 1903 role, endued the 1912 Oktoberfest with an almost neoteric character. The novelist Thomas Wolfe wrote of baseball, "Almost everything I know of spring is in it." What the Rooters knew of baseball involved a bottle and a song.

The Royalists were ruddy, raucous, defiant, and sentimental. Before Game One versus the New York Giants they marched around Times Square, singing, "Carrigan, Carrigan, Speaker, Lewis, Wood, and Stahl. Bradley, Engle, Pape, and Hall. Wagner, Gardner, Hooper, too: Hit them! Hit them! Hit them! Do boys, do" to the tune of "Tammany." (Their hit parade also included the familiar "Tessie" and "When I Get You Alone Tonight.") Four special trains had brought the Rooters and two brass bands to the Polo Grounds. After a 4–3 victory — Wood struck out 11; the Giants muffed a fly ball and double play — they returned to Boston on what the New Haven Railroad called the "John Barleycorn Excursion."

Darkness ended Game Two at 6–6. Boston lost the third outing, 2–1. Wood then beat Jeff Tesreau, 3–1, and Bedient edged Christy Mathewson, 2–1. Behind three games to one with one tie, New York won the next match, 5–2. A day later, the Giants took Game Seven, 11–4, tying the Series. Worse, Fenway was oversold — and its prosopopeia lost their seats. Forget diplomatic nicety. The Rooters refused to leave, trampled the bleacher fence, and fought mounted police. "To hell with Queen Victoria!" one shouted while standing on the broken fence.

How could the final game surpass such babel? On Wednesday, October 16, at Fenway Park, quite easily, as it occurred. The Giants scored first. In the sixth inning, Hooper crashed into the temporary right-field seats to rob Larry Doyle of a homer. New York then made two of its seventeen Series errors to help Boston tie the game, 1–1, on a pinch-double by Olaf Henriksen. In the top of the tenth, Wood, reliev-ing — and ultimately, winning his third game — yielded the lead run. The bottom of the inning spawned a denouement that, if you are a Red Sox fan, is still worthy of recall.

Leading off, pinch-hitter Clyde Engle popped to Fred Snodgrass. The center fielder saw, but missed, the ball. "I don't know why," he said later. "I just dropped it." Engle reached second. Hooper then lined to Snodgrass (who, ironically, made a diving catch), Mathewson walked Steve Yerkes (the potential winning run), and Speaker gift-horsed a pop between first baseman Fred Merkle and catcher Chief Myers. Both looked it in the mouth.

Reprieved, Tris singled, tying the game. Larry Gardner's fly to right scored Yerkes, concluding it. The ex-Pilgrims had again found Canaan: Boston 3, New York 2.

In 1925, Gardner was asked about the Giants' sudden-death fatality. He couldn't recall what pitch he hit—rather, what the hit had meant: "Four thousand twenty-four dollars and sixty-eight cents [his World Series winning share], which just about doubled my earnings for the year."

Soxaphiles felt as rich. What a break—what *timing*—for the Olde Towne Team. Was God a baseball fan? At the least, He clearly loved its unlikely, insouciant, made-in-America storylines. Til Ferdenzi urgently replayed 1912. "Who could believe it today?" he laughed. "The Sox had the gods on *their* side." Soon, in a reverse twist of fate, another break would presage the century's last eighty years and end their prepotency with a thud.

In spring 1913, Wood fell on his throwing hand and broke a thumb. Today, with surgery, he might have missed a month. Instead, he was told to exercise it. The thumb got worse. In movie theatres, Joe couldn't lift his arm above the seat. From 1913 to 1915, he was 11–5, 9–3, and 14–5; then he quit. In 1918, the one time orb of Red Sox hauteur returned to belt game-tying and game-winning homers against the Yankees. Wood's rebirth is said to have sired novelist Bernard Malamud's character Roy Hobbs—like Joe, the how-close, if-only, what-might-have-been "best there ever was."

Smoky Joe still leads Sox pitchers in career earned-run average (1.99) and winning percentage (117–56, .676). Succeeding, if not replacing him, was a mound firm rivaling Horatio at the bridge. In 1914, 1915, and 1916, Dutch Leonard, Wood, and Babe Ruth, respectively, led the league in earned run average. Twenty-game winners included Ray Collins (twenty in 1914), Ruth (twenty-three and twenty-four in '16–17), and Carl Mays (twenty-two and twenty-one in '17–18). In 1918, Mays and Joe Bush each tossed eight shutouts. Rube Foster, Ernie Shore, and Leonard (twice) no-hit opponents.

"Think of the comparison," Lee Allen urged. "You're talking pitchers like Koufax and Drysdale"—or Atlanta's Maddux and company, say, in 1995. By 1915, Carrigan's staff denied self-doubt. Six-foot-four-inch Shore and five-foot-seven Foster bookshelved lefties Ruth and Leonard. Boston's pitching was so deep that fifth starter Wood had a league-leading 1.49 earned run average—and Mays's 1.54 ERA was deported to the bull pen. "Great it was," chortled Ruth, "and we needed it all come October."

The World Series, quoting Wes Westrum, was a "cliff-dweller"—every set was decided by a run. Shore lost Game One to Grover Cleveland Alexander—until 1980, the sole Series pitcher to lose to the Phillies. Foster equaled things by winning at Philadelphia's Baker Bowl. Games Three and Four moved from Fenway to larger Braves Field, upwardly mobile before its time. Duffy Lewis hijacked Gavvy Cravath in each set to save a 2–1 victory. Said Gavvy of a place where both four-hundred-foot drives would have cleared the wall: "Why, oh, why don't we play those games at Fenway?"

In the 1915 regular season, Harry Hooper homered twice. Ibid. Game Five. Scoring thrice in the last two innings, the Red Sox overcame a 4–2 Phillies lead to win the set, 5–4, and the Series, 4–1. All Boston pitchers threw complete games—Shore (two), Foster (two), and Leonard. Lewis, Speaker, and Hooper made twenty of the Sox' thirty-eight hits and eight of twelve RBIs, and forged a Maginot Line against extra-base bids. "Their outfield play was the best I've seen in many a year," said Ty Cobb.

One hundred and twenty-nine years earlier, Edmund Burke had etched a like occasion: "Here lies the summit. He may live long, he may do much, but he can never exceed what he does this day."

The first impression was that the Red Sox and Babe Ruth were, shall we say, a tad mismatched. Unusual for the time, Boston enlisted college men—Gardner, Hooper, Lewis, Carrigan, Ray Collins, and 1917 manager Jack Barry. Ruth seemed further from academe than Sunday school in Hades.

In 1915, a teammate snarled, "Look at that big ignorant ape, making all that money."

Learned, Gardner replied: "We're all making more because of Ruth."

Dead for half a century, Ruth still seems umbilically attached to excess. Babe drank before and after games, and wolfed two steaks, a dozen eggs, three pots of coffee, and a slab of ham for breakfast. He made love to women by the hundreds. Said Carrigan, "He knew more women around the league than the rest of us put together." He smoked cigars by the thousands, and bewitched youth by the millions. Japanese soldiers in World War II thought him such the persona of America that, charging U.S. positions, they cried, "To hell with Babe Ruth!"

In 1925, the Babe ate—what was it?—a half-dozen or two dozen hot dogs and brooked, the public fretted, "the stomachache [really, gonorrhea] heard 'round the world." In 1948, as a sweltering pallbearer of Ruth's cancer-wracked remains, Waite Hoyt heard another ex-Sox, Joe Dugan, moan, "Lord, I'd give my right arm for a beer." Hoyt murmured, "So would the Babe." What remains is the legend—a sunny-dark star, the full-sized Everyman, with whopping power. "Boy," marveled Carrigan, "when he hit one, you could hear it all over the park. The sound when he'd get a hold of one—it was just different, that's all."

Ruth arrived in Boston in 1914 as a part-time pitcher. A year later, pitching, he became a part-time hitter. In one game, the Tigers loaded the bases with Bob Veach, Sam Crawford, and Ty Cobb coming up. Ruth struck them out. "Boy, did Cobb yell," he hooted. "He told the umpire I was doctoring the ball. Ty could really blow up a storm." Soon, Babe blew up the league.

In 1915, he won eighteen games, yielded only 6.86 hits per nine innings, smacked four homers (outfielder Braggo Roth led the league with seven), and batted .315 (check *Webster's* under "complete package"). The next year, his niche as baseball's best left-hander turned all-consuming: nine shutouts, a league-best 1.75 ERA, and twenty-three of ninety-one Sox victories. In one game, Ruth pitched a three-hit shutout and got three hits, including a home run and double. He beat Walter Johnson five straight times, including a thirteen-inning 1–0 marathon, and in the Series threw 13⅓ consecutive scoreless innings.

The nineteenth-century British statesman Benjamin Disraeli muttered, "It was worse than a crime—it was a blunder." By the mid-'10s, millions thought it was both that Ruth didn't bat every day. "He wanted to *hit*!" Lee Allen contended. "The fans wanted to *see* him hit. The Sox wanted him to do both." The contretemps might have lingered, but for the war of doughboys, Verdun, gas masks, and "Over There," and a Broadway financier and former bellhop named Harry Frazee.

For a moment, think of Chet Nichols, Arnold Earley, and other tatters of the early 1960s. Breathe deeply. Resolve not to curdle bitterness. In 1916, Boston pitching that was good got even better. Three years earlier, Joseph Lannin had bought the Red Sox from Jim McAleer. Now, preparing himself to sell, Lannin dealt Tris Speaker to the Indians. "Part of it was that Speaker thought he should run the club," Carrigan said. "More of it was that Ban Johnson was league president and he wanted Cleveland to have a winning team." Trisless, the Sox flagged at bat. Their team average dropped from .260 to .248; only Gardner hit more than .300. "We needed pitching more than ever, which meant we needed Carrigan," said Gardner. "In all my years in baseball, I never knew anyone who could work with a battery better."

Much of 1916 was spent toting zeroes. Boston finished two games ahead of Chicago, then again used Braves Field for the Oktoberfest. Shore won the first game. Ruth pitched all fourteen innings as Boston took Game Two. The next match went to Brooklyn, but Leonard and Shore won the last two games, respectively, at Braves and Ebbets Field. What hitting there was was done by Gardner: two home runs, including one that he didn't see: "Brooklyn's Jack Coombs was pitching and I was angry because I wasn't hitting. He throws, I close my eyes, and swing from the heels." Years later, spotting Gardner, then-Brooklyn outfielder Casey Stengel whooped, "There's that third baseman that made me show my ass to the crowd chasing those home runs."

It is not known if the Ol' Perfessor read the poet Robert Lowell, who said, "If youth is a defect, it is one we outgrow too soon." What is known is that change was the Sox' post-1916 flaw. Lannin sold the team to Frazee. Carrigan—to Ruth, "the best manager I ever saw"—retired: "I have business affairs down in Maine [banks and a theatre chain] that demand my attention." His exit removed a therapist and pugilist—also, the only Sox manager to win two Series in a row. Yellowy photos show Ty Cobb, spikes flashing, gouging catchers' arms and legs. Most catchers avoided him. Carrigan *courted* him. One day, Bill moved out of the way as Ty slid toward the plate and then punched him in the face as hard as he could with the hand that held the ball. Cobb was out—and out cold, carried out on a stretcher. "Now you know," he told reporters, "why they call me Rough Bill."

Ken Coleman formed a smile. "Here's how it was back then," he said. "Even bad things turned out good." In 1917, Ruth hit .325, won twenty-four games, and completed a league-high thirty-five of thirty-eight. On June 23, he walked the first batter and was ejected for arguing. Shore, relieving, retired the next twenty-seven Senators in a row. In early 1918, Jack Barry joined the service. When Duffy Lewis followed, Barry's successor, Ed Barrow, asked, "Babe, how would you like to play left field?"—and pitch, too. Ruth batted .300, hit a league-high eleven homers to tie the A's Tilly Walker, and won seven games in the last five weeks to finish 13–7.

In 1918, play ended early to trudge U.S. troops to war. That September, Boston beat the Cubs in six games for its fourth world title in seven years. Carl Mays had completed thirty of the thirty-three games he started, including both games of a doubleheader. He won two more in the Classic. Ruth begot the other two and a then-Series record of 29⅔ straight scoreless innings. Barrow won the World Series in his first year as manager. Calling Bud Selig: the games ranged between one hour and forty-two minutes and 1:57.

At the time, 1918 seemed vaguely messianic—an act of grace, the tie that bound—and a portent of Sox masterworks to come. Instead, it exhausted providence. "They were like the gambler who breaks the bank one night and then can't buy a break," said the late *Herald Traveler* columnist Al Hirshberg. "In one decade the Sox used up their luck."

Since 1912, Boston's winning percentage only once had dropped below .591. The Sox beat the Yankees eighteen straight times—*in New York*. Twice, they won more than one hundred games and led the league in attendance. Ruth, Speaker, Hooper, Barrow, and Herb Pennock began their treks to Cooperstown. No Red Sox shortstop played more games than 1914–21's Everett Scott.

"It was a dynasty," Ned Martin said. "It's the only word that applies." In 1927, Carrigan returned to manage a Sox outfield of Wally Shaner, Ira Flagstead, and John Tobin. That, as they say, was in another country.

4

A Ballpark, Not a Stadium

By Martin F. Nolan

The ballpark is the star. In the age of Tris Speaker and Babe Ruth, the era of Jimmie Foxx and Ted Williams, through the empty-seats epoch of Don Buddin and Willie Tasby and unto the decades of Carl Yastrzemski and Jim Rice, the ballpark is the star. A crazy-quilt violation of city planning principles, an irregular pile of architecture, a menace to marketing consultants, Fenway Park works. It works as a symbol of New England's pride, as a repository of evergreen hopes, as a tabernacle of lost innocence. It works as a place to watch baseball.

It is a ballpark, not a stadium. The Big A in Anaheim, the Astrodome in Houston, and Shea Stadium in Queens are all planned, programmed, and enclosed in neat, off-ramp packages designed by demographic studies and traffic engineers. Fenway Park laughs at traffic engineers. It is cozy, yes, but it is cantankerous, not cute.

The Red Sox are beloved nationwide (to the delight of television-ad salesmen) because for decades Bostonians and New Englanders have departed in search of economic opportunity elsewhere. This exodus has begun to reverse itself only since the last World Series here.

Shake a tree in Orange County and a half-dozen Dorchester emigrés fall out. In Baltimore, Earl Weaver used to complain that Orioles partisans at Memorial Stadium were outnumbered by Red Sox fans who had motored north from nearby Washington. Ex-Bostonians are plentiful in the capital because Boston's greatest natural resource and chief export has been politics.

Fenway has been a talisman for the poetically inclined. It is old, it is idiosyncratic, and a frequent citadel of dashed hopes—all enduring themes of literature. Fenway is the ultimate protagonist of the "lit'ry life," a survivor.

"All literary men are Red Sox fans," John Cheever told Diane White a few weeks after the exquisite agony of 1978. "To be a Yankee fan in literary society is to endanger your life." The late author saw the Yankees–Red Sox rivalry as the Trojan War, with the Red Sox as the tragic Trojans (broad-backed Yaz in a noble frieze, his poignant pop-up soaring beyond the topless towers of Ilium before the dream is dashed by the grit-gloved Craig Nettles).

The Red Sox may resemble Trojans, but as Governor William Bradford wrote in "Of Plimouth Plantation," the first New England literary work, "they knew they were Pilgrims." The franchise was known as the Boston Pilgrims before the new owner, John I. Taylor, put red stockings on the team in 1907 to exploit the lingering fame of the old nineteenth-century National League franchise. "From now on, we'll wear red stockings and I'm grabbing that name Red Sox," Taylor said.

The team's popularity outgrew its Huntington Avenue grounds, and Taylor oversaw construction of the new ballpark. With the same directness with which he baptized the team, Taylor, whose family also owned the *Boston Globe*, said, "It's in the Fenway section, isn't it? Then name it Fenway Park."

The Fens was the centerpiece of the "Emerald Necklace" of parks designed by Frederick Law Olmstead, a planned environment of babbling brooks and green vistas, a design that held out a peaceful vision for urban America. But the stronger influence upon Fenway Park—and of its literary destiny—was the unplanned, anti-pastoral engine of haphazard growth that butchered Boston's landscape, the railroad.

Lansdowne Street necessitated the improbable Wall because Lansdowne Street was squeezed by the multilined pathway of the Boston and Albany Railroad, the tracks that transported Boston's wealth and innocence westward. These roaring lines (now hemmed to a modest ribbon by the Massachusetts Turnpike) defined "the other side of the tracks."

Fenway Park is funky because of an odd circumstance of geographical neglect. The novel, play, and movie *The Late George Apley* explains why the Back Bay historically has lorded over the South End (and Fenway). Although South End houses were as grand and substantial as their counterparts in the Back Bay, Apley discovered a man sitting *in shirtsleeves* on a South End stoop. He sold his property, and the South End was degentrified for almost a century. Had Fenway not been on the other side of the tracks, it might have been bulldozed and replaced with boutiques. Fans would not have sat in shirtsleeves in the bleachers, the team would have fled to suburbia, and would the Framingham Red Sox have as much appeal?

The tracks also symbolized another enduring literary theme, treason. On one treacherous day in 1920, Babe Ruth was sold to the New York Yankees by the new Red Sox owner, Harry Frazee. New York, the symbol of capitalist crassness, that day lost future generations of poets.

Fenway, the vestibule of approach-avoidance, would win any literary plebiscite over Yankee Stadium, a self-confident garage for a juggernaut. The arrogance of easy winners against the charm of the underdog? New York neon vs. New England pewter? Trendy vulgarity vs. traditional serenity? No contest. Now playing right field for Nathaniel Hawthorne, John Updike. Now at first base for William Dean Howells, David Halberstam.

Babe Ruth's betrayal was based on Frazee's longing for the bright lights of Broadway. He needed money to finance a new musical, *No, No, Nanette*, and had already sold several Sox players, all of whom took the train to join the Yankees. The Babe had just ended a fabulously successful career as a pitcher to begin to make history with his bat.

Frazee's Boston roots were notoriously shallow, and he became a New York prototype, what the tabloids meant when they said "playboy socialite." Frazee's name in our household ranked somewhere between Judas Iscariot and Benedict Arnold. (My father was involved in show business in the 1920s and played banjo in New York bands.)

Pinstripe paranoia has been a Boston curse ever since. Since Ruth was sold, the Yankees' lead over the Red Sox in winning World Series is 22–0 [now 24]. When Joe Page lumbered out of the Yankee bull pen in the late '40s, he resembled King Kong and the Red Sox performed like Fay Wray. Tommy Henrich always made the clutch hit, or Gene Woodling did, or Yogi Berra. Although we earnestly sang, "He's better than his brother Joe, Dom-in-ic DiMaggio!" we didn't believe it. Manhattan's mark of Cain was stamped upon Boston's brow indelibly by Bucky Dent in 1978.

In 1946, the American League pennant returned to Boston after an absence of twenty-eight years. A major factor was a trade with Detroit that brought Rudy York and his 117 RBIs to first base. Although he was with the team less than two seasons, York became the prototype of Fenway sluggerdom. Instead of first basemen, the Sox favored power forwards. For decades, Red Sox policy built a row of condominiums down the right-field line — Foxx, Walt Dropo, Vic Wertz, Dick Gernert, Mickey Vernon, Norm Zauchin, Dick Stuart, Lee Thomas, George Scott, Tony Perez [and Mo Vaughn].

The team's strategy has been a prisoner of Fenway, or at least of the Wall. Big-boom right-handed hitters were always courted (many of whom dented the Wall for singles). The hit-and-run remains a rarity and the stolen base a sacrilege. Red Sox philosophy defies logic as the park defies geometry. The kaleidoscope of contrariness only adds to the charm. The park is not the only enticement for loyal Bosox rooters; so is the tradition of almost winning, the September-October malady of *gonfalonia interruptus*.

The major difference between Bosox rooters and adherents of the Chicago Cubs is not the difference between Fenway and Wrigley Field. Sox fans are used to the near miss. Cub fans inhabit the limbo between buffoonery and the quiescence of Adlai Stevenson Democrats —it doesn't matter if you lose eloquently or lose poignantly, as long as you lose.

Since World War II, the Red Sox have brought their disciples to the foothills of glory a half-dozen times. Each approach and each disappointment is documented in the minds and hearts of New England:

October 15, 1946—Enos Slaughter scores from first on a single in the seventh game and St. Louis wins the game and the Series. In his only World Series, Ted Williams is outhit by a rookie catcher for the Cardinals, Joe Garagiola.

October 4, 1948—The first American League playoff ends early as the Cleveland Indians pummel starter (at 8–7) Denny Galehouse and win the pennant, 8–3.

October 2, 1949—A team bulging with .300 hitters and two twenty-game winners heads into Yankee Stadium needing one victory out of two. They lose twice, 5–4 and 5–3.

September 26, 1950—Again with steady hitters and two 144-RBI sluggers, the Sox challenge, but the Yankees eliminate them a week early.

October 12, 1967—After the "Impossible Dream" pennant, a tired Jim Lonborg starts the seventh game, which a fresh Bob Gibson wins by scattering three hits for the Cardinals.

October 2, 1972—Two future Hall of Famers find themselves occupying third base, but Luis Aparicio wasn't supposed to be there when Yaz tripled. The Sox lose the game and the pennant to the Tigers, 3–1.

October 22, 1975—The anticlimax to the great twelve-inning sixth game as Perez takes Bill Lee downtown. The Cincinnati Reds win the game and the World Series, 4–3.

October 2, 1977—The Sox get close again, but fade in the rain, tie for second with Baltimore.

October 2, 1978—In the second-ever AL playoff, Yaz's heroics, Piniella's blind catch, and Dent's poke off Torrez end with another Yankees victory, 5–4.

October 2, 1981—Yet another tease into the "final weekend" before finishing 2½ out, eliminated by the Indians, 11–4. [This essay was written before Game Six of the 1986 World Series.]

T. S. Eliot, an undergraduate at Harvard when the Red Sox received their current name, wrote that "April is the cruelest month . . . mixing memory and desire." Yet desire has not fled the souls of Red Sox fans, not while they can maintain hope this late in the season. October in New England remained in the memory of an Amherst native who went west. Helen Hunt Jackson could have written this anthem of hope for every survivor of a Fenway season:

> O suns and skies and clouds of June,
> And flowers of June together,
> Ye cannot rival for one hour
> October's bright blue weather.

This offer not available for Series games played in the Astrodome.

Martin F. Nolan has been a Boston Globe *reporter, Washington bureau chief, editorial page editor, and—since 1991—associate editor. He is a Boston College graduate, past fellow at Harvard and Duke Universities and the Hoover Institution, and Pulitzer Prize finalist for editorial writing and commentary.*

5

The Hungry Years
1919—33

As Casey Stengel said, "You can look it up." A native of Peoria, Harry Frazee once played in Boston. Today, convention echoes writer Fred Leib, who called Frazee "the evil geenie." By contrast, the record is as clear as whitecaps off the Cape: buying the Sox after the 1916 World Series, Frazee at first seemed bent on becoming Father Christmas.

First, he signed one Holy Cross man, Jack Barry, to replace another, Bill Carrigan, as manager. Next, he was said to have offered $60,000 for Walter Johnson. "Nothing," he tut-tutted, "is too good for the Boston fans." Oh, say, Harry could even see: he was the first owner to play "The Star-Spangled Banner" before a baseball game—on September 9, 1918.

Frazee's real anthem, alas, was greed. Carl Mays won twenty-one games in 1918. The next year, he started 5–11 and on June 13 left the team. "Tell them," he said, "I've gone fishing." A day later, Mays hooked his end: "I'll never pitch another game for the Red Sox." He never did. Needing cash to bankroll plays, Frazee peddled him to the Yankees.

The Red Sox owner apparently believed that one bad turn deserves another. Soon, he turned to baseball's apotheosis.

Heywood Broun once penned, "the Ruth is mighty and shall prevail." Babe Ruth was and did in his final year in Boston.

Before 1919, baseball's home-run marks wrote a Philadelphia story— twenty-four and nineteen, respectively, by the NL Phillies' Gavvy Cravath and AL A's Socks Seybold. On Labor Day, Babe smashed number twenty-four in the second game of a doubleheader. Buck Freeman had hit twenty-five homers for the 1899 NL Washington Senators. Ruth broke that record and then a newly found mark of twenty-seven (Ned Williamson, Chicago White Stockings, 1884). "What the hell?" Babe said. "Did they pitch underhanded then?" Pitching less, Ruth was enjoying life more.

On September 20, 1919, Frazee held Babe Ruth Day. Ruth tied Williamson, passed him against the Yankees, and homered the final weekend in Washington, D.C. How Ruthian was his total? Twenty-nine home runs were only one less than the *combined* sum of the next three AL sluggers—George Sisler, Tilly Walker, and Frank Baker—and twenty-five more than the *rest* of the Sox combined. Ruth led the league in RBIs (114) and slugging percentage (.657), homered in every park in the regular season, and hit a then-record four grand slams. Even nicknames shouted carnival—the Bambino (also, Big Bambino). Behemoth of Biff. Caliph of Clout. Colossus of Club (or Sport). Goliath of the Grand Slam. King of Clout. Prince of Powders. Slambino. Sultan of Swat. Wizard of Whack. "He was the first national superstar," observed columnist George Will, "the man who gave us that category."

By any name, Ruth had less subtlety than a Jack Dempsey jab. Ahead for Red Sox Nation was a knockout to its head. On January 5, 1920, Frazee sold Babe to the Yankees for $300,000. Among the Sox owner's would-be Broadway hits was *My Lady Friends*—aptly, a farce. Noting the play's name, a critic puffed, "They're the only friends the SOB has." Babe's sale, eleven days before Prohibition, drove fans to hang signs on Boston Common and Faneuil Hall—"For Sale."

Tip O'Neill stoked a cigar. "That sign was superfluous," he said. "Frazee didn't need any ideas." Catcher Wally Schang, utility infielder/Ruth pinch-hitter Mike McNally, and pitcher Waite Hoyt—a future Hall of Famer—all were traded from Boston to the Yankees. Frazee got cash and catcher Muddy Ruel, then shipped him to Washington. Naturally, Ruel became a star. Next, Harry sent shortstop Everett Scott and pitchers "Bull Joe" Bush and "Sad Sam" Jones to the Yankees, whereupon they won pennants in '22 (Bush won twenty-six games) and '23 (when Jones won twenty-one). In return, the Sox received cash and Roger Peckinpaugh, then sent him to Washington for Joe Dugan. You know the rest: Peckinpaugh was the AL's Most Valuable Player on the 1925 champion Senators.

Each New Year's Eve, Guy Lombardo and his Royal Canadians played "The Music Goes 'Round and 'Round." Frazee's music—and money—kept winding up at 42nd and Broadway. In 1922, he traded ten-year veteran Herb Pennock and George Pipgras. A year later, Pennock helped the Yankees to their first Series title. Of New York's twenty-four players, eleven had been Red Sox. "Boston last season [1922] reaped the fruits of four years' despoliation by the New York club," *Reach Guide* mourned. "And for the second time in American League baseball history, this once-great Boston team, now utterly discredited, fell into last place, with every prospect of remaining in that undesirable position indefinitely."

"You're going to ruin the Red Sox in Boston for a long time," Ed Barrow told Frazee on learning of Ruth's sale. Dub him Nostradamus. The pre-1920 Sox took six AL pennants. They won a single flag in the next forty-seven years.

As the Sox unraveled, a free state neared in Ireland. "In Boston, that was great," said O'Neill, "since there were fewer Irish in Dublin than here." In Baltimore, H. L. Mencken rebuked the "booboise." In Indiana, the Ku Klux Klan boasted nearly five hundred thousand members. In Washington, D.C., the 1920 census read, "Population, United States, 106,466,000." Bookstores hawked *Main Street* by Sinclair Lewis, *Winesburg, Ohio* by Sherwood Anderson, and F. Scott Fitzgerald's *This Side of Paradise*. Already, Sacco and Vanzetti formed a *cause célèbre*. Alcohol's "reign of terror [was] over," quoth revivalist Billy Sunday, a former major leaguer. It yielded to Prohibition—and the hammerlock of organized crime.

The early 1920s flaunted speakeasies and raccoon coats and Clara Bow and Rudolph Valentino. Bobby Jones and Bill Tilden buoyed golf and tennis. Jack Dempsey became the Frank Merriwell of boxing. Warren Gamaliel Harding, of whom the politician William Gibbs McAdoo jeered, "He left the impression of a man of pompous phrases moving over the landscape in search of an idea; sometimes these meandering words would actually capture a straggling thought and bear it triumphantly, a prisoner in their midst, until it died of servitude and overwork," besieged the White House, his greed obscured by piety.

Admired and despised, having occupied the vestibule of legal power, Kenesaw Mountain Landis—a gaunt, white-maned prosecutor/judge—now preempted baseball's sanctum. Named commissioner in November 1920, he "got his job," jibed Will Rogers, not through the *New York Times*. "Somebody said, 'Get that old boy who sits behind first all the time. He's out there every day anyhow.' So they offered him a season's pass and he jumped at it." Meanwhile, at the Polo Grounds, his abode until "The House That Ruth Built" opened in 1923, the Bambino became Boston baseball's Banquo's Ghost. "He was . . . a burst of dazzle and jingle," Jimmy Cannon wrote, "Santa Claus drinking his whiskey straight and groaning with a bellyache caused by gluttony."

Ruth deified the home run and fulfilled his appetites and secured for baseball a messianic time. *Most* of baseball. Increasingly, the Red Sox played more like Dead Sox.

Ruth knew that Tiparillos don't feed the bulldog. "They had a Babe Ruth Day for me last year and I had to buy my wife's ticket to the game," he told reporters in 1920. "Fifteen thousand fans show up and all I got was a cigar." A cigar is more than Red Sox fans got through 1933. For fifteen straight years, the Boston American League Baseball Company ignored all entreaties to vacate the second division. Leaving little to the imagination, it left less for competition.

"I started at the bottom in this business," said actor Art Carney, "and worked my way right into the sewer." So did the 1919–33 Red Sox. Their box score: 881 victories, 1,398 defeats, and an otherworldly 692½ games out of first. Each year, you hoped that they would march—unevenly, to be sure, but *finally*—from the sackcloth of ruin. Fat chance. Their list of managers trembled between facetiousness and fellow suffering: Barrow, Duffy, Frank Chance, Lee Fohl, Carrigan, Heinie Wagner, Shano Collins, and Marty McManus. Their luck changed more slowly than autumn in Alabama.

Twice, Boston finished seventh. Five and nine times, respectively, it lost more than one hundred games and finished last. In 1922, the Sox entered the cellar for the first time. From 1925 to 1930, they owned it—six times placing eighth in an eight-team league. In 1931, Boston finished sixth; "the city fathers," said Ken Coleman, "were prepared to declare a civic holiday." It then raised impotence to a new, pre-Viagra level: the 1932 Sox won forty-three games, had a .279 "winning" percentage, ended sixty-four sets behind New York, and lured 182,150 fans—per date, 2,365—less than 1979's first nine games.

"How bad were the Red Sox?" the late Jack Redding asked. "On a scale of one to ten, about fifteen." Juxtaposed were the high deeds and heroes of many rivals. Exempli gratia: Pie, Black Mike, the Rajah, the Fordham Flash, Big and Little Poison, the Iron Horse, the Lip, Marse Joe, the Mechanical Man, the Wild Horse of the Osage, and Hack. Respectively: the Pirates' Pie Traynor, stubby and well-muscled; Mickey Cochrane of the A's, Tigers, and five championships; Rogers Hornsby, with a .358 career average; Frankie Frisch, theatric and urbane; brothers Paul and Lloyd Waner, together reaping 5,086 base hits; Henry Louis Gehrig, Old Biscuit Pants, the Pride of the Yankees, a quiet man, a hero; Leo Durocher, who stormed, "Show me a good loser and I'll show you an idiot"; Joseph Vincent McCarthy, Philadelphian by birth and Victorian by bearing, who said, "Sometimes, I think I'm in the greatest business in the world. Then you lose four straight and want to change places with a farmer"; Charlie Gehringer, of whom Cochrane mused, "He'd say hello at the start of spring training and good-bye at the end of the season, and the rest of the time he let his bat and glove do all the talking for him"; the Cardinals' Pepper Martin, who pawed the earth and slid head-first and wore no underwear; and finally, the Cubs' Hack Wilson, of whom Warren Brown wrote: "He was a high-ball hitter on the field, and off."

In 1930, Wilson smacked fifty-six round-trippers and a record 190 ribbies. Bill Terry forearmed .401. Each '30 Cardinals regular hit more than .300. The Yankees batted .309 as Ruth and Gehrig combined for 327 RBIs. No matter: Sparta finished third. A year later, Al Simmons hit .390. In 1932, the A's Jimmy Foxx hit fifty-eight home runs and McCarthy won his first Yankees pennant. In time, their lives would grow around the Red Sox like vines on a trellis. For the moment, they helped Boston pitching almost vanish in a headwater of home runs.

Red Ruffing lost forty-seven games for the Sox in 1928–29. A year later, Milt Gaston and Jack Russell both lost twenty. On June 23, 1927, Gehrig homered thrice at Fenway; he and Ruth hit fourteen round-trippers for the year. (Their thirty and thirty-eight rank fourth and first, respectively, in rival home runs at Fenway.)

Frazee's leaving didn't help. The Victorians called cloudless spells "Queen's Weather." Buying the Sox in 1923, ex-Browns general manager Bob Quinn lured mishap like Madonna does film. "Every time we get ready for a big crowd, it rains," Quinn said. "They even have an expression around here when it does. They say, 'Here comes Quinn's Weather.' " In 1933, he sold the club—owing concessionaire Harry Stevens, $150,000 to the league, and a mortgage owed to Frazee's friend and trading foil, Yankees owner Jacob "Colonel" Ruppert.

"I went to the Colonel and told him I had already laid out a great deal of cash, and I wondered if he could carry the mortgage into the following year," said Tom Yawkey, Quinn's successor as Red Sox owner. "He said yes, he was delighted to have me in the league." That year, 1933, the Sox swept a five-game series from New York at Fenway. Yawkey laughed, "The next morning my lawyer called to say it was a costly sweep. Ruppert's lawyer had just called, and they were demanding payment right now on the mortgage. Jake didn't like to lose five straight."

The next day, he sent "that SOB" a check.

"Remember TV's *The Life of Riley?*" a friend asked of William Bendix as Chester A. Riley. "He'd bellow, 'What a revoltin' development *this is.*'" Perhaps Bendix loved the Olde Towne Team.

Revoltin': On June 27, 1923, pitcher Frank "Lefty" O'Doul yielded thirteen runs to Cleveland. Boston lost, 27–3. Released, he changed leagues and, like Ruth, morphed into an outfielder. "The Red Sox could have used him," Ken Coleman whistled quietly of the two-time NL batting leader and Hub expatriate. In 1927, the Babe outhomered their entire *team*, sixty to twenty-eight.

Appalling: The Sox' version of "we all have fish to fry." In 1928, rookie Ed Morris won nineteen of Boston's fifty-seven victories. Morris won only twenty-three more before being fatally stabbed by a jealous husband at a 1932 fish fry.

Enduring: Fire, and atrocious trader. On May 8, 1926, Fenway's wooden bleachers beyond third base burned. Not replaced, they enlarged foul ground for the rest of the year. In 1930, Quinn swapped Ruffing for the Yankees' Cedric Durst. Durst hit .240 and retired. Ruffing's plaque specks the Hall of Fame.

Revealing: "Baseball is Boston's real religion," Tip O'Neill often said. Third baseman Marty McManus was attending mass when the Red Sox named him manager in 1932. Needing confession and/or absolution, McManus's teams won 95, lost 153, and swam in catatonia and disarray.

The Townies' numbers, which often seemed up, literally *were* in 1931, when Boston put them on its uniforms. (Four have been retired— Ted Williams's 9 and Joe Cronin's 4 on May 29, 1984; Bobby Doerr's 1, May 21, 1988; and Carl Yastrzemski's 8, August 6, 1989). Relief stemmed less from triumph than trivia. In 1925, Roy Carlyle hit for the cycle. In 1932, Dale Alexander hit .372 to win the batting title. Everett Scott set a franchise-record consecutive-games streak (832). In 1931, Earl Webb whacked a major-league-record sixty-seven doubles. Six Sox players from 1919 to 1932—Ruth, George Burns, Del Pratt, Ike Boone, Buddy Myer, and Smead Jolley—hit in twenty or more consecutive games.

In 1923, Lou Gehrig, at nineteen, played for Columbia against Rutgers. Back at Yankee Stadium, scout Paul Krichell told general manager Ed Barrow, "I saw another Ruth today." Having sold the original, the Sox found a copy on September 7, 1923: Howard Ehmke no-hit the A's. In his next start, he one-hit the Yankees on a disputed single by Whitey Witt off third baseman Howard Shanks's glove. Years later, Shanks told official scorer Fred Lieb, "I think it should have been scored an error." Lieb wrote, "Ever since Shanks told me that, I've had the play on my conscience." In 1929, Frazee died with New York Mayor Jimmy "Beau James" Walker at his side. The only play on *his* conscience was doubtless still *My Lady Friends*.

That season sabbath baseball was finally OK in Boston, but not at Fenway due to its proximity to a church. Until the law was changed, in 1932, the Sox played on the seventh day at Braves Field, losing Boston's first Sunday game (April 28, 1929, versus Philadelphia, 7–3) and Fenway's July 3, 1932, Sunday inaugural (to New York, 13–2).

Sunday tested the Hub's early '30s waves of loyalty. So, for that matter, did Monday through Saturday. A decade after buying Ruth, the Yankees owned Olympus. The Sox hoped merely to avoid becoming the Atlantis of the American League.

For America, despair was first minister as Franklin Roosevelt took the oath of office as America's thirty-second President—for some, the president *still*. On March 4, 1933, unemployment topped 13 million. A banking crisis shrouded FDR's inauguration. Said outoing president Herbert Hoover, "We are at the end of our string." That April, writer Rud Rennie left Florida training camp to travel north with the Yankees. "We passed through southern cities which looked as though they had been ravaged by an invisible enemy," he wrote. "People seemed to be in hiding. They even would not come out to see Babe Ruth and Lou Gehrig. Birmingham, a once-thriving, bright metropolis, looked as if it had been swept by a plague."

More than 25 percent of America's workforce was out of work. In Wisconsin, farmers dumped milk on roads to reduce supply and lift prices. In Iowa, auctions halted because of bloody protests against foreclosure. Every state had either closed its banks or reduced their capacity to act. America seemed a cross between Dogpatch and Hades. "First of all," Roosevelt countered in his inaugural address, "let me reassert my firm belief that the only thing we have to fear is fear itself—nameless, unreasoning, unjustified terror." Did the seas part? No, but curtains spread.

Slowly, America as patient began to heal. From an unseen room burst FDR as the nation's shaman—jaunty and effervescent, laughing, always *leading*—"all grin and gusto," wrote Arthur Schlesinger, "but terribly hard inside . . . who had been close enough to death to understand the frailty of human striving, but who remained loyal enough to life to do his best in the sight of God."

Even now, his persona fuses father of the New Deal and scourge of Nazi Germany—the man who created Social Security and hailed "my little dog Fala" and whom Adolf Hitler feared—his influence so huge that when he died on April 12, 1945, a part of each American died, too. "One remembers Roosevelt as a kind of smiling bus driver," Samuel Grafton said, "with cigarette holder pointed upward, listening to the uproar from behind as he took the sharp turns. They used to tell him that he had not loaded his vehicle right for all eternity. But he knew he had it stacked well enough to round the next corner and he knew when the yells were false and when they were real, and he loved the passengers."

Once, conceding a salary larger than Hoover's, Babe Ruth explained: "But I had a better year than he did!" Most Red Sox fans will tell you that 1919 to 1933 was not often better at Fenway Park.

The Pilgrims—led by Buck Freeman's 104
RBIS, Patsy Dougherty's .331 average, and
three 20-game winners—won Boston's first of
ten American League pennants. (Baseball Hall of
Fame Library, Cooperstown, New York)

*South End Grounds II, the future Braves'
home from 1888 to 1894, was flanked by railroad lines and featured a twin-spiraled roof.*
(Baseball Hall of Fame Library, Cooperstown, New York)

*Among the earliest photos of the new Red Sox
household at Lansdowne and Jersey Streets.*
(Baseball Hall of Fame Library, Cooperstown, New York)

*The bleachers fill for Game Two of the 1916
World Series, at Braves Field. Babe Ruth hurled
all 14 innings as the Sox edged Brooklyn, 2–1.*
(Baseball Hall of Fame Library, Cooperstown, New York)

*Talent or beginner's luck?
The Red Sox won four pen-
nants in the first seven years
of Fenway Park, shown under
construction in late 1911.*
(Baseball Hall of Fame Library,
Cooperstown, New York)

Throngs cram the Huntington Avenue Grounds for the 1903 World Series. The Pilgrims stunned Pittsburgh to win the first Oktoberfest.
(Baseball Hall of Fame Library, Cooperstown, New York)

Smoky Joe Wood (left) and Walter Johnson visit before their September 1912 clash in Boston. Wood derailed the Big Train, 1–0, to cap his 34–5 year. (Baseball Hall of Fame Library, Cooperstown, New York)

There may be someone more despised than Harry Frazee in Boston baseball history, but it is difficult to envision who — or why. (Baseball Hall of Fame Library, Cooperstown, New York)

On September 20, 1919, Fenway hosted Babe Ruth Day. Four months later, Boston sold the part-time outfielder to the Yankees.

(Baseball Hall of Fame Library, Cooperstown, New York)

Twice Tris Speaker threw out a record 35 American League runners in a single season. He could also hit, batting more than .300 every year from 1909 to 1915 for the Townies.

(Baseball Hall of Fame Library, Cooperstown, New York)

Tom Yawkey, with first wife Elise, reveling in his late-1930s contender. "He didn't own the Red Sox," a writer said. "He was the Red Sox" —then, and now. (AP/Wide World Photos, courtesy Baseball Hall of Fame Library, Cooperstown, New York)

Sox President Bob Quinn
(extreme right) flanks 1920s
politicians and players Nick
Altrock and Al Schacht (left)
at Opening Day ceremonies
at Fenway Park. (Baseball Hall of
Fame Library, Cooperstown, New York)

Red Sox bats in 1946 looked
this huge to opposing pitchers. By late August, Boston
had virtually clinched its
first flag in twenty-eight
years. (Baseball Hall of Fame Library,
Cooperstown, New York)

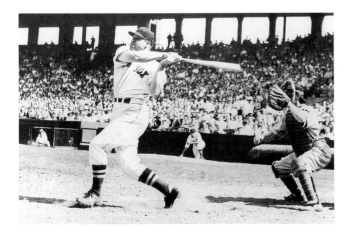

On August 16, 1940, Jimmie
Foxx bombs his 495th career
homer, passing Lou Gehrig,
to help Boston edge
Washington, 7–6, at Fenway.
(Baseball Hall of Fame Library,
Cooperstown, New York)

Joe McCarthy (left) and Casey Stengel won nineteen pennants and fourteen World Series. They are likely discussing the nightmare Sox 1949 finale at spring training in 1950. (Baseball Hall of Fame Library, Cooperstown, New York)

Splendor amid the Browns' ruins. Ted Williams flanks the scoreboard, which shows a modern big-league scoring record. Boston beat St. Louis, 29–4, on June 8, 1950. (UPI/Corbis-Bettmann, courtesy Baseball Hall of Fame Library, Cooperstown, New York)

Like Feller and DiMaggio, Williams was baseball's 1940s cover boy. Look was among many magazines to profile Number 9—and his nonpareil swing. (Baseball Hall of Fame Library, Cooperstown, New York)

*Baseball's oldest teenager: the Kid, nearing forty, drives a
miniature car during August 22, 1958, Shriner's festivities at
Fenway Park.* (UPI/Corbis-Bettmann, courtesy Baseball Hall of Fame Library,
Cooperstown, New York)

"The greatest hitter of all time," Curt Gowdy
called Williams in a September 28, 1960,
pregame speech. Number 9 proved it in his
last at bat, hitting home run number 521.
Jim Pagliaroni (left) congratulates him as he
crosses the plate. *(AP/Wide World Photos, courtesy
Baseball Hall of Fame Library, Cooperstown, New York)*

*Unlike Jim Lonborg, Mel
Parnell limited his skiing to
Fenway Park. The Sox ace
frolics after a three-inch
storm postponed Opening
Day on April 15, 1953.* (AP/Wide
World Photos, courtesy Baseball Hall of
Fame Library, Cooperstown, New York)

*On July 14, 1946, Cleveland tried a new strategy to keep Williams
from pulling safely: the Boudreau Shift, with three infielders to
the right of second base.* (Baseball Hall of Fame Library, Cooperstown, New York)

Pitcher Bill Monbouquette brightened Boston's
early 1960s. Here, the right-hander points to
the scoreboard and one day's results: a one-hit,
5–0 shutout of Detroit. (UPI/Corbis-Bettmann, courtesy
Baseball Hall of Fame Library, Cooperstown, New York)

Forget Bo Belinsky and
Frankie Avalon. Tall, dark,
and handsome Tony
Conigliaro was a region's
heartthrob—and destiny's
forgotten son. (Baseball Hall of
Fame Library, Cooperstown, New York)

Luis Aparicio, who would later (1971–73)
play shortstop for Boston, steals second
for Chicago on July 16, 1961, against the
Townies' then-shortstop Don Buddin. Note
the ball, typically eluding Buddin's glove.
(Chicago Sun-Times, *courtesy Baseball Hall of Fame Library,*
Cooperstown, New York)

In 1969, the Sox named their all-time team. Left to right: Bobby Doerr, Frank Malzone, Commissioner Bowie Kuhn, Joe Cronin, Lefty Grove, Birdie Tebbetts, and Numbers 8 and 9. *(Bowie Kuhn Photo Collection, courtesy Baseball Hall of Fame Library, Cooperstown, New York)*

A tableau for the ages: Carlton Fisk hits a Game Six 12th-inning blast to beat the Reds, 7–6, tie the 1975 Fall Classic, and make body English a universal tongue. *(AP/Wide World Photos, courtesy Baseball Hall of Fame Library, Cooperstown, New York)*

In 1967, Jim Lonborg won 22 regular-season games. Here, Gentleman Jim throws the first pitch of his one-hit victory over St. Louis in World Series Game Two. *(Baseball Hall of Fame Library, Cooperstown, New York)*

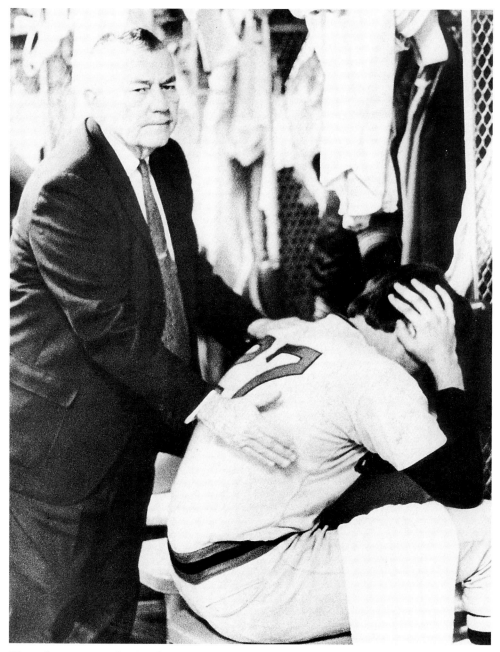

There they go again. On October 3, 1972, the Sox lost the AL *East flag to Detroit. One future Hall of Famer consoles another: Tom Yawkey and rookie Carlton Fisk.* (Frank O'Brien/Boston Globe, courtesy Baseball Hall of Fame Library, Cooperstown, New York)

*Fred Lynn parks one in the 1975 Fall Classic.
That season, he became the only American
Leaguer to be named the Rookie of the Year and
MVP. (Baseball Hall of Fame Library, Cooperstown, New York)*

*Whether pivoting on the
mound or smoking cigars in
the shower, El Tiante wowed
Red Sox Nation. In October
1975, Luis Tiant beat the
Reds, 5–4, in Game Four to
even the World Series. (AP/Wide
World Photos, courtesy Baseball Hall of
Fame Library, Cooperstown, New York)*

*Bucky Dent climaxes perhaps the greatest game ever played. His
three-run homer shocked Fenway Park, reversed a 2–0 Sox lead,
and gave the Yankees the 1978 playoff and pennant. (UPI/Corbis-
Bettmann, courtesy Baseball Hall of Fame Library, Cooperstown, New York)*

In 1861, leaving for Washington, Abraham Lincoln said good-bye
to his home people at the Springfield, Illinois, train station: "I bid
you an affectionate farewell." Too, Yaz in 1983. (Baseball Hall of Fame
Library, Cooperstown, New York)

*Mookie Wilson is about to
end Game Six of the 1986
World Series, unforgettably
and surrealistically. The
Mets' Ray Knight (22) will
shortly score on Bill Buckner's
error to beat Boston, 6–5.*
(Baseball Hall of Fame Library,

Cooperstown, New York)

*The dictionary defines logic
as the science of correct rea-
soning. Mo Vaughn became
league MVP, led the 1993–98
Sox in homers, and was then
dispatched to California.*
(Photo File, courtesy Baseball Hall of Fame

Library, Cooperstown, New York)

*New England's parlor, a region's nightclub,
and the Olde Towne Team's hearth. To generations of Americans, going to Fenway Park
has been like coming home.* (Dr. Kevin Penird,

courtesy Baseball Hall of Fame Library, Cooperstown, New York)

6

Where You Lead

1934–45

In 1934, Lou Gehrig earned a temporal prize—the Triple Crown. Pitcher Lefty Gomez revealed a more timeless key: "It's simple [pitching success]—clean living and a fast outfield." Detroit seized its first pennant since 1909. Giants manager Bill Terry asked: "Is Brooklyn still in the league?" Dizzy Dean won thirty games for the Cardinals. America embraced their Gas House Gang. In Boston, the Red Sox waved hallo to a sportsman, patrician, and patriarch. "I think that as much as he saw himself as the man who owned the team," Bart Giamatti later observed, "to most he *was* the team."

Thomas Austin Yawkey arrived in Boston through baseball's old-boy network. In 1933, the American League had gone looking for someone to save the Sox. Yawkey's uncle had owned the 1904–07 Tigers. Detroit's current owner knew his family. "They've got money," Walter Briggs told fellow owners, fixing Yawkey in his crosshairs. "I don't think the league should be a bank."

Eddie Collins knew Yawkey as a former prep schoolmate. One night at dinner, the 1915–26 White Sox second baseman, '24–26 Pale Hose manager, and '31–32 A's coach swung from the heels. "You love the game," he entreated Yawkey. "Why don't you look into the Red Sox? I know [owner Bob] Quinn will sell it to the right man." He did, for $1.5 million, and Yawkey was.

At thirty, loyal, shy, and sentimental, the new Sox owner began the task of darning hose. First, he persuaded Collins to become his vice president and general manager. "He was honest," Yawkey said. Fixing the 1919 World Series, gamblers had treated Collins like a leper at a bazaar. Yawkey then cast his net on the Potomac. Bucky Harris was Boston's 1934 manager. Collins wanted to replace him with the AL's 1930 Most Valuable Player. Joe Cronin made the All-Star team seven times, twice led the league in doubles and once in triples, and hit a lifetime .301. If not, unlike Ozzie Smith, reinventing the position, he was even more than Luke Appling and Arky Vaughan the best shortstop of the '30s.

Stolid, granite-armed, -legged, and -jawed, Cronin had led Washington to its final pennant in 1933, his first year as player/manager. How could the Red Sox lure such a paladin? Yawkey had a way. At a league meeting he approached Senators owner Clark Griffith and asked, "What will you take for Cronin?"

"Why," Griffith said, "he's just married Mildred [Griffith's niece]."

Puzzled, Yawkey—T.A. to intimates—asked what matrimony had to do with playing shortstop. Griffith dodged: "Oh, I couldn't sell Joe. I'd want too much money for him anyway."

Yawkey replied, "Put your figure down on the back of the envelope and see." Griffith did, and wrote, "Of course, I won't have anybody to play shortstop, so you'll have to throw in Lyn Lary."

The figure was $250,000. A postage stamp then cost three cents, scotch $2.50 a quart, rooms at a Boston luxury hotel $3 nightly. Yawkey said, "That's it." Cronin was now his.

In 1933, the Sox finished ahead of only the hapless Browns. A year later, placing fourth, they headed, in the argot of the day, "upstairs," not uptown. Today, Yawkey, Collins, and Cronin grace the Hall of Fame in Cooperstown. Their plaques evoke a Red Sox recovery of propriety, old-fashioned heroism, and, batting cleanup, cash.

At Fenway Park, the Red Sox executive offices open onto the shops and hordes of Yawkey Way, known as Jersey Street prior to 1977. Next to a door both medals and mettle link two pioneers.

One plaque says: "Thomas Austin Yawkey 1903–76. In Memory. From Those Who Knew Him Best—the Red Sox employees." The other reads: "A Tribute to Edward Trowbridge Collins. May 2, 1887—March 25, 1951. His ability, loyalty, and integrity as a player and an executive in the game of baseball will forever be remembered and cherished. Erected by the Boston Red Sox, 1951." You recall Collins telling Cronin in 1935, his first year as manager, "We'll get you players; you work with them."

The Sox had begun to rework Fenway straightaway on Quinn's selling. Yawkey wanted it to treat you like a guest, invoking hospitality. "All folks know is what happened after Yawkey bought it," said Til Ferdenzi. "Before then, Fenway was a joke. I grew up around here, and remember how lots of chairs didn't have bottom parts. There were bird turds on the seats. The structure itself was beautiful—just pathetically kept up. And if you wanted a long nap—boy, this was the place to go."

On January 5, 1934, a four-alarm, four-star blaze virtually ruined construction to rebuild the park. A year later, Yawkey replaced the wooden seats with concrete and steel. For $750,000 he painted fences, cleaned aisles, reinforced supports, and heightened the left-field wall. The fence was still too near for panicked pitchers. A Yankees pitcher mused: "If you were a right-handed pitcher and threw sidearm, your knuckles would scrape it." Up went a quilt of Wall advertisements. One counseled, "Be wise. Clear heads choose Calvert [whiskey]." In another, a Venus peered from atop the scoreboard: "OK," she said, "now that you use GEM clog-proof razor." To her right script read, "Lifebuoy stops B.O." In Philadelphia, a fan wrote on a like ad, "The Phillies use Lifebuoy and they *still* stink."

On Yawkey Way a third plaque reads: "New Fenway Park. Built— 1912. Reconstructed—1934. Boston American League Baseball Company. Thomas A. Yawkey, President." On April 17, 1934, the new Fenway opened. Ironically, the Cronin-managed Senators edged Boston, 6–5, in eleven innings. Quickly, novelty ushered profit to the door. That August 12, 46,766 jammed Fenway for a Yankees double-header. A week later, a Tigers twin bill lured 46,995. On September 22, 1935, a record 47,627 saw another two for the price of one with New York. Curt Gowdy explained: "Those never-to-be-equaled marks came from lax fire laws and league rules that were tightened after World War II."

The 1934 Townies more than doubled '33's attendance. Finally, you sensed, if not optimism, exactly, a sprig of opportunity. Yawkey's wallet brought catcher Rick Ferrell and pitching brother Wes to Boston. From the A's trekked reliever Rube Walberg, Max Bishop, and a madding crowd—Bing Miller, Doc Cramer, Lou Finney, Eric McNair, Mike Higgins, and Dib Williams. Slowly, Fenway again became a prism and progenitor of the archetypal fan's long-buried trust—a magical property "where you can sit for hours," John Updike said, "and feel a serenity that does not exist anywhere else in the world." At home, you could feel it, too, through a new gospel of baseball gossip.

Today, inured to instant replay, downlinking, and fiberglass antennae, the mind's eye falters at vagaries like retail radio stores erecting sidewalk speakers, or streets filled with play-by-play, like shopping malls with Muzak, or burgs from Newton to New Haven gaping wide-mouthed as the Red Sox erupted from a box.

"Understand how big radio was to us when it started in the 1920s. It's all there was—it stopped traffic," counseled Ferdenzi of his childhood home near Boston. A car-garage owner, he said, had a radio and would "turn it up and blast it around town." Literally, traffic stopped to inhale the sound.

"Radio was new," I conceded. "But why was it even bigger by, say, the thirties?"

"It's active, makes you part of the broadcast. It gets you involved. And remember, this hit us like something from another planet. It shook things up, made the world wider." He stopped a long moment. "Everything was different after that."

In 1925, Fred Hoey began a fourteen-year suzerainty as voice of the Braves and Red Sox. Six years later, he was honored with a "Day." In 1939, he exited, his time in radio spent, having (largely) made New England (arguably) America's baseball *aristoi*.

Born in Saxonville, near Framingham, a suburb of Boston, Hoey was already forty when he entered the broadcast booth. From 1909 to 1946, he wrote sports for three of the Hub's then-six daily newspapers: the *Journal*, *Post*, and *American*. Hoey refereed high school and college football, pioneered local hockey play-by-play, and above all, renewed baseball's window on the land over the Colonial and later Yankee Networks.

Hoey was repetitive. "A phrase he used all the time," said Ken Coleman, "was, 'He throws to first and gets his man.' " He also suffered the strange workings of early radio. "On the Yankee Network, every afternoon they'd break for news at six o'clock, no matter what the score. A lot of games then began at 3 P.M. It could be tied, ninth inning, bases loaded, three and two, the crowd going berserk—and if the clock struck six, the carriage became a pumpkin. Boom. You went to news."

Hoey knew his players, with their special strengths and foibles, and region, with its small shops and Indian names and cobblestones and maples. He knew how to vend for sponsors—"When you mention Fred's name," Coleman recalled, "they always talk about Kentucky Club pipe tobacco and Mobil's Flying Red Horse"—and how to imbue his public with Euripidean concern. He did not know how to elude the bottle.

"Yes, he liked the sauce, or so I've heard," said Ned Martin. In Game One of the '33 Series, exploring the borders of hari-kari, Hoey reached the booth with evident breath and fumbling. "He was bombed. In the second or third inning, they had to yank him off the air." The explanation: Hoey had a "bad cold." Perhaps he was trying to forget Boston's 1933 record—63–86.

Once sober, Hoey returned a conqueror. "He came back to Boston, where, of course, people knew about his drinking problem, and all was forgiven," said Coleman. "In fact, there'd been a flood tide of letters—literally *thousands*—written in his defense. They swamped the newspapers, saying, 'How dare you do this to our Fred?' "

In 1939, the Sox' and Braves' new sponsor dared more. General Mills wanted its own barker, not a voice sired by Kentucky Club and the Flying Red Horse—and from St. Louis sprang Frankie Frisch, fired as Cardinals manager in 1938. Hoey died in 1949, at sixty-four, in a gas-filled room, of "Accidental . . . asphyxiation," reported the *Boston Daily Globe*. "He was generally credited with building up baseball broadcasting to the lofty spot it holds in the American sports scene today."

In 1936, the Red Sox finished sixth. A year later, placing fifth, they won their most games in a season—eighty—since 1917. "They were bad, but they were getting better," Hoey said in 1942, "more entertaining, scoring more runs, and people were starting to say, 'Hey, these guys—I can hardly believe it—might win something some day.' " Yawkey thought so. A '36 poster featured players from that year's team. "After waiting 18 years," it said, "Boston now has pennant hopes." In New England, hope made the Red Sox a community peregrination.

One cause was Lefty Grove, arriving in 1934 from Philadelphia. As a boy, Grove taught himself pitching by throwing rocks. The man buoyed the '20s A's, went 31–4 in 1931, and won his three hundredth game in 1941. Poised and spiky, he was even better than his record—for crucial sets inspired Grove, their pressure immersing him. In 1935, he and Wes Ferrell each won twenty games. Lefty won ERA titles in 1935, '36, '38, and '39 with marks between 2.70 and 3.07 runs a game. In 1969, Sox fans named him Boston's all-time best left-handed hurler. Many still term him all of baseball's best.

Grove was lucky, rarely facing teammate Jimmie Foxx. Another Lefty, Gomez, who did, never decided how. One day, the son of Maryland farmers came to bat at Fenway Park. Gomez kept shaking off his catcher's signs. Finally, Bill Dickey walked to the mound. Beyond center field loomed the Buck Printing Co. sign. Spying it, he took time to sample Fenway's smells and sounds.

At last, Dickey turned to his reluctant warrior. "How the hell do you want to pitch to Foxx?" he wondered.

"To tell you the truth," Gomez said, "I'd rather not pitch to him at all."

Think of Ken Griffey Jr., baseball's Strong-arm Kid, or Mark McGwire, swinging like Big Klu by way of the Bambino. Ralph

Kramden in TV's *The Honeymooners* vowed to send wife Alice "to the moon." Some insist that's where their—like Foxx's—orbits land. His niche is steadfast: of Foxx's 534 lifetime home runs, he belted 218 with the '36–42 Sox. Hitting a Boston record fifty homers in '38, Double X was the Yawkeys' only titlist between Ruth and Williams—and only the second AL right-handed batter to twice smack fifty or more. In '38, Foxx led the league in batting average (.349), slugging average (.704), total bases (398), and RBIS (175, including 104 at Fenway Park, a Sox high and baseball's fourth-best ever). Hank Greenberg's 58 homers kept him from the Triple Crown, but not from becoming the first player to win three MVP Awards.

Al Hirshberg wrote: "His personality was one of the gentlest in the game. Foxx hated no one and no one hated him. From the day he first went into the major leagues, he was pleasant to everyone, never impatient with fans or admirers, always accessible to anybody who appreciated him." Added Bob Feller: "Jimmie Foxx could hit a home run over that wall with half a swing." Double X's problem was his full swing at life—drinking and reaching for the check; always, shunning moderation. Retiring, he met a somerset of adversity—failing as a Sox announcer, golf investor, and restauranteur. "Everyone liked him," Ted Williams said. "He was just too soft a touch." Foxx choked to death on a chicken bone when he was only sixty years old.

Pitcher Early Wynn said he'd knock his grandmother down to win. Double X made pitchers cry "uncle." Before 1938, Boston had placed as high as fourth only twice in twenty years. That year's team vaulted from fifth to second. Three Sox led the league in hits—Joe Vosmik (201), Doc Cramer (198), and Foxx (197). Cronin led in doubles. Ben Chapman was third. For a team used to a basement flat, its new niche seemed providential. Or was it accidental? The Townies had not yet reached the Ritz.

One reason was attitude—then a noun, not adjective. Once, Cronin ordered the acquired-from-Washington Chapman to sacrifice bunt. Instead, he swung and hit into a double play. Later, Chapman told reporters, "I don't sacrifice." Other expatriates were, shall we say, equally unintense. Often, Wes Ferrell entered the locker room to say, "I can lick any man in checkers"—that being his primary focus. Coach Tom Daly bought some books on the game and challenged Ferrell. He beat Wes six straight games, at which point Ferrell threw the checkerboard out the window.

A second cause was pitching. In 1938, no Sox hurler won more than fifteen games. Still another was the '36–39 Yankees, leading the nearest team at year's end by 19½, 13, 9½, and 17 games, and winning sixteen Series sets to their rivals' three. Every '36 New York regular but two batted over .300. Gehrig's forty-nine home runs led the league. Red Ruffing enacted the first of four straight twenty-victory seasons. Two years later, Joe DiMaggio (.381) won his first batting title, the last right-handed hitter to top .380. The '38–39 Sox placed second. A saw proclaimed, "The Red Sox will win the pennant in the American League, and the Yankees will win in their league."

"There used to be a saying," Gowdy said, "that players traded to New York performed better in Yankees pinstripes." By contrast, a new name helped after playing in the Hub. Pete Jablonowski pitched badly for the '33 Yawkeys. Renamed Pete Appleton, he was 14–6 for Washington in 1936.

Luck attacked other surnames, too. In September 1935, Boston had the bases loaded, none out, and Cronin up against the Indians. He lined a ball that glanced off third baseman Odell Hale's head and caromed on the fly to Billy Knickerbocker. The shortstop tossed to Roy Hughes on second base for the second out and then threw to first, completing the triple play.

Deferred, the Sox were seldom dull. On June 16, 1938, Foxx became the only AL player to draw six walks in a nine-inning game. Center fielder Cramer hit .302 in 3,111 Red Sox at bats — and smacked one home run. Who was the only '30s Sox player to hit for the cycle? Moose Solters in '34. In 1937, Daly tried to silence Buck (Bobo) Newsom. "Come on, Bobo, I'll warm you up bare-handed," said the former catcher. Daly's hands were sore for a month, but quietude prevailed. A year earlier, Heinie Manush arrived from Washington. A film of the day showed an actor trying to get to sleep in an upper berth. His technique was intoning, "Heinie Manush, Heinie Manush, Heinie Manush . . ." to the rhythm of the wheels. The uptake was predictable: on road trips, players started chanting whenever Heinie neared his berth. "I never got much sleep on a train after that."

The journalist Lincoln Steffens once visited the Soviet Union and predicted an absurdity. "I have seen the future," he said, "and it works." In 1939, the Reds won the NL pennant, baseball televised its first major-league game, and Gehrig left the Yankees' lineup — his dying cry, 2,130 straight games. At Fenway Park, the future meant a man who would become the very manifestation of the Olde Towne Team.

Each decade blazes symbols of its especial place, and time. World War II flaunted the Andrews Sisters. The 1990s blazed Madonna and Roseanne. College students of the early 1970s inhaled Cocker, Cosell, and Crosby, Stills, and Nash. Other names span generations: Ronald Reagan, scripted from radio to a 1980s presidency. Johnny Carson, lauded for hale, light commentary. Theodore Samuel Williams, winning games with his wrists and mind and more with his heart than both.

No hitter who ever lived surpassed the Seasons of the Kid. Ty Cobb flaunted average (.367 lifetime). Al Simmons and Chuck Klein crushed balls that left one zip code for another. The Yankees' Tommy Henrich panted for pressure spots: thus, Mel Allen's moniker, "Old Reliable." Williams did all of the above—and with a panache that was/is indelible.

Author Henry Berry calls him "the overwhelmingly dominant figure of Red Sox baseball." William Shakespeare presaged the Splinter in *Julius Caesar*: "Why, man, he doth bestride the narrow world, like a Colossus." Williams first played ball in the second grade in San Diego. In high school, he banged so many balls over the fence onto an adjacent roof that custodians ordered the coach to switch fields. Ted averaged .430 in high school, signed with the hometown Padres in 1936, and entered the Sox' farm system in '37. In 1938, he hit .366 with Minneapolis with forty-three home runs—already, to paraphrase Ring Lardner, treating mediocrity like a side fish Ted would never order.

Obsession—Williams loved, and lived, to hit—became his leitmotif, like Elvis Presley's hair, Barbara Bush's pearls, or Phyllis Diller's cackle. The Kid awoke at night (to rehearse his swing), wouldn't watch a film (fearing it might dim his vision), and by day walked around holding a bat (to keep its feel. Wait. Don't swing at a bad ball. Concentrate. *Think*!). In batting practice, he screamed at himself for missing a pitch or even grounding out. Fiorella La Guardia said, "When I make a mistake, it's a beaut." At bat, Ted almost never did.

Curt Gowdy shook his head. "Williams is the best fisherman I've ever seen. Best hunter. His eyes tested perfect in the marine air force. They couldn't believe how good his sight was." Hunting, Ted pronounced, "There! Watch two ducks coming at 3 o'clock." Curt responded, "Where?" Two minutes later, ducks appeared. In 1988, New England's cancer charity, the Jimmy Fund, hailed Number 9 at a seventieth birthday dinner. Among the guests was U.S. Senator John Glenn, Ted's flight commander in the Korean War. "Williams was his wingman," Gowdy said. "So I asked him, 'What kind of pilot was he?' " Glenn replied, "Best I ever saw."

Statistics are said to lie. Tell that to opposing pitchers. Six batting titles—1941, '42, '47, '48, '57, and '58 (.406, .356, .343, .369, .388, and .328). Four home-run and RBI crowns—1941, '42, '47, and '49 (thirty-seven, thirty-six, thirty-two, and forty-three) and 1939, '42, '47, and '49 (145, 137, 114, and 159, tied with Vern Stephens), respectively. Two Most Valuable Player Awards—1946 and '49. Two Triple Crowns—1942 and '47. Lifetime .344 average, 2,654 hits, and Sox-high 521 homers, including 248 at Fenway. Last man to hit .400. Hall of Fame, '66. Sox' greatest all-time player, as voted by the fans. Williams's laundry list would surfeit dry cleaners from Kennebunk to Holyoke.

"Perspective is all," a teacher once told me. The Kid's caveats surpass many careers. Eighteen All-Star games, hitting .304. Second all-time in slugging percentage. Eleven, eight, six, and three times, respectively, he drew one hundred or more walks, hit thirty or more home runs, scored 131 or more runs, and knocked in 137 or more runs. He had as many as forty-three homers, eighty-six extra-base hits, 368 total bases, and 162 walks. At thirty-nine, he hit .388 to win the batting title, and won his final crown at forty. Gowdy noted, with remembrance neither vague nor selective, "All this despite missing five years in the military"—World War II, 1943–45; Korea, 1952–53. "Add those five years to his career and there'd be no place in the record books for anyone but Ted."

Time to second-guess: perhaps statistics *can* lie. By any reckoning, Williams's childhood wish corkscrewed into vérité: "I wanted people to see me walk down a street, point to me, and say, 'There goes the greatest hitter who ever lived.'"

Memory gentled Tom Yawkey's voice. "Some say Ted made Red Sox history," he observed in 1975. "It's more accurate to say that for generations Ted *was* Red Sox history." In 1939, Ted homered off left-hander Thornton Lee. In 1960, he homered off his son, right-hander Don Lee. Williams arrived in Boston as the Third Reich swallowed Czechoslovakia, John Steinbeck's *Grapes of Wrath* was published, and cinemas starred Garbo and Barrymore and Rogers and Astaire. He left as the Soviets shot down an American U-2 plane, *The Andy Griffith Show* warmed network television, and Nixon and Kennedy staged the most theatric election of our age.

Leave it to Teddy Ballgame: his timing was nonpareil, if fallible. Born twelve days before the Sox won their last World Series, Ted struck out in his first two big-league at bats. Next time up, he touched Ruffing for a double. Already, Number 9's plots and stories and drama rounded out scenes. In 1939, Williams batted .327, had thirty-one homers and 145 RBIS, and became Rookie of the Year. His goings-on of reminiscence included tipping the cap. "Yep, he waved it," affirmed 1939–51 team-mate Bobby Doerr. "But next year they started to boo Ted for hitting fewer home runs, and Ted got mad. To him, they were fair-weather." Williams never doffed the cap again.

Instead, he buoyed a team formed largely of immigrants. In 1934, '38, and '40, Billy Werber, Joe Vosmik, and Doc Cramer rapped two hundred or more hits apiece. In 1935, Wes Ferrell won twenty-five games, started thirty-eight, and completed thirty-one. Grove won eight straight games in 1939, forging Fenway Park's highest-winning percentage (.764, 55–17) for a Sox left-handed pitcher. Foxx's '38 fiesta starred a Fenway-high thirty-five home runs, ninety-two extra base hits, 398 total bases, 119 walks, ten multihomer games, and a .349 batting title (.405 at the Fens). Said Doerr: "Mr. Yawkey kept trying to buy a pennant." Failing, he would soon build from within.

A right-handed pull hitter, Double X loved Fenway's closer-than-close left-field wall. Meanwhile, the lefty Williams hit to Fenway's yawning stretch in right-center field. Enter Williamsburg—1940 bull pens in front of the bleachers to replace the old bull pen areas in foul ground beyond the dugouts. "They were placed there for Ted," confided Gowdy. "It shortened his home-run distance [by 23 feet]." The diminution made the then-rail-thin—ergo, Splendid—Splinter more content with Fenway's contour. "He loved its tiny foul territory [many would-be outs found seats], the center-field backdrop [no advertisements littered the fence], and how seats above it weren't sold [precluding white pitches leaving white shirts]." Williams hit .403 at Fenway in 1951 and '57—and .428 in 1941. He also began a decade in which baseball became all-meaning.

Between 1939 and 1950, eleven major-league teams won at least a single pennant. The other five grasped the first division. Eight times, a pennant was decided in the season's final game. Recalling and applauding the last decade to have a .400 hitter or a pitcher complete more than thirty-five games in a season or the Indians win a World Series; the first (excluding the Cubs) to have all teams play at night (Detroit saw the light in '48) and boast a black major leaguer (Jack Roosevelt Robinson), a one-armed outfielder (Pete Gray), a team that drew more than 2 million spectators (the 1946 Yankees), and two pennant races that ended in a tie ('46, '48); the first/last in which a batter hit safely in fifty-six straight games and a "Subway (here, Streetcar)

Series" rose west of the Mississippi—one marvels at the stories in which baseball has been rich.

It is true that Fenway did not write all of them. Retrieving the past, even a cursory glance shows that few parks wrote more.

Disbelieve it, if you will. The age began with baseball's Tyrone Power aping Dagwood Bumstead on the mound. For months, Williams hammered his manager to "let me pitch. I can do anything." On August 24, 1940, Cronin let Ted throw the last two innings of a 12–1 loss to Detroit. Line score: three hits, one run, and a strikeout of Rudy York. Underwhelmed, the Sox never pitched him again. Why would they? In New England, baseball now meant the plot whose grass was/is real and bleachers that were/are full and—sorry, Bronxophiles—the rich antiquity of baseball's greatest park, true baseball, as it was/is *meant* to be played.

"Think back upon this century," Ned Martin mused in his erudite way. "Say great owners, and Yawkey comes to mind. Hitting can't mean anyone but Williams. Intimate parks—that's Fenway. It's also quite a trio." Bushwhacking boredom through 1960, they were not, of course, inviolate.

Charges flew: Ted walked too often, pulled too much, and revered the *"me"* in *"team."* "Ridiculous," Doerr fumed. "In baseball you have to score runs—Ted's walks did. Why would he change the world's best batting stroke? And how his teammates loved him." Another problem was reported to be the owner. Yawkey drank, or not enough—was too patient with players, and abiding of ineptitude. He hired hangers-on, declined to fire friends, and wouldn't know a pitcher if he poured a Narragansett. "Bull!" exploded Williams. "The Sox were dead before T.A. He brought them back to life." In sock-happy 1930, Earl Webb led Boston with only sixteen homers and sixty-six RBIs. By '36, Foxx tallied forty-one and 143. From 1939 to 1942, the Townies placed second thrice. Only the Yankees stood in the courthouse door.

Even Fenway took a curve. Its supposed curse: the Sox stocked slow pull hitters to bash the wall and then floundered on the road. "Yeah?" Yawkey might demand if still alive. "Then how did we *ever* sweep those games from the Yankees in New York?" How: see below. Where: Yankee Stadium. What: a five-game series. When: July 7–9, 1939.

That year's Yankees won 106 sets. By coincidence, Yankee Stadium would host the All-Star Game. To prepare, on July 7 American League manager Joe McCarthy, missing the first Soxfest, stayed in his hotel room.

Why not? Nine Yankees graced the twenty-five-man AL roster. New York was enduring a one-hundred-degree heat wave. What, me worry? The Bombers led Boston by 11½ games. Was Alfred E. Neuman a Bosox fan? Trick question. *Mad* magazine's cover boy was born in July 1955.

The first game showed how a body learns baseball by falling in love with a team. Cronin homered off Ruffing. Joe DiMaggio's base hit tied the score. Williams untied it by singling in one run and scoring a second. Sox win, 4–3. McCarthy laughed, "It's a 10½ game lead. This is too close for comfort." Some joke: the next day he left his room for the dugout and a doubleheader. Fritz Ostermueller scattered four Yanks hits in the opener. The nightcap mixed Double X, homering off Johnny Murphy, and Doerr, plating one run and robbing Charlie Keller of another. Each game ended 2–1. McCarthy was no longer the Good Humor Man. "Who the hell are supposed to be the world champions, us or the Red Sox?"

On July 9, the alarm rang: the Red Sox were coming—or was history in the making? A crowd of nearly fifty thousand braved Sunday traffic to see if Boston could divide another two for the price of one. Said Cronin, "We didn't dream of a [five-game] sweep—just, 'Let's win one and keep off the floor.'" After 4–3 and 5–3 wins, you had to pick Boston off the ceiling. The actors: in the fourth game—Foxx, with a triple past the center-field flagpole; and Cronin, hitting a two-run, eighth-inning, game-winning homer—and in the fifth—Double X, with a two-run blast; catcher Johnny Peacock, plating two on a New York error; "Black Jack" Wilson, with five straight scoreless innings; and another reliever, Joe Heving, blanking the Yankees for the last two innings.

Bart Giamatti said, "Baseball is an unalloyed good." To Boston it seemed so in July 1939. Three days, five victories, and ultimately, a twelve-game winning streak. Scribes were stunned: when had Boston last swept even *four* straight at Yankee Stadium? No one knew. McCarthy was furious, but only briefly: his brigade won the pennant by nineteen games. The Soxnoscenti were purified. Observed the *New York Times* on July 10: "[Yesterday's] crowd cheered mainly for the Red Sox at every turn."

"Those damn Yankees, why can't we beat 'em?" cursed Joe Hardy in a 1958 movie. In the last summer of an uncertain peace, the Boston American League Baseball Company did.

As president, George Bush gently ribbed the "vision thing." Boston's lack of vision sold Babe Ruth to New York, spurned Pie Traynor in a tryout, traded Red Ruffing for Cedric Durst, and shipped infielder Bucky Walters to Philadelphia, where he became an All-Star pitcher. (On the other hand, the Sox signed Ted Lepcio in 1952–59.) Yawkey couldn't bring them back. He could, however, build a farm system whose safety lay in numbers.

From the early '40s to 1951, four Sox-signed starters—the Splinter, Doerr, Dom DiMaggio, and Johnny Pesky—formed the Townies' core. If not enough—save 1946, it wasn't—failure stemmed from what Williams called "the Yankees' experience, defense, pitching, and probably finesse, but certainly not hitting. We could hit every bit as well as they could, if not better."

In 1940, every infield regular hit more than twenty homers and Williams hit .344. Boston flagged to fourth. In 1941–42, the Sox finished 7 and 10½ games, respectively, ahead of Chicago and St. Louis—but 17 and 9 behind the Yankees. Think of baseball as a river. Quietly, like still water shedding ice, the Red Sox flowed with Hall of Famers. (In 1940–41, five often graced the lineup—Grove, Doerr, Cronin, Foxx, and Williams.)

Doerr arrived in 1937 to thrice hit more than .300, make nine All-Star teams, five years lead the league in double plays, and six times top it in fielding and drive in more than one hundred runs. At second base, Doerr handled an AL-record 414 chances in seventy-three games without an error. At bat, he smacked 145 Fenway homers—fifth behind the Kid, Carl Yastrzemski, Jim Rice, and Dwight Evans. To Williams, Doerr was "the silent captain of the Red Sox." Gowdy thought him "one of the two sweetest men I have met in baseball. The other, King Kong Keller." Doerr and Williams fished, but had a problem. Bobby suffered migraine headaches. Williams could be dour and difficult, but a chatterbox with friends. "We'd be in the boat," Doerr laughed, "and Ted'd talk for hours." Finally, he employed a down-home rule. "Each hour, no matter what he was going on about, I got to interrupt. It's amazing how well it worked out."

In 1940, Yawkey signed a younger brother of baseball's best center fielder. Like Joe, bespectacled Dom DiMaggio was bright and fleet, but he lacked Joe's power and celebrity. "The Little Professor" hit .300 three times, but only .298 lifetime. "That troubled me," he said, "and I guess word got around. Once, Tommy Henrich caught a deep fly I hit that was a sacrifice that brought in the winning run. He didn't have to catch it, but he did." Later, Henrich confessed that the catch bothered him because he felt that somehow one hit would have given Dom a .300 average. "It wouldn't, of course. I laughed and told him to forget it."

Abiding to a Bostonian were Dom's play in center field, hitting streaks—twenty-two, twenty-seven, and thirty-four games—and his home-grown career, begun as a '30s clubhouse boy with Portland of the Pacific Coast League and evolving into a big-league player, coach, manager, and broadcaster. "It's hard to make predictions," opined Yogi Berra, "especially about the future." Not after John Michael Paveskovich's rookie year. Johnny Pesky had once shined Doerr's shoes as a clubhouse boy in Portland. In 1942, the Oregonian batted .331, led the league with 205 hits, and scored more than one hundred runs. "He was our table setter," Cronin mused, "and no one set it better."

Pesky only once batted below .300, three times led the league in hits, and six straight years scored more than one hundred runs. His arsenal linked singles off the Wall and tattoos off the right-field pole (hence, Pesky's Pole). The shortstop/third baseman earned first base the old-fashioned way: he swung—in 4,085 at bats facing just one 3–0 count. In 1950, versus Washington, Pesky stepped out to check the sign. "With Williams up next, no one wanted to walk me," he said. "But here it was—hit away. I thought [then-manager Steve] O'Neill had gone nuts."

His reaction was understandable. At Fenway Park, many managers have confessed to feeling daft.

Recalling the 1920s, the Sox' playbill of talent in the early '40s made you pinch yourself. In 1941, theater filled New York, where Joe D. made "fifty-six" a keepsake, and Brooklyn, winning its first pennant since the last year of Wilson's presidency. It avoided Philadelphia (the A's and Phils placed last) and detoured around Braves Field (seventh, for the fourth straight year) before moving down the Charles to a wonder of our big-league time.

Williams's 1941 is now as part of baseball as Joe Wood's 1912, Willie Mays playing stickball, or Gehrig's farewell ode. In early April he chipped an ankle bone and missed the first two weeks of the season. That helped: "I never hit as well in cold weather as I did in the dead of summer—*never*." Joe Dobson helped, too. Acquired from Cleveland, he wasn't pitching regularly. To keep sharp, he threw daily batting practice. "I got the most practice of my life," Williams said, "and the best, because Dobson had a hell of a curve and a good overhand fastball, and he always bore down."

In July, Williams's three-run, ninth-inning homer won the All-Star Game, 7–5, at Briggs Stadium. "What people still remember," said

Doerr, "is Ted jumping around the bases" — joyous, uninhibited, utterly aglow. The Yankees clinched September 4, so the Kid's pressure became interior: become the first since Bill Terry in 1930 to get four hits every ten times at bat. By June, Williams's average was .436; late August, .402; mid-September, .413. The final Saturday, Boston played in Philadelphia — or would have, had rain not interfered. Ted was hitting .3995 — .400 in the record book. Cronin pleaded with him to skip Sunday's year-ending doubleheader. "You got your .400. Sit it out." Ted said, "No, I don't want it that way. I'll play." John Wayne was never more Aetean on film.

Only twenty-three, Williams and friend/clubhouse attendant Johnny Orlando walked for miles Sunday morning on the dank streets of Philadelphia. The Kid was morphing from prodigy to legend. In the first game, he whacked a home run and single. Freed from ball and chain, Ted added a pair of second-set hits: His double broke the loud-speaker horn. Six-for-eight, a .406 average, and a sustaining niche in history.

How could the next few years compare? In baseball, they couldn't.

A month later, Nazi tanks drove within forty miles of Moscow. By December, crossroads. A Soviet counterassault stunned the Wehrmacht. The Japanese spawned a "day that will live in infamy." Roosevelt asked Congress to declare war on Japan. Hitler declared war on the United States of America. Replied FDR as darkness terrified: "Soon we and not our enemies will have the offensive."

In January 1942, he wrote a letter to Commissioner Kenesaw Mountain Landis. "I honestly feel it would be best for the country to keep baseball going." Players soon went to places like Burma and Bataan and Bordeaux and the Bulge. In '42, Williams won the Triple Crown — .356, thirty-six homers, and 137 RBIs — then joined the navy. A year later, Pete Fox, Doerr, and Jim Tabor, respectively, led the incredibly shrinking Hose with .288, sixteen, and 85.

By 1944, most teams were stocked with has-beens and never-weres, cast-offs and rookies, and men rejected by the service. Rosters pulsated with players designated 4-F. Douglas Wallop wrote, "The game being played on the field was recognizable, but many of the players were not." Among those who were: Doerr, topping the league in 1944 in slugging percentage; George Metkovich, hitting safely in twenty-five straight games; Tex Hughson and Dave (Boo) Ferriss, winning twenty-two and twenty-one sets, respectively, in 1942 and '45; and '43's Cronin, pinch-hitting eighteen safeties and a record five home runs. On June 17, two of his pinch-drives won a doubleheader. "I guess the old man showed them today," he said, forced to play because of talent for whom even obscurity was too pleasant an end.

In 1943–44, Doerr, Leon Culberson, and Bob Johnson hit for the cycle. (Cronin, the Kid, and Moose Solters also did between 1934 and 1946.) Williams, Carl Yastrzemski, Jim Rice, and Mike Greenwell all became Sox All-Star left fielders. The fifth man could stump *What's My Line?*: Johnson, thirty-seven in 1944. War transformed creativity (Mike Ryba played nine positions in a minor-league game, then drove the team bus to the train) to eccentricity (Ryba—a.k.a. "the Colonel of the Bullpen"—lined up its residents for the national anthem, then swapped salutes at its end).

In 1945, the A's Hal Peck made a bad throw that hit a Fenway pigeon and deflected to the second baseman. The pigeon was killed, and runner Skeeter Newsome was tagged out. That year, Boston's Tom McBride camped under what he thought was a long drive by Sam Chapman. Too late, he discovered what it was. Willie Horton and Billy Hunter later skulled birds in a game and batting practice. Williams used a rifle until the Humane Society cried *no mas*.

In the real war, America neared "the blessed hush of history." A citizen read of Yalta and Okinawa and Iwo Jima and Remagen, where a platoon from the Ninth Armored Divison crossed the Rhine, and the Elbe, where American and Soviet troops toasted one another with captured German champagne. Roosevelt died of a cerebral hemorrhage. Germany and Japan surrendered.

Returning U.S. soldiers would encounter old, unfamiliar places. Among them was not Fenway Park. The Sox had not won a pennant since the *last* war ended. Ahead lay the Church of Baseball's reward for flaunting the patience of Job.

7

Baseball Has It All

By George Bush

It is said that you never forget your first love. For me, that was, and is, Barbara. But a runner-up is baseball. My first memories of baseball came as a boy, growing up in Connecticut. I followed the game, and memorized its box scores. My favorite team was the Boston Red Sox—and their home was Fenway Park. It's nice to know that some things never change.

In a sense, the Red Sox reflect America's love affair with baseball. Millions watch it; millions more listen to, read about, and even argue over it. Each day, we become self-anointed experts. Baseball is the most democratic of sports—of course, it's also the most republican—and whether in the major leagues, or in Little League, what counts is the size of your *heart* and of your *dreams*.

Babe Ruth, whom I met in 1948 when he gave his papers to Yale University, referred to this when he said, "Baseball comes up from the youth. You've got to start from way down, when you're six or seven years old. And if you try hard enough, you're bound to come out on top." He knew that baseball enchants kids of *every* age, and evokes a tapestry of memory. We mark chapters of our lives by the baseball moments we recall.

For me, many of those moments have involved Fenway Park—and the ultimate kid, the Kid. As a teenager, I thrilled with my dad to Joe Cronin and Dom DiMaggio and Johnny Pesky. Like now, the Red Sox were New England's team—and Fenway, New England's house. Today, visiting Fenway, you see the retired number of another player I watched so often. He is a dear friend—and the greatest hitter who ever lived.

I admire Ted Williams for many reasons. The first is character. Ted couldn't stand what he termed "politicians"—phonies. On the other hand, his teammates adored him—just like his country does because of his service in Korea and World War II.

Ted confronted gunfire in thirty-six combat missions, but never complained about 5½ years robbed from the prime of his career. Service deprived Ted of even greater statistics, yet made *him* even greater in the eyes of all America.

Curt Gowdy calls Ted "the most competent man" he's ever met. I've seen that fishing and hunting. Certainly, Number 9 has never lacked for confidence. In 1939 spring training, a skinny rookie stood next to Bobby Doerr. Doerr said, "Wait til you see Jimmie Foxx hit." Replied the Kid: "Wait til Foxx sees *me* hit!" Yet Ted has a gentler side. He raised millions of dollars for charity—a point of light before my administration coined the term.

Ted got to Cooperstown via two Triple Crowns, a pair of Most Valuable Player Awards, and two others he might have won. He played in sixteen All-Star Games, hit .344, won six batting titles—and would have won another if today's walk rules applied. Tommy Lasorda often said, "I want my team to think baseball the way my wife shops. Twenty-four hours a day." That's how Ted was about hitting. He performed sport's hardest task—hitting a baseball—as well as anyone ever has.

Hitting was something I never mastered: at Yale, I batted eighth—*second* cleanup, I put it. Still, I tried to teach it after Barbara and I packed up our red Studebaker in 1948 and left the Northeast for Texas. I coached Little League for a while, and all four of our boys played. One of them, George Jr., became general managing partner of the Texas Rangers. Today, he is the governor of Texas. As for Barbara, well, even then thousands of Texas kids played Little League—and there were times I thought she was carpooling them all! Incidentally, Barbara knows how to score a ball game along with the best of them.

Even from a distance we followed the Red Sox at Fenway. Together, the Bush family—including our youngest child, Doro—marveled at the '67 Impossible Dream. Then came a game that showed how baseball is an American institution and a global affair.

In 1975, the Sox and Reds staged what has been called the greatest game ever played—Game Six of that year's World Series. Carlton Fisk smacked his twelfth-inning home run at 12:34 A.M. eastern time, giving Boston a 7–6 triumph. I was stationed in Beijing as envoy to China at the time, and recall how our embassy's Red Sox fans—nearly eleven thousand miles from Fenway Park—were cheering Fisk's homer almost as soon as it occurred.

Later, as president, I saw time and again how baseball hit a grand-slam home run. Always, it was our ambassador of goodwill—whether I was greeting Little Leaguers on the South Lawn of the White House, hailing the world champion Oakland A's in the Rose Garden, or telling Polish boys and girls in Warsaw, "Few things show America's love like bringing our national pastime to you"—linking teamwork, generosity, and dedication. Baseball has it all.

Ted Williams was a great friend of Roy Campanella, the beloved catcher of the Brooklyn Dodgers. Once, Campy explained why baseball is special. "You have to be a man to be a big leaguer," he said, "but you have to have a lot of little boy in you, too."

At Fenway Park, you see and feel what Campy meant. Like Ted, Roy, and all of us who love the game, two of the most beautiful words in any language are "Play ball."

George Bush was the forty-first president of the United States. In Curt Smith's book on presidential libraries, Windows on the White House *(South Bend, Ind.: Diamond Communications, 1997), the author writes: "[As a child] Bush loved what was then true, and real—'a nation,' he later said, 'closer to* The Waltons *than* The Simpsons.' *Losing that, we lay griefs upon America."*

8

Heart

1946–50

In 1945, the Cubs and Tigers played a World Series that starred comic-opera shortstops Roy Hughes and James (Skeeter) Webb. Said writer Warren Brown: "I don't think either team can win." (Detroit did, in seven games.) The next year, back from war, the soldiers of baseball's green and tended fields fed a land starved for peacetime heroes. "Oh, man, we were fearless," related Joe Garagiola, then a twenty-year-old catcher. "Anything you did, you felt you were ahead of the game. Not that you'd been in the trenches, necessarily. No matter *what* you'd done, you were so glad to be back"—and from the game's eastern- to westernmost posts (aptly, Boston and St. Louis) baseball as deliverance began a mad dash around the bases.

Like the game, the Red Sox were glad to be home. In 1942, owner Yawkey rued, "I'd pay the price of admission just to watch Williams come back for batting practice." In 1946, baseball broke its all-time attendance record by 80 percent. The players were recognizable again—and 18 million people turned out to see them. In the AL, six of eight teams cracked their single-season attendance mark. The Yankees, placing third, lured 2,265,512 fans. The Sox doubled their prior high—1,416,944 versus '42's 730,340.

What they did astounds. Boston had win streaks of 12 and 17 games, played 60–17 ball at Fenway Park, and won 104 games and the flag by 12 over Detroit. Doerr knocked in 116 runs. Dom D. hit .317, Pesky .335 on 208 hits. Williams left the Naval Air Force to yoke .342, thirty-eight homers, and 123 RBIs. On June 9, he hit Fenway Park's longest-ever blast—502 feet, to right field—which landed on top of the straw hat of

Joseph A. Boucher, fifty-six, a construction engineer from Albany, New York. "The sun was right in our eyes," he said. "All we could do was duck. I'm glad I didn't stand up. They said it bounced a dozen rows higher, but after it hit my head, I wasn't interested." His seat is now painted red — number twenty-one, bleacher section forty-two, row thirty-seven.

"By the time the press of Boston has completed its daily treatment of Theodore S. Williams," John Lardner wrote that summer, "there is no room in the papers for anything but two sticks of agate about Truman and housing, and one column for the last Boston girl to be murdered on the beach." Number 9 homered on Opening Day at Washington. That July, in the All-Star Game before 34,906 at Fenway, he ripped two homers, one off Rip Sewell's blooper pitch, or "eephus ball," had four of the Americans' fourteen hits, and knocked in five of their twelve runs.

"I loved watching Ted take command," Pesky said. "What people don't know is that he was out of the box when he hit the blooper pitch. It was late in the game so it wasn't called. Actually, he [Sewell] threw him two bloopers — Ted just looked at the first one. It was real high. But the next pitch was right in his wheelhouse." It was a season for dramaturgy. On September 13, Ted poked the only inside-the-park homer of his career to left field to clinch the pennant, 1–0. Mused Doerr, "There were mortal players, and there was Ted."

In '46, returning veterans enlarged rosters to thirty men per team. "Usually, you only got twenty-five," recalled Doerr. "We had ballplayers all over the place." Most were now Sox-reared. Tex Hughson again won twenty games. A year earlier, Dave (Boo) Ferriss had won twenty-one — but against whom? Only three AL regulars hit more than .300. In '46, Ferriss won his first ten games, later twelve in a row, and never lost a game at Fenway. Bo(o) knew both pitching (e.g., a league-best 25–6 and .806 winning percentage) and hitting (.250 lifetime). His mates adored him: "What a guy," said Pesky. "He's the only man I ever knew in baseball who never had an unkind word to say." He was even said to be ambidextrous — to Yogi Berra, "amphibious."

Briefly, Ferriss rivaled a blend of Walter Mitty and Walter Johnson. "He was a splendid competitor," Yawkey said after asthma and a hurt arm ended his career. "He was also a fine person." Mates included 17–9 Mickey Harris, thirteen-game winner Joe Dobson, and little-used relievers Mike Ryba, Earl Johnson, Mace Brown, and Ellis Kinder. (Bored, Ryba focused on hotel lobby-sitting. In one month, he counted thirty-five weddings.) Hal Wagner and Roy Partee caught. At third Yawkey had Pinky Higgins, and George Metkovich and Tom McBride in right. In April, Cronin turned the final screw—trading Eddie Lake for the Tigers' Rudy York.

York was a lumbering "part Cherokee, part first baseman," some-one said, who knocked in 119 runs and once chewed out Williams in the dugout for not hustling. "I've never stopped trying and I expect you to do the same."

The Kid respected the older Bunyan: "He knew all about that lit-tle game you play with the pitcher." In 1946, Williams, who also did, rarely stopped trying. What Red Sox Nation loved is that Boston rarely stopped hitting.

Imagine that Johnny Carson is hosting *The Tonight Show*. Ed McMahon says, "Williams, Pesky, Doerr, Wagner, Ferriss, Harris, Dom DiMaggio, and York." Carson, as Carnak, answers, "Which Red Sox made the 1946 All-Star team?" (The first four started.) How good were the Townies' first champions since bodies draped Verdun? They had the Kid. They had just razed the American League. It seems somehow alien to say it now, but they had never lost a World Series.

One reason was Williams's power: a pull hitter, he shunned left field like a Constitutional offense. On July 14, T. Ballgame clubbed Cleveland in the first game of a doubleheader. In set two, Tribe short-stop/manager Lou Boudreau shifted all but his leftfielder to the right-field side of second base. "He had this crazy infield lineup," Williams recalled. "It seemed everybody was over on the right side. I said, 'What the hell is this? He's trying to make a joke out of the game.' "

The dare taunted: *now*, hit one through. Quickly, the Boudreau Shift moved to other teams. In the National League, Cardinals man-ager Eddie Dyer made a note. The solution was hardly intricate: Ty Cobb, among others, urged Ted to go to the other field. The problem: Williams refused out of strategy or, more likely, pride. One day, he hit into Fenway's left-field corner. "Who is this Ty Cobb?" Ted roared, then pulled the ball his next time up.

"He'd get angry," said Mel Allen, the Yankees' 1939–64 siren of a voice. "He'd take the challenge and hit right into that shift. If he hit the other way, I think he would have hit .400 five or six times." On Wednesday, October 9, 1946, Dyer left only one player on the left side of the diamond—the Boudreau Shift. The Splinter bunted. The act, and stage, seduced—Game Three of the World Series against a team that, like the Red Sox, was not without its lure.

From 1926–34, the St. Louis Cardinals—a.k.a. the St. Louis Swifties, Runnin' Redbirds, or, more memorably, the Gas House

Gang—baited opponents, flung dirt at umpires, and disrupted hotel lob-
bies with workmen's tools on road trips. They formed a band, the
Mississippi Mudcats—carting fiddles and harmonicas, washboards
and guitars, and playing "Rock Island Line" and "The Wreck of the Old
'97" on train rides to Cincinnati and points east. They won five pennants and three World Series, and made aggression a symphony. They
were raucous, defiant, and sleek.

By 1946, Frankie Frisch and Pepper Martin and Dizzy Dean yielded
to Stan Musial, whose uncoiling stance placed infielders in jeopardy;
other infielders Whitey Kurowski and rangy Marty (Slats) Marion and
freckled Red Schoendienst of Germantown, Illinois; outfielders Terry
Moore, Harry Walker, and Enos "Country" Slaughter, playing each
inning with the full measure of his strength; and pitchers Murray
Dickson, Howie Pollet, and Harry "The Cat" Brecheen. They erased a
6½-game Dodgers lead to force the bigs' first playoff, swept its best-of-
three, then fixed to do what five other NL teams had not—beat the Sox.

The oddsmakers made Boston a seven-to-twenty favorite. It was
going to be so easy. "We want to keep our edge," Cronin said, slating
exhibitions with AL players while the Brooks and Redbirds dueled. On
October 1, Washington's Mickey Haefner hit Williams on the elbow,
which swelled to three times its normal size. "He didn't complain," said
Doerr, "but you could see it hurt." The Sox won Game One, 3–2, on
York's tenth-inning homer. Next day, reality: Ted didn't hit out of the
infield. Blanked only eight times in the regular season, Boston fell, 3–0,
to Brecheen.

Cronin wasn't worried: "We'll handle this thing back at Fenway,"
he said before Game Three. "The Sox are not going to want to come
back to St. Louis." In particular, York, Williams, and Ferriss seemed to
hear: respectively, bombing a three-run homer, bunting safely, and spacing six hits. The 4–0 shutout was the Townies' first home Series game
since September 11, 1918. To many, Game Four seemed as long: twenty
Cardinals hits in a 12–3 laugher. Rare sixteen-millimeter film of that
game shows Slaughter sliding, Doerr covering second base, and a blur
of type on the scoreboard; it etches a tenant: "Boston Yanks. Fenway
Park" as well as other scions of pro football's then-ragtag clan: "Pittsburgh
Steelers, Washington Redskins, Chicago Cardinals, Los Angeles Rams,
Philadelphia Eagles." Perhaps the turn of seasons confused the Sox, who
fumbled four errors, leading to four unearned runs.

In 1946, Autumn Occasion box and bleacher seats cost $7.20 and
$1.20, respectively. Friday, October 11—Game Five: Fenway's last Series
set until 1967—made the price worthwhile. The Red Sox whacked

eleven hits. Leon Culberson, portending, homered. Dobson beat St. Louis, 6–3. Ahead, three games to two, the Sox now had only to win one more match to repeat 1903, '12, '15, '16, and '18. The downside was Ted: he still wasn't hitting. "I'm sure due to hit one," T. Ballgame said. He would, in 1947.

That weekend, the Series returned to Sportsman's Park and its inviting 310-foot right-field porch. Brecheen made it look a continent away, winning for the second time, 4–1. A day off preceded the Sox' first Game Seven since 1903. Boston scored a first-inning run: only Moore, robbing Williams in deep center field, kept it from another. Scoring thrice, St. Louis stayed ahead on great catches by Walker (off Williams) and Moore (again, off Higgins). Behind 3–1 in the eighth inning, the Sox tied the score on a two-run DiMaggio double that brought Number 9 to bat. "It's funny," Cronin, unlaughing, said. "Three-three. Our guy up. The whole year in one moment." Against Brecheen, relieving, the Kid popped up to end the inning: he now had five singles in twenty-five Series at bats.

DiMaggio jammed his ankle sliding into second base. Culberson went to center field as Dobson, relieving Boo Ferriss, left the game, journeyman Bob Klinger relieved, and Slaughter singled in the bottom of the eighth. With two outs, Walker came to bat. What happened next forms a bridge between unlikelihood and inevitability. On a 2–1 count, Dyer ordered the hit-and run. Country sped toward second, Walker hit to left-center, and weak-armed Culberson fielded the ball. Slaughter sighted third. Culberson relayed to Pesky, who—at this point, accounts cleave—turned toward the plate and (a) was or was not startled to see Enos running and (b) did or did not hesitate before throwing the ball up the third-base line as Slaughter scored the tiebreaking run.

The Sox would not be the Sox without a final, anguished, Lucy-took-the-football tease. In the ninth, the tying run—pinch-runner Paul Campbell—reached third with one away. Roy Partee then fouled out, and McBride grounded out. Brecheen became the first pitcher in twenty-six years to win three World Series matches, and St. Louis took a Game Seven for the fourth of six straight times. "I can't understand it," said Ferriss. "Those were good pitches they hit." Cronin, stunned, said, "It was those three catches—by Moore and Walker on Williams and by Moore on Higgins—that's what beat us."

"Holding" the ball hovered like a northeasterly over the rest of Pesky's life. "Culberson really lobbed the ball to me," he invariably said. "I would have needed a rifle to nail Slaughter." Reality blurred with myth. After the Series Pesky returned to Oregon, where, seeking anonymity, he wore dark glasses to a college football game. He enjoyed it more than the quarterback, who kept fumbling. Finally, a nearby fan had a brainstorm: "Give the ball to Pesky," he thundered. "He'll hold on to it."

Pesky both was and was not a goat. The Cardinals' Joe Garogiola hit an un–Joe G.-like .316. The Sox made ten errors to St. Louis' four — but they had not made the Series on fielding. Hitting got them there — Boston batted .271 from April through September — and failed them in October (.240). Afterward, entraining at Union Station for the long ride home, Williams locked the door of his compartment and began to weep. In his distress, he failed to draw the compartment blinds. Looking up, the Kid saw more than one thousand people intruding on private grief — as public now as his .200 Series average, or Slaughter's mad dash for home.

Braves 1950–58 pitcher Ernie Johnson tells a story. "Two little ladies entered the park about the fifth inning and sat down behind a priest. 'What's the score, Father?' they said. The priest said, 'Nothing-nothing.' One lady said to the other, 'Oh, good, we haven't missed anything.' We go to the eighth inning, and a pinch-hitter bats for the local team. He makes the sign of the cross before stepping into the box. One little old lady leaned over and said, 'Father, father, will that help?' The priest turned around and said, 'Not if he can't hit.' "

Nineteen forty-six marked a dividing line that, once crossed, few would double back upon. As Slaughter tore around the bases, George Vecsey wrote, he "was like a steam engine racing his way across the country, telling the people: 'Look — look — the men are back — the war is over — baseball has survived!' " Its effect on Boston was more abiding — a belief in Murphy's Law (if something can go wrong, it will) over the Law of Averages (life is fair; things even out).

The Sox had expected to win. Losing, they began to doubt. "A dynasty," Williams laughed. "It was supposed to begin in '46. Hell, I thought for sure I'd get in another. Cobb had three World Series and only hit in one." The reverse begot others. Ted won the '47 Triple Crown: Incredibly, Joe D. was voted MVP. Two lost batting titles proved life's unfairness. In 1949, Williams lost on the last day to George Kell. (Both hit .343; Kell won on the fourth digit. "He got two or three hits that day," Williams recalled. "More power to him.") In 1954, Ted had only 386 official at bats, fewer than the 400 needed to qualify, because his 136 walks were then considered unofficial plate appearances. Thus, with a .345 average, Williams lost to Bobby Avila's .341. (Although too late for Ted, a 1957 rule change made walks official.) Above all, Boston lost two pennants it could, and should, have won.

At Fenway Park, much of 1947 was spent hoping that '46 was not an accident. The Townies fell to third. Three pitchers were hurt, in a continuum begun with Joe Wood and spun through Jim Lonborg, Jose Santiago, Bill Lee, and Wes Gardner. Curt Gowdy clenched his fist: "In 1946, Ferriss, Hughson, and Harris won a ton of games [sixty-two]. The next year they were done—gone. I felt sick that Yawkey didn't win more pennants." Bad luck compounded injury. York was traded to Chicago for Jake Jones in a farce redolent of Ruth, Pennock, and later Sparky Lyle and Jeff Bagwell. "Jones couldn't hit the breaking ball," said Pesky. "If I'd had his power, I could have hit forty home runs a year."

Instead, Pesky batted .324, hit in twenty-six straight games, and helped table-set the Kid to the RBI title. Pleased: clubhouse man Johnny Orlando, to whom Williams gave his entire '46 Series check. Also, Boston Electric: on June 3, Ferriss beat the White Sox, 5–3, in Fenway's night inaugural. Stunned: on May 17, 1947, a seagull bombardier dropped a three-pound smelt on the mound, hitting Browns pitcher Kinder in the middle of his windup. Nurtured: change. Green paint replaced ads on the left-field wall. Elevated: in 1948, Cronin, replacing Collins, to vice president/general manager. Since 1935, Cronin had managed Boston to only one nonwar losing season. As general manager, he made a terrific skipper. One writer said, "I don't think a single scout was fired when Cronin was GM." Hired: implausibly, the Yankees' former manager.

Joe McCarthy's temper imperiled jobs, careers, arms, legs, jaws, and possibly life itself. "He had the Irish in him," Mel Allen said, "and was a disciplinarian. But he was fair." He shouted "What's the score?" at a player from the dugout, then bellowed at another with his arms extended, "Where in the hell do you think you are—a canoe?" Players feared him. Few doubted that Marse Joe was hard. From 1931–46, his Yankees won ten pennants and seven World Series—four in a row from 1936 to 1939. The dynasty was retributive; some called him a push-button manager. Others bequeathed a more enduring sobriquet: the greatest field leader of all time.

"I couldn't wait to play for McCarthy," enthused the Splinter. McCarthy couldn't wait for Williams to lacerate New York. Marse Joe had made the Yankees wear suits and ties. Williams hated them. How would the new Sox manager respond? At '48 spring training, he appeared for breakfast in a bright open-necked sports shirt. "Anyone who can't get along with a .400 hitter," McCarthy said, "is crazy." Years later, Williams called him "the best manager I ever played for. He installed a more businesslike attitude in twenty-five guys than any man I ever saw."

Businesslike, or robotic? In early 1948, you couldn't tell. On Patriots' Day, the Townies lost a doubleheader to Philadelphia. Three weeks later, WBZ televised the first Red Sox game from Fenway Park. The Sox would have bombed as a TV series: by midsummer they were eleven games out. On July 4, however, they staged a pre-*Bonanza* bonanza — or was it a prevideo repeat? Williams became the first batter to face the same pitcher (the A's Charlie Harris) three times in a single inning.

A half century later, the Yawkeys' radio network coupled fifty-seven stations in New York and New England (Maine seventeen, Massachusetts twelve, New Hampshire ten, Vermont eight, Connecticut six, Rhode Island three, and New York one). In '48, it starred Fred Hoey's successor, the lyric and prickly Jim Britt, who one day grew as enraged as Williams by Fenway's wind, which often blows in toward the mound.

"A northeasterly begins and a Boston batter hit a fly ball toward the wall," recalled Leo Egan, Britt's then-analyst. "Jim yells, 'That ball is smashed and it's gone!' But it wasn't — it blew back and was caught. Later, *another* Boston hitter belted one to the wall, and Britt yells, 'Yes, it's gone!' But it wasn't. Same thing — the wind blew it back for an out."

"By now," I said, "Britt must have been beside himself."

"Yes, he had a little Felix Unger in him. Now, he was really peeved. So a little later, a *third* guy tattoos one to the wall, and Jim roars, 'It's really smashed — and I don't care what *anybody* says! It's gone!' But," and Egan was laughing, "it wasn't. *Another* out, and now Jim was berserk."

McCarthy hoped to inherit first place, not the wind. Slowly, the Sox awoke; by Saturday, October 2, Boston and New York trailed the Indians by one game. Each team had two sets left: the Yankees at Fenway, Cleveland versus Detroit. "They've been writing us off all year," McCarthy exulted. "They counted us out last week. They counted us out more than Lazarus." He smiled. "Well, there are only two games left, and we're still alive." That winter, Yawkey had bought pitcher Jack Kramer and shortstop Vern Stephens from the Browns. Stephens led Boston with 137 RBIs. On Saturday, Williams homered, Kramer won his eighteenth game, and the Sox lived, 5–1. "Now if only [Detroit's Hal] Newhouser can beat [Cleveland's Bob] Feller tomorrow," said McCarthy. Kinder, also acquired from St. Louis, added, "One down, one to go. I hope I can pitch the playoff."

The next day Detroit assaulted Feller. Meanwhile, Doerr plated two runs, Williams's two doubles included a shift-buster to left, Stephens and Dom D. homered, and Boston scored five third-inning runs: Sox 10, Yankees 5. In New York, television's *Toast of the Town* debuted with pleasant, stone-faced Ed Sullivan. In Washington, Harry Truman, a one to fifteen underdog against Thomas E. Dewey, called the GOP "Gluttons of Privilege." In Boston, Fenway primped for the AL's first playoff—its last till Bucky Dent. McCarthy was in bloom. "They counted us out!" he whooped. "They counted us out!" A reporter told the Kid that the Indians' Bob Lemon would pitch the playoff. "I don't care if he's beaten us twenty times this year," he shouted. "We'll knock his brains out tomorrow."

Lemon had already won twenty games and thrown ten shutouts; teammate Gene Beardon had won nineteen and tossed the league's best ERA. With Feller fanning 164 and Joe Gordon banking thirty-two in the seats, Ohioans filled Municipal Stadium with a record 2,620,627 patrons. Lou Boudreau was Cleveland's key—at twenty-four, its player/manager. Wrote Rud Rennie: "Boudreau can't run and his arm's no good, but he's the best shortstop in the league." On Monday, October 4, Boudreau picked Beardon, not Lemon, to face the Sox. That afternoon, Marse Joe made that surprise look smaller than a buoy on Nantucket Sound.

Late Sunday, McCarthy was still tweaking reporters. Who would start, they asked—Kinder or Mel Parnell? "You saw the bull pen today," he answered. "I had everybody out there. Maybe I'll get the word tonight in a dream. Or better still, just find some nice little man and rub his curly head." Earlier in 1948, a journeyman had thrown well against the Tribe. McCarthy thus chose Denny Galehouse—fast-forward to '78's Bobby Sprowl—to start a game where only the nerve-less need apply.

Jimmy Dudley was then a rookie Indians announcer. "Going into Fenway for the playoff," he said, "was like throwing the Christians to the lions. Lord, the Sox were so good at home!" The Christians won as Boudreau voided an all-Boston World Series by going four for four, blasting two homers, and driving in five runs. Final score: 8–3. Maybe the lions had a better pitcher.

"I think Cleveland would have beaten anybody that day," Pesky later said of the playoff. The point is, it beat Boston. As the reader knows, the Olde Towne Team has lost the World Series in the seventh game or the pennant in a playoff or on the next-to-last or last day of the regular season in 1946, '48, '49, '67, '72, '75, '78, and '86. After 1986, perhaps the worst was '49.

Not before or since have the Red Sox brandished such a dreamboat of a club. Four regulars batted over .300. The infield tied Billy Goodman (.298) at first, Doerr (.309) at second, Stephens (.290) at short-stop, and Pesky (.306) at third. The Kid batted .343, became MVP, had a career-high forty-three homers, and led the league in total bases, extra-base hits, total bases, slugging percentage, and RBIs (with Stephens). DiMaggio shaped a franchise-best thirty-four-game hitting streak. At twenty-five, Parnell won as many games—a Sox high for left-handers —and won the team's only league ERA title between 1939 and 1971. Kinder finished 23–6. Said a teammate: "Ellie could drink more bour-bon and pitch more clutch baseball than anyone I ever knew." Boston even had McCarthy. How, sweet Moses, could the Red Sox *lose?*

Their stage was a time when America worshipped the geometry of the diamond. "When they referred to the Giants, it was the New York Giants," said HBO Television's superb 1991 documentary *When It Was a Game*. "The Dodgers were a Brooklyn institution—seemingly forever. There was an American League team in St. Louis, and a National League team in Boston." Added Red Barber: "There were 3 million peo-ple in Brooklyn, and if everyone there wasn't rooting for the Dodgers, everyone seemed to be." In 1949, the Red Sox drew 1,596,650 fans— more than they ever had, or would until 1967. From Kittery, Maine, and Mystic, Connecticut, and Montpelier, Vermont, parishioners trooped to Fenway Park. Their road, over hills heavy with farmland mixed with small towns shot by Ansel Adams, was long and hard. It was a per-fect metaphor for the year.

In Ernest Hemingway's *The Old Man and the Sea*, Santiago, the older man, says to Manolin, "Have faith in the Yankees, my son. Think of the great DiMaggio." In late June, the great DiMaggio came to Boston. Because of a painful heel spur he had not played all year. Then, one day, stepping out of bed, the pain miraculously was gone. On June 28, a Fenway night-record 36,228 gathered for Joe's return. DiMag repaid them by crashing a third-inning homer off Mickey McDermott. The Yankees won, 5–4. The next afternoon Boston scored four first-inning runs, Stephens hit the screen, and the Sox led behind Kinder, 7–1. Reenter DiMag. In the fifth, he touched Ellis for a three-run homer. In the eighth, he scorched Earl Johnson to break a 7–7 tie. Pesky still remembers: "One of them went over the wall, the screen, and everything. It might have gone to the Hotel Kenmore, for all I know."

New York won, 9–7, and a day later swept the series—Parnell lost as DiMag hit a three-run belt, his fourth homer of the series, that hit the steel tower in left field. The noise was insupportable. Fenway was in a constant uproar. Above, a small plane trailed a banner. It read: THE GREAT DIMAGGIO.

In 1948, the Sox rallied on the final weekend, then lost a playoff. Three decades later, they blew a fourteen-game lead, won their final eight, then lost a playoff. In '49, Boston trailed by twelve games on Memorial Day, revived in June, then, reeling from DiMag, lost three in a row to Philadelphia, dropped a July 4 doubleheader at Yankee Stadium, and again dropped twelve games behind.

"We'd gone through this roller-coaster," Pesky said, "and in six weeks we hadn't picked up a game." In August, the Sox jelled, rising to within a game and a half of New York by Labor Day—then, well, as psychologists will tell you, human beings usually revert to form.

For almost a century, the Red Sox' fiercest rivalry has entailed a short trip from Back Bay to the Big Ballpark in the Bronx—baseball's Rommel and Montgomery, jousting at El Alamein. "It's one of those great American events, like the coming of snow or the end of school," ordained Bart Giamatti. "Fathers pass that rivalry down to their sons." Williams was more prosaic: "Christ, I wanted to beat the Yankees!"— especially in '49.

On September 24, New York led Boston by two games with eight games left, five against each other. Since early August, Kinder and Parnell were 21–1. That night, Ellis blanked the Yanks, 6–0, for his eighteenth straight starting victory. The next night, Parnell's twenty-fifth— and final—win tied the teams with six games left to play. Once Yawkey said, "A coward is supposed to die a thousand deaths. In a pennant race, you can die each night." On the 26th, Boston beat New York, 7–6; Kinder relieved at Yankee Stadium. The Sox had a one-game lead. Boston and New York then won two out of three over the Senators and the A's, respectively. Needing one victory for the pennant—again, how could the Red Sox lose?

Gowdy had an answer: "Stengel used to say of McCarthy, 'If that old man hadn't lost those three pitchers [Hughson, Ferriss, and Harris to injury], they'd 'a won a ton of pennants.' Great hitters, but no pitching in the late '40s beyond Kinder and Parnell." Another reason was the Yankees' first-year manager—by reputation a clown and semigrammarian. Only once in nine prior years as a big-league manager had Casey Stengel finished above .500—and never higher than fifth. "I became a major-league manager in several cities and was discharged," he later told a U.S. Senate committee. "We call it discharged because there was no question I had to leave."

No 1949 Yankees regular hit above .287. Only Phil Rizzuto appeared in more than 130 games. DiMag missed the first 65. Yet here they were, one match behind the Sox with two left before gigantic home audiences, Boston at Yankee Stadium on the weekend of October 1 and 2. Gowdy was then Mel Allen's assistant: "As long as I live, I'll never forget that weekend or its noise. The Yankee fans going crazy. The Red Sox fans roaring after they drove down from New England. It hurt your eardrums. I've never heard such volume from a crowd."

On Saturday, by chance Joe DiMaggio Day, Parnell faced Allie Reynolds. A reporter asked Mrs. Rosalie DiMaggio: "Which team [Joe's or Dom's] are you rooting for?" Brother Dom answered, "Mother is impartial"—unlike the 69,551 that filled the triple-tiered enormity. In the third inning the Red Sox shaped a bloop single and five walks into three runs and a 4–0 lead. Victory was tangible. Then, momentum swung. Reliever Joe Page glowed. New York rallied one single at a time. In the eighth, Johnny Lindell came up hitting .229 and sans homer since July 31. He parked Joe Dobson's second pitch into the left-field seats to break a tie and give the Yankees a 5–4 triumph.

"Two straight seasons and one final game settles it," Birdie Tebbetts said early the next day. "When Cronin sends my contract for next year, I'm gonna' specify that I not show until October. It's better to play fresh than tired." In the first inning, Rizzuto's drive off Kinder eluded Williams for a triple. Tommy Henrich's grounder plated the first run. Inning stretched into inning. In the eighth, New York led, 1–0, when McCarthy pinch-hit. Kinder, still sharp, was furious. Parnell, relieving him, had been used that week in the bull pen. "He was tired," Williams said. "He just didn't have it." The upshot: four Yankees runs—Al Zarilla misplayed Jerry Coleman's fly into a three-run double—that offset three ninth-inning Boston tallies. Tebbetts, a tired tying run, fouled out for the last out.

The games were austere and riveting; they stirred these famous old contenders. After the Sox' unhosing—a second straight pennant lost on the final day—Williams sought isolation and McCarthy a flask. "When those two games were over, I just wanted to go and hide somewhere," the Splinter mourned twenty-five years later. "They really tore me up inside. We'd beaten them at Fenway the week before: I'd hit two home runs then. Poor McCarthy, he'd taken us from so far behind, and we couldn't win one of them. That really tore me up inside."

From 1969 to 1972, Ted managed the Senators and Rangers: "I'd go up in the room and start worrying about the team and just start eating. I called up McCarthy and he said, 'You're better than I am. I used to do the same, but I'd start drinking.'" Kinder, who never stopped, thought far less of his old manager. "If he leaves me in, I stop the Yankees, they don't score those four, we get our three, and we win." On the train back to Boston he tried to punch McCarthy in the mouth.

"We were never mad that we lost the Series and then barely missed two straight pennants," Parnell maintained. "We were just disappointed. I don't think there's anything more heartbreaking than to come that close—just a game—and not get there."

If Parnell wasn't angry, much of Red Sox Nation was. How could it *happen*?—so needlessly, and heedlessly. Brecheen and Boudreau. Rizzuto and remorse. "If ifs and buts were candy and nuts," observed 1970–73 Sox manager Eddie Kasko, "we'd all have a hell of a Christmas."

Williams's ideal game, Gowdy said, was 20–18. "Always it was, 'Hitting! More hitting!'" Too little pitching caused Boston's ifs and buts. A great example was 1950. Seven regulars batted over .300. Walt Dropo hit thirty-four homers, tied Stephens with 144 RBIs, and was named Rookie of the Year. Doerr had 120 RBIs. Goodman led the league with a .354 average. Dom D. hit .397 at Fenway. On June 8, the Red Sox tied a league record for most runs when they beat the Browns, 29–4.

"Hitting! More hitting!" had failed in 1946, '48, and '49, and now failed again. Connie Mack called pitching 90 percent of baseball. By way of evidence, Boston hit an astonishing .302 and finished third, four games behind—all together, now—New York. "Why did they battle? You had the geography," Enos Slaughter explained of the Hub and Apple. "You had an inter-city rivalry with the Dodgers and Giants. There was no other American League team, so Boston was the closest." At least the 1950 Yanks spared Boston more exquisite last-game agony.

Slaughter joined the Yankees in 1954—too late to play under or against McCarthy. Four years earlier, Arthur Miller had gloried in *The Death of a Salesman*. Mrs. I. Toguiri d'Aquino—"Tokyo Rose"—was sentenced to ten years in prison. Norman Vincent Peale touted the oasis of inner peace. Lacking it, on June 23, 1950, Marse Joe resigned as Red Sox manager, replaced by Steve O'Neill, who in turn preceded Lou Boudreau, replaced by Pinky Higgins, who begot York, Billy Jurges, Higgins (again), and Del Baker—all in a single decade.

McCarthy had resigned as Yankees manager in 1946. Leaving Boston, he closed a five-year frame of Feller and Old Reliable and Country running and Joe D. hitting and John Paveskovich holding(?) the ball—an age that sired "something in the image of the Red Sox in particular," said poet Donald Hall, "that has to do not simply with mere defeat, but glorious defeat."

Once, McCarthy had yearned to change places with a farmer. Now, limp and wan, he retired to his farm near Buffalo. Some were glad to see him go. Others sought a place where perspective was more in season. Even now, people of a certain generation will gather in Searsport or Sagamore to retrieve a distant night, under a cloudless sky, with the moon jumping over the Fens. They will hoist a brew. They will revisit Boo and Tex and the Silent Captain and Mr. Yawkey. Then, shaking their heads, they will hail the dynasty that never was.

9

From Father, with Love

By Doris Kearns Goodwin

The game of baseball has always been linked in my own mind with the mystic texture of childhood, with the sounds and smells of summer nights and with the memories of my father.

My love for baseball was born on the first day my father took me to Ebbets Field in Brooklyn. Riding in the trolley car, he seemed as excited as I was, and he never stopped talking; now describing for me the street in Brooklyn where he had grown up, now recalling the first game he had been taken to by his father, now recapturing for me his favorite memories from the Dodgers of his youth—the Dodgers of Casey Stengel, Zach Wheat, and Jimmy Johnston.

In the evenings, when Dad came home from work, we would sit together on our porch and relive the events of that afternoon's game, which I had so carefully preserved in the large, red scorebook I'd been given for my seventh birthday. I can still remember how proud I was to have mastered all those strange and wonderful symbols that permitted me to recapture, in miniature form, the every movement of Jackie Robinson and Pee Wee Reese, Duke Snider and Gil Hodges. But the real power of that scorebook lay in the responsibility it entailed. For all through my childhood, my father kept from me the knowledge that the daily papers printed daily box scores, allowing me to believe that without my personal renderings of all those games he missed while he was at work, he would be unable to follow our team in the only proper way a team should be followed, day by day, inning by inning. In other words, without me, his love for baseball would be forever incomplete.

To be sure, there were risks involved in making a commitment as boundless as mine. For me, as for all too many Brooklyn fans, the presiding memory of "the boys of summer" was the memory of the final playoff game in 1951 against the Giants. Going into the ninth, the Dodgers held a 4–1 lead. Then came two singles and a double, placing the winning run at the plate with Bobby Thomson at bat. As Dressen replaced Erskine with Branca, my older sister, with maddening foresight, predicted the forever-famous Thomson homer—a prediction that left me so angry with her, imagining that with her words she had somehow brought it about, that I would not speak to her for days.

So the seasons of my childhood passed until that miserable summer when the Dodgers were taken away to Los Angeles by the unforgivable O'Malley, leaving all our rash hopes and dreams of glory behind. And then came a summer of still-deeper sadness when my father died. Suddenly my feelings for baseball seemed an aspect of my departing youth, along with my childhood freckles and my favorite childhood haunts, to be left behind when I went away to college and never came back.

Then one September day, having settled into teaching at Harvard, I agreed, half reluctantly, to go to Fenway Park. There it was again: the cozy ballfield scaled to human dimensions so that every word of encouragement and every scornful yell could be heard on the field; the fervent crowd that could, with equal passion, curse a player for today's failures after cheering his heroics the day before; the team that always seemed to break your heart in the last week of the season. It took only a matter of minutes before I found myself directing all my old intensities toward my new team—the Boston Red Sox.

I am often teased by my women friends about my obsession, but just as often, in the most unexpected places—in academic conferences, in literary discussions, at the most elegant dinner parties—I find other women just as crazily committed to baseball as I am, and the discovery creates an instant bond between us. All at once, we are deep in conversation, mingling together the past and the present, as if the history of the Red Sox had been our history, too.

There we stand, one moment recollecting the unparalleled performance of Yaz in '67, the next sharing ideas on how the present lineup should be changed; one moment recapturing the splendid career of "the Splendid Splinter," the next complaining about the manager's decision to pull the pitcher the night before. And, then, invariably, comes the most vivid memory of all, the frozen image of Carlton Fisk as he rounded first in the sixth game of the '75 World Series, an image as intense in its evocation of triumph as the image of Ralph Branca weeping in the dugout in its portrayal of heartache.

There is another, more personal memory associated with Carlton Fisk, for he was, after all the years I had followed baseball, the first player I actually met in person. Apparently, he had read the biography I had written on Lyndon Johnson and wanted to meet me. Yet when the meeting took place, I found myself reduced to the shyness of childhood. There I was, a professor at Harvard, accustomed to speaking with presidents of the United States, and yet, standing beside this young man in a baseball uniform, I was speechless.

Finally, Fisk said that it must have been an awesome experience to work with a man of such immense power as President Johnson—and with that, I was at last able to stammer out, with a laugh, "Not as awesome as the thought that I am really standing here talking with you."

Perhaps I have circled back to my childhood, but if this is so, I am certain that my journey through time is connected in some fundamental way to the fact that I am now a parent myself, anxious to share with my three sons the same ritual I once shared with my father.

For in this linkage between the generations rests the magic of baseball, a game that has defied the ravages of modern life, a game that is still played today by the same basic rules and at the same pace as it was played one hundred years ago. There is something deeply satisfying in the knowledge of this continuity.

And there is something else as well, which I have experienced sitting in Fenway Park with my small boys on a warm summer's day. If I close my eyes against the sun, all at once I am back at Ebbets Field, a young girl once more in the presence of my father, watching the players of my youth on the grassy field below. There is magic in this moment, for when I open my eyes and see my sons in the place where my father once sat, I feel an invisible bond between our three generations, an anchor of loyalty linking my sons to the grandfather whose face they never saw but whose person they have already come to know through this most timeless of all sports, the game of baseball.

Doris Kearns Goodwin is a Pulitzer Prize–winning historian who has written about Presidents Roosevelt, Kennedy, and Johnson. She is a professor of government at Harvard University, an author of numerous bestselling books, including Wait Till Next Year, *and the first woman journalist to enter the Red Sox locker room.*

10

Down on My Knees
1951–66

They began with—what?—the death of Joseph Stalin, or the conquering of Mt. Everest, or even the birth of *I Love Lucy*. Looking back, the 1950s were possessed of an innocence that seems almost artlessly kind. Even now, something remains, if but a vague recollection, of their shy and sober poise—a closeness that Ronald Reagan, among many from an earlier steppe land, felt toward his childhood home. "Everyone has to have a place to go back to," he said of his heartland Pleasantville. "Dixon [Illinois] is that place for me."

As a small-town and, in Murray Kempton's phrase, "shabby-genteel" boy growing up, I discerned an age graced by self-restraint and a Fred MacMurray affability; inadvertently ennobling, and so divorced from today as to rival a dialogue of the deaf. What one remembers is an elemental passion for the sanitary and the upright—an interest in family and friends, fondness for the everyday and familiar, and reverence for everything American. "I cannot now deny my recognition that Eisenhower's years in Washington," wrote Theodore H. White, "were the most pleasant of our time." In what Archie Bunker would call the "good old U.S. of A.," it was a good time to be alive.

Each of the banal and towering, self-assured and unself-confident, devious and trustworthy persons that are the people of the United States have something central to the timbre of their lives. For Franklin Roosevelt, it was paralysis; Mario Cuomo, the immigrant experience; Averell Harriman, noblesse oblige; Huey Long, the bruised tailbone of poverty. In the 1950s, central to the childhood of the American male was baseball, aural and wondrous.

"Back home, even among the adults," Willie Morris reminisced in his autobiography, *North Toward Home*, "baseball was the link with the outside." In the town of my youth, winter ended with catch and Little League. Summer forged pickup games in a field adjacent to a cemetery. Rites linked grass stains, broken windows, and our Holy Grail — an automatic homer — hitting a stone. Day meant my fielder's glove, small and brown and wiry. At night, smuggling a transistor radio into bed, baseball paraded across the mind. From faraway places with their rich, imposing names — Crosley Field, Memorial Coliseum, Comiskey Park, the Polo Grounds — simian sounds and static-lapped voices spun a galloping globe of big-league gloss.

Did such an age exist? It did. You do not reinvent youth at the time. In daily papers (the *Globe* called Sox players by first names) and weekly periodicals (like *The Sporting News*, the self-named "Bible of Baseball," or newly born *Sports Illustrated*, devoting entire issues to "Our National Game") and yearbooks, guides, and annuals, my friends and I read of little else. Males aped a universe (in my case, Bobby Richardson), had a favorite broadcaster (Dizzy Dean), and knew the parks of baseball's web — the ivy at Wrigley Field, the playful furnace of Sportsman's Park, the green-boxed fortress at Michigan and Trumbull, or the stretch of Forbes Field grown heavy with base hits. "They were built on a human scale," says talk-show host Larry King, who grew up in another icon, Brooklyn's Ebbets Field. Angular and intimate, they sang a larger-than-life baseball psalm.

In 1951, a fan hailed Brooklyn's Preacher Roe, with an .880 winning percentage, and the A's Ferris Fain, taking his first of two straight batting titles, and Bobby Thomson, hitting his rock of ages thunderclap, and the Yankees' third World Series in a row. Everywhere, baseball evoked chary tenderness, middle-brow and middle-class. Even in Boston, where the '50s Sox did not, shall we say, find a new Jerusalem? "Hell, yes," as Williams said. At Fenway, one would no more zap baseball than burn the American flag.

For fifteen years, Red Sox radio and television evoked a Rocky Mountaineer whose style was home-style and whose name connoted respectability, good manners, and pluck. He called a club whose mediocrity maddened loyalists, presided over the changing of the guard from Number 9 to 8, and became a near-institution for an institution of a franchise.

Regard Curt Gowdy's run as uneven bookends — 1951–60 and 1961–65. A Gallup poll says Americans would rather relive the 1950s than any decade of the century. Certainly, Sox rivals would. In seven years Boston finished third ['51, '57, '58] or fourth ['53, '54, '55, '56]. From 1952 to 1960, it never lured less than 931,127 nor more than 1,203,200 fans. Only in 1955, behind by two games in August, were the Townies in a real, live, honest-to-Marty-Keough pennant race. "Bad enough," mused Gowdy. "What came next made it look Olympian."

In 1960, as we shall see, Williams retired to Florida. The Yawkeys exited to Elba. In 1965, they lost one hundred games for the first time since 1932 and drew 461 stragglers for a September game against the Angels. Gowdy's Sox never ended less than eleven games out of first (twice, trailing by over thirty-nine), played before shrinking hordes at their Back Bay beer house (in '65, drawing 650,201, fewer than in 1909), and compiled a 1,147–1,199 record (by five-year intervals: 400–369, 385–385, then 362–445). "The longer I stayed at Fenway," Curt laughed, "the worse the Red Sox got."

Looking back, it stuns how interest survived their brutal poem of bleakness over WHDH radio's over fifty-station network and a seven-outlet TV arrangement from Kittery, Maine, to New Bedford, Massachusetts. "We didn't do much in the standings, but what personalities we had!" said Gowdy. "The Peskys, the Bobby Doerrs. Of course, Williams. That's why the Red Sox have always been fascinating. In a way, they're *like* baseball. It's not really a team game, like football. It's a game of individuals."

The age began with individuals moved, or haunted, by the cross of recent memory. "Bobby Doerr still asks me, 'Why didn't we win?' " Tommy Henrich recalled of the late '40s. "Jeez, it was something special. Red Sox and the Yankees—oh, boy, it was the highlight of the year." Especial were rivalries within the rivalry—the Kid and DiMag, Doerr and Joe Gordon, McCarthy and Stengel. Said Henrich: "You think you're not gonna fear those birds?"

Doerr wondered, "Didn't we have a good ballclub?" Henrich answered, "You scared us to death. Sure, you had a good ballclub." Doerr: "Then why didn't we win?" Old Reliable: "I don't know. I think the owner over there liked you better than our owners did us." Cadillacs, he added, festooned the Red Sox parking lot. "We had to bear down more for ours."

Some fixated on 1948–49 to the 1950s' detriment. Others shunned their agony like a locked room in a deserted mansion. Slowly, players left or ebbed. In 1950, the unofficial captain homered three times in a game at Fenway. A year later, Doerr's bad back forced him to retire. In 1950, with 83 RBIs at the All-Star Game, Williams hurt his elbow hitting the wall on a great catch off Ralph Kiner. "It took me until I came back from Korea [in 1953] to really get over that one." Pesky and York were traded for the Tigers' George Kell. "Good trades benefit both sides," said Gowdy. "This trade benefited none." Pesky and Dom D. retired. The team was breaking up.

Each year hope gleamed, and later was rebuffed. Mate: At Fenway, Clyde Vollmer and Norm Zauchin homered thrice against the 1951 White Sox and '55 Senators. Checkmate: Cleveland's Bobby Avila had a three-HR set there June 20, 1951 (also, Ken Keltner, Harmon Killebrew, and Boog Powell in 1937, '63, and '66). The long ball was the rule. In 1957, Vic Wertz homered seven times at Fenway. Hank Greenberg, Pat Seerey, Mickey Mantle, and Killebrew whacked six each in 1937, '44, '61, and '63. Pitching was the exception. Winning twenty-one games in '53, Mel Parnell has Fenway's fourth-highest winning percentage among left-handed hurlers (71–30, .703).

The 1946–49 Red Sox flaunted four twenty-game winners. The 1950–66 teams boasted two—Parnell and Bill Monbouquette, who was 20–10 in 1963. "It's too bad," a fan of this era jibed of Townies pitching, "that Abner Doubleday can't come back and make this an *eight*-man game."

Curt Gowdy rubbed his hands. "Baseball is stories," he said. "It's not the numbers, though baseball's statistical, it's the moments. In football, you remember entire games as great. In baseball, it's the incredible home run or catch, the amazing inning or year."

On July 12–13, 1951, baseball's pair of hose knit *The Longest Day[s]*. First, a twi-night doubleheader: games one and two lasted nine and seventeen innings. Boston won the opener, 3–2. Kinder threw ten scoreless relief frames to win the nightcap, 5–4. A day later, Boston's soon-to-be-traded-to-Washington Mickey McDermott hurled the first seventeen: Chicago won, 5–4, in nineteen innings. Vainly, pitchers panted to be paid by the pitch.

In 1957, baseball's Lawrence Welk shunned Geritol to bash thirty-eight homers, amass a monumental .731 slugging percentage, and win a fifth batting title at .388—the best since .406. T. Ballgame also hit .403 in the Hub, twice slammed three home runs in a game, and was intentionally walked a club-record thirty-three times. "Only Ted," a fan said, "could mix Champagne Music and Narragansett Beer."

From 1958 to 1962 Pete Runnels hit over .300 each year, won two batting titles, and flaunted Fenway as a participant, not spectator. In 1951–57, the lefty Runnels played in Washington. "He was a slap hitter," said then-Senators voice Bob Wolff, "and would make out to left field [a trolley ride of 387 feet at Griffith Stadium]." Traded to Boston, Pete blitzed the wall. "Clark Kent became Superman on a train ride to Fenway from D.C."

On June 18, 1953, at Fenway, the Sox scored seventeen runs in the seventh inning. In 1954, they beat Philadelphia, 20–10. A year later, the Indians' Herb Score blanked Boston, 19–0, after a black plastic cat, failing as a lucky rabbit's foot, was buried below a headstone in the Townies' bull pen. In 1959, a spit-spot of revenge: Boston smacked three straight homers against the Yankees. "Stories!" Gowdy mused of our oldest and greatest talking game.

Many stemmed from the Yawkeys' jock-shock '50s outfield. "I'd kid Williams," Gowdy said. " 'In right, we got Jackie Jensen, who's afraid to fly and hires a hypnotist for road trips. In left, you're not the sanest guy who ever lived. Add Piersall, and we got the kookiest outfield that ever played in the major leagues.' " Williams paused and then agreed.

Jensen was baseball's first real two-sport All-American since Jackie Robinson, another ex-USC running back. Blond and blue-eyed, he buoyed Fenway as quiessence dressed the land. A June 1955 Gallup poll revealed that 60 percent of *Democrats* wanted Republican Dwight Eisenhower as their presidential nominee. Said the man who, in reflection, emerged as a superb and civilizing leader: "Everybody ought to be happy every day. Play hard, have fun doing it, and despise wickedness." Boston scribes in the fashion of the day assured readers that Jensen went three-for-three.

Number 4 had five seasons of over 100 RBIs, and led the league in 1955, '58, and '59 (116, with Ray Boone, 122, and 112). The Golden Boy's golden year was 1958: .286, thirty-five homers, and MVP. "He drives home one hundred runs every summer," a writer said, "the way other men mow their lawns." Afield, he was a star. The problem lay above it: Jack hated flying. For half a century, the American League crowded into the USA's northeast quadrant. In 1955, moving the A's to Kansas City, it compressed time, expanded mileage, and ended train travel as a way of life. "I can still see him," said a teammate, "traveling all night by train just to get to a game on time. We'd gone by plane and got in the night before." Haggard, he retired in 1960. A year later he returned at thirty-four, and then retired to California for good—by train.

Jensen smacked eighty-six Fenway dingers. It often seemed like his 1954–58 playmate might pluck that many from the stands. "He made three of the five greatest catches I saw in baseball," related Gowdy of Jimmy Piersall. "I'll never forget him disappearing into the bull pen one day and coming up with the ball. Casey Stengel called him 'the best outfielder I've ever seen.' " Added *Sports Illustrated* in 1957: "Piersall's marvelous fielding is something to see. He is the pitcher's friend."

Piersall's ungentle life is doubtless known to the gentle reader. In 1950 he joined the Sox—quick, lithe, and jumpy. He played shortstop, struggled, and in 1952 was demoted to Class AA Birmingham. "I was in Tom Yawkey's room one night when the Birmingham general manager called," Gowdy said. " 'Mr. Yawkey, you better come get this kid. I think he's sick.' Yawkey said, 'What's the matter?' He said, 'He's squirting water pistols at home plate, and goes out and hangs numbers on the scoreboard and runs the bases backwards. There's something wrong with him. The fans love it, but I don't. You wouldn't either if you saw it.' "

The film *Fear Strikes Out* etches the scope of Piersall's pain: breakdown, prognosis, shock treatment, isolation, and, ultimately, resilience if not recovery. In 1956, he batted .293. Two years later, he won a Gold Glove for fielding skill. Neither bested manic depression. Once, imitating a pig while leading off first base, Piersall so unnerved Satchel Paige that the ancient pitcher loaded the bases and yielded a grand slam to Sammy White. Each Opening Day, Eisenhower threw out a first ball that players scurried to retrieve. In 1958, at Griffith Stadium, Piersall watched Ike toss the ball before giving him another as mates fought for the souvenir. "Mr. President," he said, "would you sign *this* ball while those idiots scramble for *that* one?"

In 1961, Piersall kicked a spectator who ran out on the field. In 1963, he ran the bases backward to celebrate his one hundredth homer. By then, the former Sox center fielder had left Fenway Park via Cleveland and Washington for the Metropolitan Baseball Club of New York, Inc.—the Mets. Perhaps much of this appears humorous now. It did not seem so at the time.

The Red Sox 1950s' briar patch bristled with thorns of schizophrenia. In 1956, Mel Parnell no-hit Chicago before 14,542 at Fenway. In 1951 and '58, Allie Reynolds and Jim Bunning no-hit the Sox. Frank Sullivan was 18–13 with a 2.91 ERA in '55. His puzzle was Boston's: he couldn't beat (0–5) the Yanks. Willard Nixon won sixty-nine and lost seventy-two, but led AL pitchers in 1957 batting average (.293). What's in a name? With Nixon, it depends. Three times, Thoroughly Modern Milhous lost Massachusetts.

Boston's strengths towered by the early '50s: Williams, Piersall, Jensen, Goodman, and later, Frank Malzone, lashing the Monster like the Third Army did Germany. Sullivan, Tom Brewer, and Ike

Delock were a combined 46–20 in 1956. Sammy White adeptly managed pitchers. One—Kinder: "Old Rubber Arm"—segued from a starter into Boston's first true reliever. "Ellis liked to stay out all night—*night* after night," said '54–60 Sox announcer Bob Murphy. "One morning they picked him up off the sidewalk at five o'clock. Guys are laughing, 'So much for using him in today's doubleheader.' All he did was save both games"—working four innings in the second.

In 1953, Kinder set then-Sox marks with twenty-seven saves in sixty-nine games. At some point—it is harder to say exactly when than how—the music died. White stopped hitting. Brewer and Sullivan became late-'50s sub-.500 pitchers. A behemoth of a pull hitter, Dick Gernert seemed sired for the left-field wall. "One year," said Murphy, "he led the club in homers and RBIs ['52, with nineteen and sixty-seven]." By 1957, he was benched. Nowhere did luck more evanesce than with a local boy who quarterbacked Boston University, signed a bonus with the Red Sox, and as a rookie in 1954 smashed four home runs in a Fenway home stand. Retrieving Harry Agganis, you recall the hypothetical.

"He grew up in Lynn [a Boston suburb]," Gowdy began. "Paul Brown [coach of football's Cleveland Browns] wanted him to succeed Otto Graham. Harry comes up here from Louisville and starts to pull the ball. We're talking All-Star first baseman for the next ten years. By 1955, he's hitting over .300 when he got pneumonia. They put him in the hospital, and one day he comes into the locker room drenched with sweat.

" 'What the hell are you doing?' I said. He said, 'Working out.' I said, 'You're crazy. You just got out of the hospital.' But he was desperate to play, and got on the plane with us for a western trip." One morning, Gowdy spotted him in the elevator with a suitcase. " 'What's the matter?' I asked Jack Fadden, our trainer. 'We don't know,' Jack said. They sent him back to Boston, and he had a blood clot in his leg that went into his lungs and killed him." The Golden Greek was twenty-five years old.

In his eulogy, Gowdy thought of Agganis's smile. Four decades later, he fixed on Boston's misery. "Yawkey had awful luck," he said. "Piersall, Jensen, injuries. But nothing was worse than this." By 1958, *Sports Illustrated* was writing, "No one has spent more money for more disappointment than owner of the Red Sox Tom Yawkey. Ten years ago he had the team everyone wanted: Williams, Doerr, Stephens, Pesky, and DiMaggio. But it won no pennant"—nor would it, for another nine.

Much of the money went for prospects—"bonus babies." Where are pitchers Ted Bowsfield, Ted Wills, Tom Borland, or Nels Chittum?

Shortstop Billy Klaus surprised by hitting .283 in 1955. Klaus didn't last. Neither did *si*'s same-year view of Don Buddin—"definitely a comer." By '59, it wrote, "Buddin has a way of making unbelievable stops and then firing the ball into Row G behind first base." Of the Sox' nearly fourteen hundred players, few failed more wondrously than their 1956 and '58–61 shortstop. Some said that Buddin's license plate should read "E-6." Others charged he had no license to *play*. For seven straight years Boston opened with different shortstops: Stephens, 1950; Lou Boudreau, 1951; Piersall, 1952; Milt Bolling, 1953; Ted Lepcio, 1954; Eddie Joost, 1955; Buddin, 1956; and Klaus, 1957. None worked—nor did other babies from Billy Consolo via Ken Aspromonte to '57's thirty-one-year-old "rookie," Gene Mauch.

For years, Goodman patrolled second. In 1958, replacing him, Runnels arrived from Washington—to *si*, "a sort of second-carbon Billy Goodman in that he plays many positions inadequately and hits singles left-handed." The magazine was harsher on Sox catchers of that year: "Samuel Charles White and Peter Harvey Daley Jr. are perfectly proper names for a couple of lawyers. But they are not lawyers, they are catchers, and last year neither one hit well enough to pass a bar exam." Only a new third baseman escaped its ire. In 1957, Frank Malzone knocked in 103 runs and "won a position on the All-Star team and a place in Boston's heart." In '57–58, he drove in 190, more than the other M and Ms—Mays, Mathews, Maris, or Mantle, and won Gold Gloves (also in '59). "He can hit, he can field, and he's the best in the league at his position. Boston just wishes he were triplets."

In 1959, the Sox finished fifth for the first time since 1937. A year later they sank to seventh. One flaw was speed—MIA. Another, pitching. Said *Sports Illustrated*: "Anyone passing by the Red Sox who happens to throw a ball left-handed is likely to be enlisted as a pitcher." Righties Monbouquette and Mike Fornieles won and graced, respectively, fourteen and seventy games. They couldn't help fielders escape the league's worst ERA. "Vic Wertz [acquired from Cleveland] can't cover the ground at first," *si* continued. "When Runnels, at second, and Buddin, at short, complete a double play, sirens go off all over New England. In left, Williams gets what is hit at him—directly at him. When Boston pitchers are being judged, it must be remembered the burden they bear is great."

Boston's defense, it concluded, "is enough to break a pitcher's heart." About time, replied an embittered Hub. The '50s had begun with hope, turned to chagrin, and ended in despair. Finally, pitchers felt like the average fan.

Choose a year—say, 1957. *Sputnik*, racial strife in Little Rock, the Asian Flu epidemic, and "Leave It to Beaver"; Joseph McCarthy's death and Jack Kerouac's *On the Road*; a postwar-high 7.7 percent unemployment rate, and congressional probes of labor racketeering— and in baseball, what New York giveth, California taketh away. New York lost the Dodgers and Giants to Los Angeles and San Francisco. Herb Score, struck in the face by Gil McDougald's line drive, almost lost an eye. The Senators' Roy Sievers blasted forty-two home runs and 114 RBIs. Mickey Mantle hit .365, highest for a Bomber since 1939. Amid change, two friends reassured—Fenway, growing younger, and an aging Kid.

By midcentury, Fenway Park rivaled family around New England dinner tables. Your first game there became a rite of passage—like Dorothy sighting Oz. Years later the visit seemed a blur of blue caps and red hose and low-cut stirrups and the ageless inscription RED SOX across the chest of heaving, billowy woolies; the vendors and police and skim of smoke across the yard; the sunlight of early summer or darkness of early fall; the timeless tableau of fielder crouched, batter cocked, and pitcher draped against the grandstand; above all, the surety that there was no place on earth that you would rather be.

At Fenway's core lived strategy, history, and continuity. Like, for instance, Yankee Stadium, it shaped the game played within. A dinger to the screen might be a long out in the Bronx' left-center field—Death Valley. A single off Fenway's thirty-seven-foot-high wall would have cleared Yankee Stadium's 296- and 301–foot foul lines. It made a difference. The initials of Yawkey and his wife, Jean R. (TAY and JRY), in Morse code graced two vertical stripes on the scoreboard. The screen behind home plate, built to protect fans and let fouls roll onto the field, was the bigs' first of its kind. To a child, the park's mass, shadows, and gentle-rowed sweep of stands overcame even the Red Sox' god-awfulness on the field. Generations of sons and dads, linked hand-in-hand, became raucous, knowing celebrants—fused, alive, and utterly alight.

In 1957, writer Robert Creamer found Fenway good: "Oddly shaped but most attractive, this is great park in which to view game. It is hard to find really bad seat in the rambling one-level stands. Sun blisters bleachers in center and right fields, but in 'wet-cold' Boston this can often be comforting. To discover why Ted Williams spits at the fans, sit in section along the left-field line and listen to the more pungent comments. Special 'skyline' boxes swing out from either side of rooftop press box. Ushers are plentiful, courteous, and helpful, and may not accept tips. The eighteen refreshment stands are easily accessible from most seats for a quick snack. Frankfurters [not-yet Fenway Franks] and beer [naturally, Narragansett] are staples, plus 'tonic' (New England talk for soda pop). Some local fans complain about special out-of-town or out-of-state parties who, proper Bostonians say, tend to overenjoy themselves to the discomfort of others. Subway from nearby Kenmore Square station connects with all parts of Greater Boston, as well as to all New England via railroad, bus, or airplane. It's easy to drive to Fenway, and there's supposed to be parking space for eight thousand five hundred cars in vicinity, but don't rely on it; parking ranges from 25 cents to $1. Leaving park area after game can be difficult. Taxis are comparatively few, and if it is day game, downtown working crowd heading for home invariably clogs way."

Neither aging legs, intentional walks, nor hapless mates could clog The Stroke. "God, I got a big kick out of leading the league," Williams said of 1957. "I was thirty-nine years old, not bad for an old guy. That year, I had a total of twelve infield hits, and Mickey Mantle had forty-eight. If I'd had the speed I had ten years earlier, I would have hit over .400, maybe .420." Few doubted it. "Whenever we'd play Boston, I'd get right up at the edge of the dugout steps when Williams was up and I'd study him," said Mantle, terming him better than DiMaggio. In 1960, Boston played the Cubs in spring training in Mesa, Arizona. An hour before the game, Ted was taking batting practice. He hit the first five pitches over the right-field wall. The Cubs watched in silence. Finally, one said, "I'll be darned if that guy doesn't play this park like a pitch-and-putt."

By the late 1950s yarns about the Kid outnumbered seagulls over Lansdowne Street. Rivals admired him. "Ted was very unselfish," Gowdy related. "Mantle would come up to him—Al Kaline when he was twenty—everyone'd ask for tips on hitting. Ted would help any way he could. Finally, Yawkey, who loved Williams like a son, gave him hell. 'Why are you aiding the enemy?' " Williams's answer struck at baseball's core. " 'Look, T.A., when you're a block away from a major-league ballpark and hear the crowd roar, somebody's just hit the baseball! It's exciting. Fans love a home run or double or triple or rundown play or a cutoff. It's all action and involves hitting.' "

Williams analyzed hitting like priests the Apostles' Creed. He studied a park's background: "There was a house beyond center field on a hill in Baltimore that had lights on at night. I couldn't see the ball." Ted complained to the league office. He dissected batting orders: "I had Foxx and Cronin bat behind me, then Jensen, but they pitched to me more often when Stephens was behind me than at any other time. Great respect. I wish Vern'd been there my whole career." He also studied pitchers. Once, in the ninth inning, the Kid faced Herb Score. "Bases loaded, full count," said the Indians' then-voice Jimmy Dudley. "Boom! Ted clears Fenway onto the Mass. Pike. Later, Score said, 'See ya' later, slugger.' Ted looked up and said, 'Herbie, do me a favor. Don't ever throw me a fastball on three and two.' Imagine—this galoot's giving the *pitcher* advice."

In 1950, the Sox hosted the April City Series with the then-crosstown NL Braves. Late in the game Ted faced Braves rookie Ernie Johnson, who threw a curveball over the outside corner. "Great decision," Johnson joked. "In seconds it's rolling to the Hotel Kenmore. Afterward we're walking through the clubhouse. Billy Southworth was our manager, and he put his arm around me, tried to make me feel good, but that's not how it came out." Southworth said, "Don't worry, he's hit them off better pitchers than you." Recalls Johnson: "I'll never forget that—and I've tried." Two years later, a veteran faced Ted at the Braves' spring-training camp in Bradenton. In the first inning Vern Bickford got him out. In the third, he told teammates, "Ted's up this inning. I'm gonna see how far that big donkey can hit one."

Johnson asked, "What are you gonna do?"

Bickford said, "Lay it in there about three-quarters speed and see what happens."

Knowledge can spawn pressure. "Sometimes, in batting practice," said Johnson, "if a batter sees a lollypop pitch coming he'll get antsy, hit it on the ground or otherwise screw it up." Williams hit the light towers in right-center field. "We're roaring as the inning ends. Bickford comes back, shakes his head, and says, 'Well, I got my answer.'"

God broke the mold *before* He made the Kid.

Try to picture '50s baseball without Number 9. You can't. The dots don't connect. Something about Williams lured contempt and adulation—capable of kindness, yet despised by much of the working press. Mused Gowdy, "Everything about him shouted excess."

Largesse began with charity. "Every time he got the chance he'd visit hospitals," said Dudley. "He'd tell the nuns, 'God bless you. Don't tell anybody that I was here.'" Once, Bud Blattner arrived in Boston to air a CBS-TV *Game of the Week*. Seeing Ted, he told of meeting a ten-year old with leukemia in a Midwest hospital. Williams mementoes crammed his room. Each day nurses sat the boy on the floor with a little bat, got on their hands and knees, and rolled a ball down the corridor. "He'd hit it," Blattner said, "and as it rolled they exclaimed, 'Oh, that's a double. That's a triple. That's a home run.' If it was a homer, it was hit by Ted!"

Returning to his room, the boy asked Bud to say hello to Ted. Hearing Bud's account, the Kid interrupted. "Oκ, here's what I'm gonna do. I'll fly in and see this boy"—he flew his own plane—"but on two conditions, and I mean this sincerely. I want to be met at the airport only by the boy's mother and father. Any media, and I'll just touch down and take right off again." The second condition was that Blattner was not to mention it on the air. The boy soon died, but not before visiting with his hero.

Excess draped batting practice. "I played, called, and viewed thousands of games," said Blattner. "I used batting practice only to visit players. Williams was the exception. I'd go to Fenway just to see him. His skills—unbelievable." The Senators' Bob Wolff marveled at how Williams stopped practice. "He was the only player I ever saw where both dugouts paused to watch him. It was like a one-man pregame show. Mesmerizing"—and volcanic. "Ted could be so convivial stepping into the batting cage. If he didn't do well, he'd come out storming, 'Get out of my way!' " Wolff waited, then approached Vesuvius—not inactive, but cooled.

Excess: On April 30, 1952, the Sox held "Ted Williams Day" to hail his brief return from Korea. Williams smashed a two-run homer. In 1954, he broke his collarbone diving for a ball, missed five weeks, and didn't play until a doubleheader in Detroit. "Ted played both games," said Sox then-announcer Bob Murphy, "went eight for nine, hit two home runs. The only time he made an out was when Al Kaline climbed the fence to rob him of another." Hyperbole: Once, Cal McLish fanned Williams twice. In the dugout, T. Ballgame said, "Next time I'm up, he's gonna throw me that sidearm slow curve and I'll hit it in the upper deck." He did. Embroidery: "Ted could be sick," Murphy observed, "but the very first day back he'd hit a home run. I remember a monster shot he hit off Tom Morgan into the center-field seats at Fenway. Uncanny." He laughed. "He was explosive, temperamental, dramatic. When I joined the club Gowdy told me, 'You haven't lived till you've seen Williams.' "

Somewhere in the 1950s excess turned and stung its subject. Baseball, as opposed to hitting one, became a chore. "The Red Sox are young and full of ginger," one writer presaged, inaccurately. "But Ted Williams is their big man, and he is old and full of bitterness." Some stemmed from pride: he hated how even a .400 hitter fails six times in ten. Some, anger: at age, near-misses, front-running fans, glad-handing phonies, more than five years lost to service—"He wanted to go to World War II, but Korea? Younger players weren't drafted," said a friend. "He thought politicians had singled him out." Much of the New England press, especially columnist Dave "the Colonel" Egan, dubbed him spoiled and self-absorbed—a defense-shunning, Sox-harming, draft-dodging (!) brat. Unfair, the charges stung.

On August 7, 1956, in the eleventh inning of a scoreless game against the Yankees, the Kid was jeered at Fenway for misplaying a fly ball. Two batters later he made a diving catch for the third out. Nearing the Sox dugout at the end of the inning he spit toward occupants of the ground-level seats, entered the dugout, came out, and spit again. The next night, Ted bombed a long home run. Crossing home plate, Williams put his hand over his mouth. "Ted Spits at Fans!" screamed the *Globe*. General manager Joe Cronin was said to be furious. Hub radio and television stations raged. Yawkey fined Ted $5,000. "In *front* pages across the country," said Wolff, "everybody was talking about 'that Williams, there he goes again.' "

In 1958, Williams threw a bat and accidentally struck Gladys Heffernan, Cronin's housekeeper, in the face. That Christmas, Ted sent her a peace offering—a $500 diamond watch. A year later, a columnist urged, "Let the small letter *i* represent the American League. The Yankees, of course, are the dot, so the best the Boston Red Sox can hope for is a place near the top of the stem. Much depends on whether life truly begins at forty for Ted Williams." In 1959, he hurt his neck and hit .254. On June 17, 1960, Williams hit his five hundredth home run. For the year he hit .316 and homered almost every eleven times at bat. Abysmal, the '60 Sox drew more than 1.1 million customers, the last time they passed 1 million till 1967. Most came, as John Updike wrote, to "Bid the Kid Adieu."

By now, Boston's love-hate affair with Williams had matured into a special bond of warmth, respect, and faith. "For so long," said Gowdy, "he'd been too stubborn to go halfway to meet the Red Sox fans." Only now, as Ted vended baseball buttons, Ted's Root Beer, Moxie soda, and the Jimmy Fund and graced baseball cards and covers from *Sportfolio* to *Who's Who in Baseball* to *The Sporting News* and *Sport* and fans faced a future they had never deigned to confront—preparing to leave baseball, the Splinter seemed to corkscrew *into* baseball—did New England yield to the impulses of its heart—to wit, in Ted's last at bat, a lyric note in baseball's scale.

The Splinter's final swing gilded myth and cast his legend, its plot as recalled as last rites, or first love. On Wednesday, September 28, 1960, on a dank day at Fenway Park, Williams played his final game. The Sox retired Number 9 and gave him a silver bowl, plaque, and $4,000 check for the Jimmy Fund. Gowdy, emceeing, ad-libbed his salaam. "I didn't get to see Ty Cobb, Paul Waner, or Rogers Hornsby, who hit .400 four or five times, but I don't see how they could be better than Ted Williams," he said. "I could have pages of batting records up here, but what really made Ted was pride. He had an intense pride that every time up he wanted to produce a hit. Not only for himself, but for the fans at Fenway whom he secretly loved, who stood behind him amid ups and downs. Pride is what made him go and why he's here. The greatest hitter of all time, Ted Williams."

In the 1980s, true believers chanted, "Let Reagan be Reagan." No one had to tell the Splinter. His speech twitted reporters ("Despite some of the terrible things written about me by the knights of the keyboard up there, and they were terrible things—I'd like to forget them but I can't"), praised Yawkey, Cronin, and past and present mates, and voiced the silent language between the Kid and Red Sox Nation. "My stay in Boston has been the most wonderful part of my life. If someone should ask me what one place I'd want to play if I had it to do all over again, I would say Boston, for it has the greatest owner in baseball and the greatest fans in America."

The game with Baltimore followed, meaningless and all-meaning. Williams walked, then flied to center. In the fifth inning he hit to Orioles right fielder Al Pilarcik, who clutched it against the fence. "If that one didn't go out," Ted told Vic Wertz, "none of them will today." In the eighth inning, Williams, forty-two, batted against Jack Fisher, twenty-one, born as Ted made the Red Sox in spring training 1939. It was raining. The lights were on. The ball wasn't carrying. "The count one and one on Williams," Gowdy said over WHDH. "Everybody quiet here at Fenway Park after they gave him a standing ovation of two minutes knowing that this is probably his last time at bat. One out, nobody on, last of the eighth inning. Jack Fisher into his windup, here's the pitch."

It is said that Fisher grooved his pitch. "He didn't," Gowdy insisted. "It wasn't a good pitch. Williams never swung at a bad pitch. His thesis was, get a good pitch to hit, and you'll be a better hitter; don't swing unless it's a strike. This time he did, and when I heard the crack of the bat and the ball started to right, I knew it was gone. I was choked up. My heart was pounding." The call: "Williams swings—and there's a long drive to right field! That ball is going—and it is gone! A home run for Ted Williams in his last time at bat in the major leagues!"

Ten thousand, four hundred and fifty-four Fenway (dis)believers had tonsils redder than T. Ballgame's hose. Ted crossed home plate, refusing to tip his cap. "I just couldn't do it," he said. "It just would not have been me." Updike offered a more angelic gloss: "God does not answer letters."

In 1958, a writer noted: "Williams is the greatest hitter since Babe Ruth, and last year was in his many ways his finest. Because of him, Boston finished third. Without him, it is hard to say how far they could sink." The Athens of America was about to find out.

Compare the 1950s and John F. Kennedy's early 1960s. Living as contrasted to recalling, them, you thought of polarity, not uniformity, and how America changed: from Main Street to New Frontier; an administration of businessmen to academics, unionists, and civil-rightsers; a Protestant-only presidency to more of an equal-opportunity post. Politicians once equated success with legislation. That changed with JFK. After Dallas, chic wrote the prose of the legend that was Camelot.

In shorthand code, those who disdained the quiescent '50s—like Adlai Stevenson, tarring their "green fairways of indifference," or John Kenneth Galbraith, torching "the bland leading the bland"—regarded the early '60s as an epoch that reawakened the senses. America pre-Kennedy, they said, had been hypocritical and puritanical, somnolent, inhibited. Naturally, the Age of Ike disagreed. Both ignored the close working agreement that bound the then-opposing camps. Their pillar was the keeper of the faith and defender of the peace, the guardian of West Berlin and scourge of "Godless Communism."

The Yawkeys' early- and mid-1960s evoked a similar continuum. The difference: the Sox wilted in the rain. "In this case, no change meant a bummer," said Ned Martin, joining them in 1961. Number 9 receded. Boston lost. Number 8 arrived. Boston lost. Dick Radatz became the fireman. Don Schwall was named '61 Rookie of the Year. Dick Stuart hit balls over tall buildings in a single bound. Boston lost. Gradually, boredom assailed the Olde Towne Team.

The 1961–66 Sox placed sixth, seventh, and twice eighth and ninth. Their best years, to use the term liberally, were 1962–63 (eight and ten games below .500). Their worst: the grotesque 1965 of sixty-two wins, one hundred losses, and forty games behind Minnesota. In 1960, mourning the Kid's good-bye, a Boston writer wailed, "Let's face it, what are we going to write about now?" As 1960 managers Billy Jurges, Mike

Higgins, and Del Baker yielded to 1961–62's Higgins (again), who begot
'63–64's Johnny Pesky, who preceded '64–66's Billy Herman and Pete
Runnels—as 1947–58 general manager Joe Cronin resigned to become
AL president, replaced by '59–60's Bucky Harris, yielding to '61–62's Dick
O'Connell, who was replaced by '63–64's Higgins, who resigned on
September 16, 1965 (his replacement [whew] O'Connell)—as Yawkey
changed chairs, shuffled the cabinet, and counted losses—increas-
ingly, the writers wrote about what was wrong with the Sox.

   Fingers pointed at three fall guys. One was the left-field wall,
alleged to scare Sox left-handed pitchers (rival pull-hitters found the
Monster a magnet) and hypnotize righty hitters from Foxx through
Jensen (changing their swing to locate the screen). "Bull!" said Mel
Parnell. "The wall never bothered me. The wall never bothered a
good pitcher—left or right. You just threw down and away and made
them hit to right, that's all." Hypnosis is suspect, too. The wall actually
helped lefties like Goodman, Runnels, and '61 rookie Carl Yastrzemski,
plucking outside pitches to the opposite field. "The wall is a great
equalizer," explained Radatz, relief's 1963–65 Everyman. "A lot of
cheap homers, but also singles off it that would have been doubles or
triples anywhere else. It balances out." *Talent* outs.

   The second villain was the owner—now, without a pennant for
almost two decades. Yawkey was said to run a country club; its handi-
cap, tolerance. In 1961, Robert Creamer wrote, "Yawkey has spent
much money buying established stars (Jimmie Foxx, Lefty Grove, Joe
Cronin, etc.), much more on bonus players, but so far has had only a
pauper's return." The farm system bottomed out. Prospects from Don
Gile to Tracy Stallard flopped. Yawkey pals like Harris were unhosed
by rivals; in 1960, he dealt Sammy White to Cleveland for Russ Nixon,
whereupon White retired, at which point Indians General Manager
Frank Lane convinced Commissioner Ford Frick that the Tribe should
keep Nixon. Yawkey was left with four catchers who had caught a total
of twelve big-league games: six-foot-six Gile; six-four Haywood Sullivan;
six-three Jim Pagliaroni; and five-eleven Ed Sadowski. He would have
gladly traded all for five-eight Yogi Berra. "Baseball," said Bill Veeck,
"is the only game where you don't have to be seven feet wide or seven
feet tall."

   Curt Gowdy grew angry. "People have always called the Red Sox
'country club,' " he said. "To me they were family." In 1951, the Sox lured
him from New York. His first two games, both losses, were, ironically,
at Yankee Stadium. Curt began to get telegrams—"Go back to New
York, Yankee-lover"—blaming him for the start. Worse, he had mis-

pronounced towns with an English accent—Worcester, Swampscott.
"The Sox hired a speech tutor. I start thinking I should have stayed in
the Bronx." The next day the phone rang: Yawkey wanted to see him.
Terrified, Gowdy approached his office. "I'd never met him," Curt said.
"I open the office and, well, here's this multimillionaire, but dressed
in khaki pants and faded shirt, he looks like he doesn't have a dime."

Yawkey rose and said, "Curt, I just want to welcome you to the Red
Sox. I followed you in New York and liked it." Not a whiff of
Swampscott: Listening, Gowdy felt reborn. He asked the owner what
kind of broadcast he wanted. Yawkey said: "Look, they've had major-
league baseball here since the 1876 Braves. The Red Sox came into the
American League in 1901. New England knows baseball; just give 'em
the game. I don't want line drives made into pop-ups or excuses for
errors." That was, and is, Gowdy's style: "No cheering," T.A. said. "Tell
it straight."

In time, Gowdy loved Yawkey like a father. "He had great ethics,"
Curt observed. "When Bob Feller was eighteen, he signed a contract
with the Indians. Judge Landis declared it illegal and put him on the
free market. Landis called Yawkey and said, 'Tom, I don't want you to
bid for Feller.' He knew Yawkey had money and could literally buy all
the great players. Yawkey agreed—he cared about the welfare of the
game." In 1957, Gowdy reinjured his back and missed the whole year.
Yawkey told a neurosurgeon, "I don't care how long this kid misses, his
job is ready. One year, five years, he's got a permanent job here."

Curt's eyes reddened. "Tom Yawkey is the most marvelous man I
ever knew."

"They always accused him of paying too much," Gowdy continued.
"But life would be a lot better if more Tom Yawkeys were around." Life,
yes; the Townies, maybe. Color the Sox' third fall guy black-and-white:
they were blind, not color-blind.

The Dodgers broke the race barrier in 1947, signing Jackie
Robinson. The Indians signed Larry Doby; the Cubs, shortstop Ernie
Banks. Yawkey might have signed either: likely, Banks could have
unseated Billy Klaus, Billy Consolo, or E-6 Buddin. Instead, the Sox
remained slow and segregated—by plan or accident, it is still not clear.
On July 21, 1959, infielder Pumpsie Green ended Boston's cachet as
baseball's last all-white team. It was hardly worth the wait. Green hit
.253 that year at Minneapolis, and .246 in his Boston career. Slowly, the
Red Sox welcomed Reggie Smith, George Scott, Jim Rice, Mo
Vaughn—slowly, and belatedly. "I keep thinking about the '50s and

'60s," said a friend. "Other clubs get Clemente, Aaron, Frank Robinson, Don Newcombe. What will the records say? 'Boston, American League. Elijah (Pumpsie) Green.' "

Phillies manager Danny Ozark once malapropped of a losing streak, "No problem. Even Napoleon had his Watergate." The Sox' early and mid-1960s problems did not include Yaz's 1963 batting title (.321); Number 8's, Eddie Bressoud's, and Lu Clinton's 1962, '64, and '65 twenty-game hitting streaks; the first of Yastrzemski's eighteen All-Star Games and last of Malzone's eight; and Don Schwall's 1961 (15–7, 3.22 ERA). That July, Schwall graced the All-Star Game, before 31,851 at Fenway Park, allowing all five NL hits and its only run. (The game ended 1–1 after nine innings because of rain. Other Sox all-stars were pitcher Mike Fornieles and Higgins, who served as a coach. Williams, flanked by Cronin, threw out the first ball.)

A frequent early '60s Fenway visitor was the then-JFK aide, unofficial "Undersecretary of Baseball," and later director of Boston's Kennedy Library, David Powers. At the time, his boss flaunted a parquet of imagery: The World War II boat *PT-109* and the book *Profiles in Courage*. Hatless, coatless health. An accent made for mimicry. A rocking chair to ease back pain. Sailing off the Cape, and touch football at Hyannis Port, with a clan large enough to man both teams. Wife Jackie's elegance. Son John-John. Daughter Caroline, riding pony Macaroni. By reputation, Kennedy put forth irony, a fluent phrase, and a graceful front when under pressure. Emphatic and sensitive by nature, he was not a hater, and sought endlessly to grasp other points of view. "He just inhaled information," said Powers. A minor job was to "keep Jack briefed on baseball."

A photo of JFK and Powers at the Senators' 1961 home opener shows them studying *The Sporting News*. If you were a Sox fan, it could even make for pleasant reading. That May 12, Monbouquette set a then-team mark for strikeouts — seventeen, at Washington. In June, Boston scored eight ninth-inning runs to beat the Senators, 13–12. Dick Stuart led the '63 AL with forty-two homers. The Sox contended until June. In '64, Radatz — the Monster, a one-man Red Cross — won sixteen games, had a 2.29 ERA, and fanned 181 — and rookie outfielder Tony Conigliaro bloomed like Agganis. "Again," said Gowdy, "All-Star for the next ten years." On April 18, at nineteen, Tony C. wafted the first Fenway pitch thrown him for a homer. In August, leading the AL with twenty-four, he broke his arm. A year later, Conigliaro became the league's youngest home-run titlist. In 1962, Earl Wilson and Monbo no-hit the Angels and

Chicago. On September 16, 1965, only 1,247 Fenway patrons saw Dave Morehead no-hit Cleveland. Waterloo, or Watergate: the problem was that little lasted—success, or careers.

"It was so frustrating," Ned Martin mourned. "In 1961, my first year at Fenway, we had a fine rookie second baseman, Chuck Schilling. You think he's set, and he loses it. Same thing, Schwall and Radatz. Jensen's back, and then he jumps ship, goes home. Morehead throws a gem, and then reverts to form. Tony C. seemed set for Cooperstown"—until Jack Hamilton began his wind. Schwall walked 121 in 1962—third-highest in team history. Welcome a tater tear: Wilson yielded a then-record thirty-seven homers in 1964, Gene Conley allowed thirty-three in '61, and Monbouquette thirty-one or more in 1963, '64, and '65. Forlorn, the Sox embraced trivia and/or arabesque: Carroll Hardy, Tracy Stallard, Conley, and Stuart.

On May 31, 1961, Hardy became the only man to pinch-hit for Williams (September 21, 1960) and Yastrzemski. That October 1, Roger Maris hit a fourth-inning Stallard fastball into the Stadium's right-field seats to exorcise a ghost. In 1927, Babe Ruth hit sixty home runs in 154 games; in 1961, Maris torched his sixty-first in game 163 (the Yanks played one tie). Conley came from Philadelphia in baseball's biggest-ever two-man trade—the six-foot-eight Oklahoman for six-seven Frank Sullivan, who said, "I am in the twilight of a mediocre career." Gene lived in a sixty-foot trailer, played for the NBA Knicks and Celtics, and pitched for the 1961–63 Sox—winning fifteen games in '62. That July, the team bus stopped in Manhattan's traffic wilderness. Conley and Pumpsie Green got off, purportedly to search for a rest room, and instead headed more or less for the promised land.

Three days later, Conley tried to buy an airline ticket to—accounts diverge—Tel Aviv or Jerusalem. Accosted, he was summoned to Yawkey's office. "Gene, we would all like to do what you did, but we can't," T.A. said. "I'm going to fine you $1,500. But if you stay in line for the rest of the year, I'll give it back." Conley, and Yawkey, did. "Good thing, too," said Gene. "We really needed the money."

Stuart needed a glove, a talking-to, and mace to combat teammates. "Dick was ten years too soon with Boston," said Dr. Strangeglove's 1963–64 manager, Johnny Pesky. "He would have been a great DH." Instead, he was a menace. "Just didn't have any interest at all. Nobody could hit well enough to make up for what he cost us in the field. He'd just wave at balls." Stuart kidded Pesky that he'd hit under .260 against 1960s pitching. The joke was on the Red Sox. One day Dick got a standing ovation for picking up a windblown hot-dog wrapper without dropping it. "Whenever Stuart was on the field," said a '63–64 Soxer named Dick Williams, "there you had constant chaos."

Camp or macabre—what *was* it with these guys? Later, Conley summed up the pre-1967 sad-sack Sox. In '63, Gene hurt his arm, was released, and joined the Indians, who banished him to the minors. What was he to do? His arm, and thus, his vocation, was spent. One day Conley noted a church service next to the hotel his club was staying at. He entered the church, found a pew, and began crying openly.

A kind man moved into the pew beside him. "What's the matter, son?" he whispered. "Did you lose your dad or your mom?"

Conley looked at him and sobbed, "Neither, sir. I lost my fastball."

In 1966, few had heard of est, Tom Hayden, Zen, My-Lai, "Do your own thing," "If it feels good, do it," "Honk if you want peace," or "Don't trust anyone over thirty." A streetwise meanness would soon forge a triumph undreamt of in the age of Ike or JFK—America as horror house, coming apart at the seams. Right versus left. Hard hat against hippie. Main Street versus the radical Jerry Rubin, who opined, "So we struggle, in our humble way, to destroy the United States."

At this point, few had heard of Darrell Brandon or George "Boomer" Scott or Jim Lonborg or Jose Tartabull. That would also change, indelibly and unforgettably. In 1966, Gowdy left Fenway for a sustaining run at NBC. "Looking back [to 1951], I can't believe I thought about going back to New York," he mused. "Williams, Fenway, six states, great fans. My fifteen years here were the greatest of my life." Replacing him, Ken Coleman described a team that batted only .251, lost ninety-two games, and whose every pitcher had a losing record. Or was the glass half full? Boston won ten more games, drew 158,971 more people, and finished fourteen games nearer first than in '65. Said Coleman: "It didn't get much notice, but the Sox began for the first time in a long time to play some ball."

One reason was Lonborg, the six-foot-five would-be dentist and future "Gentleman Jim" who led the staff in K's and innings. Others: Jose Santiago, who won twelve games, and Lee Stange, who had a 2.67 ERA and completed eight games. Reggie Smith, Mike Andrews, and Scott debuted in center field, at second base, and third base. Another rookie, Joe Foy, led the team in walks, runs, and triples. Tony C. domineered club stats: homers (twenty-eight), RBIs (ninety-three), extra-base hits (sixty-one), slugging percentage (.487), and total bases (272)—reducing Fenway to Williams's pitch-and-putt. One day he hit a net-finder that Ralph Terry called "the hardest ball hit off me ever. It struck about two feet from the top. There was this crash, like a car accident, and the ball dropped straight down." Tony C. got a single. "If the wall wasn't there, it would have gone over five hundred feet." The above Sox were good. Better, each was young.

By now, Rico Petrocelli was Boston's best shortstop since Pesky. Shy and quick-wristed, the natural pull hitter lashed curves toward the wall like heat-seeking missiles. "Rico had the perfect swing for Fenway," said scout Bots Nekola, who introduced him to Yawkey, who charmed the would-be Townie—vital in baseball's predraft early '60s. "A couple clubs were after me, but my family and I were so impressed by Mr. Yawkey and how well they treated us that I said, 'This it it.' " Rico endured the Eastern, Carolina, and Coast Leagues before becoming Sox shortstop in 1965. "We were getting better. The pitching just wasn't there. The main problem was the attitude—it was a losing one." In '65–66, his Bostons lost 190 games.

On September 27, 1966, the son of a Long Island potato farmer lost his 535th Sox game. In 1960, Creamer wrote, "A word should be said about the youngster who almost certainly will be tomorrow's hero, Carl Yastrzemski. Boston fans may find his name hard to pronounce, but they will not find him hard to take." What the twenty-year-old second baseman found hard was the Townies' futility. "People called us country club," he huffed. "Bunk. The reason we were lousy the first six years I was on the team was we had lousy players—just plain lack of talent." Looking back, the wonder is that Yaz even joined the Sox.

The Phillies had envisioned Yaz clearing the right-field wall at baseball's first steel-and-concrete plant—Connie Mack Stadium (née Shibe Park). "I took a lot of batting practice there," he said. "It was a much better park for a left-handed hitter." A friend urged him to think anew. The Sox had baseball's kindest owner (Yaz could get rich) and near-worst team (opening their lineup). Convinced, Carl signed with Boston for $100,000 and led the Carolina League his first year with .377 and 102 RBIs. In 1960, he topped the American Association in hitting when Boston played an exhibition game in Minneapolis. "The Millers were our top farm club," Gowdy said, "so we were all curious. I'm standing around and ask a guy, 'Which one is Yastrzemski?' He pointed to a figure swinging a couple of bats, and I said, 'That little guy?' Not really, but I expected a giant after seeing Williams in left for so long."

Mickey Mantle was once asked Yastrzemski's strength. "Consistency," he replied. "Lots of guys were streak players. Not Yaz. He was always good." Not in early '61. He was proclaimed the next

Williams, the Kid redux. Try succeeding/replacing a deity: "I'd be as equally as willing," quoth Henry Higgins, "for a dentist to be drilling." On April 11, Yaz got his first of 3,419 hits. By June he was hitting around .200. He straightened up, tried to pull the ball, and climbed to .266. "Without patience," said Number 8, "he [manager Mike Higgins] would not have stuck with me as long as he did that first year. He was great with young players, but not the kind of manager to make big things happen. Remember, he had lousy teams." We do.

From 1962 to 1965, Yaz batted between .321 and .289. "I was not satisfied with myself in those first few years," he said. "My rookie year was very difficult. I put a lot of pressure on myself. I was playing left field, where Williams played, and there was that pressure, too." Yaz's defense was nonpareil. "Forget what he was hitting," Gowdy urged. "Boy, could he field. Joe Cronin always said that Al Simmons was the best defensive left fielder in the game's history, and he rated Yastrzemski equal. Yaz had been an infielder in the minors, and that's how he played the outfield. Charging grounders. Flinging strikes to the bases." Four times Number 8 led the league in assists. "Any ball hit down the line—it's a single, believe me."

In 1966, Yaz hit .278 with sixteen homers and eighty runs batted in. "Yaz's power came later," Curt remembered. "He made himself into a complete player." After six years, Carl seemed an above-average player on a below-average club. He could not foresee a season that would turn him from a singles into a power hitter—and his abyssal duckling of a club into America's parlor team.

That year, the Braves moved to oval and antiseptic Atlanta Fulton County Stadium. The Cardinals traded one Busch Stadium for another multisport lookalike. The Reds and Phillies readied to swap Crosley Field and Shibe Park for generic Riverfront and Veterans Stadium. The Pirates primed to junk Forbes Field. One by one, football stadia invaded baseball's soul. Fenway seemed a dinosaur.

In Boston, nitwits built a bandwagon. Forget intimacy! Give *us* a cookie-cutter! Fenway, Steinway—tear it down! Caution, impelled others: Fenway was "one of the best-maintained parks in the majors," said *Sports Illustrated*. "No advertising on fences. . . . Most seats are on one sprawling, far-reaching grandstand level. Fenway Park—named for swampy fens that once dominated area—is in city's Back Bay section, a short drive from downtown Boston. The MTA transit system is the best way to go to the ball game in Boston. Regular spectators come from all six New England states to cheer for the Sox." In short, the magazine seemed to state, baseball was throwing sanity a curve.

Could Fenway regain its hold on New England's fealty? In late 1966, it was not clear that Boston realized what it had. As we shall see, it took '67's Impossible Dream to make Fenway a jewel, not a dowager—evoking, as the writer Ellen Glasgow said, "an infinite feeling for the spirit of the past, and the lingering poetry of time and place."

For the moment, many recoiled at another ill-spent year. A favorite story of Edmund Muskie's etched their unease. A man stuck in the mud with his car was asked by a wayfarer whether he was really stuck. "Well, you could say I was stuck," said the man, "if I was going anywhere."

11

Rapt by the Radio

By John Updike

Forty years ago and four hundred miles from Boston, I sat in my father's Chevrolet, in the Shillington (Pennsylvania) High School parking lot, and listened to the seventh game of the 1946 World Series, the Red Sox versus the Cardinals. Eighth inning, score 3–3, Cardinals up, Enos Slaughter on first base, Harry Walker at the plate; there's a hit to center field, Leon Culberson (substituting for the injured Dom DiMaggio) throws to the infield, shortstop Johnny Pesky cuts it off—Slaughter is being waved around third! Pesky hesitates, the throw is late, Slaughter scores!! The Cardinals hold on to win the game and the World Series. I don't know if I cried, sitting alone in that venerable Chevrolet, but I was only fourteen and well might have. Dazed and with something lost forever, I emerged into the golden September afternoon, where my classmates were jostling and yelling, nuzzling their steadies, sneaking smokes and shooting baskets in a blissful animal innocence I could no longer share.

What had led me, who had never been north of Greenwich, Connecticut, and didn't know Beacon Hill from Bunker Hill or Fenway Park from Park Street Under, to attach my heart to that distant aggregation? Ted Williams had made a dent in my consciousness before the war, but it was the '46 Sox that made me a passionate fan. What a team that was!—Ted in left, Dom in center, Doerr at second, Pesky at short, big Rudy York having a great twilight season at first, Boo Ferriss and Tex Hughson on the mound. Though the Cardinals squeaked by them in that Series, the Sox looked sure to cruise to pennants at least until I got out of high school in 1950. But in fact they didn't, coming perilously close in '48 and '49 but not quite having it in the clutch. The postwar pattern of thrills and spills was set, and whenever they came to Philadelphia, there I was, hanging by the radio.

With its nine defensive men widely spaced on the field, baseball is an easier game to visualize than a fast shuffle like basketball and hockey, and until girls and a driver's license got me by the throat, I spent many an idyllic summer day indoors huddled on the family easy chair next to the hoarse little Philco. The announcers' voices in their granular shades of excitement, and the wraparound crowd noise, and the sound in the middle distance of the ball being hit (not to mention the uproarious clatter when a foul ball sailed into the broadcast booth) made a vivid picture in ways superior to what I would see when, once or twice a summer, I was bused the fifty miles to Shibe Park's bleachers. I even kept box scores of my audited games, and listened on the rain-out days when the play-by-play of some remote and feeble contest like the Browns against the Senators would be verbalized from a teletype whose chattering could be heard in the lulls. The two Philadelphia teams were pretty feeble themselves, and created the vacuum into which my irrational ardor for the Red Sox had flowed.

My barber was a Yankees fan; that was the other choice in Pennsylvania. As his scissors gnashed around my ears and his hair tonic corroded my scalp, he would patiently again explain why Joe DiMaggio was a *team* player, and why as a team the Yankees would always *win*. But they didn't like Roosevelt or Truman at the barbershop, either, and I would rather lose with Boston than win with New York. When my college choices came down to Cornell or Harvard, the decision was obvious. And yet, those four years in Cambridge, it rather rarely seemed to have dawned on me that the Red Sox were only two ten-minute subway rides (or, on a sunny day, a nice walk along the river) away. Living in New York, though, I would risk the subway up to the Bronx and from within the cavernous shadows of the Stadium admired the aging Williams as he matched strokes with Mickey Mantle, who had replaced DiMaggio as the hood ornament of the on-rolling Yankees. The '50s Red Sox didn't leave much of a mark on the record book, but they seem to have inspired a quixotic loyalty in me. While it is not entirely true that I moved from New York to New England to be closer to the Red Sox, it is not entirely false either. I wanted to keep Ted Williams company while I could.

Lying in backyards or on the beach, driving in the car or squinting into a book, I listened to the games and internalized Curt Gowdy. That ever-so-soothing and sensible voice, with its guileless hint of Wyoming twang, relayed pop-ups and bloop hits, blowouts and shutouts to my subconscious. My wife's parents had a retreat on a far hill of Vermont without electricity or telephone but with plenty of pinecones and bear turds in the woods. We parked our car on the edge of that woods, and there I would go, many an afternoon, to sit in the front seat and tune in the Red Sox. Curt's voice came in strong from (I think) Burlington — so strong that one day the car battery wouldn't turn the starter over, and we were stranded. I must have been the only man in New England who, rather than lose touch with the Red Sox, marooned his family in a forest full of bears.

The older you get, the stranger your earlier selves seem, until you can scarcely remember having made their acquaintance at all. Whatever held me there, rapt by the radio, all those precious hours? Ted, of course, who was always doing something fascinating. But the Red Sox around him had a fascination, too; generous-spending Yawkey saw to it that there were always some other classy performers, and some hopeful passages in every season. Yet the wheels inevitably came off the car, or were lubricated too late in the season, and the Red Sox had that ultimate charm, the charm of losers.

All men are mortal, and therefore all men are losers; our profoundest loyalty goes out to the fallible. Chris Evert, for example, did not win our hearts until Navratilova began to push her around, and I know a man who to his own evident satisfaction has been a Chicago Cubs fan for fifty years. As a boy in Pennsylvania, I felt sorry for Mr. Yawkey, that all his financial goodness couldn't buy a World Series. I felt sorry for Williams, that he didn't go five-for-five every day and that spiteful sportswriters kept cheating him out of the MVP Award. The Red Sox in my immature mind were like the man in the Hollywood movie who, because he's wearing a tuxedo, is bound to slip on a banana peel. They were gallantry and grace without the crassness of victory. I loved them. I might have loved some other team just as well — an infant gosling, if caught at the right moment, will fall in love with a zoologist instead of its mother, and a German, if kicked often enough, will fall in love with a shoe — but the Red Sox were the team I had chosen, and one's choices, once made, generate a self-justifying and self-sustaining inertia. All over the country, millions of fans root and holler for one team against another for no reason except that they have chosen to. Fanship is *acte gratuite* hurled in the face of an indifferent (or at least preoccupied) universe.

Since Williams retired — dramatically, as usual — my Red Sox ardor, with its abuse of car batteries, has cooled. But I have not been unaware, in the quarter-century since, of the pennants of 1967 and 1975 and, just as in 1946, the subsequent seventh-game disappointments in the World Series. I remember, in fact, on a late-September Sunday of 1967, crouching with some other suburban men in an interruption of a touch football game, around a little radio on the grass as it told us that the Twins were losing to the Red Sox while the Angels were beating the Tigers, thus allowing our Yastrzemski-led boys back into their first pennant in twenty-one years. And I remember, as well, in 1978, when my wife and I, heading for a Cambridge dinner date, parked along Memorial Drive and listened to the last innings of the Yankees–Red Sox playoff. We heard about the poky Bucky Dent home run, and we heard in living audio the foul Yastrzemski pop-up. It was Slaughter rounding third all over again.

The memoirs of a Red Sox fan tend to sound sour, a litany of disappointments and mistakes going back to the day when Babe Ruth was traded. But the other side of this tails-up coin is that time and time again the team, as its generation of personnel yield to one another, has worked its way to the edge of total victory. Yaz's famous pop-up, for instance, was preceded by a heroic week of solid victories, forcing the Yankees to a playoff, and in the game itself, we (notice the reflexive-possessive pronoun) had fought back from a 5–2 deficit to 5–4 and the tying run on third. In sports, not only do you win some and lose some, but twenty-five competitors, in a twenty-six-team sport, are going to come in lower than first. What makes Boston — little old Boston, up there among the rocky fields and empty mills — think it deserves championship teams all the time? Having the Celtics is miracle enough, perhaps, not to mention a Patriots team that finally won in Miami. The founding Puritans left behind a lingering conviction, it could be, that earthly success reflects divine election, and that this city built upon on a hill is anciently entitled to a prime share. Certainly the scorn heaped in the Boston columns upon imperfect Red Sox teams approaches the self-righteous.

Now this summer's team, casually relegated by most April prophets to a fourth- or fifth-place finish, has made it to the playoffs. It seems a strange team to us veteran Red Sox watchers — solid, sometimes great pitching, and fitful, even anemic hitting. Where are the home runs of yesteryear? Wade Boggs singled his way to some batting championships, and now Jim Rice has choked-up on the handle and is hitting for average, too. This nervous-making crew, with its gimpy veterans and erratic infield, has shown toughness and courage and internal rapport, and like last year's Patriots did better than anyone dared to hope. These Sox were spared that burden of great expectations carried by so many of their star-crossed predecessors; now they have nothing to lose but the marbles. Once again, I'm tuned in.

John Updike is a novelist, short-story writer, poet, and essayist. To many, his name evokes The Centaur, The Witches of Eastwick, *and his contemporary Everyman, Harry "Rabbit" Angstrom. Writing this essay before the 1986 World Series, he could not imagine how "nervous-making" that year's Red Sox would become.*

Been to Canaan
1967–74

In 1940, only England stood between Adolf Hitler and the abyss of a fascist age. Addressing the House of Commons, its new prime minister, Winston Churchill, concluded: "Let us therefore brace ourselves to our duties, and so bear ourselves that, if the British Empire and its Commonwealth last for a thousand years, men will say: 'This was their finest hour.' "

Assume that baseball lasts even a hundred more years. The Red Sox may win a World Series; Bill Clinton will fall again, Richard Nixon rise again, and Jupiter align with Mars; Newt Gingrich may become a social worker, Jane Fonda a patriot, and the Rolling Stones retire; the Sphinx could erode, the Thames reverse course, and Mary Poppins become a madam; Jim Baaker might rejoin the ministry, Billy Graham become a rabbi, and Drew Barrymore a nun; Pete Rose may scream *apologia*, Bob Uecker find the front row, and the National League return to Boston—all this will occur before baseball knows a finer hour than the year nineteen hundred and sixty-seven.

Ninth in 1966, the '67 one hundred-to-one Townies forged a witching power that even Ripley would disbelieve—ending "one of baseball's great rags-to-riches stories," the *New York Times*' Joseph Durso wrote, by winning their first pennant since 1946 on the final day. On Broadway, *The Man of La Mancha* flaunted "The Impossible Dream." The Red Sox' dream transfixed a region, made baseball cool again, revived the Boston American League Baseball Company, and turned Fenway Park into a funhouse of precocious peals.

In 1967, Matty Alou hit .330 or over for the fourth straight season. Child's play. Lonborg won another. Roberto Clemente won the NL batting title at .357. Kid's stuff. Yaz just went deep. The Cardinals linked Lou Brock, Tim McCarver, and Orlando Cepeda to become "El Birdos" and win an unlikely flag. Who cares? How's Tony C.? In the larger world, riots scarred Detroit—forty-three died—and more than two hundred other cities. Thousands protested U.S. Vietnam policy by marching on the Pentagon. Arson, sit-ins, and bombings split campuses where panty raids once seemed bravura. The Red Sox took a fractured time and briefly made it whole.

"Even a restrained backward look at this season must appear hyperbolic," Roger Angell observed of the Yawkeys' wonderwork. From a distance of more than thirty years, you recall its leaves and splashing hues and spooked-up nights that cradled the imagination. Once, Leonard Bernstein said, "Music is something terribly special. It doesn't have to pass the censor of the brain before it can reach the heart." Like music, the Sox of 1967 disdained the finite, crying "Gotcha" to the soul.

Go ahead. Pinch yourself. You still do not believe it.

In early 1967, the Red Sox' chances to win a pennant seemed smaller than Tiny Tim's singing bass in *The Barber of Seville*.

"Well, we don't say 'Wait till next year' anymore,' " pledged general manager Dick O'Connell. His new manager was an ex-Sox pinchhitter. "The talent was there," mused Dick Williams of 1963–64, "but they couldn't play together as a unit." In 1965–66, Williams managed Boston's Triple-A affiliate. Joining the Sox, he vowed, "The only thing I guarantee is that we'll have a hustling ballclub. And, they won't quit. They didn't quit on me in Toronto. I don't intend to have anybody quit on me here." Fans yawned. They had heard it all before.

John Keats once wrote, "Where are the songs of spring?" For Ken Coleman, the spring of 1967 still croons magic and rebirth. "People forget how down the Red Sox were," began the Sox then-announcer. "Talk of leaving Boston. The bottom had fallen out." He recalls to the ticket how few—8,324—specked Fenway's opener to see Rico Petrocelli lash a three-run blast and Lonborg beat Chicago. Next stop, New York, and a kid pitcher from Toronto. "Billy Rohr, April 14," Coleman repeated like liturgy. "That's where the story started."

Rohr, a rookie, had never hurled a major-league game. His rival, Whitey Ford, would pitch in 498. With one out in the ninth inning— well, do what we did in '67. Hop on, and enjoy how for the last third of this century New England's waves of loyalty to the Red Sox have seldom ebbed.

"Billy Rohr on the threshold with a tremendous performance today," Ken canted over Bosox radio. "Eight hits in the game—all of them belong to Boston. Rohr winds—here it comes. Fly ball to deep left. Yastrzemski is going hard, way back, way back! And he dives . . . and makes a tremendous catch! One of the greatest catches you've ever seen by Yastrzemski in left field! Everybody in Yankee Stadium on their feet roaring as Yastrzemski went back and came down with that ball!" The next batter, Elston Howard, singled. The rookie won only two more big-league games. That fall, WHDH Radio broadcast a paean to the Sox, "The Impossible Dream." Released as a record, it became a must-buy Christmas gift. Of Rohr's near-miss, Coleman narrated: "The fans began to sense it. This year was not quite the same."

In Florida, Williams said, "We'll win more than we lose." Few guessed that any schoolboy could soon recite his lineup. At third, Joe Foy led off, started a triple play, and hit two grand-slam homers. In June, the Sox acquired Jerry Adair. When Petrocelli broke his wrist, Adair replaced him. When Mike Andrews was hurt, Adair moved to second— to Coleman, becoming "the kid and the quiet man." Loud were other bats: George Scott's, moved to first, shortstop Petrocelli's, and those of baseball's peerless outfield. Conigliaro was the "ballplayer," said authors Bruce Chadwick and David M. Spindel, "every woman in New England had a crush on." Originally a second baseman, Reggie Smith moved to center field and won a Gold Glove in 1968. Yaz had merely what Coleman called "the greatest season I've ever seen a professional athlete have."

Local boys vied to catch: Mike Ryan, of Haverhill, and Fall River's Russ Gibson. Dalton Jones keyed reserves. Lonborg, Jose Santiago, John Wyatt, and Sparky Lyle led an otherwise vapid staff. Minnesota, Detroit, and Chicago boasted Dean Chance, Denny McLain, Gary Peters, and Joel Horlen, among others. The Sox had Darrell Brandon, Dave Morehead, Lee Stange, Jerry Stephenson, Bill Landis, Gary Bell— acquired in June from Cleveland—and Gary Waslewski, stuck in the minors since 1960. "It's true," Williams laughed, "we weren't Cy Youngs." Morehead, Stephenson, and Waslewski started twenty-eight games—and completed one. Boston's 3.35 earned run average was eighth in the ten-team league.

Former broadcaster Ned Martin chuckled. "Historians will look at the pitching and ask how they won it." Williams helped—and Yaz and Intervention. Also, the junior circuit's junior year. The Sox finished first with a .568 winning percentage, at that time the lowest ever for an AL champion. In 1946, Detroit won ninety-two games and trailed the Townies by a dozen. In '67, playing eight more games, Boston won ninety-two and the pennant.

"We played very well in the last two months of 1966," Brandon recalled. "We felt strongly that we could do it back in September of '66. We thought we had a chance the whole season long." Hardly anyone else did. For one thing, the 1966 Red Sox had finished a half-game from the cellar. For another, no member of the '67 roster had ever played with a .500 Boston team.

"Remember, I'd been there as a player a couple of years before," Williams counseled. "We put in bed checks, the whole thing. It was a point of getting back to fundamentals, on the field and off." He let/made Yaz step down as captain. "We'll have only one chief. All the rest are Indians." He clashed with Tony C., who answered with a two-out, two-run, eleventh-inning dinger to beat Chicago, 2–1. Williams put Foy on a diet, and benched Scott when the Boomer swelled. Amused, the Angels' Jim Fregosi said, "We have nine managers in the league and one dietitian." On October 1, Williams said: "Well, the dietitian won."

July marked the rubicon—even now, a recording, photos, magazine stories, and faded cartoons retrieve its events. The Red Sox lost six straight before the All-Star Game to fall six games behind Chicago. "Same old Sox," the muttering began. Lonborg checked it, Yaz homering, by beating Detroit the Sunday before the break. "Williams wanted to stop the slide so that guys wouldn't think of losing during the layoff," said Martin. "You look back at big games. That was one." What ensued was what many refused to cotton: their team in an honest to goodness, praise be, hallelujah *pennant race*—the Sox versus their patina of bad luck and brooding insecurity. Given history, the outcome still astounds.

To a viewer, coffee and anecdote eased the Nationals' 2–1 All-Star victory. The next day, the Red Sox left Logan Airport for a ten-game road trip. The earth turned flat. The Great Salt Lake became fresh. Boston won every game, including a doubleheader at Cleveland, 8–5 and 5–1. The Townies returned to Logan, where ten thousand greeted them like Lindbergh at Orly Field. Ask any New Englander alive during the next two months: barbecues and work and PTA begot the Sox. "A whole region went insane," Coleman marveled. "That's what '67 really did—it recharged baseball in New England. On the street, in a restaurant, turn on a TV—it's all there was. People talk about other upsets. Believe me, they're nothing compared to 1967."

It was said of the Greek playwright Sophocles that he saw the world "steadily, and he saw it whole." By contrast, 1967 returns in twinklings. One tenth inning Smith batted with the bases loaded, whereupon a radio listener refused to enter the Sumner Tunnel until he learned how Reggie did. Soon, a conga line of autos trailed him—their drivers listening, too. On August 19, TV's *Game of the Week* showed Fenway at its lushest. "The pitch by Stephenson," said Martin. "A chopper. Over the mound. May be tough. Charged by Petrocelli. Throws to first. He's out! The ball game is over! A clutch play by Rico Petrocelli ends it all as Jerry Stephenson gets a save in a wild and woolly ball game in a twelve to eleven win by the Red Sox!" Something was happening—but what?

Casual fans became addicts. Babies were born, and sermons given; marriages were begun, and divorces decreed; dinners grew cold, and were warmed again—all to the fabric of the Red Sox on the air. On beaches, you heard the games from a hundred different radios. From Boston to Nova Scotia, pilots traced the Sox' West Coast pilgrimage via lights in homes below. Williams now said, "We'll win"—and that the race would end on the final weekend. August arrived. On August 13 five teams were within 2½ games.

"In '67," jibed the *Globe* columnist Marty Nolan, "the Red Sox came as close as anything I've seen in sports to a sense of community." One late-summer night, they also trekked nearer death than a pacific game should go.

"Then, one August night, the kid in right lies sprawling in the dirt," said Coleman, narrating "The Impossible Dream." "The fastball struck him square, he's down, is Tony badly hurt? The doctors say he'll be OK, but he won't be back this year. If Tony's through, what can they do? Who'll carry them from here?"

Save Yaz for a moment; you know who carried them. Instead, freeze-frame August 18: Conigliaro, with a league-high twenty homers, batting against Jack Hamilton. "He threw inside," Tony said, "and I moved my head back so quickly the helmet came off." The ball broke Conigliaro's cheekbone, causing a grotesque wound around the eye. "I didn't freeze. The ball got me where I wasn't protected." Out a year, Tony returned in 1969 to an Opening Day record crowd—35,343. In 1971, he smacked thirty-six homers, then faded. A last revival failed in '75. Seven years later Tony C. had a heart attack, went into a coma, and died in 1990, at forty-five. "Maybe it figured," said a fan. "With all the good luck they had that year [1967], that tragedy would even things out."

One would-be replacement, Jim Landis, signed August 23, homered the next day, and was released on the 28th. Another, Ken "Hawk" Harrelson, deplaned from Kansas City. "Charlie [owner Charles Finley] doesn't like me, wanted to humiliate me, so he put me on irrevocable waivers," said the first baseman and outfielder. "This makes me a free agent, so I can sign wherever I want"—ultimately with Boston, for between $75,000 and $150,000. On September 1, Harrelson homered, tripled, and doubled against the White Sox. It was a rarity: Hawk hit .200. In the argot of the age, the next year he became a "happening" (and led the league in RBIs).

A former role player, Williams now juggled, berated, platooned, and prayed. "I like underrated guys," he said. In 1963, Williams pinch-hit sixteen for forty-eight. A year later, he got eleven hits, including five homers, and homered with Tony C. back-to-back to beat the Yankees. Elston Howard arrived from New York to steady the pitching staff. Lee Stange won five straight complete-game victories. Increasingly, non-headliners took to scripting the implausible. You could hear it in the voices of the patrons cheering and announcers speaking: Few believed what they were seeing.

Two days after Tony C.'s injury, the Sox fell behind California, 8–0, on Sunday, August 20. Fenway was silent; the bottom was falling out. "Trailing 8–0, Reggie Smith homered in the fourth to make it eight to one," Coleman said. "Yaz had a three-run homer in the fifth, and they got four runs on three hits in the sixth and tied it." Then, "Fly ball hit deep into left-center field, and it is . . . a home run! Jerry Adair has hit his second home run of the 1967 season and the Red Sox, who trailed 8–0, are now leading in the eighth inning, nine to eight!" A new moniker arose: the Cardiac Kids.

A week later, Boston led, 4–3, in the ninth inning at Comiskey Park. With one out, Duane Josephson batted against Sox reliever John Wyatt. The White Sox had the tying run at third. "Josephson, a right-handed batter. [Ken] Berry, a fast man at third," explained Martin. "Wyatt looks at him and throws. And there's a little blooper to right field. [Jose] Tartabull coming, has a weak arm. Here comes the throw to the plate. It is! Out at home! He is out! Tartabull throws the runner out at the plate, and the ball game is over!" The Red Sox' weakest arm made the season's primo throw.

In 1945, Detroit had won its most recent pennant. On September 18, the Tigers hosted the Yawkeys at the corner of Michigan and Trumbull. In inning ten, the ultimate reserve faced Mike Marshall. "Jones raps one deep toward right, and it's up, and it is gone!" Coleman cried. "Home run, upper deck, for Dalton Jones! The Red Sox take the lead!" The poke meant a two-game swing in standings, and towered on October 1.

Norm Siebern cracked a three-run pinch-hit triple. Andrews bunted home a tying run. Howard blooped a ninth-inning single to beat the Senators. Lonborg slowed a slide by winning the opener of an August 29 twi-night doubleheader at Yankee Stadium. "And the fans here in New York," exulted Coleman upon its final out, "you'd think you were in Boston." Still, analyzing the contenders—Detroit had Al Kaline; Minnesota, Tony Oliva; the White Sox, pitching—a critic had little choice but to sniff of the Townies, "No way." Your response fell back on the left fielder with the encyclopedic name. "The man," Coleman said, "who served as the leader in the field and at the plate, with his glove and hustle, with his bat and muscle, was the fabulous Number 8."

Someone may have a greater season than Carl Yastrzemski's 1967—although how and when, it is difficult to imagine. "I never saw a man have a season like him," Coleman said of Yaz's MVP and Triple Crown year—forty-four homers, 121 RBIs, and .326 average.

"He was phenomenal," added Williams. "He did everything that year—hitting, running, fielding, throwing, hitting with power, and he did it consistently." Dick played with '50s Dodgers Roy Campanella and Duke Snider and Jackie Robinson. "But I never saw anyone have the year that Carl had in '67."

"His numbers were awesome," catcher Russ Gibson conceded, "but they don't tell half the story. He was the greatest clutch hitter I ever saw. It was like he was waiting all afternoon just so he could get up and win the game for you." Time has deepened surety. "I'll tell you. Nobody ever had a season like Yaz in '67. Nobody."

Off-season conditioning helped. Number 8 tried to pull more than in 1961–66. Scott and Smith bloomed; pitchers couldn't work around him. Still, logic cannot define how Yaz singly carried a team, made the impossible routine, and spawned an era of good feeling. "Who can explain it?" Ezio Pinza warbled in *South Pacific*. "Who can tell you why? Fools give you reasons. Wise men never try."

Yaz's, which was Boston's, paradise began with April 14 thievery in New York. "I thought it was gone," he said of Tom Tresh's ninth-inning drive off Billy Rohr. "I leaped as high as I could and lost my balance coming down, but I had the ball. I may have made better catches, but I don't remember any." Soon memory jerked at Yastrzemski's awakening; he warred with different weapons.

One day, he was beating Cleveland with his fielding. (In 1967, Yaz won his third of seven Gold Gloves.) "Here's a ball hit toward left," said Martin. "But Yastrzemski is back, still back, he runs, he's got it! A great catch!" Another time he knifed California with his arm. (In '67, he led AL leftfielders with thirteen assists.) "A base hit to left field. Charged by Yastrzemski. Runner is being held. He runs past the sign. The throw—he's out at the plate!"—the plate being where Yaz led the AL in hits (189), extra-base hits (seventy-nine), slugging percentage (.622), total bases (360), and runs (112).

In early September, Williams urged him to rest after going zero for eighteen. "Hit deep toward left-center field," said Martin of Yaz's reply. "Way back goes Howard. He won't be able to get that one! It is gone! Home run number thirty-seven!" White Sox manager Eddie Stanky called Yaz "a great ballplayer from the neck down." Number 8's riposte: six for nine, including a home run, in a doubleheader at Chicago. Rounding third base, he tipped his cap to the Brat. Blue, it mimed Stanky's face. On August 30, Yaz homered in the eleventh to beat the Yankees in the Bronx. In September his ninth-inning blast into Tiger Stadium's upper-deck overhang tied the score at five and prepared the way for Dalton Jones.

"The nice thing about having memories," wrote William Trevor, "is that you can choose." One remembers Yaz charging balls, tumbling as he threw—feigning catches, then playing it off the wall—above all, hitting daily, fiercely, as if pressure were a pet. "There'd be two on base and Yaz would homer," recalled Gibson. "The game would be tied in extra innings, and we'd have a guy on second and Yaz'd drive him in with a double off the wall." Once, Yankees manager Ralph Houk told sportscaster Howard Cosell, "You're like sh– –. You're everywhere." In fall 1967, Yaz adorned $5 bills and Yaz buttons and straw hats and Carl Cups—inimitable, indomitable, incorrigible, and *ours*.

Tom Gilmartin was a longtime Fenway usher. "In a way, you know the Red Sox will break your heart in the end, but you love them anyway," he said. "That's what being a fan is all about, isn't it?" Not in the season of The Yaz.

In early 1968, Number 8 was named president of the Arnold Bread Sportsmanship Club. Its rules ordained, "Success in sports—and in life—is spelled 'hard work.' " Other maxims: "Defeat can help—if you learn from it." (Yaz had.) "Be good to your body, it's the only way to live." (He was, via workouts.) "Don't forget, the name of any game is FUN." (Not for the Red Sox before 1967.)

In 1979 and '83, Yastrzemski became the sole American League player to get a four hundredth homer and three thousandth hit and the oldest man, at forty-three, to play center field, respectively. He ranks first lifetime in games (3,308), third in total at bats (11,988) and walks (1,845), sixth in total bases (5,539), and ninth in RBIs (1,844). "He's got all kinds of longevity records," Gowdy mused. "Some guys say the work ethic's dead. They should have told Yastrzemski."

In 1989, near "the mountains [that] stood in their native dress, dark, rich, and mysterious," James Fenimore Cooper wrote in *The Deerslayer*, "while the sheet glistened in its solitude, a beautiful gem of the forest," on a seamless day in the recesses of the Mohawk Valley, that ethic brought Yaz to Cooperstown. Visiting the Glimmerglass, a then-record crowd of twenty-five thousand packed Cooper Park and heard Carl give a talk bereft of dogma and cliché. People hung from shrub and trees. Families oozed Sox caps and pennants. Suddenly, in a moment rich with feeling, a tune wafted from near the rear of the Hall of Fame Library.

In 1967, Boston radio/TV's Jess Cain composed "Yastrzemski Song" to the melody of "The Hallelujah Chorus." A saw observes, "It's so bad, it's good." By that measure, "Yastrzemski Song" rivals "Maggie May" and "Messiah" as the greatest aria of all time. Clearly, induction spectators thought so. Singing, they recalled the man—and his year:

Carl Yastrzemski, Carl Yastrzemski, Carl Yastrzemski,
the man we call Yaz, we love him.
Carl Yastrzemski, Carl Yastrzemski, Carl Yastrzemski,
what power he has.

Our Boston team is always on the beam, 'cause we got Yaz!
We Fenway fans, we stop and clap our hands at Yaz's jazz.
Those rival pitchers on the mound all shake.
They dread each windup that they have to take.
When Number 8 is standing at the plate, and then he swings!
Wow! There it goes again!
Wow! There it goes again!
Wow! There it goes again!

A rival batter hits one off the wall;
And there's Yastrzemski going for the ball.
They try for two, the runner knows he's through;
Ah, look at Yaz!
Wow! He threw him out again!

Carl Yastrzemski, Carl Yastrzemski, Carl Yastrzemski,
the man they call Yaz.
Carl Yastrzemski, Carl Yastrzemski,
he's the idol of Boston, Mass.
On Beacon Hill, he gives them quite a thrill;
In Southie, too, there's lots of woopdie-doo;
In the North End, they call Carl friend,
and they hope the season'll never end.

From Wellesley way, they come to watch him play.
And on Cape Cod, they take a holiday.
From all about, they come to shout,
yell for Yaz to hit one out!
The state of Maine is going quite insane.
And in Vermont, it's only Yaz they want.
From every state, they come and wait,
to see Yastrzemski at home plate.

Our Boston team, it's always on the beam, 'cause we got Yaz.
We Fenway fans, we stop and clap our hands at Yaz's jazz.
Although Yastrzemski is a lengthy name,
it fits quite nicely in a Hall of Fame.
We love him so.
In Boston, we all know that when he swings,
yeah, here we go again!

At that instant, hundreds thought of Yaz's final out in the 1975 World Series and '78 playoff; or his league records for at bats, games, plate appearances, and intentional walks; or how no one outtoiled Carl Yastrzemski's son. More likely, they recalled the most glorious juncture in Boston's baseball suzerainty—the fall of 1967—to which we now return.

How many Soxaphiles truly expected to win the pennant? Looking back, the Yawkeys embody the fox taken as a naif who winds up taking the taker. Russ Gibson's first two big-league games had been Rohr's near–no-hitter and an eighteen-inning marathon at Yankee Stadium. In September, he observed, "That second night, when I went to sleep, I said to myself, 'Jesus, playing for the Boston Red Sox is going to be fun.'"

With one week left, Boston and Minnesota shared first place at 90–68. Chicago trailed by ½ game (89–68), and Detroit by 1½ (88–69).

At Fenway, the Sox lost to Cleveland Tuesday and Wednesday. Advantage, White Sox—until the hitless wonders, batting .225, dropped a Wednesday doubleheader to Kansas City and three games at Washington. Advantage, Detroit, home for the last four games—until it rained Thursday and Friday, forcing weekend twin bills. "If the Tigers won all four," Yaz added, "they were guaranteed at least a tie. But it's harder to win two doubleheaders than four single games." Advantage, Minnesota—leading by one game with two left at Fenway—Saturday, September 30, and Sunday, October 1. "Of course we were nervous, particularly Thursday and Friday when we were waiting," said Number 8, "but it'd been like this for three months."

Stores closed. Churches opened. Most of New England's humanity knew the truth and consequences: Minnesota, 91–69; Detroit, 89–69; Boston, 90–70. In 1958, *Sports Illustrated* wrote, "The Red Sox are New England's pride and despair. Annually hope rises that this year the Sox will finally upset those top-dog New York Yankees, and annually there is frustration." One defeat would extend it. Two victories might end it. Ghosts surfaced: At home, on the final weekend, needing to sweep their rival, the Yawkeys' niche mirrored the '49 Yankees'. Asked which game Lonborg would start, Williams snapped, "What difference does it make? We have to win them both."

On Saturday, the Twins scored a first-inning run. In the third, a vital break: pitching to Jose Santiago, Jim Kaat heard something in his elbow pop. Replacing him, Jim Perry yielded run-scoring hits to Adair and Yaz. Minnesota tied the score, 2–2, before Scott batted in the sixth. "Here's the pitch," Coleman chorused, "and Scott hits one deep into center field. This one is back! This one is gone!" An inning later, Jim Merritt faced Yastrzemski. "The three-one delivery," Martin said. "Hit deep toward right field! This may be gone! It's outa' here! Home run!" Fenway's girders throbbed. The noise was insupportable. Yaz's three-run poke broke Williams's '49 team record of forty-three homers. "If you've just turned your radio on, it's happened again," Ned continued. "Yastrzemski's hit a three-run homer, and it's six to two, Red Sox."

Boston won, 6–4. The teams were tied (91–70). Whoever won Sunday would make a playoff. Dividing Saturday's two-for-one, 90–70 Detroit needed a sweep to force it. In 1949, Kinder faced Vic Raschi in game number 154. In '67, Lonborg and Dean Chance dueled in set 162. Earlier that year, Chance no-hit the Sox and Indians. Now, he took a 2–0 lead on Oliva's first-inning double and Yaz's third-inning error. In the sixth, Lonborg led off. The Twins least expected one of baseball's oldest plays. "Chance throws," said Coleman. "Lonborg bunts it down third. Tovar in, no play! He's safe!" Adair and Jones followed with ground singles to fill the bases. Yastrzemski then lined a base hit into center field. "One run is in, Adair's around third, he will score. Going to third is Jones. It's tied, 2–2!"

The Twins resembled the late-'40s Sox. On one hand, they could club you to death. On the other, defense was not exactly a strength. Harrelson hit a ball directly at their shortstop, who hesitated and was lost. "High chopper to [Zoilo] Versalles," said Coleman. "No chance at a throw to the plate. Safe! Jones scores! The Red Sox lead, 3–2!" Yaz went to second, scoring on two wild pitches by reliever Al Worthington. Harmon Killebrew's error gave the Townies a 5–2 lead. "The Red Sox are out in the sixth inning," Ken said, finally. "But what a sixth inning it was!"

In the eighth, Superman for the final time tugged at Minnesota's cape. With two out, Oliva on first, and Killebrew on second, Bob Allison lined a ball into the left-field corner. Harmon scored, and Oliva rounded second. Unlike Versalles, Yaz reacted instantly. "I knew Allison wasn't fast, and he probably figured I'd go home to try to stop Oliva. I stuck my foot against the wall and threw to second." Out! The Twins' rally—and season—died. Rich Rollins batted in the ninth. Ned Martin's call still has a spectacle to its stride:

"Lonborg is within one out of his biggest victory ever . . . his twenty-second of the year . . . and his first over the Twins. The pitch . . . is looped towards shortstop. Petrocelli's back, he's got it! The Red Sox win! And there's pandemonium on the field! Listen!" We are, more than three decades later.

As the ball settled in Rico's glove, Lonborg was clutched at, rushed at, hoisted, crushed. The students and working men and academics and housewives on the field became a wave, hundreds of bodies rocking, collectively and ecstatically. "I was terrified," said Gentleman Jim, now 22–9, fearing that Fenway might resemble a hospital tent at Shiloh. The mob was a crowd, though, not a beast. Inside the clubhouse, teammates turned on a radio. What they heard—at 7:24 P.M., Dick McAuliffe hit into a double play and Detroit lost the second game, 8–5, and the pennant—uncorked confetti in New Britain and Nashua and a jangle of noise in Blue Hill and Brattleboro and a blur of past and present in Wakefield and Woonsocket—joy, utter joy, unmatched since V-E Day.

Jerry Adair dried champagne and said, "This is undoubtedly the greatest day of my life." Bobby Doerr, the first-base coach, shook his head. "I was sure we'd have a playoff." Williams told the press, "I'm here, just listening and sweating, like you are . . . and I'd like to thank God." Yawkey must have remembered 1946, '48, and '49: "All I can say is that it's really just the most terrific thrill I've ever had. I don't see how anything could surpass it. Other than that, I don't have words that can describe my feeling. It's just a terrific, fantastic thing." Yawkey hadn't had a drink since 1963—"but I'll have one now."

Emotion warps reason. Reflection bronzes it. The Sox won the pennant in July (19–10), August (20–15), September (15–11), and October (1–0). Lonborg had a 3.16 earned run average, threw eight ten-strikeout games (the Sox' third-best ever), led the league in starts (thirty-nine) and strikeouts (246)—the team's sixth- and fifth-best ever, respectively—and won the Cy Young Award. Santiago finished 12–4. Wyatt graced sixty games, saving twenty, with a 2.60 ERA. Petrocelli hit seventeen homers. The Boomer added nineteen and tripled seven times. Smith stole sixteen bases. Yaz had five multihomer games, and his first of three years of forty or more—forty-four, forty, and forty again in 1967, '68, and '70. Number 8 had twenty-three hits in his last forty-four at bats, ten in his last thirteen at bats, and seven in his last eight, and went four-for-four on October 1. Recalled Johnny Bench, then nineteen: "Just having him at the plate gave them an edge."

The October 2 Boston *Record-American*'s cover bannered: "CHAMPS!" above a drawing of two red socks. Next, the World Series—climactic, or was it? 'Sixty-seven's followed a tough act, like Sinatra preceding Vic Damone. The Cardinals had won 101 games. Said Williams: "They had an All-Star team"—an outfield of Lou Brock, Curt Flood, and ex-Yankee Roger Maris; infielders Orlando Cepeda, Julian Javier, Dal Maxvill, and Mike Shannon; Tim McCarver catching and Bob Gibson pitching.

"Who *are* these people?" Yaz mused of the corporate suits, replacing regular ticket holders, who watched Fenway's first Series game since October 11, 1946. Gibson beat Santiago, 2–1. Brock stole his first of seven bases. Anticlimax, indeed.

A black-and-white photo of Yaz, swinging, caught the next day's difference. McCarver's glove is held high and inside. Inside, Dick Hughes's pitch wasn't high enough: Yastrzemski pulled it in the seats. "He's back!" a fan whooped as Number 8 homered twice and robbed Flood on a leaping, lunging catch. At the time, the theft saved Lonborg's no-hitter. Javier's eighth-inning double ended it. Boston won, 5–0, then met hardship in St. Louis: Nelson Briles beat Bell, 5–2, and Gibson again beat Santiago, 6–0. Behind, three sets to one, Lonborg threw a three-hitter against Steve Carlton for a 3–1 win. Smith, beating McCarver's tag, scored the Sox' final run. A picture shows Williams, hands raised in the dugout, like a football referee's "good!"

The Occasion returned to Fenway, where Boston bats revived. Rico hit the screen in the second inning. In the fourth, Yaz, Reggie, and Petrocelli homered. Gary Waslewski pitched the Sox into inning six with a 4–2 lead. St. Louis scored twice in the seventh. The Sox then touched four pitchers for four bottom-of-the-inning runs. Game, Boston, 8–4; the Series was tied, three-all. The next day, October 12, Red Sox Nation prayed for rain. Gibson would pitch with three days' rest; a tired Lonborg, two. The Cardinals belted the Gentleman around the lot. Gibson and Javier homered. Lonborg left trailing, 7–1. "And though Sox followers saddened as each Cardinal rally crossed," narrated Coleman, "one sportswriter called it 'the Series nobody lost.' "

The Red Sox dispersed to homes in Boston and Greenville, Mississippi, and Rio Piedras, Puerto Rico. The nation busied itself with reliving an Ozymandian year. Citizens could buy, and did, Sox stuffed dolls, plastic dolls, bobbing dolls, and piggy banks; Sox beach caps, baseball caps, pennants, and old ink pens shaped like bats; date books, photo decal glasses, popcorn megaphones, and newspaper foldouts. "It was a great off-season," Yawkey said. "People dressed and decorated their homes in Red Sox."

In 1966, Fenway welcomed 811,172 customers. In '67, the Sox set an all-time attendance record—1,727,832—and led the league four times through 1971. Fenway had been an early- and mid-'60s *Game of the Week* oddity. Baseball's Main Street now rediscovered its charm. "It's terrific on TV," said NBC's late director, Harry Coyle. "You got to love the nooks, crannies, the camera angles." From 1968 to 1989, Fenway hosted *Game* more than any ballpark. An '80s *Mason-Dixon* poll asked southerners their favorite club: the Red Sox trailed only the Atlanta Braves.

Fenway's primacy, in turn, helped baseball. As we shall see, to those who discussed such things, it had become an act of '60s faith that the sport was too mild to survive an age of violence and an ethical laissez-faire. Its condition was clearly terminal; with luck, the patient would outlast the '70s. By contrast, the Sox brandished a plot (Arthurian), surface (God's grass), and lure (real baseball, not gaudy hip-hop or in-your-face).

"Karl Marx, who said religion was the [people's] opiate, would have revised himself had he watched the Red Sox unite to throw off their ninth-place chains," the *Globe's* Bud Collins wrote in 1967. "The

Red Sox are the opiate right now, Karl, baby, although you might clas-
sify them as a religion."

Not bad for one year's work.

The Sox' (*especially*, the Sox') luck couldn't (and didn't) last. Two days
before Christmas 1967, Lonborg fell while skiing on a California mountain near Lake Tahoe and tore a pair of ligaments in his left knee. He
won only six games in '68. That July, Santiago went on the disabled list.
"After that, we were through," Williams said. "Of course, George
Scott's falling apart [.171] didn't help any." Remember Ronald Reagan:
"There you go again." Like Joe Wood, Tex Hughson, and Boo Ferriss,
Lonborg and Santiago faded. By dint of irony, pitchers' legs/arms have
been Boston's Achilles' heel.

It is no yarn to say that division remained America's. In 1968, more
man-hours were lost to strikes than any previous year. At the Democratic
Convention, antiwar protestors clashed with club-swinging police.
Students tuned in, turned on, and dropped out. Many aped filmmaker
Oliver Stone's '90s advice: "Have no fear, make no plans, test and
enjoy the limits of life." In baseball, pitchers *derided* limits. Gibson
twirled a 1.12 ERA. Don Drysdale hurled 58⅔ straight scoreless innings.
Both leagues sustained a record 339 shutouts. Only one ALer topped
.300—Yaz at .301. Only rarely did events lift a year of zeroes. Cincinnati
batted .273. The Tigers' Jim Northrup bombed four grand-slams. In
Boston, Harrelson bought a Nehru jacket, plopped on a cowboy hat,
swung a booming bat—and dubbed himself "the Hawk."

"In '67, I didn't hit much after leaving Kansas City. Didn't have to—
not with Yaz," he said, wryly. "That winter I went home, and worked
my butt off. Only one thing was on my mind, and that was beating Yaz.
The next year it all happened—great year [thirty-five homers, 109 RBIs,
and .518 slugging percentage]. Better, I became a personality. The fans
wanted something to latch on to, so I decided to give it to 'em—a guy
bigger than statistics, flamboyant, the clothes, bigger than life."

To Harrelson, other years were Great Danes to admire. 'Sixty-
eight towered, the spaniel who stole your heart. "Fans were different,
more forgiving, salaries weren't that big. So when I made up my mind
to be a public guy—'the Hawk'—it clicked." He attended charity
events, signed hundreds of pictures daily, and got mail addressed to, simply, "Hawk." It became his *alter idem*. "I'd be in the on-deck circle and
say, 'Get out of Hawk's way and let him go.' " In 1975, Hawk entered
Red Sox television. "In a good game, I'd let Ken do the play-by-play.
But in a rout you need some entertainment—so I'd tell myself, 'Get out

of the way. Here's Hawk.' " He laughed. "That's what Red Sox baseball does."

In 1968, Hawk's hitting barrage richened Ray Culp and Dick Ellsworth, acquired via trade. "We had to rebuild our pitching staff," said Williams. "They were our big two." Culp led in earned run average, innings, complete games, and strikeouts. He and Ellsworth each won sixteen games. The Red Sox finished fourth, drawing 1,940,778 pilgrims. A year later, Harrelson went to Cleveland for—more pitching—Vicente Romo and Sonny Siebert. Culp won seventeen, rookie Mike Nagy led in ERA, Lyle graced seventy-one games, and Petrocelli flowered—.297, .589 slugging percentage, and a league record for homers (forty) by a shortstop.

Rico loved, but was sensitive about, the wall. "I'm a pull hitter, and if I hit a ball that just makes the net someone will say, 'Oh, what a cheap shot!' " he mourned. "What they forget is most of them are so high up they'd be out of a lot of other parks. What you do get is a lot of base hits against the wall that might be caught in other parks, but home runs, no—you lose as many as you get; they even each other out." He liked Fenway as it was, and had company. Hordes were now jamming the Olde Towne team's cabash.

Through 1974, the Sox won between eighty-four and eighty-nine games, contended only in 1972 (losing by 1½ games) and '74 (leading until August), and placed third four times (1969, '70, '71, and '74) and second twice (1972–73) in baseball's new six-team AL East division. Attendance belied post-'67's fall. Boston topped the league in 1969, '70, '71, and '74—drawing from '70's 1,595,278 to '69's 1,833,246. In 1968 alone, four crowds of 35,610 or more packed the AL's smallest park to see the Tigers, Twins, and Yankees (twice). It was the '50s all over again: as often as not you paid to watch the individual, not the team.

Yaz twice crashed forty homers, played 350 straight games, and won his third batting title—and almost a fourth, losing on his final 1970 at bat to the Angels' Alex Johnson. In 1971, the Sox peddled Andrews to Chicago for shortstop Luis Aparicio, who promptly went zero for forty-four. Petrocelli moved to third, playing a then-league-record seventy-seven straight games without an error. That season, Siebert topped Boston with sixteen victories, Tony C. amazed with 116 RBIs, and 35,710 crowded Fenway to see the A's Vida Blue debut. From 1969 to 1973, Reggie Smith led the Sox at least once in average, home runs, RBIs, hits, doubles, triples, extra-base hits, slugging percentage, total bases, runs, and stolen bases. George Scott became Falstaffian in girth and legend:

e.g., the second basemen's "teeth"—in truth, beads and shells—that Boomer wore around his neck.

"Hitting! More hitting!" Ted Williams had cried. Weak pitching again consigned Boston to so-so on parade. From 1968 to 1971, Culp won sixty-four sets and each year led the Sox in strikeouts and innings. Roger Moret fashioned Fenway's second-highest career winning percentage for a lefty (.720, 18–7). At the other end, Gary Peters, traded from Chicago, left his stuff on the tarmac at O'Hare. In 1969, Dick Williams was fired. Said Yawkey: "He has a communication gap with his players." His less-martinet-than-minister successor made vanilla seem risqué. "I loved [Eddie] Kasko," Yaz confided. "No controversy. He would have been a great manager with a good team." Neither he, nor they, were.

Kasko was the Sox' Triple-A manager when, on July 20, 1969, the Townies hosted Baltimore and Neil Armstrong walked on the moon. Reporting it, P.A. announcer Sherm Feller spawned a wave of noise that soon encased the park. The umpire called time. Brooks Robinson, due to bat, couldn't hear what Feller said and started for the plate. Seeing him, the umpire explained the applause, whereupon Brooks dropped his bat and began to clap. At that point a fan in Fenway's left-field corner—with its door and angles, dubbed "No-Man's Land"—stood and began to sing "God Bless America."

In a moment Fenway became a park full of loud and teary carolers. Caruso or Pavarotti have never sounded better.

It is hard for post–baby boomers to grasp how in the early '70s Richard Nixon fused person and president like no chief executive since FDR. Nixon as Grant Wood versus temporal fashion etched what *Newsweek's* Meg Greenfield called the age's "traumatic clash of cultures." As it lodged in the White House, in a man who despised—and was despised by—America's hip, camp, and pop-art intelligentsia, it split families, politicians, above all, generations, and cemented his rapport with the great middle classes before, to mix classical analogies, like Icarus perishing from Promethean fire, helping to bring about his fall.

As one doubted whether a middle ground was possible, Anwar Sadat hinted at a peace accord with Israel, cocaine vied with the Jesus movement, and forty-eight men died at Attica Penitentiary. Nixon became the first U.S. president to visit Moscow, planted the roots of America's foremost scandal, and ended decades of estrangement in Beijing, Hangzhou, and the Forbidden City. Upheaval tinged values and morality, civil rights, feminism, drugs, and whether police were pigs, love should be free, grades abolished, and America—as George McGovern urged—should "come home." The age seemed, if nothing else, *alive*. Baseball, on the other hand, again receded.

The 1972 season began with a players' strike that lopped thirteen days and eighty-six games off the regular season. The walkout upended schedules (Boston lost seven games, Detroit, six) and cost baseball at the gate (the pre-August Sox drew poorly; both playoffs abided empty seats). "Those players, making all that money," huffed citizens. The anger would go underground, then return.

For those who cared, the Townies stoked the hot-stove league. In '71, they finished eighteen games back of Baltimore. Alarmed, General Manager Dick O'Connell began to trade. One worked: Scott, Lonborg, and Ken Brett to Milwaukee for pitcher Marty Pattin and outfielder Tommy Harper. Another didn't: Yankees first baseman Danny Cater for Sparky Lyle. "I don't really feel I'm wanted around here anymore," Lyle said. He soon would be, reaping a league-leading thirty-five saves for New York. Cater, previously a Red Sox–killer, promptly forgot how to hit (thirty-nine RBIs). Sadly, Bob Montgomery never learned how to throw. On April 19, Kasko sacked him for Carlton Fisk. "He may be inexperienced," said Kasko of Fisk, "but at least he has an arm."

Fisk batted .293 with twenty-two homers, became the only pre–Nomar Garciaparra player unanimously voted American League Rookie of the Year, swapped red for white hose after a 1980 contract dispute, and played more games and hit more homers as a catcher than anyone. Tall and granite-jawed, Number 27 rivaled Tony C. as a heartthrob.

Luis Tiant was neither. Red Sox Nation wouldn't care. In 1968, the then-Indians' starter twirled a 1.60 ERA. He hurt his arm, tumbled to the minors, and resurfaced with the Red Sox the same day that Fisk cracked the lineup—in relief, fanning four in two innings. In time, the balding, bulging, English-breaking, cigar-in-the-shower-smoking, pirouetting-as-he-threw Cuban evolved into Carmen Miranda via Bobo Newsom turned Arthur Murray—El Tiante. In 1972, he embodied Casey Stengel's portrait of the '69 Miracle Mets: "They did it *slow*, but *fast*."

Luis won eleven games, including seven straight, in August and September to become the AL ERA leader (1.91), Boston's first since Mel Parnell in 1949, and Comeback Player of the Year. Slowly, fans returned to see the Sox, 47–47 on August 1, win thirty-eight of their last sixty-one games. On September 20, Marty Pattin beat Jim Palmer and Tiant blanked Mike Cuellar at Fenway against the Orioles. Rookie Dwight

Evans, twenty, got two hits in each game. "It was the biggest thing I'd seen," said Evans. "Of course, I remember those games in Detroit [at season's end], but why talk about them?" Yaz began to hit: of his twelve home runs, eight buoyed September. Pattin started 2–8, but finished 17–13. Fisk and second baseman Doug Griffin won Gold Gloves. Harper and Petrocelli topped the Sox with 141 hits and 75 RBIs, respectively. "We weren't that powerful," said Yastrzemski. "But we still should have won it." You could almost hear McCarthy speaking.

On September 28, Boston led Detroit by half a game. That night, the Tigers lost and John Curtis beat Kansas City in Fenway's final game. Boston was 82–67, Detroit 81–69. A day later, the Tigers won and Yaz homered to beat Baltimore. Ibid. the 30th: the Townies still held a 1½ game lead. Five years earlier, Lonborg won the pennant on October 1. Presently, that date upbraided fate: Boston lost, Detroit won—again a half-game lead. Both readied for their season-ending series—three games at Tiger Stadium. "That schedule!" scolded Yaz. "The strike made us play one fewer game than the Tigers." The half-game meant nothing. The '72 Sox had dropped six of seven games in the place where Goslin dazzled, McLain cavorted, and Gehringer simply played ball. They now needed to win two of three for the flag.

More than fifty-one thousand packed Detroit's boxy silhouette for the October 2 opener. In the second inning, one old warrior—Al Kaline—touched Curtis for a homer. In the third, another replied. With one out, Harper and Aparicio singled to left. Yaz then lashed a drive to center field—baseball's deepest, its vast turf shrouding the horizon— over the head of Mickey Stanley. Harper scored easily. Not Aparicio, who lost his balance nearing third base, regained it, turned third, fell down, and retreated to the bag, where—as TV's Gomer Pyle would say, "Surprise! Surprise! Surprise!"—he found Yaz staring him in the face. "He had at least a triple," Kasko mused, "maybe an inside-the-park homer." Boston should have led at least 2–1 with one out and Number 8 on third. Instead, Yaz was put out, Smith fanned to end the inning, and the score stayed one-all.

Even for Boston, the burlesque amazed. Little Looie! Stumbling like a derelict! Losing a pennant on a running botch by probably the greatest base runner of his time! "If we had that one, and we should have," wondered Yaz, "we would have been certain to win one of the next two. We lost it right there. We had Mickey [Lolich] on the ropes and we let him bounce back." They lost the game, 4–1, and the AL East the next night, 3–1, on Kaline's single before 54,079 patrons. The final game didn't matter. Naturally, the Townies won.

"We had a good team," Tom Yawkey said. "I liked our pitching. We just stopped hitting." In 1946, the Sox had stopped hitting. The '72 debacle rivaled '48 and '49. Boston had wavered, fallen, and rallied as in a tease—before, with success in the bank, again proceeding to empty its account.

As Aparicio slip-slid his way into Detroit's Monday-night delight, I mused in my college dorm about "second" teams—the franchise you adopt if/once your ball club fails. The Red Sox are millions' second team. The Tigers—like the Sox, a regional club, from Grosse Point to the Upper Peninsula—are another. Many hoped that Detroit might purge the A's in the playoff—to Madison Avenue, the "League Championship Series." Its loss meant that even after Kaline's three thousandth hit, Mark "the Bird" Fidrych's rise and fall, and the debut of baseball's longest-running keystone pair—Lou Whitaker and Alan Trammell—the Tigers entered 1984 sans a pennant since '68.

The Sox' wait was shorter. In politics, power corrupts. In baseball, it can disperse. In 1973, team leaders included: Smith (.303), Fisk (twenty-six homers), Yaz (ninety-five RBIs), its first designated hitter, Orlando Cepeda (244 total bases), and Harper (ninety-two runs and fifty-four stolen bases, breaking Speaker's '12 mark of fifty-two). Tiant's twenty victories, twenty-three complete games, and 206 strikeouts were the most by a Sox pitcher between 1968 and 1985. Left-hander Bill Lee had a 2.75 ERA in 285 innings. Nuff' ced: the Townies won eight straight games in August to fall *further* behind Baltimore, which took fourteen in a row. Kasko was fired, replaced by Darrell Johnson, who joined O'Connell to treat age with less than a diffident respect.

By now, Boston's farm system had been reborn. In the off-season, O'Connell dealt Smith to St. Louis and released Aparicio, Cepeda, and Bolin. "We believe," he said, "that our young players can carry us." They did—by '75. In 1974, Evans and Griffin were injured. Fisk hurt his leg in a June 28 collision at the plate and was lost for the year. In response, Boston acquired Deron Johnson and Dick McAuliffe to help Yaz, Rico, Harper, and Montgomery—fellow thirty-somethings. Experience counts, say campaigners. It seemed to as the Sox flew to an eight-game lead in late August before, like the *Hindenburg*, collapsing.

The crash dwarfed 1972's. Never before had Boston lost a pennant after leading by so much so late in the year. Hints arose (on August 12, Nolan Ryan fanned a league-record nineteen Yawkeys) and quickly were dismissed. Too many Sox hit like infielder Mario Guerrero. "Who," the A's Reggie Jackson wondered, "are all these Mario Andretti guys?" On

September 6, Boston lost its eighth game in a row. "The Red Sox fan, of course, is mad mostly at himself," wrote the *Globe*'s Leigh Montville as the Sox were blanked for twenty-nine straight innings. "He finds he was tricked again by those beguiling storm-door and aluminum-siding salesmen from Lansdowne Street. He bought their whole damn package. . . . The Red Sox fan had forgotten his inbred pessimism, his rooting heritage. He had stuffed it in a drawer." Out it came. The Yawkeys finished third, seven games behind.

"Our young players weren't old enough," a fan remarked. "Our older players were no longer good enough." Added Darrell Johnson: "Termites grabbed our bats"—and age. Now thirty-five, Yaz led the Townies in average (.301), RBIs (seventy-nine), total bases (229), slugging percentage (.445), and home runs (fifteen, with Rico). Invariably, each statistic was a 1960s–70s club-worst. The Sox as they had been, and would be again, peopled Pawtucket, their Triple-A affiliate. Jim Rice, twenty-one, became the International League's Most Valuable Player. Fred Lynn, twenty-two, jumped to Fenway in September and went eight for fourteen in a four-game blitz. Evans was twenty-two; Fisk, twenty-six; shortstop Rick Burleson, twenty-three. Tiant was thirty-four, but Lee and Moret twenty-seven and twenty-four. Only Number 8 and Petrocelli remained from '67.

The 1975 Red Sox would so enthrall New England, a critic wrote, that if the light were to appear in the Old North Church again its signal would transmit: one if by Rice, two if by Lynn. Looking ahead, you wandered back. To many, even the '75 Sox did not, could not, match the wonder of another apostolic year.

In *Casablanca*, Bogart tells Bergman, "We'll always have Paris." In the burgs, sunburnt hills, and backcountry of Red Sox Nation, we will always have 1967.

13

The Impossible Dream

By Beth Hinchliffe

There's an image from childhood that stays pure in my memory and captures all the promise of that time of breathtaking innocence. It's the thundering deluge of emotions that swept me away when I walked up the crowded cement gangway into the right-field stands one Friday night in 1967 and suddenly saw Fenway, mythmaking Fenway, spread out before me.

Forget my friends who wanted to meet John or Paul. Being there, in the cathedral of the team at whose cleats I worshipped, was my own dream come astoundingly true. If I could be there—so close I could smell that rich, newly mown Fenway grass, could see George Scott's huge jowls flop as he worked his chewing tobacco, could feel the crunch of roasted peanut shells underfoot, could hear the bellows from undershirted fans and the slap of the ball against the catcher's mitt and the deeply satisfying crack of a bat when it connected—if I could be there for all this, and have my Red Sox in a pennant race on top of it, well, of course, any dream could come true.

To be suspended for one last summer in the world of childhood in Boston that year meant that life was full of possibilities, life was good, and Carl Yastrzemski was God. For the summer of 1967 was like none other. Ever.

When did we know there was magic to come? During the off-season, when Jimmy "the Greek" gave one hundred-to-one odds on our winning the pennant, and Dick Williams chewed out his immortal "we'll win more than we'll lose"? During spring training, when I did my Latin homework to the roar of the Winter Haven crowd over the transistor radio my Dad made for me? (*"Amo, amas, amat"* has never been quite the same.) On April 12, when we won our home opener against the Chicago White Sox (and our principal, Mr. Peebles, announced the score over the school P.A. system)? Maybe it was when they became "our boys," during those long, lovely summer evenings when the lawns in our neighborhood burst alive with shared barbecues, games of catch, and sleepy-eyed children stargazing to the accompaniment of a dozen radios tuned to WHDH. You could take a walk around the block and never miss a play.

More than three decades later, I might not even know all the names on the '99 team, but I can still recite that classic 1967 lineup without looking at a clipping: Joe Foy leading off at third; Mike Andrews, second base; Yaz, left field; Tony C., cleanup and right field; George Scott, first base; Reggie Smith, center field; Rico Petrocelli, shortstop; Elston Howard, catcher (though we could never really accept or forgive him, since earlier that year when still a dreaded Yankee he had stolen Billy Rohr's no-hitter with two out in the bottom of the ninth). And for sheer style to round it out: Jim Lonborg, pitching.

The players were kids and their fans became kids again, caught up in the heady joy of playing a game not for money but for the sheer love of the dirt flying when you slide into first or the sight of a ball puffing the net above the Green Monster or the team erupting out of the dugout to clap you on the back as your feet touch home plate. To us, the Red Sox weren't distant professionals—they were our own personal Little League team playing with the sandlot grins and guts that make baseball a game of love, a bond and a pledge between players and fans.

For me, the drama of '67 was even more thrilling because I was hopelessly in the thrall of my first crush, enacted with all the obsessive passion an adoring adolescent girl could muster. I knew I was destined to marry Tony Conigliaro. I wore his picture (cut from a chewing-gum card) in the antique locket my grandmother had given me. I sent him a cross on a chain (which looked like real gold) I'd bought with baby-sitting money, and fudge I'd cooked myself. In my room (the walls covered with posters and magazine covers), I crafted tribute scrapbooks while I listened endlessly to the 45s he'd cut: "You're Just Too Good to Be True," "Why Don't They Understand?," "Playing the Field" (I chose to believe that referred only to his baseball exploits). And I begged and whined as only a teen can to be able to go to a game and see him *in person* (and have him spot me in the stands).

That's how I came to be at Fenway on August 18, 1967 (the ticket stub is still in scrapbook number two). No matter how many times I go to the park, whenever I hear its name I still see that brilliant first glimpse: giddy with heart pounding I push up the gangway and then — bam! — unbelievable, there it is before me, smaller and closer than I ever could have dreamed, almost suffocatingly intimate, drenched in breathtaking colors, how do they make them so bright? The players are shagging balls a few feet away! I could touch them . . . I almost do. I can't get enough of everything, can't squeeze it all into my senses, and then the game starts and the action is right in front of me, just for me. I screech at Tony his first time up and he gets a hit, but he doesn't see me. I shift against the wonderfully uncomfortable slats of the old wooden chairs, gaze up at the Green Monster (thirty-seven feet high, I knew that), chant along with organist John Kiley as he plays chords to pump up the crowd, and copy everything my father and grandfather are doing, so proud to be initiated into the Red Sox ritual of generations.

Now, it's the fourth inning, scoreless with two out and Tony's on deck. I don't even pay attention to Reggie Smith in the batter's box. Three weeks ago Tony hit his one hundredth home run; at twenty-two the youngest ever to reach that milestone. You can do it again, I urge him telepathically. You've been in a minislump, but tonight we can break out of it. When he steps up to the plate, owning it in that gloriously cocky, taunting stance of his, I focus fiercely on his face through binoculars (I don't need them because we're practically on top of the umpire, but I want to see every expression, and I watch him pop a big pink bubble of chewing gum). I can hear the crowd roar all around me as the first pitch is hurled by right-hander Jack Hamilton.

That's the instant my story becomes everyone's tragedy. Because, of course, what I saw through the binoculars was the impact of an out-of-control pitch that exploded into his unsuspecting face, nearly killed him instantly, broke our spirit, and set the stage for an anguishing series of setbacks, near-comebacks and disillusionments that eventually trapped him in that big athlete's body, the symbol of lost dreams and the reality of a brave boy who died of a broken heart.

The numbness of that August night haunted the rest of the season — even when the hazy days of August turned into a crisp, tight September pennant race that exceeded the excitement even the most loyal fans had scripted. To the strains of "The Impossible Dream," we started to believe we could be in our first World Series in a generation.

Nerves taunted as four teams were within one game and it became a playoff every night. Strangers stopped others on the street to ask for scores, and we knew the pitching rotation and every injury of Detroit, Minnesota, and Chicago. We watched in awe as Yaz's heart and talent grew in proportion to our need and he closed in on the Triple Crown. Kenmore Square came colorfully alive as the designated heart of Red Sox Nation, lucky ticket-holders and thousands of others merging into a pulsing, celebrating throng after each game. We felt like we were one with the players and each other, all of us thrown together on this improbable joyride we never wanted to end.

Final week: We were a half game back of Minnesota. We laughed at Hubert Humphrey's quote: "We're really up against it. We've got to beat Cardinal Cushing and the entire Kennedy family as well as the Red Sox." He should have added, "and the population of New England." Final weekend: The cardinal, the Kennedys, and all the rest of us had to beat those Twins twice. On Sunday, Jim Lonborg was carried off by the most magnificent mob in the history of the city.

Only a few more hours to go. Radios from beaches to backyards were tuned in unison to the doubleheader that pitted the Tigers against the Angels. Our collection of unknown scrappy kids sat in their locker room after their own triumph, their fate for the first time this season out of their hands. When the Tigers lost the second game, the Red Sox won the pennant. Just when we thought we couldn't celebrate anymore, we did.

For us the World Series was almost anticlimactic. After all, we'd come this far on a shoestring and a prayer . . . but we'd deluded ourselves into forgetting the legendary comment of Ray, of the Bob & Ray comedy team: "On my tombstone it's going to say, 'Cause of Death: Boston Red Sox.'" The National League champion Cardinals even had the weather gods on their side.

Seventh game: our hopes all resting on Gentleman Jim, who had to pitch after two days' rest, impossible like the rest of this year—and this impossible dream was finally one too many. The skies were threatening, the forecast dubious. So the weather was all we could talk about: it's got to rain, the game will be postponed a day, it will be Jim with three days' rest against Gibson, the classic matchup, the way it should be. If we'd known how to do rain dances, we would have. But it didn't rain, the dream was over, and we all woke up. Mark Hays smuggled a radio into school and Mr. Sands let us listen during science class. Our buddy Mr. Peebles announced the score every inning. As the afternoon slowly passed, we grew resigned and we grew up.

Three decades later, the promise-drenched first glimpse of Fenway that August 1967 night is what I cherish, the last purely perfect memory. For those of us who came of age with those boys of that summer, those men of that fall, it was our defining moment, when our worlds divided between childhood and the rest of our lives.

We'll never forget those sweet days when Ned Martin's voice made time stand still, when good guys could win and heroes could live forever: before dreams and cheekbones could be shattered in a dreaded instant, before Jack Hamilton's pitch and the rain that wouldn't come, before Kent State and Watergate and Haight-Ashbury, before Bucky Dent and Bill Buckner, before the World Series at night and free agents selling their loyalty and Pete Rose selling his soul, before kids grew up too fast and lonely in a harsh-edged world eager to teach them that it's folly to believe in an Impossible Dream.

Beth Hinchliffe is an author, award-winning playwright, and former speechwriter for President Bush who now writes for cabinet secretaries and members of the British government. The Wellesley College and University of Cambridge graduate is a fourth-generation Sox fan who grew up three doors away from Pete Runnels.

The Red Sox have played at Fenway Park since 1912. Here it's the mid-1950s, and Ted Williams is still tearing it up.

Andy Jurinko, *Above Fenway Park*, 1998

Copyright © Andy Jurinko

Summer 1941, Fenway Park, the home team's clubhouse: Could this be the Splinter's stall?

Bill Williams, *Vintage Fenway Flannel*, 1994

Copyright © Bill Williams

April 29, 1986: Twenty-three-year-old Roger Clemens has just frozen Seattle's Phil Bradley in the ninth inning to notch his twentieth strikeout, setting a major league record for strikeouts in a nine-inning game.

Bill Purdom, *Rocket's Red Glare*, 1996

Copyright © Bill Purdom

*Saturday, September 30,
1967: Carl Yastrzemski
has just launched a
seventh-inning pitch from
Minnesota's Jim Merritt
into the bleachers. The
three-run shot gives Yaz
enough homers (44) to
capture the Triple Crown.*

Bill Purdom, *Triple Crown Clout*, 1995

Copyright © Bill Purdom

July 17, 1987: The Townies are hosting Oakland, and Dave Stewart is pitching to shortstop Spike Owen.

Andy Jurinko, *Fenway Park Diptych*, 1990

July 19, 1987: Curt Young is pitching to Wade Boggs. The view is from the lower-deck seats.

Andy Jurinko, *Fenway Park Triptych*, 1988

Midsummer 1991: A fantasy game between the Yankees and the Red Sox. Wade Boggs is batting in the first inning.

William Feldman, *Fenway Park Matinee*, 1992

Copyright © William Feldman

*Memorial Day week-
end 1989: Angels vs.
Red Sox. The view is
from the third-base side.*

Bill Purdom, *Fenway Park
Panorama*, 1989

Copyright © Bill Purdom

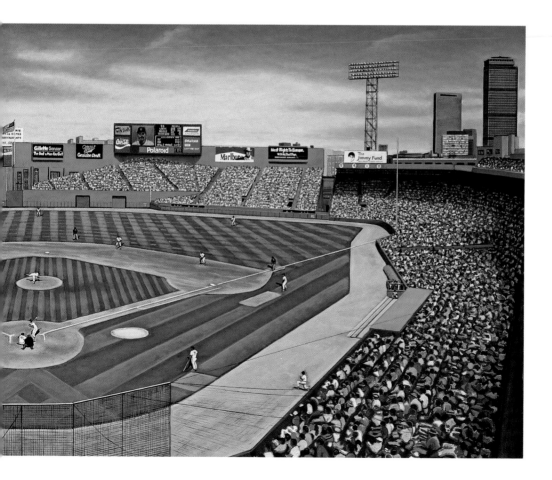

*July 14, 1946: The Indians employ the
Boudreau Shift to thwart the Splendid
Splinter. Williams was 1 for 2 in the game,
with a double, two walks, and two runs scored.*

Andy Jurinko, *Fenway Park Gold*, 1992

*May 25, 1955, at
Fenway: Ted Williams
is following through
on his swing in a game
against Washington.*

Andy Jurinko, *Ted Williams,
1955*, 1995

14

Where's That Rainbow?

1975—86

Ralph Waldo Emerson wrote of Napoleon, "He was no saint—to use his word, 'no Capuchin,' and he is no hero in the high sense." Not saints, the Red Sox of 1975–86 were possessed of a surpassing identity and ability to relate. However general and arbitrary memory may be, many will concede in trying to recapture this era that they were lucky through sheer accident of birth. A boy knew little of things like original sin and Calvinism and mysticism and the Babe's farewell curse. What mattered was that if you couldn't fantasize about being Looie or Dewey or the Rooster or Yaz, you were squaresville, freaked out, a nerd, out of it—but good.

Baseball is subjective: what appears vanilla to me may seem like chocolate to you. By any taste, the '75–86 Red Sox played, and lost, three of baseball's arguably five greatest games of the television, which is modern America's, age. We know them by rote: Game Six of the 1975 World Series, the '78 playoff against the Yankees, and Game Six of the '86 Oktoberfest. The other two: Bobby Thomson's blast, and Bill Mazeroski's against the Yankees. (Contenders: Don Larsen's perfect game, Kirk Gibson's 1988 reprise of *The Natural*, Joe Carter's ending the 1993 World Series, and Dave Henderson's thunderbolt in 1986.) Never before, or since, was the republic so umbilically attached to the Boston American League Baseball Company.

Fenway Park is New England's tribal meeting place. Television in our time is America's—the grounds where members congregate, then leave to savor and debate. In a 1964 Lou Harris survey, 48 percent of those polled named baseball their favorite sport. In early '75, 17 percent did. Reasons fused. The bigs did little marketing. Pro football played the networks like a cello. Many of baseball's finest teams—to wit, Oakland's 1972–74 world champion A's—drew poorly, played far from New York's electronic core, and/or had a mausoleum of a park. In television's creative colony, network baseball became a leper.

"That's how people were talking then," Bowie Kuhn said in 1984. "That baseball was dull, and because of that dead or dying." Reenter a sort of Eastern yeasty turbulence: from 1975 to 1986, the Red Sox—and the Mets and Yankees—helped America rediscover the rhythms of a game, ironically, more balletic than slam-bang or cutting-edge. In 1975, more than 124 million watched all or part of the Boston-Cincinnati World Series. By 1986, Game Seven of the Mets-Sox Classic was seen in 34 million homes, luring an estimated 81 million of the devoted and the curious—easily, the most-watched baseball game of all time.

"It helped," Kuhn said of baseball's going back to its future. "In person or on television, you love to see tradition, the up-close, and roaring fans." Without wishing to besmirch the latter, televised games at, say, Olympic Stadium rival a stroll through Kmart. On the other hand, Fenway inveigled with its dark-green grass and light-green wall and jammed and hopeful grandstand and ricocheting balls and intruding fans and low camera shots and up-close portraits and seamless web of angled blocks and nooks and triangles and planes.

Increasingly, the carousel at Lansdowne and Yawkey became the place that denoted the national game. "It comes down to this," NBC's Harry Coyle said in 1980. "The Red Sox mean Fenway—and to millions Fenway means great TV baseball." For argument's sake, accept Yankee Stadium as baseball's most famous park; Wrigley Field, its most beautiful; Ebbets Field, revered; and Camden Yards, visionary. Between Carlton Fisk and Bill Buckner, Fenway became its most beloved.

In 1974, batting catatonia lit New England's September collapse. Few expected a better '75. The year began with the Yankees' signing of Jim Hunter, from the A's, after arbitration deemed the Catfish a free agent. There followed the majors' first black manager, Frank Robinson; Nolan Ryan's fourth no-hitter; Rod Carew's fourth straight batting title; and an October celebration/genuflection—to baseball, recompense for the past decade's slights and lost prestige.

Ned Martin's voice softened. "Nobody had picked them to go anywhere that year," recalled the man whose "Mercy!" wrote his calling card. "Baltimore was supposed to win." Four years earlier, Hawk

Harrelson had quit to become a golfer. In early 1975, struggling, he retired to become a Sox TV voice. That March he did his first spring training game. "I was uptight, but we got through the first few innings," he said. Montreal then pinch-hit Tim Foli, leading partner Dick Stockton to call him "a pepper pot." Ad-libbed the Hawk: "He's a feisty little guy. Got a lot of balls." Stockton's jaw dropped. As Harrelson tells it, suddenly even golf looked good. Quickly, he learned that Red Sox Nation is a forgiving, which is not to say, forgetting lot: most letters called it a first-year mistake, adding, "Please don't do it again." Hawk learned never to refer on-air to gonads. The Sox had learned that Dorian Gray never faced a curve.

"They've always needed pitching," mused the *Globe* contributor and ESPN-TV analyst Peter Gammons. " 'Seventy-four taught them you needed youth, too." In 1975, pitching meant Bill Lee (17–9), Roger Moret (14–3), Reggie Cleveland (13–9), the florid El Tiante (18–14), and Rick Wise (19–12), acquired from St. Louis. Jim Willoughby landed to anchor the bull pen. Youth meant the "Gold Dust Twins"—rookies Jim Rice and Fred Lynn—flanking rightfielder Dwight Evans (.274) to form the best Sox outfield since Lewis, Speaker, and Hooper. Rice (.309, twenty-two home runs, and 102 RBIs) was so strong he broke his bat while checking a swing. Lynn (.331, twenty-one, 105, and a Gold Glove in center field) led Boston in ten categories from stolen bases to slugging percentage—the first same-year Rookie of the Year and MVP.

Yaz, now a first baseman, hit .310 the first half but finished at .269. Rico Petrocelli slowed and the next year retired—eleventh on the Sox' all-time list in hits; ninth in at bats, walks, and total bases; eighth in games; and seventh in extra-base hits, RBIs, and homers (210). Fisk shook off a broken wrist to hit .331. Rick Burleson and Cecil Cooper batted .252 and .311, respectively. Denny Doyle arrived in June to hit in a league-high twenty-two straight games (Lynn had twenty) and steady second base. Boston had only 134 homers, but led the league in batting average, slugging percentage, and on-base percentage. "A good, but not typical, Sox club," said Bobby Doerr. "No tattooing the wall. Just singled and doubled and tripled you to death."

On Opening Day, a northeaster struck Boston. "They're all up as the groundswell continues for Tony C. in his comeback in a Red Sox uniform," said Martin. Then, "There's a line drive, base hit to right field! Tony's got a base hit!" In May, he hit his last home run. By June 1, the Sox were 23–9. Three weeks later, the Yanks crashed Fenway for a four-game series. Fisk, returning to the lineup, crashed a ball into the screen. "Way back!" growled announcer Jim Woods in his booming, whiskied voice. "Back! It is gone! Carlton Fisk has his first home run of the year! And look at him jump and dance! He's the happiest guy in Massachusetts!" Winning three, the Yawkeys grabbed first—to stay.

Baseball's wild card of recent bent devalues its daily, gnawing pennant race—the Giants and Dodgers in 1951, or the Phillies folding in late 1964. By contrast, '75 fused date and deed. On July 2, Wise pitched a no-hitter for 8⅔ innings. On the 17th, Rice became the fifth player to clear Fenway's center-field back wall. "Out of sight!" Woods chimed. "Over the American flag and out of here!"

In mid-month Boston won ten straight games and then visited New York for another four-game set. Already, Lynn had staged a nonesuch night: "And there goes a shot deep to right field!" Martin cried on June 19 in Detroit. "High in the air, and we watch this one go into the upper deck! His third home run of the night as he goes five-for-six with three home runs and ten runs batted in!" Now, like a postscript, Lynn wrote touché by day.

The teams split games Friday and Saturday. On Sunday, ahead, 1–0, in the first game of a doubleheader, Lee pitched to Graig Nettles in the ninth. "Drive to left-center field," said Martin. "May be a gapper! Lynn is running, Lynn is going! He's got it in a great catch! A great catch by Freddie Lynn! Oh, mercy, what a catch by Lynn! He outran that ball in the alley in left-center and Red Sox fans are going ape out here. This is World Series time!" Moret blanked New York, 1–0, in the second game. Good or typical, take your choice: the Sox now led by ten.

When the Red Sox run a pennant race, the Townies' lure expands until a goodly portion of the land cares whether at last this year they will strike down a vengeful deity and christen their ode to joy. It also evokes angst, panic, parched throats, and moist palms. If this is Fenway Park, collapse is the address.

In August, Boston won nine of fifteen road games and then began to lose. Worse, the Orioles started to win. Arriving in Baltimore, a columnist dubbed them the "Great Boston Chokers" akin to Albert DeSalvo, the Boston Strangler. A disc jockey for Baltimore station WFBR flew to Nairobi to ask a witch doctor to apply a hex. The price: $200 and two cases of beer. The rites were more byzantine than Tiant's windup: an autographed baseball was chanted over, encased in human hair, and put in a monkey's paw. The Sox swept the two-game series to lead by eight. A Nation sighed: This was not your father's 1974.

On September 16, the teams met in Boston. Fisk and Petrocelli homered. Tiant beat Jim Palmer, 2–0. Cries of "Loo-ie! Loo-ie!" from 34,724 filled the ancient yard. "We've crawled out of more coffins than Bela Lugosi," tut-tutted Earl Weaver, the O's bantam manager. On Saturday, the 26th, the door slammed as Baltimore lost a doubleheader. In 1982, voting of fans chose the Sox' all-time team: four of the players picked—Yaz, Fisk, Petrocelli, and Evans—played on the '75 AL East champion. "It's always nice to win a title," Yastrzemski said years later. "But with the team we had we expected to win a hell of a lot more."

On Saturday, October 4, the playoff began for the AL pennant. The A's paraded Reggie Jackson and Sal Bando and Joe Rudi and panache. Reading, you thought Boston had little but ancient mariners (Yaz and Luis) and Baby Hueys (Rice and Lynn). Oakland was jaunty, tested, and heavily favored. In the first game convention took a fall. Oakland made three first-inning errors. The Sox scored five seventh-inning runs. Tiant spliced three hits to win, 7–1. Said Jackson: "Luis Tiant is the Fred Astaire of baseball."

The next day, Fenway reverted to a shooting gallery. Jackson bashed a long two-run homer. Oakland fronted, 3–0, till Yastrzemski hit a two-run net-finder to the opposite field. Later, the Sox scored single sixth- and seventh-inning runs to lead, 4–3. In any park but Boston's, Yaz's poke might have been an out. Fenway was scene and actor: it mattered where the game was played. In the eighth, another veteran hit to whom the wall gave life: "Fly ball, left field," canted Woods. "Don't know whether it's deep enough or not. And Rudi will watch it go into the screen for a home run! Rico Petrocelli has homered into the screen! Boston leads, 5–3, and Fenway Park is an absolute madhouse!" The play-off was then a best-of-five series. Moret, relieving Cleveland, gave the Townies a 2–0 edge.

Two days later, the A's fell not with a win but with a rally. Early in the game, Yaz threw out Jackson trying for a double. In the eighth, Boston led, 5–2, when with two on Reggie lined a pitch to left-center field. Yaz dove, held him to a single, and kept a second run from scoring. Dick Drago then relieved Wise.

"Bando on third, Jackson on at first," said Woods. "Drago is set. Here's the pitch. Ground ball hit down at Burleson, on to Doyle for one, on to first. They've got two." The noble 6-4-3 ended the Oakland dynasty. Boston won, 5–3, and, incredibly, swept the series. When Tom Yawkey had last visited California (1930), Hoover was president, *The Rudy Vallee Show* buoyed radio, and *The Green Pastures*, a slapstick

critique of Negro Bible lore, starred Richard Harrison as "de Lawd."
Now, calling Yaz the best player in Sox suzerainty, T.A. drank champagne from a paper cup.

Jackson agreed. "Yastrzemski is a superstar," he said, "and you can
keep on saying that all night." Before October, Number 8 had not
played left field all year. Returning, he turned off Oakland's faucet and
hit a team-high .455.

Spying a calendar, you spotted a mistake. The year should have read
1967.

Boston's upset began a postseason that regained much of baseball's grip
on burgs time zones from Fenway Park. "The Sox had always been a
folk team throughout New England," Martin said. "Now in the playoff and, especially, Series, people saw what we saw every day—the
small park, the depth of fans' knowledge of the game. In other words,
baseball like at Ebbets Field or Shibe Park. Baseball like it was *meant*
to be."

The 1975 World Series opened at Fenway on October 11. Again, the
Sox were likened to the boy falling off a turnip truck. Cincinnati had
won 108 games, swept Pittsburgh in the NL playoff, and fielded an All-
Star team—two Hall of Famers (Joe Morgan and Johnny Bench), three
should-be inductees (Tony Perez, Dave Concepcion, and perhaps Pete
Rose), and will-be Hall member manager Sparky Anderson, a.k.a.
"Captain Hook." None helped the Reds in Game One. Tiant scattered
five hits and singled to start a six-run rally. Boston won, 6–0, and the
next day led, 2–1, when rain doused the seventh inning. "Lee was hot,"
said Evans. "The delay broke his rhythm." In the ninth inning, hits by
Bench, Ken Griffey, and Concepcion broke the Townies' back. Reds
win, 3–2.

The Grand Event now moved to Riverfront Stadium in Cincinnati,
where events eclipsed the dreary sameness of its gray-and-concrete
bowl. Concepcion and Cesar Geronimo homered back-to-back, the first
time that had happened in the Series since Game Six of 1967. The Reds
grabbed a 5–1 lead behind Gary Nolan, the first of five Cincy pitchers.
Evans then hit the set's sixth homer—a two-run, ninth-inning blast—
to tie Game Three at 5. In the tenth, Geronimo reached first. Pinch-
hitter Ed Armbrister bunted, at which point Fisk threw the ball into
center field. "Armbrister interfered [with Fisk]!" exclaimed Darrell
Johnson, charging plate umpire Larry Barnett. "Poppycock!" Barnett
cried, more or less. Morgan, the next batter, singled to score the winning run.

A night later Boston scored five fourth-inning runs on six hits, including another Tiant single. Pitching gamely, bravely, the Sox' best pressure hurler between Ruth and Clemens threw 163 pitches to win, 5–4. Game Five went to Cincinnati, with Don Gullett pitching and Perez homering twice: Reds 6, Townies 2. If play had ended there, we might recall it as limply, say, as 1959's White Sox–Dodgers Series. (L.A. won in six.) Instead, as the Classic returned to Boston, God proved that He is a baseball if not a Red Sox fan. For three days it rained. The delay was thought to dampen interest. Instead, it heightened pressure.

On Tuesday, October 21, the weather cleared, Yaz and Fisk reached base in inning one, and Lynn found the bleachers for a three-run homer. The Reds scored three in the fifth, added two in the seventh, and led, 6–3, when Geronimo banked an eighth-inning blast. In the bottom of the inning, Lynn got an infield single and Petrocelli walked. With two out, pinch-hitter Bernie Carbo barely fouled a 2–2 pitch, then arced a memorable, epochal, implausible blast. "The pitch," NBC Radio's Gowdy said. "Carbo hits a high drive! Deep center! Home run! [bedlam for fifteen seconds] . . . Bernie Carbo has hit his second pinch-hit home run of this Series. That was a blast up in the center-field bleachers. It came with two out and the count two and two. And the Red Sox have tied it, six to six."

Millions leapt to their feet as Carbo's drive soared toward center. Incongruity startled: Bernie, yea, Bernardo Carbo, of the punk-rock hair, .257 average, and pre–hippity-hop culture. How was it possible?—but it was. Farce vied with reverie as 11 P.M. skipped to midnight. In the ninth, Lynn popped to short left with the bases loaded and none out. Third-base coach Don Zimmer told the base runner, "No, no, no!" Denny Doyle thought Zim yelled, "Go, go, go!" George Foster caught the ball and threw toward Bench. "He's out!" said Gowdy. "A double play! A double play—Foster throws him out!"—quintessentially, the Sox. Two innings later, Morgan pulled a one-out, one-on curveball toward right—good for a triple or home run. "Back goes Evans—back, back!" said Gowdy. "And . . . what a grab! Evans made a grab and saved a home run on that one!" The best AL right fielder of his time stopped, turned, and threw to first for a double play.

Fisk led off the twelfth, the game four hours old. "Game tied, 6–6, Darcy pitching," Martin began. "Fisk takes high and inside, ball one. Freddie Lynn on deck. There have been numerous heroics tonight, both sides. The one-oh delivery to Fisk. He swings. Long drive, left field!" The ball was far enough, but was it fair or foul? "Home run! The Red Sox win! And the Series is tied, three games apiece." Moments later, Gowdy added, "Carlton Fisk has hit a one-nothing pitch. They're jamming out on the field. His teammates are waiting for him. And the Red Sox have sent the World Series into Game Seven with a dramatic seven-to-six victory. What a game! This is one of the greatest World Series games of all time."

Fisk's drive caromed off the left-field foul pole for a game-winning, Series-tying, Falstaffian home run. The Fens were alight with rapture. The Townies lived. The Good-God-Almighty, one-rip-roarious-play-after-another game ended at 12:34 A.M., tied the seventy-second Classic at three games each, and, as it delayed bedtime for 62 million viewers, revealed how "when there is a game that means something," wrote the *Times*' Dave Anderson, "baseball is the best game of all." Memory freezes the Red Sox catcher, draped against the night, swinging and lancing the ball, employing hand signals and body English to push or force or pray it fair—and when it was and the Red Sox had won this sensational, spectacular, unanswerable game, seven to six, leaping high in the air as Fenway exploded with a noise that mocked the pastime's alleged demise.

After Game Six reached its coda, "I went home," said Sparky Anderson, "and I was stunned." He returned for the finale of this resounding struggle. The necropsy: The Sox led Game Seven, 3–0, but stranded nine runners in the first five innings. In the sixth, Rose upended Doyle on a potential double play to extend the frame. Fisk ordered a curve to the next batter, Perez. Lee upheld his handle— "Spaceman," a loopy chatterbox—by tossing a blooper that Tony bashed over the screen: 3–2. In inning seven, Rose singled off Moret to tie the score. Willoughby relieved, was pinch-hit for, and in the ninth inning yielded to a rookie. "Veterans were ready to pitch, and [Darrell] Johnson picks Jim Burton," mused Peter Gammons. "Only with the Sox."

The Reds won the Series on a run more redolent of dead-ball restraint than the slugging, crowing Big Red Machine. Griffey walked, was sacrificed to second, moved to third on a groundout, and scored on Morgan's game-winning lob to center field. Burton, the loser, pitched in one more big-league game.

In 1998, *TV Guide* listed its "Fifty Greatest TV Moments of All Time." Game Six topped the list:

FAIR BY INCHES (October 21, 1975). Every little boy who has ever played on a sandlot has dreamed of winning a World Series game with a last at-bat home run. Even better: do it in front of the rabid fans of the team you grew up rooting for. In short, do what Red Sox catcher Carlton Fisk did at Boston's Fenway Park in Game Six of the 1975 World Series against the Cincinnati Reds. Leading off the bottom of the twelfth, Fisk got under a Pat Darcy sinker and drove it in a tall, lazy parabola down the left-field line. NBC director Harry Coyle kept the scoreboard camera on Fisk, creating one of the medium's most famous reaction shots. As if in a trance, the catcher bounced up and down near home plate, waving at the ball, willing it to stay fair. And when the ball obeyed, caroming off the foul pole, he leaped into the air and began his trot around the bases, both fists raised—just like a kid on a sandlot. A generation later, Fisk's home run remains the ultimate moment in TV sports, not for its drama (the Red Sox lost the seventh game) but because of its sheer beauty—an American dream come true.

Ned Martin calls Game Six "a keeper." It was also a changer. The success of Fenway's first Series night game presaged baseball's current all-prime-time Oktoberfest. A Classic-record 75,890,000 Americans watched Cincinnati win the seventh game, 4–3. On Madison Avenue, baseball was removed from TV's critical list. The reaction shot of Fisk changed sports coverage. "Since then," said Coyle, "everything's up-close, the human side, not just the play but people's reaction to it." Only with the Red Sox: it stemmed from a rodent within the wall. "The shot happened by accident," recalled NBC cameraman Lou Gerard. "My camera was inside the wall. My task was, no matter what—follow the ball. As Fisk swung I saw a rat four feet away. I didn't dare move, which is what I had to do to shift the viewfinder." Instead, he kept the lens on the ball—something, in terms of focus, the Sox found hard to do.

Veterans spied the hourglass. Years later, Yaz confessed, "I thought we should have won that Series in five games. I really did." In six of seven games the winning team came from behind. Five games were decided by one run, two in the ninth, two in extra innings. The Sox led in every match. Pups like Lynn and Evans thought the final game a blip. Said Dewey: "I thought we'd win a lot of Classics." Game Six changed Boston fans. For once, they felt like conquerors. Usher Tom Gilmartin was standing in a walkway when Fisk homered: "The woman sitting in front of me jumped up, turned around, and kissed me." They were not alone. Months later, the *New Yorker* reflected: "The Series, of course, was replayed everywhere in memory and conversation through the ensuing winter, and even now its colors still light up the sky."

Even Fenway changed. In Game Six, Lynn hit the center-field concrete wall chasing George Foster's double. The already bound-for-

Cooperstowner crumpled to the grass. Many thought of Agganis and Tony C. The next year Yawkey padded the outfield wall base, replaced left-field's tin with plastic, reduced the built-in-'34 left-field scoreboard by dropping NL scores, and moved it twenty feet to the right. Novelties included a new press box and commercial message board in center field. (In 1982–83, private suites were built atop the left- and right-field stands.) Alarmists grumbled—or were they seers? Years later, a group called "Save Fenway Park" equated the message board with lost innocence. "Money, that's what it became," said John Valianti of Marshfield, Massachusetts. "The board, the suites. When Fenway started playing by others' rules, it began not being Fenway."

At the time, change was seen as meteorological, not commercial. Before 1976, Fenway's wind blew mostly in or out. Trapping it, the new press box and message board made currents ricochet around the park. "Foul pops used to all find the seats," said *Globe* columnist Marty Nolan. "Now they can blow toward them, catch the wind, and end up fair." Even numbers bespoke transition. For years, the distance to Fenway's left-field pole—315 feet—suffused a child's imaginings. It was sacred, steadfast, like the rock at Plymouth Point. On October 19, 1975, the *Globe* used aerial photography to measure the distance as 304.779 feet. In 1997, the Sox revised it to 310. It was, a friend said, like waking up one morning and being told that one plus one equals three.

America in the wake of Watergate had a quirky, scattered feel. Leisure suits dressed a gender. With a burst of fireworks a million people celebrated the country's two hundredth birthday by watching a grand flotilla of tall ships in New York Harbor. *Taxi Driver* and *Rocky* graced theatres. Americans found passing idiocy in discomania and citizens-band radio. Twenty-nine persons died of a mysterious ailment called "Legionnaire's Disease" after staying at Philadelphia's Bellevue-Stratford Hotel for an American Legion convention. Aptly, Darrell Johnson stayed there while managing the AL team in the 1976 All-Star Game.

By then, baseball had begun an age that years later, as Washington Irving wrote of the Hudson Valley, "[still] holds the spell over the minds of the people"—tying, as it did, the end of a plantation order (under free agency, athletes could now play an option year and sign with another team), familiarity (the 1976–78 Yankees and Dodgers won five of the frame's six flags), domination (only five clubs won division titles from 1976 through '78), and the AL's first playoff game in thirty years (October 2, 1978, Boston versus New York).

For Boston, the era started badly. Lee, brawling with the Yankees, hurt his arm. Eight times the '76 Yawkeys crawled to within a game of .500, then lost. "With the talent we have on this club, playing .500 is a disgrace," said Yaz. Tiant's wins (twenty-one), ERA (3.06), and innings pitched (279) paced a patchwork staff. Lynn, Rice, and Yaz led the Sox in average (.314), homers (twenty-five) and RBIs (102). The team won fifteen of its last eighteen sets to finish 83–79. Ignoble, the year claimed a nobleman: Thomas Austin Yawkey, seventy-three, died at 4:20 P.M. on Friday, July 9, of cancer.

His wife, Jean, became Sox owner. In 1978, she sold a large interest in the club to a group—JRY Corporation—headed by ex-catcher Haywood Sullivan. "Since then," *Globe* columnist Dan Shaughnessy wrote of Yawkey's death, "Red Sox ownership has displayed the smarts and stability of a banana republic."

Perceptive, he was perhaps unfair. No one could replace a man who played pepper with clubhouse men, made the Red Sox the league's flagship team, and chased a World Series like Ahab did Moby Dick. Bart Giamatti, among others, knew what Yawkey was and meant: "In his moves over the years [he] really established the team that the Sox became and their place in history. I can't think of another owner in baseball so closely identified with a team."

Ask your nearest seven-year-old boy what baseball nicety he likes. He will eschew, I predict, the pitchout, hit-and-run, and the vagaries of the slider. He likes the long ball, the soul-crushing poke, the prodigious deed—the homer. We were all seven in 1977. That year, the Boston American League Baseball Company—a.k.a. "the Crunch Bunch"—belted a team-record 216 dingers. Five Red Sox hit more than twenty-five taters. Their ninth-place hitter, Butch Hobson, whacked thirty. "It was a fun club," said Rice, leading the club with thirty-nine (and .320 average, 114 RBIs, and in five other categories). The Sox went downtown thirty times in a ten-game stretch, sixteen in three sets versus the Yankees, and eight once against Toronto. In eight games they bombed five or more. For the first time Boston drew more than 2 million customers. "Pitching! We needed pitching!" Yaz caroled. Reliever Bill Campbell topped the Sox with thirteen victories. Starter Ferguson Jenkins led with only eleven complete games, 193 innings, and a 3.68 ERA. In New York, Sparky Lyle won the Cy Young Award. The Yawkeys' .602 winning percentage—their first over .600 since 1950—tied Baltimore at 2½ games behind the Yanks.

In 1974–76, Don Zimmer was Johnson's fine third-base coach. In 1976–80, as Boston manager, he remained a fine third-base coach. His Gallipoli, which became New England's, was of course 1978. Nineteen seventy-eight. The phrase stands alone, needs no embroidery—a Woodstock or Waterloo, *Sputnik* or Chappaquiddick. Spoken in the tone usually reserved for a drunken spouse or wayward child, it became freighted with connotation—so affixed to the Sox and baseball that even non-Townies grasp the pursed lips, the raised eyebrow, a plaintive sigh. Some define Game Six of the 1986 Oktoberfest as the Dante of Sox damnation. I disagree: '86 was surrealistic, otherworldly, could only have been decreed by God. Thy will be done. By contrast, '78 rivaled a greyhound who, lacking food and water, veers hidebound toward the finish in angst and shock.

Clearly, that was not Zimmer's plan. To his credit, he recalled 1974's collapse. In 1977, Mike Torrez had won sixteen games for the Yankees, including a Series-winning two. Boston bought him for $2.5 million. Whip-armed Dennis Eckersley arrived to become an author (of Eckspeak) and stopper (a staff-best 20–8 record, sixteen complete games, and a 2.99 ERA). From Milwaukee landed a reacquired George Scott. From the Angels came Somerset, Massachusetts, second base-man Jerry Remy, an oxymoron—a fast Boston regular. Never again, Zim vowed of '74, unveiling a solution: forge such a lead that even Murderers' Row would crumble.

We will come shortly to the anguished verdict. For now, recall the mock suspense with which Sox fans awaited October's laying-on of hands. Boston gained first place on May 26, went 23–7 that month, 18–7 the next, and won twenty-six of its first thirty sets at Fenway. By July 9, the Townies led Milwaukee by nine. "If Boston keeps playing like this," said Reggie Jackson, "even Affirmed couldn't catch them." A year earlier, Reggie had fought manager Billy Martin during an NBC *Game of the Week* at Fenway. Now, Martin scorched him and owner George Steinbrenner: "One is a born liar, and the other's convicted." Fired, Martin was replaced by Bob Lemon. By July 20, trailing the 62–28 Sox by fourteen games, the Yankees seemed like Alydar.

Boston threatened to kill its club with love. Strangers talked base-ball statistics. Pubs and restaurants derided the Yanks. The bleachers teemed with beach balls and abiding knowledge of the game. Sox fans knew players intimately: Yaz and Remy (stealing thirty bases), and Eck and Rooster (Burleson, steadying the infield), and Looie and Pudge (Fisk, hitting thirty-nine doubles), and Spaceman and Dewey (Evans, possessed of power, a Gold Glove mitt, and a Winchester of an arm). Seven Sox made the All-Star team: Fisk, Lynn, and Rice started. Talk likened the Gold Dust Twins to Maris and Mantle. Lynn bashed a then-left-handed high twenty-seven Fenway homers (ibid. Mo Vaughn in '96. Lynn leads with twenty-eight in '79). Rice had a leviathan of a season—forty-six homers, including twenty-seven at Fenway, and 139 RBIs, eighty-six extra-base hits, and 406 total bases in a big-league record 163 games—the only AL player to exceed the 400 mark since Joe DiMaggio in 1937. It was '49 all over again. How could the Townies *lose*?

Some cracks were medical. Burleson hurt his ankle sliding into second base. Remy cracked his wrist. Evans grew dizzy after a Mike Parrott beaning. A year earlier, Hobson succeeded Petrocelli at third. Hurt, he took to rearranging bone chips in his elbow between pitches. "What a gamer!" said Zimmer, who refused to rest him—or Fisk, playing 155 games with a cracked rib. "He wouldn't bench the regulars," mused Remy. "It was always keep pushing, build that lead." Other cracks were mental. Zimmer quarreled with Torrez. Lee lost his seventh straight, was yanked from the rotation, and called Zim a gerbil—fat, balding, and unglib. The Sox went 2–8 on a road trip. The Yanks picked up six games in eight days. Boston went to the West Coast, came home, and lost three straight for the first time. The Yanks were now five sets out. One day, Orioles coach Jim Frey asked Scott what was wrong. Boomer replied, "Some of these guys are choking, man."

Even in hindsight, what followed amazed. From August 30 to September 16, Boston played seventeen games, lost fourteen, hit .192, had a 4.58 earned run average, made thirty-one errors, and wrote what Dan Shaughnessy called "the apocalyptic Red Sox collapse against which all others must be measured." Its Stalingrad was the "Boston Massacre." On Thursday, September 7, arriving for a four-game series, New York had won thirteen of its last fifteen to draw four back of Boston. By Sunday night, the visitors had outscored the hosts, 42–9, outhit them, 67–21, and won by scores of 15–3, 13–2, 7–0, and 7–4. The Yanks had led by 12–0, 13–0, 7–0, and 6–0. It was sad, grotesque, and mesmerizing.

In the first game, Thurman Munson had three hits before Boston's ninth hitter—Hobson—batted. In Game Two the Yanks knocked out rookie Jim Wright. The next afternoon, the Yankees scored seven fourth-inning runs. Tableaus mimed a car wreck: Thursday, Yaz slumped against the wall; Friday, Evans, woozy from a beaning, dropping a fly ball; Saturday, Lou Piniella's windblown pop falling among five Sox fielders who aped drunken sailors after a night on the town. A man at a Cambridge bar said, "Today was the first time in history that a first-place team was mathematically eliminated." A woman at mass was asked to pray "for your own personal intentions." She said, "Lord, hear my prayer. May the Red Sox snap out of it." Yankees fans taunted the Sox locker room in a tunnel under the stands.

The Yankees trailed by one. Sunday afforded a final chance to avoid what Burleson called "the abuse we have taken and the abuse we must be prepared to take." That morning, Yaz begged Zimmer to start the veteran Lee—12–5 against New York. The Sox manager refused. He hated Lee, had exiled him to the bull pen. Leaders must lead from the head. Zimmer was guided by the heart. In spring training a rookie had been shot in the arm, recovered, and later called up from Pawtucket. Bobby Sprowl became Zim's choice to start: Denny Galehouse in '48 made more sense. "The kid's got ice water in his veins," Zimmer told Yastrzemski. Sprowl walked the first two Yanks, got Munson to hit into a double play, yielded a single and two more walks, and never threw another pitch for the Red Sox—nor won a game in the majors. Maybe it was tap water.

Boston was living its worst nightmare. New York had won sixteen of its last eighteen. The Sox had blown a fourteen-game lead. Players sought reporters to "Tell me, what's wrong with us?" Said Torrez, in his own (0–6) forty days of wilderness: "It [the Massacre] was so lopsized that you wouldn't have believed it if it had happened to the original Mets." On Wednesday, September 13, Boston lost, 2–1, falling to second, then ventured across the Harlem River from where the '62–63 Mets played. On Friday, the Yankees won, 4–0. Next day, the score was tied at 2–2 in the ninth. Mickey Rivers tripled over Yaz, playing too shallow in Yankee Stadium's insatiable left field, and scored on Munson's sacrifice fly. "I don't feel sorry for them," Lyle said of his former team. "I pity them." The Townies, behind New York by 3½ games, had lost 17½ games in the standings in fifty-eight days.

Boston won the next day, 7–3. Scott got a hit after thirty-six straight outs. Go figure: the Sox now turned and won eleven of their last thirteen sets, including their final eight. "It was our last chance," Remy said, "to not have this over our heads for the rest of our lives." More than New England reawoke. In 1943, Wendell Willkie wrote the bestselling *One World*. In late 1978, the late Archbishop Humberto Medeiros used a recess of the College of Cardinals to ask a Boston television journalist how the Sox were doing. When Pope Paul I died on September 28, a Boston TV station teased its upcoming newscast, "Pope Dies, Sox Still Alive."

That week, the Sox moved within a game. Both Boston and New York won through Saturday, the 30th. The season ended the next day: Cleveland at New York, Toronto at Fenway. Tiant won, 5–0, in his final Red Sox game. Radio was reliever Bob Stanley's pre-ESPN link to the Yankees' goings-on. In the bull pen, a transistor beside his ear, Steamer cheer-led the bleachers. Rick Waits beat the Yankees' Catfish Hunter, 9–2. Both clubs now had a 99–63 record. The next afternoon Fenway Park would host a one-game playoff for the AL East title—the league's first since October 4, 1948.

"Stairway to Heaven" or "Plenty of Nothing"? In Boston, both vied as baseball readied for a day that has long ago settled in its bones.

October 2, 1978, broke crisp and sunlit—a postcard, autumn foliage, Norman Rockwell New England day. The weary Sox were pleased to be playing baseball. The Yankees were pleased to be playing Boston. "When you were the Yankees, you just handled the Red Sox," Reggie Jackson said years later. "You knew you were going to beat them. The Red Sox players didn't expect to play well." Today, they opposed a the-atre of the elements: wind, pitching, and above all, luck. Lee under-stood. "If you don't bear down all the time and don't have your act together," he said, "Fenway Park will bite you, eat you up, and spit you up." He could have been describing a gerbil.

Zimmer chose Mike Torrez to avenge his ex-mates. Bob Lemon picked '78's transpontine hurler: left-hander Ron Guidry—"Lou'siana Lightnin' "—bidding for win twenty-five. "Few so ballyhooed sporting events ever match the anticipation," Peter Gammons wrote. "This one did." It began with the wind. Jackson hit a likely first-inning homer that dropped off a shelf into Yastrzemski's glove. "That was no wind," Lee would say. "That was Mr. Yawkey's breath." An inning later, the ageless Yaz pulled Guidry inside the foul pole for a homer: 1–0. The crowd roared, then stilled, recalling '75's Game Seven (the Sox stranded nine runners) and '78's last month (losing five 1–0 games, they failed twenty-four times to score a runner from third with less than two out).

In the third, Scott led off with a double and was left at third. In inning six, Burleson doubled into the left-field corner. Rice's single plated him: 2–0. The Yanks then turned their first of several screws. With runners on first and second, Lynn, a non-pull hitter, pulled the ball into the right-field corner—a double certain to score two runs, except that Piniella was there, but why? "I was over twenty feet to right of normal," he said. "[Catcher] Munson told me [Guidry's] slider was slowing up, acting like a curveball."

In the seventh inning, Bucky Dent hit with two out, two on, and a .244 average with four home runs. Dent fouled Torrez's second pitch off his foot. In pain, he asked for time. At that moment, another turn: on-deck hitter Rivers noted a small crack in Dent's bat, ditched it, and plucked another. Torrez threw a fastball, Dent swung, and Mike trudged toward the dugout. "I thought it was a simple fly," he admitted. Tip O'Neill was watching from a box-level seat: "He hit that goddamn pop fly. Everybody stood up and I thought it was an easy out." Fisk sighed in relief as he walked toward the mound. "I thought, 'We got away with that mistake pitch.' I almost screamed at Mike. Then I saw him looking up and I said, 'Oh, God.'"

Like the wall, Fenway's wind giveth and taketh away. Changing an inning or two earlier, it now blew toward the Monster. "Deep to left!" Yankees announcer Bill White said. "Yastrzemski will not get it! It's a home run! A three-run homer by Bucky Dent! And the Yankees now lead by a score of three to two!" Fenway rivaled a dark, unseen room. The only sounds stemmed from the Yankees' colony. "Another half inch in on his hands and I may have broken his bat," Torrez said. Ifs and buts: New York, 3–2. Stanley, relieving, was rocked by Munson for a run-scoring double. In the Sox seventh, aging Bob Bailey pinch-hit against Goose Gossage, relieving Guidry. Believing his bat to be connecting tissue, Bailey kept it on his shoulder for three fastball strikes. "Typical," said a fan. "Over the hill, didn't swing, goes down without a fight. 'No-standing' zones should be renamed 'No-Bailey.'"

The Sox did not go without a fight. Jackson's eighth-inning parabola gave New York a 5–2 lead. Remy began the bottom of the frame by doubling over the first-base bag. Yaz singled to score him, and Fisk and Lynn singled: 5–4. Fenway trembled between joy and reminiscence. Hobson flied out and Scott—"Some of these guys are choking, man"— fanned to end the inning. The Yanks went softly in the ninth. Ahead: the Sox' final turn at bat, during which, wrote Gammons, "the Red Sox–Yankee competition reached a peak of intensity rare even in that legendary rivalry."

Burleson drew a one-out walk. Remy next lined to right, blinding Piniella in the sun. "I just thought, 'Don't panic. Don't wave your damn arms and let the runner know you've lost it.'" As he feigned, Rooster waited, then reached second while Piniella grabbed at and somehow stabbed the ball. "If it had gone to the wall," Lou said later, "those two scooters would still be running around the bases"—the pennant won on an inside-the-park homer. Instead, two runners perched with one away—and Rice and Yastrzemski up. Rice flied to center,

Burleson reaching third. Yaz then approached the plate—the final out, the Sox' final hope, and as it occurred, his final chance for a World Series ring.

You can't stop the clock, Boswells say of baseball's speciality. Fenway's stopped as Goose faced Yastrzemski. Fisk, the on-deck hitter, looked at its 32,925 loyalists. They were standing. "You know, they should have stopped the game right then and there and said, 'Okay, that's it,'" he said. "'The season is over. You're both world champions. We can't decide between you, and neither of you should have to lose.'" Specters fused: Pesky, Boudreau, Burton, Aparicio. Yaz had flown out to end the '75 Series. Now, he wafted Gossage's second pitch toward third baseman Graig Nettles.

"I was trying to will the ball to stay up," said Fisk. Slowly, irreversibly, like a 78 rpm record played at 33, it came down. The congregation remained, standing. No one moved, as if they could will a different end. Later, Yastrzemski wept. Zimmer cursed ifs and buts. Most fixed on Dent's thunderclap. "Anywhere else, that would be the third out," said Guidry. "The wind took it over, though. We were just amazed."

All of us were by 1978.

In 1978, Jim Rice played 163 games, missed only one at bat, and rapped 213 hits to top three straight years of 200 or more. That off-season, he was named Most Valuable Player over Guidry, a brilliant 25–3. All twenty-eight MVP voters named Rice first or second. Boston won its most games since 1946, and drew a then-record 2,320,643. More pivotally, the 1977–78 Townies won 196 sets—and nothing. After Dent's homer, a New Haven bar owner moaned, "They [the Sox] killed our fathers and now the sons of bitches are coming to get us."

Looking back, the playoff marked a Pickett's charge of pre-McGwire lure, though few knew so at the time. "This is baseball's Golden Age," *Sports Illustrated* said in its April 9, 1979, issue. "Indeed, there is impressive evidence to suggest that the old game . . . is now enjoying unsurpassed popularity and prosperity. . . . Pro football is still very much in the picture, but the latest polls show baseball to be *the* sport these days. And statistics suggest that upward curve has been steep and is almost surely still climbing." It was, for a while. By 1982, baseball achieved a rough equivalency with the NFL—leading, 23 to 20 percent, in a Gallup poll as the sport Americans followed most closely and had the greatest interest in.

In August 1979, 136,364 crowded Fenway for a four-game Pale Hose series. That year the Sox broke their one-year-old, single-season attendance mark. On September 12, Yaz touched the Yanks' Jim Beattie for his three thousandth hit—a single to right field. Lynn won a batting title (.333) and Gold Glove (Evans and Burleson did, too) and like Rice hit thirty-nine homers. Yaz and the Twins started the '79 Mid-Summer Classic. Evans played 380 straight games in 1980–83. On the whole, however, the Sox' niche scent of post–high tide, a time of last things and farewell hugs. Increasingly, the Townies lacked baseball's new self-confidence—a turning away from the game's late-'60s and early-'70s inferiority complex of stricture and passivity.

In 1979, El Tiante signed with the Yanks; he still ranks third all-time in Sox starts (238) and strikeouts (1,075) and fourth in shutouts (twenty-six) and wins (122). Zimmer sent Bill Lee—sixth in games (321) and eleventh in wins (ninety-four)—to Montreal for the redoubtable Stan Papi. Lee went 16–10. Sox '79 lefty starters won a single game. In late 1980, Boston acquired Jim Dorsey, Frank Tanana, and Joe Rudi for Burleson and its career eighth-best hitter, Fred Lynn (.308). At the same time, it failed to send Fisk's contract on time to preclude free agency. On March 9, 1981, Fisk, a Sox leader in homers (tenth, at 162, tied with Tony C.), slugging percentage (tenth), and extra-base hits (thirteenth) signed with the White Sox. "You couldn't help but understand what was going on," mourned Yaz, "and it hurt." This glorious team—Boston's best since Speaker and Smoky Joe and the Babe and Rough Bill—was breaking up.

Zimmer was fired, leaving his demons and ghouls, replaced by 1980's Pesky, who preceded 1981–84's Ralph Houk, who begot '85's John McNamara. In 1978, Haywood Sullivan succeeded Dick O'Connell as general manager, then tumbled to '84's Lou Gorman. It didn't help. Boston placed second in the second half of 1981's strike-split season. Otherwise, it placed third through fifth from 1980 to '85—flunking .500 (76–84 in '83) for the first time since 1966. Carney Lansford won the '81 batting crown. Blooming under Houk, Evans won his eighth Gold Glove, took the '81 home-run title (twenty-two, with three others), and became the sole ALer to hit twenty or more each year from 1981 to '89. Starting and relieving, Stanley corkscrewed onto the Sox all-time list: first in games (637), saves (132), and relief wins (eighty-five), sixth in wins (115), and third in losses (ninety-seven).

"Looking back," laughed announcer Joe Castiglione, "it was easier to root for certain players than for those teams." Rice led the league in 1983 with thirty-nine homers and 126 runs batted in. On August 29, he homered three times at Toronto—his last, a ninth-inning, game-winning poke—six years to the day after dinging Oakland thrice at

Fenway. Outfielder Tony Armas led the AL in '84 with forty-three homers and 123 RBIs. Eck was traded for Bill Buckner, who in 1985 hit forty-seven doubles. Like in the '50s, young hurlers surfaced. Bob Ojeda. John Tudor. Bruce Hurst, ultimately, fourth and seventh all-time, respectively, in Sox K's (1,043) and starts (217). Finally, Dennis "Oil Can" Boyd, a bit on the blockhead side. One day a game was postponed in Cleveland as fog rolled off Lake Erie. "That's what you get," said the Can, "when you build a stadium on the ocean." Observed a rival: "Even London couldn't match his fog."

On May 1, 1982, the Sox held their first Old-Timers' Day. The outfield linked Ted Williams (then sixty-three), Jimmy Piersall (fifty-three), and Jackie Jensen (fifty-five). "Lloyd's of London," one writer said, "couldn't insure what their salaries would command today." All would have starred on the '83 team, whose torpor was contagious. One night, Cleveland scored twice in the eighth inning to take a 3–2 lead. Said Ken Coleman: "Here comes the tying run and the winning run, and the Indians win." Spying the mound, he saw Stanley standing there. "It was then," Ken said, "that I realized I'd goofed. Baseball is a nine-, not eight-, inning game." Blunders, vapid teams, power hitters, pitching babies: Barbra Streisand sang, "We have been this way before." Where were Uncle Miltie, hula hoops, Buffalo Bob, and beloved Ike?

"In the '50s," said Curt Gowdy, "the Red Sox had great players cursed by mediocre clubs." In the early '80s, Britain won the Falklands War, a U.S. amphibious force invaded Grenada, and Sandra Day O'Connor joined the Supreme Court. The Hub obsessed more with its purest hitter since the Kid. In 1982, Wade Boggs joined the team and began hitting singles and doubles to every field. He was superstitious. "He'd eat chicken at all his meals," said '82–90 second baseman Marty Barrett, "and run sprints at the same exact time each night." Boggs was a bit lacking, shall we say, in judgment, enduring girlfriend Margo Adams's showing and telling all about their extramarital affair in *Penthouse* magazine. Above all, Boggs was a Merlin at the plate.

From 1983 to 1991, Number 26 led the Sox in batting. Four and three times, respectively, he hit 154 and forty-five or more singles and doubles. Seven years he had 200 or more hits, climaxing in 1985's team-record 240. Wade won batting titles in 1983 (.361), '85 (.368, Boston's highest since Williams's .388 in 1957), '86 (.357), '87 (.363), and '88 (.366). That year, he rewrote Sox (187 singles), league (758 plate appearances), and baseball records (batting safely in 135 games). Boston finished 81–81. Norm Zauchin would have understood.

On Saturday and Sunday, October 1–2, 1983, perhaps the greatest Red Sox career ended, as it began, in the shadow of the Wall. Later, Carl Yastrzemski would say, "The fans in Boston were, and are, the most knowledgeable in America." That weekend, he played his first outfield game since 1980 in his last big-league game.

It is said that leaders make a difference because they will, not wish, it. Not hulking, like Williams, nor as strong as, say, Foxx, Yaz willed himself to batting practice and ceaseless work and playing caroms off the Monster. On Saturday, he fought tears to tell the crowd, "I saw the sign that read, 'Say It Ain't So, Yaz,' and I wish it weren't." Both days, he ran around Fenway Park to touch the fans "who made this all possible."

It was simple, not self-absorbed, and heartfelt: Yaz—after the Golden Year and near-misses and road trips and hitting streaks and hope that Next Year was This Year and twenty-three years with a single team—the quintessence of the New England Sox. At Cooperstown, his plaque reads in part:

> YAZ. Boston, AL 1961–83. Succeeded Ted Williams in Fenway's left field in 1961 and retired . . . as all-time Red Sox leader in 8 categories. Played with graceful intensity in record 3,308 AL games. Only AL player with 3,000 hits and 400 homers. Three-time batting champion, won MVP and Triple Crown in 1967 as he led Red Sox to "Impossible Dream" pennant.

It might have added: "He's *still* the idol of Boston, Mass."

"I've always felt that managers are largely victims of circumstances," Coleman allowed. In 1942, Casey Stengel's Braves won 59 games. His 1949–60 Yankees won ten pennants and seven World Series. He was less wizardly with the '62 Mets, losing 120. "If we can make losing popular," Stengel confided, "I'm for it." Warren Spahn once said, laughing, "I knew Casey before and after he was a genius." Voluble and street-hard, he invented Stengelese. Paid by the word, the Ol' Perfessor might have owned the world.

No one will name a language after John Francis McNamara. Plain and stolid, the proverbial "good baseball man," he became Red Sox manager after stops in Oakland, San Diego, Cincinnati, and Anaheim. In 1985, his Boston club went 81–81. In March 1986, *Sport* magazine wrote, "The Red Sox are the most boring team in baseball." Then, on Good Friday, the parish team affirmed its religious gloss by trading Mike

"The Hit Man" Easler for Don Baylor—the first Sox-Yankees trade since Sparky Lyle became New York's in 1972. "As soon as he walked into this clubhouse," said pitcher Roger Clemens, "there wasn't any doubt who the leader was."

On April 7, 1986, it was Evans, banging the first pitch of the year for a homer off Detroit's Jack Morris. No one had done it before, he was told. "Big deal," he jousted. "We lost." Boston also lost its Fenway opener, 8–2, to Kansas City, then rode Roger Clemens to first place. A Tom Seaver pitch-alike, college All-American, and Boston's best mound prospect in thirty years, Clemens brooked shoulder surgery in 1985. He revived to hurl thirty-eight double-figure strikeout games in the decade. (No other Sox pitcher has more than Smoky Joe Wood's eighteen.) On April 29, Clemens left off-Broadway before just 13,414 on a dank night at Fenway. Said the Rocket, beating Seattle, 3–1, "The strikeouts just kept coming."

By now, Ned Martin had traded radio for a TV swaddling—cable's NESN (New England Sports Network). That night the basketball Celtics were playing at the Garden. "It was a big game," he said, "so our TV audience was limited, and so was the crowd." Before the game, catcher-turned-analyst Bob Montgomery said, "This Seattle club has been striking out a lot. The way Clemens is throwing, we may see a few K's." On radio, talk addressed the recently released Red Sox yearbook. "I see here that Roger's favorite singer is Steve Nicks," Coleman told partner Castiglione. "Ken, I believe that's Stevie Nicks," Joe countered. Ken said, "Well, I know him well. I call him Steve." Castiglione said, "Uh, Ken, Stevie is a girl."

By the fifth inning, Clemens had fanned twelve Mariners. Word filtered to the Garden, which started emptying: the Rocket was on a roll. Word-of-mouth recalled baseball's nine-inning record of nineteen strikeouts, held by Steve Carlton, Nolan Ryan, and Tom Seaver. Could Clemens break it? Inadvertently, Baylor helped. "He was usually a DH," stated Sox TV voice Sean McDonough, "but this night was playing in the field. Here comes this foul pop-up, and Baylor dropped it." Still alive, the batter fanned. Whenever Clemens pitched, a fan in right field posted a "K" on the wall to celebrate each strikeout. Tonight, missing several innings, he suddenly appeared for the Sox' most-ever special K. In the ninth, Roger struck out two to set a record of twenty, including a league-tying eight straight. "And here they come up at Fenway! A new record!" cried Martin. "Clemens has set a major-league record for strikeouts in a game! Twenty! What a performance by the kid from the University of Texas!"

Incredibly, Clemens walked zero Mariners. Maxwell Smart would have loved the Rocket: control, not chaos, works. Winning his first four-teen, Roger didn't lose until July. The Sox, picked to finish in the second division, grabbed first place on May 15. Castiglione laughed, softly. "We weren't a powerful club, not a lot of home runs, but fate seemed to like us"—until that October night in Queens. One day, Boston had thirteen walks but trailed Texas by a run as the Sox' Marty Barrett and Steve Lyons both slid into second base. "Me from one direction," Lyons said, "Marty the other." Nothing in outfielder George Wright's past had prepared him for this puzzle. He threw the ball into the Rangers' dugout. Both runners scored. Sox win, 2–1.

In 1978, Peter Gammons had named The Who's "Won't Get Fooled Again" the Townies' official anthem. In mid-July, the Red Sox stumbled. By August, only 2½ games behind, the Orioles domineered the rearview mirror. One journal wrote, "Poised for another El Foldo?" The buzzards circled. The Nation braced. Then, the damnedest, not damnation, happened: Boston won eleven straight. On August 17, it traded a slick for a steady shortstop—Rey Quinones for Seattle's Spike Owen—and outfielder Dave Henderson. Boggs won his third batting title. Baylor clubbed thirty-one homers, twenty-two away from Fenway. Rice added 110 RBIs. At first base, Bill Buckner hit .267 with eighteen homers and 102 RBIs—oh, irony! a favorite. "Fans loved how he gutted it out," Owen observed, his ankles hurt, rebuilt, and gouged again.

As ever, the Sox played station-to-station ball. For a change, however, they beat you the unsung, fundamental, overachieving way. "Pitching!" crowed Castiglione. "What a rarity—we had it." Boyd and Hurst finished 16–10 and 13–8, respectively. Clemens's year rivaled Joe Wood's 1912: a league-leading 24–4 and 2.48 ERA, 238 strikeouts in 254 innings, Cy Young and MVP awards, and All-Star Game starter. From June to August three-game crowds of between 104,339 and 105,037 filled Fenway for the Tigers, Yankees, O's, and Royals—four of Boston's top-ten throngs of the '80s. "On weekends," said souvenir salesman Marc Talbot, "just about all of my business is fathers buying souvenirs for their kids and telling them stories about how it was when they'd come to Fenway with their own fathers. Three generations coming to Fenway telling baseball stories." The Sox drew 2,147,641, up 361,008 over McNamara's first year.

On September 28, the Sox thumped Toronto, 12–3, for their first division title in eleven years. "A high pop-up! This may do it! Buckner is there!" Martin said. "It's all over! The Red Sox are the new divisional champions." Fans rushed the field. Teammates embraced. Billy Buck caressed the ball. In a time of cold fish, prima donnas, and glamor boys, the Hub and the man with the gimpy gait and high-topped shoes seemed thoroughly warmed.

The '86 Angels, Mets, Astros, and Red Sox won their divisions by husky margins. Next came a glorious autumn of taut playoffs (the Mets won in six sets, the Yawkeys in seven) and a seven-game World Series (true to form and the sins of their forebears, another shattering, self-fulfilling, unbelievable Sox loss) and baseball over an extended stretch as it has rarely been played before—a lyric mix of poetry, comedy, and Ferris wheel of drama—"baseball at its summit, [raising] the sport to new levels of courage and endurance," wrote *Newsweek*'s Pete Axthelm. "Even [now], millions . . . are still savoring their rendezvous with base-ball at its pinnacle. It leaves you breathless."

The now-best-of-seven AL playoff began Tuesday, October 7, at Fenway. Bad karma: Clemens lost, 8–1. The next afternoon, Rice homered, the Sox got thirteen hits, and the Angels pratfalled. Three errors helped Hurst cruise, 9–2. On Friday, Boyd and John Candelaria met in the Halos' football-redesigned and -ruined pad. The Angels' Dick Schofield and Gary Pettis homered. Boston lost, 5–3. The next night, in Game Four, routine faded with the sun. Clemens led, 3–0— until Doug DeCinces homered to begin the ninth and Schofield and Bob Boone singled. Replacing Clemens, Calvin Schiraldi got Pettis out on a fly to left—until Rice lost it in the lights. "This series," ABC-TV's Al Michaels enthused, "is getting interesting." Schofield scored to make the score 3–2. Schiraldi walked Ruppert Jones to load the bases, fanned Bobby Grich, and threw two strikes to Brian Downing. Future reference: One strike would win the game. Instead, a 1–2 pitch hit Downing in the ribs, tying the game. Grich's eleventh-inning hit won it, 4–3.

"Indeed," said Voltaire, "history is nothing more than a tableau of crimes and misfortunes." Game Four shouted Boston's. Repeating history, the fifth set changed it, too. In the fifth frame Dave Henderson replaced the twisted-his-ankle Tony Armas. An inning later, the Sox led, 2–1, when Grich hit a drive to center. Henderson raced back, leaped, nearly caught the ball, but knocked it over the wall for a two-run homer. "A half an inch more in his glove, and he makes the catch," a Halos infielder observed of Hendu—or was it Torrez versus Dent? The Angels led, 5–2, in the ninth. Buckner then singled and Baylor hit a two-run homer. Evans popped up. Score: 5–4 Angels. One out would win the game—and California's first pennant.

Think of heretical role reversals: Kate Smith becomes Cher. Dan Quayle becomes Mick Jagger. On Sunday, October 12, 1986, the Angels became the Red Sox. Their manager, Gene Mauch, yanked Mike Witt for Gary Lucas. Lucas hadn't hit a batter in six years. His first pitch plunked Rich Gedman. Replacing him, Donnie Moore faced Henderson. The count went to two and two. With the Sox a strike from elimination, fans poised to assault the field, horses and dogs there to thwart them, and champagne chilling in the California clubhouse, Moore threw a forkball. "Deep to left and Downing goes back! And it's gone!" chorused Michaels. "Unbelievable! You're looking at one for the ages here! Astonishing! Anaheim Stadium was one strike away from turning into Fantasyland! And now the Red Sox lead, 6 to 5!"

Henderson's two-strike, two-out, and two-run ninth-inning *voila* stilled the Big A, capped a four-run rally, and stunned into schizophrenia Red Sox Nation. "This is supposed to happen *to* us," said a friend, "not *for* us." It almost did. In the Angels' ninth, Grich batted with the bases loaded and one out. Grich, then DeCinces, failed against reliever Steve Crawford. "I got no place to sleep tonight," Mauch later laughed, "because I bet my house DeCinces would get the run in from third." In the eleventh, Henderson's sacrifice fly scored the winning run, 7–6. To this day Michaels dubs Game Five the best he has seen, or called. "The highlights could last till midnight, but there were so many twists. Take Crawford. Ninth guy on a ten-guy staff, mops up, gets a save now and then, trying to save a pennant. Afterward, he tells a reporter, 'If there was a bathroom on the mound, I'd have used it.' Baseball has the unlikeliest heroes. One day: Steve Crawford's moment in the sun."

The Angels had receded, though it is doubtful that Mauch knew it. At Fenway, the Sox won Game Six, 10–4, behind Boyd and sixteen hits. The next night became an exception, wrote columnist Mark Shields, to the rule that "to be born a Boston fan is to learn early that life is not going to work out." In the fourth, Clemens led, 4–0. "He swings—there's a fly ball to left!" CBS Radio's Ernie Harwell said. "It's deep! Going back is Downing—looking—it is long gone! A home run for Rice! A three-run homer, and a seven to nothing lead!" The Townies' victory (8–1) was their first in a winner-take-all game with a division flag, pennant, or World Series at stake since 1912, the year Fenway was built, and their first seventh-game postseason triumph in eighty-three years. "What can you say?" Johnny Mac asked of their revival. "You know what the poets say: 'Hope springs eternal in the human breast.'"

Three years later, Donnie Moore committed suicide. His agent, David Pinter, said, "Ever since Henderson's homer, he was extremely depressed. He blamed himself for the Angels not going to the World Series." It was a feeling, and event, with which the Olde Towne Team could sympathize. "Baseball is not a matter of life or death," wrote then-*Globe* columnist Mike Barnicle, "but the Red Sox are."

"Their MTV video has more stars than Hands Across America," *Washington Post* reporter Richard Justice wrote of Dwight Gooden, Darryl Strawberry, Keith Hernandez, and Gary Carter, et al., "which is perfect for the New York Mets and another reason they present opponents with special problems." They and minor meteors helped the '86 Flushings thump their division by 21½ games, beat Houston in the playoff, and enter the World Series as a 2½-to-1 favorite. Not from the Bronx, they were still of New York. In 1948, New York had helped force a playoff. In '49 and '78, New York applied the choke. Would the snake charmer still seduce the snake? "History, hell," glowered McNamara, who should have been more careful.

The Classic whimpered to a Saturday, October 18, start. Mets second baseman Tim Teufel's error scored the only run. Spacing four hits, Hurst became the first Sox left-handed pitcher since Ruth to win a Series game. Walter Alston was once asked what he learned in twenty-three years as Dodgers manager. He said, "You make out your lineup card, sit back, and some very strange things happen." The first game ended 1–0. In Game Two, Boston littered Shea Stadium with eighteen hits. The Red Sox won, 9–3, as Evans and Henderson homered. In '46, Cronin said, "We'll handle this [the Series] back at Fenway." Up 2–0, the Sox flew home. Only the '85 Cardinals had won the first two sets on the road and proceeded to lose the Classic. What was there to handle? Len Dykstra, for one: Tip O'Neill threw out Game Three's first ball. Dykstra hit Oil Can Boyd's third pitch downtown. New York scored four first-inning runs and won, 7–1. Carter, for another: The next night, he went long twice, Ron Darling spaced four hits in seven innings, and the Mets evened a more dull than Grand Event, 6–2.

Game Five ended with Hurst facing Dykstra. "And a swing and a miss!" said CBS Radio's Jack Buck. "He chased a bad ball high! And Boston has won it to take the lead, three games to two — the final game they'll play in their home park this year! Here's the final score: Boston four, New York Mets two." When Hurst beat Gooden, becoming, in another laurel, the first Sox lefty since Ruth to win a Series game at Fenway, the Townies moved twenty-seven outs from their first world title since 1918. "Is this the threshold of a dream or the eve of destruction?" Dan Shaughnessy wondered in the next day's *Globe*. "Are baseball's heartbreak kids finally going to keep a promise, or are they just setting you up for one final apocalyptic, cataclysmic fall?"

The region of Cotton Mather, Jonathan Edwards, and hope receding into Calvinistic tragedy replaned for Shea Stadium—and once more approached the abyss.

It began rather commonly, as epic theatre goes. Behind Clemens, Boston took a 2–0 Game Six edge, had the Mets score twice, but retook a lead when Barrett scored on a seventh-inning force play. As in a tragic play, certain moments presaged disaster. Rice, lumbering, thrown out at the plate on a single by Rich Gedman. Boston, stranding fourteen runners. In the eighth inning the Rocket, ahead 3–2, sustains a blister on his pitching hand and leaves, Schiraldi relieving. With the bases loaded, McNamara lets left-handed Buckner bat against southpaw Jesse Orosco. Billy Buck lines out to center, leaving his sixth, seventh, and eighth runners of the night. In the bottom of the eighth, the Mets score the tying run, 3–3.

At 11:59 P.M. Eastern Time, Henderson swung, bashed a tenth-inning ball off a *Newsday* billboard beyond left field, put Boston ahead, 4–3, and reached the dugout as the Shea clock read midnight. A Barrett walk, Boggs hit, and Evans groundout scored a fifth Townies run. Insurance, you might call it, except that Sox policies rarely redeem—even when Wally Backman and Keith Hernandez flew out to begin the Mets' tenth inning, the Shea message board prematurely blazed, "Congratulations Boston Red Sox," Bruce Hurst was named Classic MVP, the World Series trophy and twenty cases of Great Western champagne entered the Boston clubhouse, and the Nation, believing that it had seen the worst, was ungently disabused.

One out would win the Series. All year Dave Stapleton had replaced a defensive millstone in the later innings. Few noted that Billy Buck was still at first. The wives of Red Sox players stood hugging, cheering. Only Rich Gedman's spouse, Sherry, born forty miles from Boston, sat, recalling '72, '74, and '78.

Carter slapped a 2–1 pitch to left field. You remembered that night's NBC pregame guest: Dick Casey, ninety-two, scribe of the 1918 World Series. "Every day since," he said, "I've prayed to God that the Red Sox would win one more World Series before I die, so now I guess I'm going to die soon." Was he—or the Sox? Kevin Mitchell singled. Ray Knight went to 0–2. One strike would end the famine. Knight singled, Carter scored, and Mitchell took third. A friend turned to Gammons and prophesied, "They're going to do it. Just when we thought that we had been freed at last, they're going to create a way to again break our hearts that goes beyond our wildest imagination." Boston led, 5–4. Shea was throbbing. McNamara ditched Schiraldi for a once-comer turned aging hard-luck kid.

Bob Stanley had thrown only one wild pitch all year. His fifth pitch to Mookie Wilson—again, a strike away, the thirteenth and last pitch that could have won the Series—drifted in, knifed off Gedman's glove, scored Mitchell, and tied the game at five. Knight reached second. Wilson fouled off four pitches, then readied for another. "So the winning run is at second base with two out!" NBC-TV's Vin Scully said. "Three and two to Mookie Wilson! . . . A little roller up along first . . . behind the bag. . . . It gets through Buckner! Here comes Knight! And the Mets win it!" As Wilson's grounder went through Buckner's legs, giving the Mets a 6–5 triumph, "Forty-one years of Red Sox baseball flashed in front of my eyes," wrote Gammons. "In that one moment, Johnny Pesky held the ball, Joe McCarthy lifted Ellis Kinder in Yankee Stadium, Luis Aparicio fell down rounding third, Bill Lee delivered his Leephus pitch to Tony Perez, Darrell Johnson hit for Jim Willoughby, Don Zimmer chose Bobby Sprowl over Luis Tiant, and Bucky (Bleeping) Dent hit the home run." The final act had reached its denouement. The country, exhausted and disbelieving, shook its head.

Tip O'Neill watched Game Six on television. "I didn't sleep for three months. I'd wake up every night seeing that ball go through Buckner's legs. Of course we were cursed that time." The curse withered lives. In 1978, Stanley had gone 15–2 with a 2.60 ERA. The wild pitch completed his evolvement in popular view into an ill-starred, luck-scarred, overfed oaf. Years later, spotting him, a Boston driver tried to ram his car. Buckner corkscrewed into the Sox'—indeed, sport's—poster child of the ultimate victim and/or goat. In spring training 1987, he huffed, "I'm not going to talk to anybody about it. What bothers me the most is the way the media has blown it out of proportion." On July 23, Billy Buck was released. "I would have to say that things were good for me here up until after the sixth game of the World Series. After that, it just went down." Ultimately, he returned to California and later Idaho. In public, McNamara was defiant. "I don't know nothin' about history," he exploded after Game Six, "and I don't want to hear anything about choking or any of that crap." Privately, he reeled. Later that week five hundred thousand mourners graced a Sox parade through Boston. "For me it took away some sting," said Castiglione. "Not for Mac." At Fenway, Joe entered the manager's office to say good-bye. McNamara was disconsolate. "Why me, Joe, why me?" he said. "I go to church — have my whole life. I don't understand why this had to happen."

Game Seven was washed out on Sunday. The Nation waited, sensing what lay ahead. "After they lost the sixth game," Yaz said, "you just knew somehow they wouldn't win the seventh game." Even when rain stopped and Monday's set began and Hurst allowed only one hit in the first five frames and the Olde Towne Team carried a three-run lead into the bottom of the sixth — even then, wrote the *Baltimore Sun*, "You knew the ending. You just didn't know how. They are the Red Sox. You change the ending and there's no more mystique. Just as Hamlet dies every night, the Red Sox die every time they take the stage."

In the second, Evans and Gedman homered back-to-back to give Boston a 2–0 lead. Boggs's same-inning single plated a third. In the sixth, behind, 3–0, Hernandez hit with one out and the bases full. Castiglione was doing play-by-play. "I told myself, 'If Hurst retires Hernandez, the Red Sox win — if Keith gets a hit, the Mets will win.'" He singled to left-center, scoring two.

As reliever Sid Fernandez glowed, New York scored a tying run, and Knight batted in the seventh inning, the inevitable began to pronounce itself: the Sox would lose their fourth straight World Series. "Schiraldi's . . . behind on the count to Ray Knight," said Jack Buck. "The pitch — swing and a fly ball, left-center field, well-hit! May not be caught! It's gone! It's gone! Over the fence in left-center! A home run by Ray Knight to give the Mets their first lead of the evening, 4–3!"

Two days later the *Washington Post* perceived: "They [New York] win 108 games in the regular season, pull off a string of late-season victories, take the World Series in seven games [final game, 8–5], and how will they be remembered? They will be remembered years hence as the other team in the Series the Red Sox blew. That is the triumph of enduring notoriety over fleeting fame; the Red Sox always lose in the end, but in ways that are so imaginative and heartrending as to be more memorable than victory." Evans shook his head. "I don't believe in history, either, but maybe I'm starting to. Sixty-eight years is a long time — 1918 was a long time ago. It does make you wonder."

Again the Olde Towne Team had wanted in the worst way to amount to something, and did; but not quite in the way it had expected, or hoped.

Baseball didn't care, basking in a sort of "ooh-ah" approbation. On October 27, the World Series had opposed ABC's *Monday Night Football* for the first time. NBC's Game Seven coverage blitzed the Rozelles in audience share (55 to 14 percent) and Nielsen ratings (a boffo 38.9 to 8.8). In Los Angeles, New York, and Boston, the Series swaggered, 4-, 7-, and 19-to-1. Observers seemed immune to Fenway's pain. "The 1986 Series seized the nation like no other in recent years," mused Shirley Povich. "It was baseball as Americans know and love it—a throbbing, good-God-what's-next World Series that had Americans' hearts pumping in every time zone—the kind of theatre that no other sport can generate."

Columnist Dick Young had covered the 1950s' Every Year Is Next Year Brooklyn Dodgers. Now, he penned a salute to baseball's dream-stuff fall: "The four divisional races were a drag. Not one hot finish. Then, two breath-holding playoffs and one excruciating seesaw World Series. Always, it seems, the game has something to redeem it. As the Natural said, contemplating the end of his career, 'God, I love baseball.'"

So did Red Sox Nation, often against its will.

15

The Wonder Years

By Ned Martin

The first time I saw Fenway Park was in January 1961, hardly baseball weather. I'd just been named a Red Sox announcer and I came to Boston to accompany players like Bill Monbouquette on the Red Sox Caravan—a ticket-selling type of thing. The only time I'd even seen Fenway on TV was in the 1948 playoff between the Indians and Red Sox in television's infancy. Now, I left the Kenmore Hotel and walked over the bridge and railroad tracks to see it in person. It looked like a brick-yard from the outside, not at all like a baseball park. The next week I met people like Art Gleeson, the announcer, and public-relations direc-tor Bill Crowley, and Helen Robinson, who is still there as a phone receptionist. The first time I went to work was Opening Day, the first game to be played in the major leagues by some leftfielder named Yastrzemski.

I was thirty-seven years old by then, and spellbound to be in the bigs. But you talk about tough starts. During my first five years at Fenway, there weren't many people. The Red Sox were on the down-side, and only the Yankees drew. New England wanted to see Mantle and company. Everyone remembers specific things: I remember how the Red Sox endured. Earl Wilson and Dave Morehead threw no-hitters. Often an opposing player starred. One day Dick Williams hit a long drive toward the bull pen. Crack of the bat—there went Al Luplow, right fielder of the Indians, who leapt at the wall. He fell into the bull pen, a couple of Red Sox raised their hands, and you couldn't tell for a moment if Luplow had caught the ball. But he had, and the umpire said, "You're out." To this day it's the greatest catch I've ever seen at Fenway.

Still, it was the home team that made those '60s memorable. Once a Cleveland outfielder fell down with the bases loaded, and Gary Geiger got a grand-slam homer. Or how about another inside-the-park homer, by—Mercy!—Dick Stuart? Now, Stuart was no Jesse Owens as a runner. And it looked as if he'd get an ordinary single, maybe a double, when he hit a typical high shot off the left-field wall. Well, it came off of the wall at an angle and hit the center fielder for Cleveland in his Adam's apple. The outfielder fell down, and the ball ricochets off him past the left fielder, who was charging over to get the ball. The ball goes into the left-field corner as Stuart keeps running—running uphill—and got what may be the shortest inside-the-parker ever hit—certainly at Fenway Park.

Maybe 1967 was fate's way of making up for all of that. The club caught fire, the crowds came back, everybody in New England reveled in that marvelous summer. The ten-game winning streak, thousands turning out to greet the club at Logan Airport, then that garrison finish and the final weekend. What a wonder year that for me really ignited excitement at coming to the ballpark. And the great thing is, the excitement never stopped. I remember a classic game between Vida Blue and Sonny Siebert in 1971. We'd gotten Siebert from Cleveland in the Ken Harrelson deal, a darn good pitcher, and this night he's pitching at Fenway, people are hanging from the rafters, and the Red Sox win when Dave Duncan, catcher for the Athletics, hit one that looked like it would win the ball game and instead it went foul.

I called '67 a wonder year. The two others, of course, were '75 and '78. You can't have better theater than what happened with the Red Sox, or meant more to fans around the country. Heartbreak, ecstasy, amazing events, and the Townies were at the core. No will ever forget the excitement of Luis Tiant, scheduled to pitch every fourth day, leaving the bull pen before games in '75 and waddling across the field. And people chanting "Loo-ie! Loo-ie!" and folks coming into the ballpark, or even passing by on Boylston Street, heard it, and that gave you an idea of something big going on. Tiant was the absolute pivot of that pitching staff, and the crowd ate him up. Later, the cries became "Dewey! Dewey!" for Dwight Evans, who in '75 was starting to make waves with his acrobatics in right field.

That year's World Series was maybe the greatest ever. I'd waited a long time to do a network World Series, and talk about luck—I had the fortune to call Carlton Fisk's homer on NBC Radio. Certainly Game Six was indescribable—Fisk, Carbo, Denny Doyle. Evans's great play where he caught the ball off Joe Morgan, almost fell into the right-field stands, then had the presence of mind to throw to Yaz for a double play. Dwight had a lot of plays like this because of Fenway's structure—low fences, you could dive into the stands. Many consider right field in Boston to be the toughest in the league. The afternoon sun was bad, and so was the wall because the ball got to you so quickly you didn't have time to see how close it was. Evans mastered it. People got to where they loved to see balls hit out there. Once, we got to talking and Evans said he was proud of how runners wouldn't run on his arm on even medium-deep fly balls. Arm, speed, grace—like Freddie Lynn.

I once said that Lynn playing center field was like Frank Sinatra singing Cole Porter. He played it beautifully. He had a gangling kind of lope toward the ball and always got there. You think of '75 and remember his catch off Graig Nettles in New York, or running into the wall in the Series. He went down, the whole park quieted—memories you don't forget. Which brings us to a year of memory—1978, and the best Red Sox club in my time there. It started in '77, almost an unbeatable offensive team, the kind that broke home run records and pitchers' hearts. By '78, you saw some of the most intense hitting anyone's ever seen, enormous crowds, a whole lot of charisma. Everybody remembers how they had a fourteen-game lead over the Yankees and a thousand games over everybody else. Don Drysdale came into the booth in Anaheim and said, "You guys can't lose. I haven't seen a team this great in a long time." And Drysdale saw some good teams.

Talk about having it all. 'Seventy-eight had the thunder of Lynn and Rice and Yastrzemski, Butch Hobson batting ninth with all those homers. And the pitching of Dennis Eckersley, a favorite then and years later when he came back as a relief pitcher. You wish the story could end there—before the doubts and the defeats and the Boston Massacre. All of a sudden the roll ended, and the Yankees started to move. New England can still recite the collapse, and what happened on October 2, maybe the most exciting and crushing game I ever broadcast at Fenway Park.

Personally, that playoff was difficult, because it was the last game that Jim Woods and I did on Red Sox radio due to a sponsor conflict. What a voice Possum had—one of the all-time greats. And what a way to leave—with a game to be treasured as long as baseball. The National League at one time had a best-of-three playoff for the pennant. The American League played a single game, and the Yankees didn't want to play in Boston. They lost the flip of the coin, and the Red Sox vaulted to a 2–0 lead. Then Bucky Dent and his borrowed bat, and a little fly ball into the net, and all of a sudden the silence in Fenway was deafening. Maybe its greatest silence of all time—unless you were honoring someone who had passed away.

People forget that Reggie Jackson's homer actually was the winning run off Bob Stanley. They never, ever forget Bucky Dent. Dent, or Fisk—the losses were as big as the wins of this crazy, antiquated little park. But it went beyond balls and strikes to the people. I think of old-timers' games, which were always a little more fun in Boston than any-place else. One year, Williams made a catch in left field that brought down the house. I was doing television when in 1983 Yaz retired. Later, his number was retired. Always, this quiet superstar from the heart made some noise. It's like a laying-on of hands, the tradition, from Williams through Yaz to now. The players know it—and the ball-park, too.

Players talk about Fenway as a good park and a bad park. A fair park and an unfair park. A line drive to left field might be a home run at Yankee Stadium—a single, here. On the other hand, sometimes in Fenway a pop fly to left field that would be an out in twenty-nine other ballparks would be a homer here, like Bucky Dent's. But it had, and has, a beauty and the splendor of the old ballparks and has always been a drawing card. People come to see what it's like: You mean the wall is that close? You're damn right.

Once, Ralph Terry of the Yankees pitched and won a long game at Fenway. Afterward he said, "Pitching here is like spending three hours in a telephone booth." Get behind by four runs, no problem. Ahead by four in the eighth, delay the champagne. Nothing was, or is, certain, not even a pitcher sailing along. One little hit, an error maybe, can open a door to a pop-fly homer into the net. A walk and then a triple to right, maybe something down the line, can change the whole thing for or against the home team.

That's the magic of Fenway Park. That's why people love it so. Come to think of it, at Fenway almost *every* year is a wonder year.

Ned Martin was born eighteen miles from Center City but fated not to be in Philadelphia. Instead, arriving at Fenway in 1961, he climbed a Jacob's ladder of appeal. Fans hailed radio's 1974–78 duo of Martin and Jim Woods before Ned turned to TV from '79 to '92. Mercy! What a void the Pennsylvanian leaves.

16

The Green Fields of the Mind

By A. Bartlett Giamatti

It breaks your heart. It is designed to break your heart. The game begins in the spring, when everything else begins again, and it blossoms in the summer, filling the afternoons and evenings, and then as soon as the chill rains come, it stops and leaves you to face the fall alone. You count on it, rely on it to buffer the passage of time, to keep the memory of sunshine and high skies alive, and then just when the days are all twilight, when you need it most, it stops. Today, October 2 [1977], a Sunday of rain and broken branches and leaf-clogged drains and slick streets, it stopped, and summer was gone.

Somehow, the summer seemed to slip by faster this time. Maybe it wasn't this summer, but all the summers that, in this my fortieth summer, slipped by so fast. There comes a time when every summer will have something of autumn about it. Whatever the reason, it seemed to me that I was investing more and more in baseball, making the game do more of the work that keeps time fat and slow and lazy. I was counting on the game's deep patterns, three strikes, three outs, three times three innings, and its deepest impulse, to go out and back, to leave and to return home, to set the order of the day and to organize the daylight. I wrote a few things this last summer, this summer that did not last, nothing grand but some things, and yet that work was just camouflage. The real activity was done with the radio—not the all-seeing, all-falsifying television—and with the playing of the game in the only place it will last, the enclosed, green field of the mind. There, in that warm, bright place, what the old poet called Mutability does not so quickly come.

But out here, on Sunday, October 2, where it rains all day, Dame Mutability never loses. She was in the crowd at Fenway yesterday, a grey day full of bluster and contradiction, when the Red Sox came up in the last of the ninth trailing Baltimore, 8–5, while the Yankees, rain-delayed against Detroit, only needing to win one or have Boston lose one to win it all, sat in New York washing down cold cuts with beer and watching the Boston game. Boston had won two, the Yankees had lost two, and suddenly it seemed as if the whole season might go to the last day, or beyond, except here was Boston losing, 8–5, while New York sat in its family room and put its feet up. Lynn, both ankles hurting now as they had in July, hits a single down the right-field line. The crowd stirs. It is on its feet. Hobson, third baseman, former Bear Bryant quarterback, strong, quiet, over 100 RBIs, goes for three breaking balls and is out. The goddess smiles and encourages her agent, a canny journeyman named Nelson Briles.

Now comes a pinch hitter, Bernie Carbo, onetime Rookie of the Year, erratic, quick, a shade too handsome, so laid-back he is always, in his soul, stretched out in the tall grass, one arm under his head, watching the clouds and laughing; now he looks over some low stuff unworthy of him and then, uncoiling, sends one out, straight on a rising line, over the center-field wall, no cheap Fenway shot, but all of it, the physics as elegant as the arc the ball describes.

New England is on its feet, roaring. The summer will not pass. Roaring, they recall the evening, late and cold, in 1975, the sixth game of the World Series, perhaps the greatest baseball game played in the last fifty years, when Carbo, loose and easy, had uncoiled to tie the game that Fisk would win. It is 8–7, one out, and school will never start, rain will never come, sun will warm the back of your neck forever. Now Bailey, picked up from the National League recently, big arms, heavy gut, experienced, new to the league and the club; he fouls off two and then, checking, tentative, a big man off balance, he pops a soft liner to the first baseman. It is suddenly darker and later, and the announcer doing the game coast to coast, a New Yorker who works for a New York television station, sounds relieved. His little world, well-lit, hot-combed, split-second-timed, had no capacity to absorb this much gritty, grainy, contrary reality.

Cox swings a bat, stretches his long arms, bends his back, the rookie from Pawtucket who broke in two weeks earlier with a record six straight hits, the kid drafted ahead of Fred Lynn, rangy, smooth, cool. The count runs two and two, Briles is cagey, nothing too good, and Cox swings, the ball beginning toward the mound and then, in a jaunty, wayward dance, skipping past Briles, feinting to the right, skimming the last of the grass, finding the dirt, moving now like some small, purposeful marine creature negotiating the green deep, easily avoiding the jagged rock of second base, traveling steady and straight now out into the dark, silent recesses of center field.

The aisles are jammed, the place is on its feet, the wrappers, the programs, the Coke cups and peanut shells, the detritus of an afternoon; the anxieties, the things that have to be done tomorrow, the regrets about yesterday, the accumulation of a summer; all forgotten, while hope, the anchor, bites and takes hold where a moment before it seemed we would be swept out with the tide. Rice is up. Rice, who Aaron had said was the only one he'd seen with the ability to break his records. Rice, the best clutch hitter on the club, with the best slugging percentage in the league. Rice, so quick and strong he once checked his swing halfway through and snapped the bat in two. Rice, the Hammer of God sent to scourge the Yankees. The sound was overwhelming, fathers pounded their sons on the back, cars pulled off the road, households froze. New England exulted in its blessedness, and roared its thanks for all good things, for Rice and for a summer stretching halfway through October. Briles threw, Rice swung, and it was over. One pitch, a fly to center, and it stopped. Summer died in New England and like rain sliding off a roof, the crowd slipped out of Fenway, quickly, with only a steady murmur of concern for the drive ahead remaining of the roar. Mutability had turned the seasons and translated hope to memory once again. And once again, she had used baseball, our best invention to stay change, to bring change on. That is why it breaks my heart, that game—not because in New York they could win because Boston lost; in that, there is a rough justice, and a reminder to the Yankees of how slight and fragile are the circumstances that exalt one group of human beings over another. It breaks my heart because it was meant to, because it was meant to foster in me again the illusion that there was something abiding, some pattern and some impulse that could come together to make a reality that would resist the corrosion; and because after it had fostered again that most hungered-for illusion, the game was meant to stop, and betray precisely what it promised.

Of course, there are those who learn after the first few times. They grow out of sports. And there are others who were born with the wisdom to know that nothing lasts. These are the truly tough among us, the ones who can live without illusion, or without even the hope of illusion. I am not that grown-up or up-to-date. I am a simpler creature, tied to more primitive patterns and cycles. I need to think something lasts forever, and it might as well be that state of being that is a game; it might as well be that, in a green field, in the sun.

A. Bartlett Giamatti was a Renaissance scholar and former president of Yale University and the National League. The author of six books, including A Free and Ordered Space: The Real World of the University, *he served as baseball's seventh commissioner, from April 1, 1989, until his death on September 1, 1989.*

17

The Man Named Yaz

BY PETER GAMMONS

There were hundreds, maybe thousands still out on Yawkey Way when Yaz came out of his final press conference in the dining room atop Fenway Park. He was signing autographs for some security guards and ballpark workers who were waiting for him on the roof when he heard the "We Want Yaz" roar from the street and looked down.

He stepped to the edge of the roof and waved out to them with another papal gesture in his uniform pants, team undershirt, and shower clogs, then turned to Red Sox public-relations director George Sullivan and suggested that he'd like to go down into the street, and ten minutes later, there were women and children and red-eyed truck drivers in a line that stretched down around the corner of Van Ness Street.

The people came in through an entrance, two-by-two, and he signed one program and poster after another for forty minutes until there was no more line. When he had finished that, he came back into the park and signed autographs for people who get paid by the hour to work in the ballpark. It was 6:22 P.M. and dusk when he'd finished signing whatever they had for him to sign, then he stood atop the Red Sox dugout, pulled the cork out of a bottle of champagne, raised it, turned to survey Fenway and toasted them.

An hour later, as he came out to the parking lot to go to a party that [agent] Bob Woolf had for him at the Marriott, the hundreds still out on Van Ness chanted, "Yaz, Yaz, Yaz," and he signed a few more programs, shook a few more hands, climbed into the car, and pulled out around the corner.

As the car turned onto Ipswich Street, he was former Red Sox player Carl Yastrzemski. He was history—.285 average, 3,419 hits, Hall of Fame history. He had driven into that parking lot for the first time, with a sixth-place team, being asked to replace Ted Williams, and he left with a sixth-place team under a cloud of the Updike good-bye of Williams.

And he had outdone Ted; he had outdone anyone who ever wore the uniform or possibly ever played in any sport in this city. No one really cared that, in his last at bat, he threw himself at a Dan Spillner pitch in his eyes and popped out to someone named Jack Perconte, or that in his good-bye he had grounded to second, singled to left, walked, and popped up that final 3–1 pitch, or that his last home run in a Red Sox uniform came September 12 off Jim Palmer and was erased when rain wiped out the game in the third inning. Yaz didn't have to do something worthy of the ABC Network News. He was never Ted, only Yaz, never celluloid, only calloused flesh. On the day Hub Fans Bid Yaz Adieu, he didn't have to hit a Jack Fisher or Dan Spillner pitch into the bleachers. Playing left field and holding Toby Harrah to a single on a ball off the Wall—his Wall—was exactly what he should have done.

He had outdone Ted or anyone else because in the last two days of a twenty-three-year career Yaz had thrown his arms and his emotion to the people. He passionately explained that he understood what makes the Olde Towne Team what it is as if he'd worked at the mill on the Nashua River and paid his way in. He said that it isn't the stars— only two baseball teams have gone longer without a championship— or the general or limited partners or titled executives that made the Red Sox the Red Sox.

It's New Englanders. "As I stepped out of the box that last time at bat," he explained, "I tried to look around at every sign and every face to say 'thank you' to the people of New England who make this the greatest place to play baseball in the world."

He didn't ride around the park in a limousine. He ran around the park to touch the fans "who made this all possible" on Saturday, and long after he'd been replaced by Chico Walker in left field in the eighth inning yesterday as Ted had been replaced by Carroll Hardy twenty-three years before, he came out after the game in his jacket and did it again. "The people at the park today weren't the same people that were here yesterday," he said. Because so many things he couldn't control happened—Tony Conigliaro, Jim Lonborg, and Jose Santiago being lost within ten months around The Impossible Dream, then the Messersmith Decision coming one game after the sixth game of the

1975 World Series—he could never give New England what he wanted
to give them, so he did the next-best thing.

He touched and signed and repeatedly broke down and cried,
explaining to every kid in Bellows Falls and Otisfield and Jewett City
that what made all those records so great was to have done them for
the team that they have made what it is. To the media, for whom he
brought in bottles of champagne and toasted them for their fairness,
he in penultimate taste remembered those who'd passed away, like
Harold Kaese and Ray Fitzgerald and Fred Ciampa and Bill Liston and
George Bankert and Larry Claflin. He remembered the times he could
have left and made the big money. Like in October 1976. As a ten/five
man, he could refuse to go in the expansion draft, but both Toronto and
Seattle called him and told him he could sign for "any contract I
wanted," and that they could deal him to the two New York teams; the
Blue Jays had a deal worked out that would have gotten them a kid
pitcher named Ron Guidry.

"I called Woolf and told him to go to Toronto to talk," Yaz recalled,
"but I thought about it, remembered that I'd given Mr. Yawkey my
word that I wouldn't leave and told Woolf to forget it." In 1979, he could
have made big bucks from George Steinbrenner, and in 1981 both
Steinbrenner and Ted Turner had let it be known to him that they'd
pay him "three times what I could make here. But I didn't want to leave.
I liked it here. I liked the Red Sox. And what they are."

The pregame ceremony was emotional, and simple. He walked out
to the mike between the first-base coaching box and the dugout, then
had to circle away to fight the tears. When he came back he said, "I saw
the sign that read, 'Say It Ain't So, Yaz,' and I wish it weren't. This is
the last day of my career as a player, and I want to thank all of you for
being here with me today. It has been a great privilege to wear the Red
Sox uniform the past twenty-three years, and to have played in Fenway
in front of you great fans. I'll miss you, and I'll never forget you."

He lifted his cap and turned, waving to the fans, as he would do
each at bat. The park swelled when he reached out and tapped a Bud
Anderson fastball into left in the third inning, and when it came to the
bottom of the seventh and two out and Wade Boggs on first and everyone from Eastport to Block Island knew it was Yaz's adieu, they'd have
loved a home run. They stood again. Yaz stepped out again, and he swallowed hard to fight back the tears.

Spillner and all the Indians' pitchers understood the moment and
the ground rules. "We were in the bar with the umpires Friday night and

Rich Garcia told us, 'Look, fellows, if he doesn't swing, it's a ball," said Indians pitcher Lary Sorensen. "I could see Spillner was trying to aim the ball, it was coming in at eighty miles an hour," said Yaz, but home-plate umpire Vic Voltaggio called them balls until it was 3–0 and Spillner "aimed" a pitch over the plate but up around the bill of Yaz's cap.

"I was trying to jerk it out," Yaz admitted, and he popped up to end the inning. He returned to left field, then, as Yastrzemski and Ralph Houk had planned earlier, Walker ran out to take his place, and Yaz came in, shaking hands with his teammates, the umpires, and the Indians as he came across the infield. He stopped at the dugout, turned back to the first-base coach's box, turned 360 degrees as he waved again, then started his dash to the dugout unbuttoning his uniform ("I wanted to let them know that was really it"). He stopped to hand his cap to eight-year-old Brian Roberts of Needham, "because I wanted to give it to a kid and if I threw it into the stands it would have been havoc."

He'd done what he had to do. Carl Yastrzemski won't be remembered for a specific hit; the closest would be the ninth-inning homer off Mike Marshall in Detroit in September 1967, and that game was eventually won on a Dalton Jones homer. Even he listed his greatest memories as his diving stop off Reggie Jackson in the third game of the '75 playoffs; the throw that cut down Bob Allison on October 1, 1967; and the '67 catch off Tom Tresh that kept alive Billy Rohr's no-hit bid that was lost in the ninth but symbolized New England's leap out of the Dark Ages. "I wanted to make a diving catch out there," he said. "And I wish the ground had been more solid. . . ."

In the second inning, in his first time in left field since he cracked his ribs on August 30, 1980, hitting the Wall catching a Jim Essian line drive, he charged an Essian single with Alan Bannister rounding third. "I really wanted to throw him out," said Yaz, "but my foot gave out. I wanted to hold onto the ball, pump fake and get Essian going for second, but the ball slipped out of my hand." And rolled in.

He got no fly balls, per se, but in the seventh inning Harrah, who'd reached third in the previous inning, lined a ball off the Wall. Yaz didn't play it quite the way he used to, but he stretched for the carom, whirled, and fired in toward second. Harrah stopped thirty feet past the first-base bag, turned, and went back.

The 33,491 people in Fenway stood and roared. They once might have booed him so badly that he had to wear cotton in his ears to left field, but after twenty-three years they understood what made Yaz Yaz, and Yaz turned back to them and, fighting back the tears, told them that he understood what makes the Townies the Townies. He, who so long played stoically, was in the end as emotional as the emotional fans he once saw give Garry Hancock a standing ovation as he approached the plate for his first major league at bat. "You know what was great?" he beamed afterward. "The standing ovation for Jim Rice. Give Red Sox fans something, and they'll give it back to you many times over."

Hours afterward, he admitted that he felt "super, the best I've felt in a long, long while. I feel ten years younger than I did fifteen minutes ago."

For the two-day Easter celebration was over, and Yaz was a former Red Sox player. He knew he had expressed what he wanted to express, and because he'd even cared enough to try to do so, he turned off Van Ness Street onto Ipswich out of the sight of the hundreds that stood in the dark chanting, "Yaz, Yaz, Yaz," the most popular man who ever wore the uniform of the Olde Towne Team.

*Peter Gammons is arguably America's preeminent baseball journalist—*ESPN's *studio analyst, a* Boston Globe *columnist, and regular* Baseball America *contributor. The University of North Carolina alumnus and former* Sports Illustrated *writer is a three-time National Sportswriter of the Year.*

18

A Touch of Fenway

By Joe Castiglione

ptly, I first saw Fenway Park in the summer of 1967. I was about to enter my senior year at Colgate and was working with WDEW Radio in Westfield, Massachusetts. We carried the Yankees, but it was Red Sox fever that afflicted me forever. I went to some games, then in 1983 became a Red Sox announcer. No year since then is more enduring in memory than 1986.

Let's start with April 29. There wasn't a whole lot of focus on this early-season outing at Fenway because the Celtics had a playoff game in town, on the way to their last world championship. And on top of that, it was a chilly, misty night, with the temperature below fifty degrees. The kind of game that brings out only the diehards—and the announcers.

I was keeping warm in the broadcast booth, calling the balls and strikes against Seattle, when I started to get a funny feeling. "Something's going to happen," I told my partner, Ken Coleman. I knew Roger Clemens was completely on his game that night, because batters usually hit a lot of foul balls off him. But Seattle just wasn't connecting at all. Swings and misses everywhere. "Something's going to happen in the middle innings," I said to Ken, and we watched. Sure enough, we watched history.

That evening in a shivering, ignored ballpark we watched strikeout after strikeout and I felt a thrill like I've never known in baseball. Eight consecutive strikeouts: record tied. By the end of the night, twenty strikeouts: record set. That was the most memorable game of the most memorable season of my life.

And what a season '86 was, right up to the end. We got Don Baylor in a trade, and he became the team leader. One night, the Red Sox trailed California in the twelfth inning as Baylor came up. He hit a routine pop fly between home plate and third base. Rick Burleson, of all people, was then playing for the Angels at the end of his career. He dropped the ball, the tying run scored, and then a balk scored the winning Red Sox run. That's how it was—one eerie and unusual win after another.

The '86 playoffs were brilliant. After Clemens was beaten by the flu and Mike Witt in Game One, the Red Sox simply had to win Game Two at Fenway. I remember a moment from that game as if it were a photograph—former New Englander Kirk McCaskill pitching for the Angels and losing a ground ball in the sun, helping the Red Sox stage a big rally to win. The Angels won the next two games. Then, Game Five, do-or-die, and thanks to Dave Henderson's homer the Red Sox had an even bigger miracle than the Mets' later comeback in the World Series.

When Boston came back to Fenway, you knew they were going to win those last two playoff games. The Red Sox scored a ton of runs in Game Six [ten, on sixteen hits], then came out the next night to finish the job. [Jim] Rice homers, Wade Boggs hits a line drive that hits the second-base bag, and Clemens was outstanding. It always bothered me when people said he didn't win the big games, because they don't come a whole lot bigger than the seventh game of the American League championship with a ticket to the World Series on the line.

Ah, yes, the Series. The Red Sox won the first two games at Shea Stadium. The Mets tied it, then the Sox won Game Five at Fenway. I remember in that game being on the CBS Radio "Home Town Inning" with Sparky Anderson. Henderson was on first base and I said that Dave was our fastest runner. Sparky said, "If you think that guy's fast, that shows you how slow your team is." What I remember about Game Six is being down in the runway watching champagne come into the [Boston] clubhouse when the ball went through Bill Buckner's legs. The only thing I can say is thank goodness that game was at Shea. We can leave the horrid memory there and be grateful Fenway wasn't stained by that game.

My other favorite year was 1988, when Morgan Magic brought the most regular-season excitement of any team I've followed. Now, Joe Morgan is my best friend, so you can imagine how tremendous it was for me when he took over the helm after [John] McNamara was fired on the day play resumed following the All-Star break. You had to love

Joe's comment: "Interim is not in my vocabulary. I am the manager until they tell me otherwise."

The next two and a half weeks were, as the nickname implies, sheer magic. It started with Clemens leading a doubleheader sweep of the Royals. The Sox were off and running on a twelve-game winning streak. Twelve games in a row in the middle of the season, and all the first games of their new manager! I remember homers by Kevin Romine and Todd Benzinger, all sorts of comeback wins. The greatest stretch I've experienced. A decade later, I'm still waiting for something to match it. Watching Mo Vaughn hit long home runs will always be a treasured memory, but I yearn for a playoff win right here at the beloved park that has such a special place in our hearts.

I've been with the Sox at Fenway for more than fifteen years now, and every day it's still a thrill to go there. It's just fun. I've often thought it would be a great place to play hide-and-seek. There are some passageways and shortcuts I know of that most fans never even see—makes me feel like a kid to go through the little door that leads behind the scoreboard, or under the left-field wall where the grounds crew keeps their equipment, or up the back staircase with players for interviews, or into the batting cages or even the bull pen.

And what this grand old park brings to the game itself! First and foremost, there's the Wall. Think of the excitement that's given. From the broadcasting booth, I always have to wait a little bit longer on a fly ball to the outfield before I call it a home run or an out. You never know, the ball might scrape the paint on the way down. That's the most frustrating thing for pitchers, those fly balls hit by left-handed batters that would be outs in any other ballparks but that manage to sneak by and just scrape the paint on the way down, turning into singles or doubles.

In all my years at Fenway, I have to say that Wade Boggs was the very best I've seen at hitting the Wall—a healthy twenty-five times a year during his good seasons. I keep the stats, and I remember figuring out my first clue that he'd passed his prime one season when he didn't hit the Wall for the first time until a dismally late May 22. That showed me right there that he'd lost a lot of his power to the opposite field.

No one can control Fenway. It makes for an unpredictable ball game, and that's even more fun. You want the balls to travel well? Hope for the wind to blow out—or for no wind at all. You want to see fielders stretched to their limits? Try sending a few hits into the Triangle. You want a ground ball to bounce over first and go for an inside-the-park home run? Can't get that anywhere but Fenway.

A lot of us who've been around many ballparks are a little bit in awe of this place. I think Bart Giamatti described it best when he spoke of his fondness for its "eccentric angularities." He meant the wall and the padding and the nooks and crannies and the whole spirit of this wonderful place, built and squeezed in to fit the contours of a neighborhood. There's no other place like it.

It's a privilege to have it be my "office," to have the opportunity to be there every day. I get a kick out of knowing the vendors, the groundskeepers, the ushers, the people who make their livelihood at the ballpark. I never tire of seeing the fans who get there three or four hours before the game starts, patiently waiting for autographs. I always look for that one old peanut vendor who's been here forever, and the sausage guy right across the street. They're all part of the lure of Fenway—the feeling of a real city neighborhood spilling over into the park itself.

As I finish my tribute to unforgettable Fenway, I want to leave you with my favorite image, a moment that never fails to thrill me. When I come home from one of those late trips when we have a night game on the road, I often don't get back to Fenway until two or three in the morning. The place is dark. It's mystical, even magical.

To walk alone up one of those gangways by first base, to look out at the field lit only by the clock, to look up and see the lights of the city streets out on Ted Williams Way, to watch Fenway in the darkness just before dawn—well, it's breathtaking. I'll always be grateful to have had Fenway be a part of my life.

Joe Castiglione grew up in Hamden, Connecticut, and did Indians and Brewers TV from 1979 to 1982 before returning to the turf of John Winthrop and William Bradford. A Red Sox' radio announcer since 1983, Castiglione teaches a broadcast journalism course at Northeastern University. "Why not?" he says. "In New England, the Sox are required study."

19

After the Ball

1987—

In early 1987, Joel Krakow of the Newton, Massachusetts, Captain Video Store unwrapped a shipment that included the 1986 World Series highlight film. Recalling Game Six, he chose to place the tape in the horror/science fiction section. John McNamara, who might have agreed, was unlikely to buy a copy. That October, he sat in the dugout before the last regular-season game: "You know, I sit here thinkin' and I *still* can't believe we lost the sixth game of the World Series. There's a part of me that just doesn't believe it: one f— — out. That's all we needed was one f— — out." Profane, his take was proper.

The '87 Townies repeated 1947, '68, and '76—folding after the past year's pennant. In March, Clemens left camp when his pay was renewed at $400,000—half Stanley's salary. Said Gorman, untroubled: "The sun will rise, the sun will set, and I'll have lunch." Daily, teams proceeded to repast on the Sox. The Steamer pitched Opening Day. Returning, the Rocket blew a 9–0 lead at Yankee Stadium. A year before, Oil Can Boyd had flaunted antics that ran counter to self-denial: pumping his arms on K's, pointing at infielders, and stalking in circles around the mound. In '87, he hurt his neck and shoulder and won just one game. The bull pen went seven weeks without a save. Rich Gedman hit .205. On July 17, McNamara had to stick left fielder Mike Greenwell behind the plate. Fans threw up their hands. Even Don Gile looked like Johnny Bench.

Not all Red Sox were paste-up jobs. Clemens won his second straight Cy Young Award. Evans became a symbol of the perfect meritocracy: .305, thirty-four homers, and 123 RBIs—all career highs. Youth should be served, and was. Greenwell homered in his first at bat. Ellis

Burks seemed a righty Lynn, able to roam center field and cannonade the Wall. In 1987, he hit twenty homers and swiped twenty-seven bases—Boston's first twenty/twenty rookie. Baylor and Henderson were traded. One Goliath's coming eclipsed their going: Sam Horn, the first Townie to homer in his first two games. *Sport* magazine spied Horn's fourteen dingers in 158 at bats and picked him to win the 1988 title with "fifty-home-run potential." Its forecast was as off (Horn hit two) as '87's Yawkeys (78–84 and twenty games behind).

Still, the Sox could effect a gracious gesture. In September, the retiring Reggie Jackson batted at Fenway for the final time. Sherm Feller was the club's public-address announcer of exaggerated mimicry and soulful understatement. Introducing Jackson, he said, simply, "Number 44, Mr. October." The moment befit a year in which even spring had reeked of fall.

When Ronald Reagan was shot in March 1981, he told his wife, "Honey, I forgot to duck." From 1981 to '89, millions forgot to check mythy faith at the door. Their trust rose from flag-waving, Reagan's charm, America's remembered and/or reinvented past, and concern for its New Jerusalem. As president, Reagan refilled the "Hollow Army," championed the Strategic Defense Initiative, spun the first strategic arms reduction treaty, and assigned Communism to history's dustbin. In 1988, the Cold Warrior strolled through Moscow's Red Square. "If that can happen," said a friend, "the Sox can win the Series. . . . Sure."

That March, Greenwell accosted Boston's full moon of history. "You can't play on [the Red Sox] without someone, every day," he said, "bringing up names like Joe Cronin and Ted Williams and Cy Young"— and Steamer and Bucky and Billy Buck. "This stuff is from a long time ago, so nobody pays much attention to that in the dugout. Only writers remember that"—and fans. Both gawked as now-Cubs skipper Zimmer continued to aid other clubs, swapping premier reliever Lee Smith for Calvin Schiraldi and Al Nipper in December 1987. "When he's with the Red Sox, he helps the Yankees," said a writer. "In Chicago, he helps the Sox." Hired help can fumble. On Opening Day, Smith lost by yielding a tenth-inning homer to Alan Trammell. Bannered the next-day's *Boston Herald*: "Wait 'Til Next Year."

In time, Smith saved a team sixth-best single-year twenty-nine games. Time, however, was not a bar where Johnny Mac imbibed. The Sox had youth, Boggs, and Clemens. They expected to contend. "Salaries were rising," said Gammons. "That meant more money was needed, which meant more pressure." From 1987 to 1990, Fenway was resodded, a new souvenir store (The Lansdowne Shop) and restaurant (Diamond at Fenway) were built, and a color scoreboard with a black-and-white message board was installed in center field. Six hundred and ten stadium-club seats (The 600 Club) dislodged the press above the grandstand behind home plate. The ticket office and both dugouts were renovated, and weight and multipurpose rooms were built in the Sox clubhouse. Win now! the green eyeshades said. Boston joined baseball's new fixation with cash.

Castiglione recalled McNamara's postparade torment. "He didn't have much margin for error," he said of early 1988—or luck. Boston homered eight times in its first twenty-three games. Gedman's dinger off the right-field pole was mistakenly ruled foul. McNamara's band mixed miscue and double standard. Clemens stayed into one seventh inning to brook fifteen hits and nine earned runs. Evans was put at first and called the manager's pet. "What we need," Greenwell said, "is a new manager." In California, Rice missed a game—the cause, "injured rib"—but played thirty-six holes of golf that day at Pebble Beach. In Baltimore, Barrett pulled the hidden-ball trick and stole home. He was an anomaly. The Sox embraced .500.

On June 3, Margo Adams, the married Boggs' ex-girlfriend, filed a $6 million breach-of-oral-contract suit. Her public coming-out pre-saged Monica Lewinsky's: the media couldn't get enough. Adams took to TV's *Donahue* to confide that Wade had crashed teammates' rooms and shot photos of them with other women. Said Margo: "They called their maneuvers 'Delta Force.'" No force could save the hapless Mac. As the Sox dropped nine games behind, radio talk shows blared "Knife the Mac!" and Evans and Boggs fought on the team bus in Cleveland, Mrs. Yawkey convened a meeting. Fired, McNamara left Fenway to jeering fans on July 14—Bastille Day. At least he exited with his head.

"Those games," Phillies manager Danny Ozark once malapropped, "were beyond my apprehension." Joe Morgan, an ex-hockey player, Massachusetts Turnpike employee, and Walpole, Massachusetts, native replaced Mac as "interim" manager. What happened next tested comprehension. Boston swept an eleven-game homestand, had its longest winning streak since 1948 (twelve sets), took nineteen of twenty, and broke an AL record by winning twenty-four straight games at home (June 25 through August 13). Rice cowed McNamara. Morgan confronted him. The Sox' unofficial captain was miffed when Morgan pinch-hit Spike Owen for him in a bunt situation. Rice yanked the new manager into the dugout runaway. Trading shoves, Morgan surfaced sounding like Ring Lardner: "*I'm* the manager of this nine."

The help began working overtime. Margo's beau hit .366. Burks mixed speed and power—eighteen homers and twenty-five stolen bases. Greenwell had baseball's third-best average (.325), added an AL record for game-winning RBIs (twenty-three), trailed only Oakland's Jose Canseco in MVP voting, and led the team with eight triples, twenty-two homers, and 119 RBIs. "The complete package," said Ned Martin. "We thought, here's a star for years." Mike Boddicker arrived from Baltimore to go 7–3 with a 2.60 ERA in the last two months. The Red Sox grabbed first place on Labor Day, lost six of the last seven in their requisite way, but finally clinched on September 30 when Oakland beat second-place Baltimore. The air felt settled by a Wilsonian itinerary. Clemens's eight shutouts were the Sox' most since Ruth's nine in 1916. Boston won two flags in three years for the first time since 1916–18.

The rightness of things seized you: the Townies in the playoffs. Sadly, they soon wailed a soundless cry. Boston muffed Game One, 2–1, to Oakland. Boggs, batting twice with the bases full and once with two on, vended a sacrifice fly, two strikeouts, and seven left on base. The next day longtime *Globe* writer Cliff Keane threw out the first ball. "They've got to do it soon," he said. "I'm running out of time." The Sox were, too, losing the second game at Fenway, 4–3, on three ninth-inning singles. Four A's homered as Boddicker blew a 5–0 Game Three lead and the Sox lost, 10–6, in Oakland. Hurst, who dropped the first game, also lost the 4–1 finale. In four sets, Boston massed twenty-six hits. The Crunch Bunch seemed as far away as the gas masks at Verdun.

In 1998, opening on Good Friday, the Sox would ban alcohol at Fenway for the first time since Prohibition. "The only thing worse than watching the Red Sox," said a fan, "is watching them sober." The '88 Townies hailed Oakland's four-game sweep by boarding their plane to Boston and uncorking a bender. The Mormon Hurst, disgusted, left the plane. "It's not my greatest time as a baseball player when guys get a little boxed and if they get out of hand." Hurst soon got out of town, spurning a larger Sox offer to sign with San Diego.

That December, Clemens, appearing on local TV, complained as viewers sat widemouthed about having to carry his own luggage and how "There are a lot of things that are a disadvantage to a family here." Wade and cargo. Booze and broads. The Sox were becoming less the Olde Towne Team than a union of Jerry Springer and Lewis Carroll.

Bruce Hurst won eighty-eight games as a Boston left-hander, one less than Ruth. In 1989, the Red Sox had to take thirteen of their last sixteen sets to win even eighty-three. In the larger world, the Berlin Wall fell. Lech Walesa was voted Polish president. The ex–Evil Empire held its first multicandidate election. Later, Germany was reunited. "It's amazing," marveled President George Bush, "the changes that occurred in a blink of history's eye." Fenway's opener suggested that Sox changes would be depressing: the Rocket was booed.

All year Boston straddled extremes. Gorman traded for John Dopson, reliever Rob Murphy, and first baseman Nick Esasky. Dopson became the third starter. Murphy graced seventy-four games. Esasky hit .277 with thirty homers and 108 RBIs. In April and May, Clemens and Nolan Ryan staged Lone Star duels in Texas and at Fenway. Ryan and the Rocket won, 2–1 and 7–6, respectively. On June 4 Boston led Toronto, 10–0, and lost, 13–11. Another night, Ed Romero threw a container of Gatorade on the field after Morgan pinch-hit Gedman.

Pitcher Wes Gardner was arrested for assaulting his wife. Clemens fell to 17–11 and threatened to punch reporters if they wrote about his family. Under "self-absorption," include Boyd filing for arbitration after winning ten games in his last two years. Under "bad timing," cite the Sox raising ticket prices to the highest in the bigs. Improbably, they drew a record 2,510,012, with three of 1967–98's top fifteen three-game series. From August 29 to September 1, the age's second-largest four-gamer (138,810) packed Fenway for the Orioles. Margueritte Brennan, in her '60s, of Warwick, Rhode Island, explained the conundrum. "People say they've loved the Red Sox all their lives, and will love them until the day they die. That's not a true fan. The true fan, like me, will love the Sox long after they're in the grave"—precisely where Boggs must have thought he was in spring 1989.

"What a zoo!" Castiglione wondered. In March's *Penthouse* magazine Margo Adams shed all to entertain. Boggs confessed that he was addicted to sex. The helpful Boyd called him "a sex fiend." In Tampa, a bomb threat forced the Sox to change planes. Around the league, fans flogged Boggs with chants of "Mar-go!" From 1983 to '91, the Chicken Man led the Sox in average each year. He tops Boston in games at third base (1,521) and is second in average (.338); third in on-base percentage; fourth in doubles; fifth in hits; sixth in runs, extra-base hits, and total bases; and seventh in at bats and games. No matter. Trying to trade Boggs in '89, Gorman found no takers. They wished to leave him to late-night TV.

By August 29, a nine-game win streak pulled the Townies within four. The precipice startled. Ultimately, they placed third in a sad-sack division. Greenwell called his mates "wimps and fairies." Their *manager* dubbed it "a pretty good assessment." Old warriors wondered what was going on. "I know I'm going to live long enough," Pesky told himself, "when we're gonna be world champions." Doerr countered with a gnawing sense of the theoretical: "You'd think the law of averages would sort of even out—that they would win one."

Stanley, who never did, retired. The Sox released one left fielder— Jim Rice: third in team homers (382), ribbies, hits, and total bases; fourth in games, runs, and extra-base hits; and fifth in slugging percentage— and hailed another. On August 6, uniform number 8 was placed on the facade atop the right-field grandstand. The retired numbers now scrawled a taunt: 9-4-1-8, the month of the last Red Sox world title.

The final decade of the American Century began for the Sox with a case of man bites dog. Seeking to redeem himself, Buckner remade the team, was cheered on Opening Day, and released in June. Boggs hit only .302. Gedman and Esasky departed. One night, Dewey batted with 2,299 career hits. On ESPN-TV, the Sox' Sean McDonough said: "Here's Dwight Evans, who's one shit high of 2,300 hits." Partner Ray Knight began laughing. Amended McDonough: "I did say he's one hit shy of 2,300, didn't I?" Two weeks later a man greeted McDonough when the Sox visited Texas. "Will you do me a favor? Just say 'one hit shy' for me."

McDonough, and the Sox, survived. Clemens went 21–6, starter Dana Kiecker and catcher Tony Pena spurred the pitching staff, and Burks led Boston with twenty-one homers, 90 RBIs, and in six other categories. Reliever Larry Anderson, acquired from Houston, keyed the bull pen. The cost: minor-leaguer-turned-future-MVP Jeff Bagwell in a deal suggestive of Ruth, Pennock, and Lyle. Carlos Quintana helped at first base. Providence did too, an unlikely friend: Boston won a game after hitting into two triple plays.

On September 4, the Townies led by 6½ games. At that point, the Rocket hurt his shoulder. Boston sustained a 2–8 road trip and by September 23 was 1½ sets behind. "Everything goes against the Red Sox," Gorman said of dropping eight games in twenty days. "They're star-crossed lovers in a sense. The wrong thing always happens to the Red Sox." Evoking 1978, they confounded: Boston rallied to tie Toronto, then beat the Jays twice at Fenway, and took a two-game lead with three left. The Sox split two sets with Chicago and met the Pale Hose again on September 30: one up, and one to play.

Boston led, 3–1, with two out in the ninth. The crowd recalled Schiraldi and Knight: one strike to go. Reliever Jeff Reardon got two strikes on future Cub Sammy Sosa, who singled. Scott Fletcher was hit by a pitch: still one out to go. Ozzie Guillen then sliced to right. In '78 outfielder Lou Piniella had kept Jerry Remy's drive from becoming a pennant-winning inside-the-park homer. Tom Brunansky now crossed the same turf to attempt a pennant-winning catch. "If the Gods truly had it in for the Boston Red Sox, as New England has assumed for seven decades, Brunansky would have lost Ozzie Guillen's drive in the full moon that hung over Fenway Park," wrote the *Chicago Tribune*'s Andrew Bagnato. "Or he would have slipped as he stepped on the warning track. Or dropped his glove as the ball hit the webbing." Instead, he made a tumbling grab to give Boston a 3–1 victory, clinch the AL East on the final night, and send the Sox forth against the A's.

For those who recalled 1988, the playoff wrote a script already banned in Boston. Clemens left the first game at Fenway leading, 1–0; Oakland battered the bull pen to win, 9–1. Boston lost twice, 4–1, then imploded in Game Four. Behind, 1–0, Roger walked Willie Randolph, argued the call, shoved one umpire (Jim Evans), and threatened another (Terry Cooney). Players, in turn, scuffled. Anderson sped from the bull pen to restrain a raging Rocket. Did T. S. Eliot grasp the hit-and-run? October had become the cruelest month. The Sox lost the game, 3–1, and the series, 4–0, scoring one run in each set.

A *Boston Herald* cartoon drew Clemens as a baby on a pitching mound, a bottle in one hand, shouting "Bleep!" The word draped Boston's collapse. The Sox made five errors, scatched twenty-three hits, and plated one of twenty-two runners in scoring position. Said ex-Townie Carney Lansford: "The Red Sox are a disgrace."

Two months earlier, Saddam Hussein invaded Kuwait and dubbed it Iraq's nineteenth province. Bush forged a U.N. armada, and in January 1991 began "Operation Desert Shield." Yellow ribbons dotted America. Headlines blurred: smart bombs and Scuds and Patriot missiles. Many Townies were at spring training in Winter Haven, Florida, as Hussein's Mother of Battles became the Orphan of Defeats.

For the Sox, peace at the center had *already* flown south. For one thing, three flags since 1986 had failed to check the division. For another, the last link back to '75, Evans, had been released—second in all-time Sox games (2,505) and at bats; third in runs (1,435), doubles, extra-base hits, total bases, and walks; and fourth in RBIs (1,346), hits, and homers (379). Clemens won eighteen games and his third Cy Young Award. Free agent Jack Clark bashed twenty-eight homers and eighty-seven RBIs but was an albatross in the clubhouse. The Sox finished second and drew another record, 2,562,435. The front office wanted more — Morgan's job.

Homey and unorthodox, Morgan was Boston's most popular manager since 1967. The next three years likened him to Dick Williams, Ted Williams, and *Zorro*'s Guy Williams: successor Butch Hobson never topped .500. Even wins assumed a drowsy, ugly influence. One day at Fenway the Red Sox won a nearly four-hour game on the rival third baseman's ninth-inning error. Ned Martin, on Sox cable, broke to commercial and turned to partner Jerry Remy. "Boy," Ned said, "that [the game] sucked." Remy pointed to the live mike. The next day the station general manager hauled Martin to a meeting. "I just wanted to know if you said it," he asked. Ned said yes, and that he meant it. The G.M. told him not to worry: "I don't blame you. It did."

It seemed like 1964. Jody Reed's seven steals led 1992's stone-footed Townies. Brunansky's .266 with fifteen homers and seventy-four ribbies paced a banjo team. On April 12, Matt Young no-hit Cleveland and lost, 2–1. Boston fell to seventh. The next year, Clemens slumped, but Danny Darwin won fifteen games, Frank Viola had a 3.14 ERA, and Mo Vaughn burst from the minors to embody a physical burgeoning in all its diversity: six-feet-one, 240 pounds, and the first of from four to six straight years leading the Sox in homers (twenty-nine), RBIs (101), total bases, slugging percentage, extra-base hits, walks, and runs. Boston finished fifth, then fourth as 1994 boasted a major-league record for homers — or would have, had a players' strike not intervened. Mo knew why: "Because we're hitting them hard."

On April 19, 1994, Vaughn and Tim Naehring twice hit back-to-back homers to beat the A's, 13–5. "The ball's been flying around the ballpark," Naehring said. "But whether it's juiced or not, I don't know. I missed that class in college." Like the thread of an old thought, the Sox cherished a tomorrow that might be neither bogus nor offensive. That month, Scott Cooper hit for the cycle. "Yeah, it's humiliating," said Royals catcher Mike Macfarlane after the Sox won, 22–11. "But you've got to look at the positive side. We scored eleven." On July 8, Sox shortstop John Valentin made only the tenth unassisted triple play in big-league history. None helped win a pennant.

"Fenway Park," said Bill Lee, "is a shrine where people come for religious rites." Failing baptism, try burial. In 1994, several fans held a mock ceremony at Fenway to entomb *The Curse of the Bambino*, Dan Shaughnessy's book about the Sox' macabre and comic past.

By 1995, as we shall see, Fenway had spawned Baltimore's Oriole Park at Camden Yards, which spun heirs in, among other places, Atlanta, Cleveland, and Denver. Each had luxury suites, corporate boxes, and hip cuisine, and spurned a sense of pedestrian look and feel. In response, the Sox began tours, renovated restrooms, installed energy-efficient lighting, heating, and cooling, and put a metal awning roof above the left- and right-field roof seats. Suddenly, Fenway's ineluctable attraction had a catch-up '90s gloss.

The Sox added to it. Kevin Kennedy replaced Hobson. Tim Wakefield knuckled his way to a 16–8 year. Obtained from Oakland, Jose Canseco batted .325 after the All-Star break. Valentin homered thrice in a game at Fenway as Brunansky and Clark had in 1990 and '91—and Vaughn did twice in 1996 and '97. Mo fused a .300 average and league-lead-tying 126 RBIs and thirty-nine homers (including twenty-four at home) into an MVP award—Boston's first since Clemens's in '86. The Townies forged an eight-set lead, slumped, then spurted in mid-July. On September 20, they beat Milwaukee, 3–2, before 32,653 at Fenway to clinch their fourth AL East title in ten years. After the game Vaughn mounted a police horse, upon which he sauntered around the field.

"I'll never ride a horse again," said the Sox first baseman. "Everybody was saying, 'You gotta ride the horse, you gotta ride the horse, the horse is good luck.' The horse is *not* good luck." The Sox met Cleveland in baseball's born-of-the-wild-card first best-of-five Division Series. Vaughn went zero for fourteen. Boston played like Rip Collins's '38 World Series Cubs versus New York: "We came, we saw, and we went home." Game One took an endless five hours and one minute. Valentin, Naehring, and Luis Alicea homered, vainly: ex-Sox Tony Pena pricked Boston's seventh pitcher, Lee Smith, for a thirteenth-inning blast to win, 5–4. The next night four Tribe pitchers beat Erik Hanson, 4–0. Two days later 34,211 filled Fenway to see the Sox fall, 8–2. "Maybe we should stop playing on October 1," mused Greenwell of Boston's six runs in three games, eleventh straight playoff loss, and third postseason sweep.

By this time Vaughn seemed the very practitioner of the Townies' courtesies and codes. "When I heard I won the MVP," said the ninth Sox to earn it, "that ride from my house in Canton [a Boston suburb] to the Red Sox offices was the best ride I ever had." In '96, Mo banged a maze of sunny pleasantries—.326, forty-four dingers, 143 RBIs, 207 hits, and led the club in five other categories—the greatest season by a Sox since Rice

(1978), Yaz ('67), or Williams (pick a year). Wakefield and Aaron Sele won fourteen and thirteen games, respectively. Heathcliff Slocumb's work in seventy-five games was less puzzling than his name. The Townies finished third, and a Kennedy was fired. To politicos, it seemed a sacrilege.

That November, Braves third-base coach Jimy Williams replaced him as manager. On December 13, 1996, the Sox' greatest pitcher bolted Fenway for the phony turf, devalued coin, and somnolence of Toronto's SkyDome. Where to begin? asks the mosquito in the nudist camp. With Clemens, the 1986 MVP; '86, '87, and '91 Cy Young Award winner; '86, '90, '91, and '92 ERA titlist; '88, '91, and '96 strikeout king; and single-game K record-holder (tied by Kerry Wood in '98). Next, with Roger leading Boston eight times in wins; nine times in innings, complete games, and earned run average; and ten times in strikeouts. Close with numbers that to a Sox fan are required reading—first all-time in innings (2,776), wins (192, with Young), games started (382), K's (2,590), walks (856), shutouts (thirty-eight), and ten-strikeout games (sixty-eight); second in games (383, trailing Stanley) and losses (111, one behind Young); fourth in winning percentage (.634); ninth in complete games (one hundred); and tenth in ERA (3.06). His leave-taking for Toronto made even heretics wince.

"Dan Duquette wants robots. He drove me out," Clemens said of the Sox' general manager. The New England native returned the mud by calling Roger washed up at thirty-four. Ducking, you recalled the Rocket's April 29, 1986, twenty-strikeout game—to McDonough, "the greatest individual performance I've ever seen"—or was it September 19, 1996, when Clemens fanned twenty in Detroit? His exit left a void that the Sox had not foreseen.

In late 1995, Greenwell left to play in Japan—eighth all-time in Sox doubles; tenth in average (.303); eleventh in games, at bats, and RBIs; and fifteenth in homers (130). His exit closed an epoch: since 1939, only four left fielders—Williams, Yaz, Rice, and Greenwell—had patrolled the Wall. Fans adjacent to the Monster soon missed him. John Fay, a company executive from Braintree, Massachusetts, has had season tickets in section 32, row LL, since 1986. "You can hear the left fielder, shortstop, and third baseman call each other off on a pop-up," said Fay, laughing. "They can hear you, too. Greenwell was famous for his rabbit ears."

Two years later, the Red Sox' yearbook posed questions to honor their new mascot, Wally the Green Monster. Below, Wally wonders—and responds.

Questions:
1. How tall was the original left-field wall when Fenway opened in 1912?
2. What was the name of the 10-foot grassy rise that fronted the wall?
3. What part-time left fielder hit eleven homers in 1918 and twenty-nine homers in 1919?
4. What year was Fenway's current left-field wall built?
5. How tall and wide is it?
6. From what material is the wall made?
7. What was the most popular feature of the new wall in 1934?
8. What year was the screen installed above it?
9. How are balls retrieved from the screen?
10. What year was the left-field wall painted green?
11. What year were lights added above the wall?
12. What year was the first television camera used inside the wall?
13. What year was the old scoreboard renovated?
14. What size and weight are the number placards used in the scoreboard?
15. What is the biggest number on either a hit or a run placard?
16. What is the highest-number placard ever used for a half-inning?
17. Whose initials are spelled out in Morse code dots and dashes on the scoreboard?
18. What year was the protective padding installed along the base of the wall?
19. What three Red Sox left fielders won awards as the American League MVP?
20. What is the length down the left-field foul line from home plate to the wall?

Answers:
1. On Opening Day, April 20, 1912, the wall measured ten feet tall.
2. Duffy's Cliff, named after Sox left fielder Hugh Duffy.
3. Babe Ruth, topping the American League each year.
4. The current wall was finished in time for the 1934 season.
5. It measures 37 feet, two inches high by 240 feet wide.
6. Concrete. Prior to 1934, it was made of wood.

7. A long scoreboard that showed inning-by-inning results of each major-league game.
8. The twenty-three-foot-seven-inch-high screen was added in 1936.
9. A Fenway grounds-crew member climbs a ladder next to the scoreboard.
10. In 1947, after the tin advertising signs on its facade were removed.
11. In 1947, in time for Fenway's first-ever night game of June 13.
12. Luckily, the 1975 World Series, which caught Carlton Fisk's twelfth-inning Game Six homer.
13. In 1976, it was reduced in size by about half and moved twenty feet to the right.
14. Hit or run placards are sixteen inches (three pounds). Others are twelve by sixteen inches (two pounds).
15. These placards go up to the number nineteen.
16. Seventeen—the number of runs the Sox scored in the seventh inning on June 18, 1953.
17. Longtime team owners Thomas A. (T-A-Y) and Jean R. (J-R-Y) Yawkey.
18. 1976. The wall's tin facade was also replaced with a plastic covering.
19. Ted Williams (1946, '49), Carl Yastrzemski (1967), and Jim Rice (1978).
20. 310 feet, changed from 315 feet after a remeasurement in 1995. Where there's a wall, there's a way—and a sudden magic place to treasure.

Think of sumo wrestling, beery pickup games, or *Kansas City Bomber*, film's panegyric to roller derby. The 1996 overweight, overpaid, and over-the-hill Red Sox could have breezily staffed them all. Duquette wanted punch. Thus, Canseco, Mike Stanley, and bloated Kevin Mitchell trooped to Fenway. It didn't work. The Townies allowed the league's most unearned runs. A year later, the Sox ditched slow-pitch softball. Lucille Ball was once asked what movie star she most admired. "It's not any of the stars," she said. "It's the character people. *They* are the great ones." By trade or waiver came Shane Mack and Rudy Pemberton to join Reggie Jefferson, Troy O'Leary, and Wil Cordero. Some were character people; others, players on the fringe.

Unlike Mitchell, most could catch the ball. Unlike Canseco, most were inexpensive. "[Duquette] has a well-deserved reputation for picking up good, cheap talent," a writer mused of the Expos' former GM. Under "you get what you pay for", the ex-softballers finished 78–84—twenty games behind. Increasingly, the Sox dubbed Fenway a dinosaur. Wrote Gerry Fraley: "In the era of cash-cow parks, the Red Sox can't generate enough revenue—no matter how high they raise the price of the American League's most expensive tickets." Sele won thirteen games. Jeff Frye played at least one game at eight positions, including DH. The entire outfield hit fifty homers. Compounding unease was Clemens, now a Blue Jay, who led the league in victories (twenty-one), earned run average (2.05) and strikeouts (292), and won a fourth Cy Young Award.

"It's time," Naehring said, "to start winning again in Boston." In 1997, several Sox shed their bargain basement image. Naehring batted .286. In 1986, John Valentin had hit ninth on the Seton Hall team as a freshman walk-on. Now, batting second for the Sox, he clubbed an AL-leading forty-seven doubles. Another ex–Seton Haller hit .315 with thirty-five homers and ninety-six RBIs. Vaughn loved Fenway (clubbing seventy-one 1995–97 dingers) and the Boston area (his loci of community work: Dorchester's Mo Vaughn Youth Center). At twenty-nine, Boston's cleanup hitter was the Big Dog, a sure Sox lifer, the team's flagship player—or was he? "Griffey's [Ken Jr.] the best," Ted Williams said in 1998 when asked the AL's top player. "But I'm not sure the shortstop in Boston isn't the second best."

Save center field, shortstop is baseball's most high-hat position. "It gives you the stage," Johnny Pesky observed, "but you need range, speed, and a good arm to play it." Such combinations are hard to find. In 1996, a California-born, Georgia Tech–educated, '92 U.S. Olympic team walk-on homered in his first full big-league game, off future Townie John Wasdin, before his family in Oakland. "The dream finally came through," said Nomar Garciaparra. "It could have ended right there, and that would have been enough." The next year, he fused quick hands, a strong arm, a senior's poise, and a whippet of a bat into thirty homers, ninety-eight RBIs, twenty-two stolen bases, and a .306 average.

Nomar's 1997 took Don Buddin, spit him out, and stomped on his "E-6" license plate. He set a team at bat record (684), hit in thirty straight games (second in Sox history to Dom DiMaggio's thirty-four), trailed only Foxx, Rice, and Williams in single-year extra-base hits (eighty-five), and led Boston in seven categories. Garciaparra topped the AL in hits (209) and triples (eleven) and was second in runs scored (122) and total bases (365)—its first unanimous Rookie of the Year since Carlton Fisk. "He went by all our great players," averred Duquette.

"He had the best [rookie] year of any player this team ever had." *Sports Illustrated* added: "There's nothing not to like about Garciaparra. He's smart, friendly, a winner. If only the Red Sox could clone him." Watching, you recalled a writer say of the 1940s Cardinals' Marty Marion, "He's out there at shortstop, movin' easy as a bank of fog."

That winter, the Sox spent $46.8 million on multiyear pacts with Valentin, O'Leary, and Frye but, notably, not Vaughn. Nomar signed a seven-year deal to keep him content, and theirs. "The Red Sox are back in business!" vowed Duquette, investing $152 million in player salaries through 2003. The 1997–98 payroll leapt from $40 million to $54.2 million. Thinking changed: to leverage a *new* high-revenue Fenway, the Olde Towne Team would have to win. Novelties included a renovated batting cage (under the center-field bleachers), a twenty-five-foot Coca-Cola contour bottle design on the left-field light tower (the Jimmy Fund benefited from balls hitting the bottle or screen), and Wally the mascot perhaps presaging the apocalypse. A *mascot*, at *Fenway*? Next, Vaughn would be asked to leave.

By April 1998, the Sox had won more games than they lost versus the Orioles, Angels, White Sox, Tigers, Brewers, A's, Mariners, Rangers, and Blue Jays. Boston was under .500 against three Middle American teams (the Indians, Royals, and Twins) and another from a foreign city-state (the Yankees). Seven men had become popes, twenty presidential elections held, and forty-one Olympics staged since the Townies last won an Oktoberfest. Said T. Ballgame: "I don't know what it's going to take for the Red Sox to win a World Series."

Take Vaughn, whose off-season read like a tale out of Stephen King. First, he was arrested for drunk driving. The Sox withdrew a long-term contract offer—and demanded that Mo be tested psychologically for alcoholism. Vaughn felt insulted, was acquitted, and spurned a new two-year $20 million pact. "I want a longer deal," he said. "Not for security, but respect. Look at how many flags New York has won. It's almost like it means nothing. But there would be nothing better than to be with the Red Sox when they win because it would be so rare." Would he, and did they want him?

For his part, Duquette wanted to replace the Rocket; in November, he traded two prospects, including Carl Pavano, for the Expos' Pedro Martinez. "They picked the right guy," said Dennis Eckersley, now forty-three, rejoining Boston for a final year. "He's the best in the business"—leading '97 baseball in ERA (1.90), complete games (13), and rival batting average (.184) and winning the Cy Young Award. Knowing

Martinez from Montreal, Duquette signed him to a six-year, $75 million pact.

In the movie *The Razor's Edge*, Bill Murray says of life, "There is no payback. Not now." The wonder of 1998 is that payback straightaway began.

On July 13, 1999, Fenway Park will host its third and perhaps last All-Star Game. A year earlier, unveiling the Classic's logo, the Sox painted it on the dugout roofs and wall above the scoreboard. Club CEO John L. Harrington chatted about the pregame FanFest, Home Run Derby, and game. Then, league president Gene Budig said, "This is one of the original American League franchises. It's nice to be back. It's been a while [since '61]." Listening, you lauded the Sox' record at the '98 All-Star Game—52–33. (Martinez, Vaughn, and reliever Tom "Flash" Gordon made the team.)

After the break, Boston went to Baltimore and brooked its first four-game sweep in thirty-six years. A man looked at peewee Camden Yards and said, "The Nation is getting nervous. If we can't hit here, where can we?" In 1978, pitcher Jim Corsi was a Newton, Massachusetts, high school student. The Sox pitcher looked at Jin Ho Cho, a Korean import: "I'm sure he doesn't know about the Boston Massacre."

You couldn't call it a pennant race, exactly. The Townies won twenty-one of thirty-four games, awoke on August 18, and trailed the 91–30 Yankees by twenty sets. Acclimating to the wild card, they wrestled Baltimore, then Toronto and Texas, for the last playoff spot. To Eck, it evoked '78's dark humor. "I haven't been in the mix for a while. But I remember that baseball and the Sox were serious [expletive]. Passion is a nice word for it." It was as if baseball when it meant something had never been away.

Exempli gratia: On July 15, Martinez blanked the Indians' Bartolo Colon, 1–0, in an ESPN telecast—Fenway's first Sox 1-0 complete game since the Rocket's in '87. Scorned for Clemens's exit, Duquette curred I told you so. "You have to have a good farm system to make trades [like Martinez's]. If you don't develop a Carl Pavano, you're not able to . . . trade for Pedro Martinez." By August 15, Martinez was 15–4, Wakefield 14–5, and Bret Saberhagen 11–6. (Saberhagen had accepted a make-good pact after radical shoulder surgery sidelined him for two years.) The Sox became a halfway house for suspects shunned by other teams. Clicking: infielder Mike Benjamin and outfielders Damon Buford, Darren Lewis, and Darren Bragg. Flopping: pitcher Robinson Checo, designated hitter Jim Leyritz, and infielder Mark Lemke. "Some are going to work out, some aren't," shrugged Duquette. "If they don't work out, move on to the next piece of the puzzle."

In June, a key piece missed sixteen games with a separated right shoulder. Returning, Garciaparra was moved to the cleanup spot. Nomar replied with a .352 average, eight homers, and twenty-seven RBIs in his next twenty-two games. Turning twenty-five, his legend grew. "If I could have any one player today and were starting a team," said Braves assistant general manager Bill Lajoie, "I'd start it with Garciaparra." One night, doubling to beat Minnesota, he obsessed over an eighth-inning error. Mused a teammate: "Talk about a perfection-ist." One writer asked how Nomar had adjusted to cleanup. Jim Corsi stopped a belly laugh: "I don't think he has much of a problem with this thing called baseball."

On July 18, at Detroit, Nomar, Donnie Sadler, Lewis, and Vaughn, now batting third, homered with two out to set an AL record. Mo accused Sox-hired detectives of tailing him, snubbed a three-year $37 million contract offer, and said he hoped to follow Clemens to Toronto. Martinez confessed he was upset over profanity at Fenway Park. Vaughn, inured, said, "If I'm booed, I understand why." *Baseball America* surveyed players and managers and named Vaughn Sox duce. Bragg dubbed Mo "our man of steel."

On August 13 and 14, the Townies scored twenty-five runs on thirty-two hits to twice beat the Twins by a run. By then, Duquette had said, "It took us a while to replace him [Clemens], but ten million dollars [presumably, Mo's salary] will get you a pretty good hitter." It might not replace the man who one day learned that a group of disabled children and adults had arrived at the park. Vaughn signed autographs during batting practice. Later he found the group, requested a show of hands, and signed for those he missed. Martinez called Mo "our most valuable player." Both ingrained baseball with a thank-God-they're-not-all-like-Albert-Belle nonjiving, non-trash-talking, and distinctly '90s charm.

On Sunday, August 30, a sellout crowd sang "Happy [80th] Birthday!" to the Kid, watching the game at Fenway from his Hernando, Florida, home. Later that week, beating Seattle, 7–3, Nomar's grand-slam made him the fifth big-leaguer to hit thirty or more homers his first two years. (The others: Rudy York in 1937–38, Ron Kittle in '83–84, Jose Canseco in '86–87, and Mark McGwire in '87–88.) The next weekend—by coincidence, the Massacre's twentieth anniversary—Boston arrived at SkyDome nine games ahead of the Blue Jays. The Sox

Cindy Loo

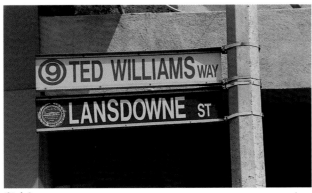

Cindy Loo

Cindy Loo

Cindy Loo

Cindy Loo

Beth Hinchliffe

Cindy Loo

Beth Hinchliffe

Cindy Loo

Cindy Loo

William Polo

William Polo

William Polo

William Polo

Cindy Loo

Beth Hinchliffe

Cindy Loo

Cindy Loo

Cindy Loo

William Polo

William Polo

William Polo

William Polo

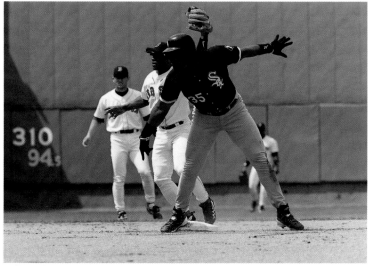

William Polo

William Polo

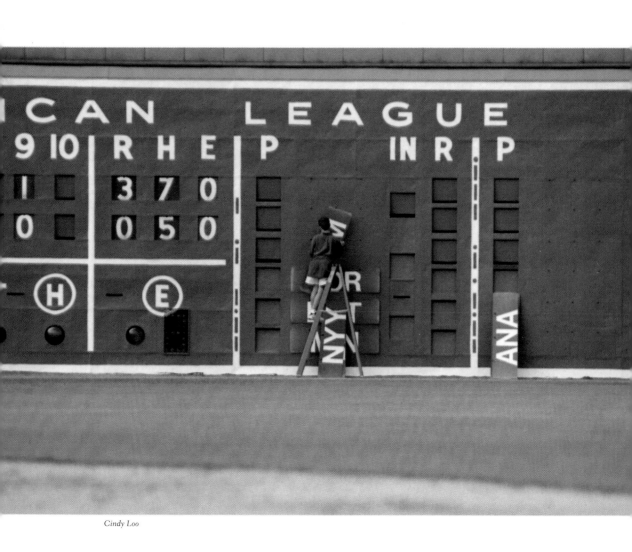

Cindy Loo

lost four straight, three by one run, including Clemens's eighteenth victory. On Labor Day, September 6, McGwire hit his sixty-first home run, tying Roger Maris, and Toronto clubbed Cleveland, 15–1, to draw 4½ sets behind. In the Hub, a talk-show host blared, "The wheels are coming off."

Jennifer Power of Boston admitted she expected the Sox to fold. "Yeah, unfortunately," she said. "That's what has happened in my lifetime— and you can extend that to my father, who is sixty-seven, and my grandfather. He was eighteen when they last won the World Series." That night, the Yankees vaulted to a 3–0 lead. What the *Times* termed "eighty years of baseball shell shock" stilled the Fenway crowd. The season then pivoted: Boston rallied to win, 4–3, on Valentin's eighth-inning homer into the center-field seats. Said Jimy Williams: "Finally, we got one."

On Thursday, September 24, the Sox got a wild-card spot, beating Baltimore, 8–3, before 32,644 at Fenway on Vaughn's two hundredth hit, Garciaparra's two homers, and Gordon's big-league record forty-second straight save. Mo had forty home runs, 115 ribbies, and 205 hits, and at .337 barely missed the batting title. Nomar added thirty-five dingers, 122 RBIs, and a .323 average. Valentin had an off-year (.247), but scored a team-high 113 runs. Naehring, Lemke, and Lou Merloni were hurt, but Benjamin batted .272 and O'Leary smacked twenty-three home runs. Dealt to the Yankees, Stanley was traded back and finished with twenty-nine. Buford, Bragg, catcher Scott Hatteberg, and Lewis hit .282, .279, .276, and .268, respectively.

In 1967, Boston's 92–70 won a pennant. In '98, the same mark trailed New York by twenty-two games. "We've had clubs with more punch," said Vaughn. "It's the pitching that turned around." The Townies finished third in the AL runs (876) and average (.279) and fifth in homers (205). Their fifty-three saves led the league, and a 4.18 earned run average was second. Martinez had a 2.89 ERA, 215 K's, and a 19–7 record. Wakefield (17–8 and 2.48 ERA) and Saberhagen (15–8, 3.96) sealed the Sox' best trifecta since Clemens, Boyd, and Hurst. Eckersley's 1,071st pitching appearance broke Hoyt Wilhelm's all-time record. On the other hand, Boston made only 106 double plays, stole a mere seventy-two bases, and led the bigs with thirty-five passed balls.

"It's a small step," said Nomar of the wild-card berth. "We understand that." On September 29, a larger step greeted them: the Division Series with Cleveland. In 1995, Mo went zero for fourteen in the Tribe's playoff sweep. In Game One, he had two homers and seven RBIs,

Nomar whacked another and drove in four, Martinez and Corsi seven-hit the Indians, and Boston won, 11–3, to end a thirteen-game postseason losing skein. A day later, tradition tripped its cord: David Justice's three-run homer helped Cleveland win, 9–5, at Jacobs Field. Back at Fenway, three dingers off Saberhagen, Travis Fryman's run-saving catch, and Manny Ramirez's ninth-inning blast off Eckersley tore the Sox, 4–3.

Behind, two games to one, Williams thumbed fashion by hurling the recently acquired Pete Schourek over Martinez. "He [Martinez] hasn't pitched with three days' rest this season," Williams said. "If it was your son out there and he'd thrown 3,000-plus pitches and 115-plus pitches a game and his career is on the line and you panicked and pitched him too soon and hurt him, I don't think you would be too happy."

For seven innings, the Townies were. Pitching brilliantly, Schourek and Derek Lowe forged a 1–0 lead. The hard part done, Boston then muffed the easy part. In inning eight, Williams opted for the reliever with forty-six saves. Already, Justice had made a sliding grab and thrown Valentin out at the plate. Now, he tagged Gordon for a two-run double — Flash's first blown save since April 14. Cleveland's 2–1 decision won the playoff, three games to one. Nomar knocked in a playoff record eleven runs. Boston outhit the Tribe, .252 to .206, outscored them twenty to eighteen, forged a 5.00 Cleveland ERA — and lost. The Sox now had a *new* three-game postseason losing streak.

Vaughn hit .412 in the playoff. "I just don't understand why he isn't signed," wondered Valentin, who averaged a series-high .467. "I don't know who we could ever bring in here to do what he does for us." That fall, the Red Sox spurned their fifteen-day exclusive bargaining window: Entering free agency, Mo received a six-year, $72 million contract offer from the Angels. Boston bid five years and $62.5 million — but by now Vaughn's and Duquette's animus aped Williams and the '50s press.

"Mo's rejected our [final] offer," said the Sox general manager. "It looks like he's going to play for someone else." Countered Number 42, scoring leak, barb, and stall: "I believe there's a right and wrong way to do things, and I think after all this time, who knows if I would have accepted *any* contract because of how this whole business had come down?"

Valentin was "shocked." Merloni called Vaughn's exit "a personal thing between Mo and Duquette." Headlines bannered: Did Mo want to leave, or had the front office packed his bags? Wrote Dan Shaughnessy: "His is a huge loss. The Black Bambino has just left town, folks." On Thanksgiving Eve, Vaughn penned an $80 million Halos pact — like

Ruth, Fisk, and Clemens, lost *sans* a player in return. An hour later, all-star free agent Bernie Williams, whom Duquette thought all but signed, blindsided Boston: "In a move as stunning as it was secretive and swift," read the *New York Daily News*, the Yankees matched the Sox' $87.5 million over seven years to keep Williams in center field.

"Where do we go now?" said Duquette, sounding eerily like Harry Frazee. "We'll probably take a look at pitching." Weeks earlier, Boston had signed a quick but strikeout-prone, singles-hitting, defensively challenged free agent. "Who has the Dom Perignon on ice so we can all celebrate the Jose Offerman Era?" the *Globe* now sniped. Critics roiled their clientele: The Red Sox shopped at Fools 'R' Us; Mo/Bernie equaled the Thanksgiving Eve Massacre; when Duquette said, "Ten million dollars will get you a pretty good hitter," he meant Willie Tasby, not Willie Mays.

In February 1999, capping the Sox' Alfred Hitchcock of a winter, Clemens left Toronto—for the Yankees! Red Sox Nation, which thought it had seen everything, shook its head. Up and down. Back and forth. A fan could only marvel at the Olde Towne Team's massy, light and dark, bewitching and enduring pull.

On August 22, 1998, Fenway Park hosted the Jimmy Fund's Fantasy Day. For a $1,250 donation even a noncitizen of the Nation got fifteen swings at the Green Monster and, said ESPN *Magazine*, "a chance to tell your grandchildren how you felled the behemoth with one mighty stroke." Doyens disputed how long it would take to clear the Wall. One, Dr. Raymond Dagenais of the Illinois Mathematics and Science Academy, said that a ball would have to travel at least 350 feet to hit the screen. The task was to smack it at a minimum speed of seventy-two miles per hour at an upward angle of 45 degrees.

Valentin etched the how-tos of playing Screeno. "Get as far back in the box as possible so you can get a good, long look at the pitch. And step right up to the plate, because an inside pitch is easier to pull. Don't uppercut. Even if you make contact, it's not going to carry. You want to stay on top of the ball because forward spin will help get it up in the air. Then haul off and whack it."

Rice, the Sox' hitting coach, treated Fantasy hopefuls like pitchers —with contempt. "They're all kids and old men. There's no way they can hit it." Nomar was more pleasant: "Have fun. Remember to stay back, stay within yourself." Finally, Valentin: "And swing out your ass."

One entrant, Charlie Orcutt, forty-eight, had already hit the Wall. "I opened my stance and pointed my left foot toward the Wall," he said.

"That helped me see the ball longer. I also tried to swing up, like the home-run hitters do." Many batters hit the Monster. Several cleared it. Going long, all longed to preserve the intimacy that made Fenway, like Ebbets Field and the Polo Grounds, a baseball paradise.

A decade earlier, Bart Giamatti first saw a model of the Orioles' new park. "He liked it, but wanted it to be more idiosyncratic," recalled an O's official. "So he sharpened its quirks, made its angles odder"—like Fenway. "When this park is complete," Giamatti said, "*every* team will want one." Corkscrewing into Camden Yards at Oriole Park, his view writes baseball's current lingua franca: "If you build it [right], they will come."

Fenway's lineage came in 1992 to Camden Yards; from '94 to '98 to Arlington, Atlanta, Cleveland, Denver, and Phoenix; and future sites in Cincinnati, Detroit, Houston, Milwaukee, Pittsburgh, San Francisco, San Diego, and Seattle, and perhaps Miami, Minneapolis, Montreal, New York, and Philadelphia—new old parks all. Each recalls the half-century after 1910. In the bigs' then-ten cities, the sixteen fields where ballclubs merged (Cleveland used two parks, and in St. Louis two teams shared one), and moreover in farms, burgs, and villages, the Golden Age of Ballparks knocked boredom down.

A parishioner did not go to see thick-haired mascots, glitzy promotions, or exploding scoreboards in the night. Baseball was the attraction, and its wonder was the mix of drama and detail. Carl Yastrzemski was a teenager in the 1950s. "You *cared* about the players because you *knew* them," he said of sites heavy with individuality. "The fans were down close. They could see guys sweat, and hear 'em curse. And it was because of places like Boston's. You felt like actors in the field of play."

A decade later, baseball embraced multisport mausolea from Queens to Anaheim. "Be with it!" trendies said, no matter how inane. Mocked were Ebbets Field's surf of sounds, the monuments at Yankee Stadium, and the steep-walled rectangle of Comiskey Park. "Since then we've had cookie cutters built more for bullfights than baseball," Number 8 said in 1983. "You don't know whether you're in Cincinnati or Pittsburgh or Mongolia or Des Moines."

Yaz is a stoic man. Mention "cookie cutters," and he spits contempt. His Medina was/is Fenway; his hope, retrieving a time when each field was special. In the 1990s, baseball's new fields plucked parts from each classic park. None was copied more than its oldest and perhaps best. "Every time you see a 'new old' park," Ted Williams added, "remember who started it. They're all trying to imitate Fenway Park."

Bob Costas was seven when he first glimpsed the triple-tiered enormity of the Sox' Bronx inferno. "Fenway or Yankee Stadium," he said, "seeing your first major-league game is an initiation experience—a boy becoming man." Like its namesake, the "House That Ruth Built" split the public. Millions thought it Mecca. Others, echoing Irving Howe, jibed, "We know the nightmare is ours." It *was* in another park— Griffith Stadium of the lowly "first in war, first in peace, and last in the American League" Senators—which sat one mile from the White House and virtually outlawed the long ball.

In Chicago, a Cubs fan liked Wrigley Field's bleachers, nearby el tracks, ivy vines on the brick outfield wall, and flag atop the scoreboard with a white *W* (on a blue background) or blue *L* (against white) to show the day's verdict. On the South Side, white-cubed Comiskey Park, fifteen miles from the stockyards, seemed closer when gales blew from the west. Rail took you to St. Louis, whose Sportsman's Park housed two tenants. Until 1954, the AL Browns played Anna, a salaried governess, to the Cardinals' wealthy Palace of Siam. In 1944, they had their first home sellout in nineteen *years*. "These peanut guys is going through the stands," announcer Dizzy Dean said one day of a vendor. "They is not doing so good because there is more of them than there is of customers."

Fenway's nearest clone was Brooklyn's temple of the underdog. "Just being in Brooklyn was amazing," said 1940–58 Dodgers shortstop Pee Wee Reese. "The fans, we joked with 'em on a first-name basis." It was akin to entering a bar and saying, " 'Hi, ya, Ben,' or 'How you doing, Joe?' The damn stands were right on top of you." The Dodgers fled west in 1957. Enduring is a Flatbush of the mind.

Ebbets Field linked Hilda Chester (ringing her cowbell) and teeny size (the deepest corner of right-center field was 399 feet from home plate; the upper deck of the left-center grandstand lured fly balls like flypaper) and combination cement wall/scoreboard/wire-mesh screen in right. One ad penned a Dodger parable—"Watch for Danny Kaye in *The Secret Life of Walter Mitty*." Another named clothier Abe Stark at the scoreboard base—"Hit Sign, Win Suit." Once, a bird flew out of Casey Stengel's hat. Daily, the Dodger Sym-Phony Band blasted caravans of noise. "Anything can happen at Ebbets Field," Red Barber would say, "Yes-suh, and usually does." Ibid., other outposts of baseball's early-Fenway trace.

At Cincinnati's Crosley Field, outlanders saw the bigs' night inaugural (May 24, 1935), the first pitcher to toss two straight no-hitters

('38's Johnny Vander Meer), and the only player to row over an outfield fence (Lee Grissom, during the Ohio River's 1937 flood). At
Philadelphia's Shibe Park, boo-birds made megaphones of popcorn
boxes, pitched beer bottles on the field, and knew baseball more than
breeding: the 1938–49 Phils placed last. For years, the hapless Tribe split
games between Cleveland's too-tiny League Park (twenty-two thousand
capacity, 290 feet down the right-field line) and too-large Municipal
Stadium (capacity: 74,208). For success, you motored to Tiger (née,
Briggs) Stadium (née Navin Field). Housing more than fifty-four thousand, it seemed smaller. Said my sister: "I feel like I'm back in Lassie
League!"

Joe Falls is a columnist. "When you walk into Detroit's ballpark,"
he could have written about any pre–cookie cutter, "you know you are
no place else in the world." In 1955, the Athletics fled Philadelphia for
a sturdy mirror of Mid-America in Kansas City. Their new playpen—
30,611-capacity Municipal Stadium—had turquoise seats, a pitcher's
feel, and a children's zoo in foul terrain. A mechanical rabbit popped
out of the ground behind the plate with balls for the umpire. A mule—
Charlie O., named for Kansas City owner Charles O. Finley—grazed
beyond the right-field fence. Fans knew the real jackass.

Each old park had personality. Forbes Field was Pittsburgh's suburban cabin, with an ivied left-field wall, double-decked pavilion, sun-
baked infield, and Sahara of an outer garden. No old park was more
gloriously absurd than the Giants' oblong cabash at 157 and 159th
Streets and Eighth Avenue, flowing gently to the sea. To this day, the
Polo Grounds denotes baseball. It had a farcical name (polo was never
played there; from 1891 to 1957 and in 1962–63, baseball was); burlesque
dimensions (the left- and right-field foul poles were 279 and 257 feet
from home plate); a grid of girders, pigeon stoops, and roofed bull-pen
shacks; and a gaping center field—483 feet away.

"That's how it was in every park," said Johnny Pesky. "Built for
baseball. Distinct, different." At Ebbets Field, Gladys Gooding played
the organ. In Pittsburgh, live bands were—ouch—instrumental. In
Milwaukee, the burghers sang with gusto equal to their beer. Before ballparks became stadia, even the national anthem threw conformity a
curve.

In this meridian of baseball temples, few dreamt that a player would
one day say, "When I'm at bat, I can't tell whether I'm in Cincinnati,
Philly, or St. Louis." Richie Hebner, native of Walpole and 1989–91 Sox
coach, hated the thought and the age of cookie cutters.

Yeasting began when in 1964 the Mets traded the Polo Grounds for the cold orb of Shea Stadium. By 1970, lookalike parks included those in Atlanta, Cincinnati, Houston, Philadelphia, Pittsburgh, and St. Louis. "Most of these places are sterile," said Stan Musial. "Most have Astroturf. No corners for balls to take strange hops. No odd places where anything can happen."

In the next thirteen years, Seattle peopled the Kingdome, the Expos left Jarry Park for gaping Olympic Stadium (the Big O, as in zero), and Minnesota dealt Metropolitan Stadium for the tomblike Metrodome. How could baseball have been so wrong? Quite easily. "Teams of this era wanted something new, jazzed-up," said Costas. "They didn't have a *clue* about what in old parks they had." Giamatti did. "What I don't understand is the lack of imagination in ballpark design," he added in 1988. "Why can't we build an idiosyncratic, angular park, for a change, with all the amenities and conveniences, and still make it better than anything we have?" For two decades, multipurpose plots entombed the pastime's corpse. Then, with hope more fainéant than the Dick Stuart Sox, Fenway's lines went deep.

From 1954 to 1991, the Orioles played in a place built for the transplanted Browns. Memorial Stadium was uncovered, double-decked, horseshoe shaped, and looked like a football bowl. In 1992, its successor opened near historic Camden Railroad, only a short fly ball from the Inner Harbor. Camden Yards—no one calls it "Oriole Park"—has Giamatti's suggested angles, outfield quirks, and asymmetrical distances. Beyond right field soars the longest building on the eastern seaboard, the restored red-brick Railroad Warehouse. Its size enfolds the field, like the buildings on Lansdowne Street flank Fenway Park.

State-of-the-art, Camden Yards sits at the head of baseball's class of the '90's. "They took the best of all the new parks," mused Brooks Robinson, "and put it into one." Its arches and brick expanse mime old Comiskey Park. Left-field is double-decked like Tiger Stadium's. The ivy and center-field scoreboard leap gently from Wrigley Field. Look at the right-field wall—twenty-five feet high. Recall Yaz in left playing singles off the Monster. Plow turf, and you'd find the former site of Ruth's Cafe, a saloon owned by George Herman Ruth Sr., father of behemoth Babe.

Disraeli said, "What we anticipate seldom occurs. What we least expected generally happens." Unexpectedly, Camden Yards went back/forward to 4 Yawkey Way. Bull pens showcase relievers warming up. Smoke wafts from Boog's Barbecue on Eutah Street—a mid-Atlantic midway between the warehouse and park. Standing-roomers pay $3 to watch from behind the right- and left-center walls. Like Fenway, the Yard spurns what *fails* (domes, fake turf, interior walls, and the nonidiosyncratic) for what *works* (the irregularity of sites that once formed baseball's web). Peeking, you hope it sways the next millennium.

In 1994, the Texas Rangers opened a 48,100-seat park. Box seats are forty-four feet—a pickoff throw—from first and third bases. A manual scoreboard and "ticker-tape message" board, respectively, drape left and left-center field. In right-center field, a corner off the Rangers' bull pen veers hits away from fielders. The park lies below street level, and meshes with the neighborhood. "The only question in judging, say, Three Rivers and Riverfront Stadium," laughed former Brave and Tiger Darrell Evans, "is which to detonate first." Rating the Yard and The Ballpark at Arlington, on the other hand, is like comparing Joe Cronin and Nomar Garciaparra. Missing: Johnny Pesky. Then, in 1994, the Indians replaced Municipal Stadium with Jacobs Field, which seats forty-two thousand, abuts downtown streets, and is antipodal in its charm.

The Jake inverts Camden Yard's design—strutting a field-level, out-of-town left-field scoreboard and upper deck in right. It has walls of different heights (twenty feet versus eight), varied decks of seating (three down the first-base line, two on the third), opens to a skyline view much of left and center field, and like Fenway, has an outfield jutting out more quickly in right than left. For years, only visitors made sounds in Municipal Stadium's dreary somnolence. Jacobs Field doubled back to an earlier age. On soft, springy-green afternoons, you could sit anywhere at League Park and watch the players without binoculars. "You were right on top of 'em," recalled Herb Score, the Tribe's onetime slingshot of a southpaw, his fastball fast and pure. "It was a more intimate feeling they had with the players and the game."

In 1995, another new old park opened, in Denver. Among Coors Field's curiosa are $4 center-field bleacher seats. "The [Colorado] Rockies could sell out each game," said an executive. "But the spur-of-the-moment fan matters. So we sell the bleachers on game day—and you should see the jostling. People beating up each other—anything for a seat." You think of Walter Matthau explaining Lucy Ricardo's universality: "There's no dream she wouldn't reach for, and no fall she wouldn't take."

When Frank Sinatra sang, "There used to be a ballpark," he bespoke shrines—it may off-put; no other word will do—passing from parent to child the joy of rooting for, truly caring about, the hometown team.

Baseball of the past quarter-century has welded sameness and Murphy's Law. Now, by dint of hope: Phoenix's 1998 Bank One Ballpark (BOB), with a period path between home plate and the pitching mound; the Astros' 2000 downtown park, its left-field wall forged from a train terminal; the Giants' Pacific Bell Park, home runs to right plopping into San Francisco Bay. All suggest that the scales finally have fallen from baseball's eyes.

Think of Crosley Field, Griffith Stadium, Sportsman's Park, the Polo Grounds. Each, now gone, recalls the matronly librarian, uptown soda fountain, and streets of leaves, stick dams, and unlocked homes. So does Fenway, lingering as pleasance and pioneer, model and example. More than any, the Sox' plot has sired baseball's going back to the future. The irony would be if its heirs—the Jake, Coors Field, The Ballpark, Camden Yards—hasten the day wreckers crumple the park to rubble.

20

Finale

"The Red Sox tell us that what they need is luxury boxes, gourmet concession stands, nicer bathrooms, and more high-priced seats," wrote the *Globe*'s Charles A. Radin in March 1998. "What they don't need, they say, is Fenway Park." For years, Fenway's pull kept the faithful coming, the TV and radio public abiding, and sponsors queuing to vend the Olde Towne Team. Now, parks like Camden Yards turned that specialty on its head. By aping it, they devalued it. "The logic is: Bigger—and better—stadium, more revenue; more revenue, better players; better players, more success on the field; more success on the field, a more stable attraction, well into the future, for the city," explained another team's public-relations aide. Unlike Fenway, old *new* parks could link nouveau and tradition.

Early in 1998, Duquette announced but would not detail a "spectacular plan" for a new park to replace Fenway. The Sox, said Dick Bresciani, their vice-president of public affairs, were too fixed on the '99 All-Star Game to etch how, or when. "Everything [else] has slowed down right now, pretty much to a stop." That July the *Globe* reported that the Townies would at some point build a new park abutting Fenway on a triangular fifteen-acre parcel boarded by Yawkey Way, Brookline Avenue, and Boylston Street. (Other ideas included a new park on the South Boston waterfront, near the Gillette plant and the Fort Point Channel, or near the old incinerator off the Southeast Expressway.) The ersatz plot would house forty-five thousand seats, boast the requisite luxury boxes, and yet "look and feel like Fenway," and rise over several years while the Sox played at their 1912 arcade.

The plan, the newspaper stated, was straightforward but not simple. Most of Fenway would crumble upon the new field's opening. In its place: cash-spawning development. The rest would become a museum and park. Fans could walk from Kenmore Square down the third-base line, next to a preserved Green Monster. The report said that revenue would stem from ticket and luxury-box sales and probably a private partner. "We have to have a new park," said Duquette, not denying it. "Our fans complain about narrow seats and lack of modern amenities [restrooms, ticket windows, and concession stands]. What's more, without corporate boxes, there's no way to get money to compete."

Most grasp how Camden Yards' and other new old parks' success threatens Fenway's survival. The Orioles and Rockies routinely draw 3.5 million customers a year. Entering 1999, the Indians had sold out a record 292 straight home games. Most perceive that Fenway, if razed, would exert a witching power on its successor. "Build a new park if you must," observed Ken Coleman. "Get your new deck, loges, the better amenities. But keep the outfield exactly as it is. This is what people see on TV, how they know Fenway—the wall, bleachers, Triangle, the low right-field wall. Height, distance, look, feel—from one pole to another don't change a thing."

The Red Sox insist that rebuilding Fenway would be quixotic. Too expensive. Little parking. The structure sags. Luxury suites can't squeeze into a Wilsonian shoebox. The park was built to shoulder one deck, not two. Assume renovation. Where would the Sox play? Answers charge, not reply. A new park would clog the neighborhood, bend the infrastructure, cloud traffic and the air. Above all, why desert baseball's cathedral of the outdoors? "I hope the Red Sox never leave Fenway," Curt Gowdy said by way of reminiscence. "They could probably draw more people. Some of those Yankee–Red Sox games I did could have done one hundred thousand a game. That doesn't matter, only this: Take the team out of Fenway Park, and they're no longer the New England Red Sox."

A decade ago Bart Giamatti was NL president, soon to be commissioner. "I just don't get it," he said of generic bowls. "A ballpark should be a box, not a saucer—everybody knows that. . . . Why can't we think up a stadium that would have some of the virtues of a Fenway Park—a place of weird angles and distances and beautiful ricochets? It could be done," and was.

Baseball won that debate. Today's asks: Is it easier to rebuild Fenway's soul in a new park, or its core in Fenway Park? The debate, by turns clichéd and Talmudic, has often talked past, not to.

In July 1998, hundreds flocked to Lansdowne Street to convert a non-believer. "Save Fenway Park" read their signs and green bumper stickers. Were they visionaries, or innocents unabroad? Entreating the curious, they struck a passerby as both. "Sure, it's a dream," said John Valianti of Marshfield, Massachusetts. "But we're dreamers here. This is our field of dreams." All feared that, with Fenway leveled, a generation would look back and rue: "*There* lies the Sox' heart and lure, if only you had known it."

A year earlier the *Globe*'s Internet home page asked why people frequented Fenway. More than half (51.9 percent) said they visit to see the park; 31.5 percent, the Townies; 16.4, visiting clubs. Andrew Pate, a salesman from Melrose, Massachusetts, was not surprised. "I've been to 'em all," the "Save Fenway" picket said of Camden and the Jake. "They're all patterned after Fenway." Elizabeth Dooley, a then-fifty-four-year resident of Box 36, vowed defiance: "I stand firm that it can be done." Scott Hardy of Concord, New Hampshire, marched with signs blaring "Save Fenway Park." Many pledged to lie in front of any bulldozer. "My sister did it to save a railroad depot in Melrose," said Valianti, whose fiancée swore to chain herself to the park if the Sox tried to wreck it. Camdens were copycats. *Here* was the original.

To those hardened by emotional removal, "Save Fenway" was a movement not without its mystery. "This is something we're passionate about," said Pate. Explaining, he seemed thoughtful, not plaintive or sore. "People make fun of us. Even my boss. They say we have no life. It's an uphill fight, but I think we can make a difference." Others, agreeing, were practical or self-absorbed, depending on your view. Locals call a new park intrusive to the neighborhood. Developers say it would block a proposed Boylston Street "Main Street" boulevard of shops. According to the *Globe*, merchants on Yawkey Way and Brookline Avenue would be bought by the city, relocated pro tempore, or promised a lush location. Like Queen Victoria, they were not amused. "People have been coming here for years—people from out of state know about us," said David Paratore, manager and co-owner of Who's on First, a bar across Yawkey Way. "If we move we'd have to start over again from scratch."

Should the Townies move, that is exactly what some wish to do. A few strays urge Boston to reacquire a National League franchise and house it in Fenway. "The new league," predicts one, "would take about as long to get used to as the absence of a designated hitter." More workaday (Armageddon will dawn before Boston gets an NL team) is the idea of Fenway's becoming a baseball chapel—the permanent site for national playoff and title games from peewee and church leagues to colleges and corporations. "I don't want to be a bad fan, but I love the Fenway experience," said Richard Soden, past chairman of the Boston Municipal Research Bureau, with left-field box seats since the 1970s. "I'm not sure I couldn't warm to another team." The concern was/is: Can Sox fans warm to another park?

In 1918, the French were losing the second battle of the Marne. "My centre is giving way, my right is in retreat," observed Marshal Ferdinand Foch, "situation excellent. I shall attack." It is true that "Save Fenway"ers lacked funds and leverage. Also plain is that they mimed a Sox fan's fear, worry, and confessions of the heart. For evidence, look at Fleet Center, which displaced Boston Garden. "It is comfortable, pricey, clean, and wildly generic," wrote Dan Shaughnessy. "The new Garden is a building without soul." Even the Internet hit away. On one side: "Fenway is an icon. These parks mean more than simply fan convenience. . . . Taking away one of the jewels of the game for money is wrong. . . . RENOVATE FENWAY!" On the other: "New facilities are in order. . . . There is no way the Sox would renovate. . . . Play seven or eight games a year in Fenway. The rest of the time it could be used as the Baseball Hall of Fame." A question coursed through the argument: Who could ensure—how was it possible—that a new Fenway might match the old?

Let us return to the park of the Silent Captain and Number 9 and Captain Carl and Mr. Yawkey. It is Saturday, July 4, 1998—Independence Day. The Olde Towne Team hosts the White Sox. People ready to laud the flag, inhale a Fenway Frank, and put on their hose. Bunting drapes box seats. Players grace the green and shadowed field. Are we retrieving the past, or reversing it? Today, no one can tell. In the bleachers, near the batting cage, at a concession stand, on the street, Fenway casts a spell of sweetest song and saddest thought.

"Maybe they're going to win, maybe even Buckner will end up the hero," Peter Gammons told a friend before Game Seven of the 1986 World Series. "But before we could find out what it feels like to win, we have to be made to suffer one last, excruciating time." The citizens of Red Sox Nation have suffered much. Only five clubs surpass Boston's thirty-three members of the Hall of Fame—three executives, six managers, and twenty-four players, sixteen of whom graced more than two hundred Townie games. Today, people trooping to Fenway Park would trade them all for the Sox' first World Series ring in the lifetime of most living.

Many faces are lined and weary. A man strokes a forehead crease—that's McCarthy, in 1949, pinch-hitting for Ellis Kinder. His wife applies makeup to her wrinkles—that's Little Looie, in '72, stumbling past third. Before their first game, children lack knowledge of such angst. Saint Francis of Assisi said, "Give me a child until he is seven, and you may have him afterward." The Sox now have him. How will they treat him? Today, the bond is sealed.

Few come by car, for parking is limited to a few gas stations, private lots, or contested on-street spots. Most take public transportation, primarily the MTA trolley and bus routes and commuter trains to Fenway or Kenmore Square, several blocks away. Emerging, you pass a bevy of shops, apartments, and industrial buildings. Ahead lie Fenway's single deck and light towers and sidewalks chockablock with verve.

At Lansdowne Street, the Number 9 circled on a sign inscribes it as Ted Williams Way. A poster reads, "Bleachers Straight Ahead," as if Charlemagne were again nearing Spain. Crusaders hail bagels and baseball and beer while waiting to buy same-day bleacher seats. Cars crowd one-way streets. Charter buses import parishioners from the far outposts of the Nation. Nearby, they pack bars and eateries from Who's on First to The Diamond at Fenway to Cask 'n' Flagon. You remember Jimy Williams, on Opening Day 1998 (Good Friday), when alcohol was banned: "I make it a point never to drink on the bench."

Aromas blend: fried dough and Cajun chicken and hot pretzels and Italian sausage. Stores sell baseball cards and autographed balls and bean bags and bobbing dolls. A giant Red Sox cap tops the door of one exterior. Inside, patrons buy jackets and jerseys and Sox title pennants and photographs of Vaughn, Martinez, Garciaparra, "Friendly Fenway," Foxx, Doerr, Wood, and Williams: the Kid up close, swinging in '42, with Ruth and the great DiMag, and in his last at bat. Infidels buy a photo of the '32 Yankees.

Leaving, you note Fenway's diagram on a nearby building front. Across Yawkey Way, tarriers wrestle at the main ticket windows. The discerning bought them long ago. Everywhere, talk fixes on the 1:20 P.M. match with the "Pale Hose" of quaint childhood usage. "Give me baseball as a carnival," said former White Sox owner Bill Veeck, "every day a Mardi Gras, and every fan a king."

On a stoop affixed to Fenway Park sit a father, Donald Singleman, and his daughter, Hannah. The girl, four, from Melrose, Massachusetts, is eating pizza half as large as her face and wearing a too-large cap around her ears.

Donald asks, "Who's your favorite player?"

"Mo Vaughn," Hannah says, almost sotto voce.

"Who's your second-favorite player?" he asks next.

Dutifully, she answers, "Nomar Garciaparra." Her father beams. Hannah wipes pizza off her face.

"OK," he says. "Now the biggy. Who *don't* you like?"

"The *Yankees!*" she shouts triumphantly. In New England, they teach children early—and raise them well.

Today, baseball on Yawkey Way cleaves into dowry and bequest. Kids wear baseball gloves and Red Sox shirts and pants and wrist-watches and caps. Fathers take their hands, find the tickets, and glimpse the Red Sox, league, and American flags. Neither seats nor field are visible from the street. Slowly, by twos and threes, like citizens in a town hall, you enter Fenway through ground-level archways in its red-brick facade. Then, into the tunnel, up a walkway, and toward the field. Out of the blue comes Russ Gibson, saying: "When I made the big leagues, my hometown [Fall River] tossed a day for me. I was a rookie." Here baseball is family, sure and certain of its place.

Cheerily offhand, baseball loves ritual. Finding your seat is timeless, yet antipodean. Box ushers escort you to your chair. In obstructed seats, tilt your head and praise your luck: you could be in the top deck at Shea Stadium, or the Big O in Montreal. Down the right-field line, some seats point to center field, not the infield. Take Ben Gay and crane your neck. The disabled have special seating in the grandstand. The politically incorrect shun sections 32 and 33, which ban smoking and alcohol. Try left-field sections 30 to 33, which turn back toward the field. "I like the perspective," said Mark Gornstein, a footwear importer from Framingham, Massachusetts. "This gives me a good angle into the [Sox first-base dugout] to see what's going on."

One seat—number 16 in section 33, row 3—adjoins the Monster. From the left-field corner, you can reach over and touch the pole. "It's the only seat in the park where you can do that," said Frank Stevens of Quincy, Massachusetts. "You have a great angle to see the balls hitting off the wall. I ask for that seat whenever I can get it," about eight or nine times a year. If you read the *Boston Herald*, you head toward one of the twelve favorite seats writer Mike Shalin announced in 1998. Among them: field boxes that abut the screen and Red Sox dugout; upper box and reserved and rooftop seats, putting geography in relief; the bleacher seat, now painted red, that cites T. Ballgame's [and Fenway's] longest homer, 502 feet from the plate. "It's baseball's Holy Grail," said Gowdy, "kept like a Japanese Garden"—tended, painted, and without a bad seat in the house.

In 1960, Fenway seemed goliath when, at nine, I first saw the Townies. Now, it evokes a parlor, intimate and dear. In right, you recall Dewey Evans, still twenty-one, racing toward Pesky's Pole. Front-row left-field seats rise above the fielder—surely, Yaz. From behind the plate you can see a curve. Today's pitcher: Jin Ho Cho, the Korean import—or is it Tex or Spaceman or Gentleman Jim? By rote, tableaus reemerge. No ball has cleared the right-field roof. In center the roped-off seats, Conig's Corner, elicit the doomed Tony C. A friend replays Mike Higgins's smash off the loudspeaker horn that once topped the left-center wall. Memory conjures the Prudential Building, and the Citgo sign on Beacon Street. "Aren't many parks where one sign is a landmark across the country," Gowdy says. The Jimmy Fund's is a different kind—New England's crucible versus cancer.

The Monster, of course, towers, as real as any relative. Yesterdays buzz like cicadas around the wall. Start with the hand-operated scoreboard of AL scores and pitching changes and Boston's inning-by-inning passage and bulbs to signal balls, strikes, outs, hits, and errors. The eye catches its upper left corner and baseball's only "in-play" ladder: climbing up, the groundskeeper plucks batting practice homers from the net. In the 1950s, Jim Lemon's fly ball ricocheted off the ladder into center for an inside-the-park homer. Above it, seven players have hit the uprights (Conigliaro, Jackie Jensen, Brooks Robinson, Frank Malzone, Mickey Mantle, Mike Easler, and Gene Conley). Removed in Fenway's late-'67 resodding, bluegrass graced Yaz's lawn at his former Lynnfield home. Today's turf is rich, not worn, for baseball is the only guest.

The 1933–36 Boston Redskins played football here until leaving for Washington. The Boston Yanks used Fenway before perambulating to New York and Dallas and becoming the Indianapolis [née Baltimore] Colts. Other tenants included Frank Leahy's Boston College, Harry Agganis's Boston University, and the 1963–68 New England (then Boston) Patriots. All now are gone. Envision baseball in Texas Stadium. You can't. Move basketball to the Montreal Forum. The swap doesn't fit in intellectual baggage. Yin and yang. Round holes and oblong pegs. Exclusivity breeds continuum. Today could be 1978 or '58 or, in a similar fashion, 1938—Rice, Jensen, or Double X's golden year.

"Fenway isn't old, it's sacred," said Dick Johnson, executive director of the New England Sports Museum. "For the city or state to tear it down would be like the government of Greece tearing down the

Parthenon." It was the Greeks, he will remind you, who said, "Let the games begin."

Today's game does, under a blue sky, before a near-sellout crowd. "Walking through the crowds into that great small old stadium, and there they were in the flesh," said the poet Donald Hall. "I can see them now in their baggy old pants, the players that I had heard about, of whom I'd seen photographs, but there they were, really walking around, live people, and the absolute enchantment, the enthrallment, the tension of starting the game, 'Play ball.'"

The flag blows gently in from left-center field—a pitcher's wind. Somewhere El Tiante is smoking a cigar. In center, the message board says: "Welcome to Fenway Park: Home of the Red Sox." Later, it will air averages, player photos, instant replays, and TV's "This Week in Baseball"—also, ads for Right Guard and Dunkin' Donuts and Priority Mail and, aptly, John Hancock, a company named after the famed signer of the Declaration of Independence. The sound system blares "Born in the USA." You forgive that Bruce Springsteen is a Yankees fan.

Other tunes befit the date—the Beach Boys' "Surfin' USA" and Don McLean's farewell bow to youth, "American Pie," and a Fourth of July medley—"God Bless America" and "It's a Grand Old Flag" and "Battle Hymn of the Republic" and "The Caissons Go Rolling Along" and "Yankee Doodle." The wave, starting in the bleachers, seems alien: swell for Three Rivers, it should be unconstitutional here. You spy the Triangle, Williamsburg, the Yawkeys' Morse code, the belly. Pennants and retired numbers grace the upper level. Numbers double back to the points of your youth: from left to right—distance, 310 (née 315), 379, 420, 302; height, 37 feet to 8 to 5 to 3.

The game itself is quick, but spartan. Chicago's Frank Thomas crashes a ball off the Monster. A Mike Benjamin blast barely curves foul. By the fourth inning you join the all-consuming lines at the bathrooms and concession stands. Mike Cameron homers: White Sox, 1–0. Scott Hatteberg throws out an enemy runner. A Midre Cummings single almost beheads a pitcher. You return with kielbasa and roast beef. The Pale Hose's Greg Norton homers. Boston collects only five hits, stranding seven. Injury, as augury, scratches Mo Vaughn from the lineup. Pitching well, Cho loses, 3–0. Since 1901, the Sox are 77–56 on July 4.

The organ plays as the crowd empties to watch fireworks on the Esplanade. Police corridor the field. Ushers hurry stragglers. Donald

Singleman turns to his daughter. "We'll get 'em tomorrow," he says of the Red Sox as bobbed cork. Hannah smiles to gird herself for tomorrow, next year, a new millennium—then, shyly takes his hand and looks at the lush and humming earth.

The Red Sox may someday win a World Series. The engine to build a new field may or may not run out of steam. Today, that can wait. "So we beat on," F. Scott Fitzgerald wrote in *The Great Gatsby*, "boats against the current, born back ceaselessly into the past." At Fenway Park, the past rows the current named tomorrow.

SOURCES

Grateful acknowledgment is made for permission to reprint excerpts from the following:

Beyond the Sixth Game, by Peter Gammons, 1985. Reprinted by permission of Houghton Mifflin Company.

Boston Red Sox, by Henry Berry, 1975. Reprinted by permission of Rutledge Books.

FDR: A Centenary Remembrance," by Joseph Alsop, copyright the Viking Press, 1982. Reprinted by permission of Thames and Hudson Limited.

"Fenway: From Frazee to Fisk," by Martin F. Nolan, 1986. Reprinted by permission of the *Boston Globe*.

"From Father, with Love," by Doris Kearns Goodwin, 1986. Reprinted by permission of the *Boston Globe*.

"Hit the Monster," August 27, 1998. Reprinted by permission of *ESPN Magazine*.

North Toward Home, by Willie Morris, 1967. Reprinted by permission of Houghton Mifflin.

"Rapt by the Radio," by John Updike, 1986. Reprinted by permission of Alfred A. Knopf.

Red Sox Yearbook, 1997. Reprinted by permission of the Boston Red Sox.

Rhubarb in the Catbird Seat, by Red Barber with Robert Creamer, 1968. Reprinted by permission of Doubleday and Company.

Seasons to Remember, by Curt Gowdy with John Powers, 1993. Reprinted by permission of HarperCollins.

Sports Illustrated, issues of April 15, 1957; April 13, 1959; April 11, 1960; and April 10, 1961. Reprinted by permission.

The Gas House Gang, by J. Roy Stockton, 1945. Reprinted by permission of A.S. Barnes and Company.

The Great American Baseball Card Flipping, Trading and Bubble Gum Book, by Brendan C. Boyd and Fred C. Harris, 1973. Reprinted by permission of Little, Brown and Company.

"The Impossible Dream," 1967. Reprinted by permission of Fleetwood Recording Company.

"Tv's 50 Greatest Sports Moments," July 11–17, 1998. Reprinted by permission of *TV Guide.*

When It Was a Game, 1991. Reprinted by permission of Home Box Office.

"Yaz, to the End, True to Himself," by Peter Gammons, 1983. Reprinted by permission of the *Boston Globe.* Appears in this book under the title, "The Man Named Yaz."

"Yastrzemski Song," 1967. Reprinted by permission of Jess Cain.

Play-by-play commentaries in *Our House* are reprinted with the expressed permission of the Boston Red Sox. Grateful acknowledgment is also made to ABC Television, ESPN Television, CBS Radio, and CBS Television.

Alsop, Joseph. *FDR: A Centenary Remembrance*. New York: The Viking Press, 1982.

Angell, Roger. *Five Seasons*. New York: Simon and Schuster, 1978.

———. *Late Innings*. New York: Ballantine Books, 1982.

———. *The Summer Game*. New York: Popular Library, 1978.

Armbruster, Frank. *The Forgotten Americans*. New Rochelle, N.Y.: Arlington House, 1972.

Astor, Gerald. *The Baseball Hall of Fame 50th Anniversary Book*. New York: Prentice-Hall, 1988.

Baldassaro, Lawrence, ed. *The Ted Williams Reader*. New York: Putnam, 1991.

Barber, Walter (Red), with Robert Creamer. *Rhubarb in the Catbird Seat*. Garden City, N.Y.: Doubleday, 1968.

Berry, Henry. *Boston Red Sox*. New York: Rutledge Books, 1975.

Broeg, Bob. *Super Stars of Baseball*. St. Louis: The Sporting News Publishing Company, 1971.

Chadwick, Bruce, and David M. Spindel. *Boston Red Sox*. New York: Abbeville Press, 1992.

Creamer, Robert. *Babe*. New York: Simon and Schuster, 1974.

Durso, Joseph. *Yankee Stadium*. Boston: Houghton Mifflin, 1972.

Enright, Jim. *Chicago Cubs*. New York: Rutledge Books, 1975.

Falls, Joe. *Detroit Tigers*. New York: Rutledge Books, 1975.

Gammons, Peter. *Beyond the Sixth Game*. Boston: Houghton Mifflin, 1985.

———. "Game Six," *Sports Illustrated*. New York: April 6, 1989.

Gowdy, Curt, with Al Hirshberg. *Cowboy at the Mike*. Garden City, N.Y.: Doubleday, 1966.

——. with John Powers. *Seasons to Remember*. New York: HarperCollins, 1993.

Halberstam, David. *Summer of '49*. New York: William Morrow, 1989.

Hirshberg, Al. *What's the Matter with the Red Sox?* New York: Dodd, Mead, 1973.

Holmes, Tommy. *The Dodgers*. New York: Rutledge Books, 1975.

Honig, Donald. *The American League*. New York: Crown, 1983.

——. *Baseball's 10 Greatest Teams*. New York: Macmillan, 1982.

Hutchens, John K., and George Oppenheimer, eds. *The Best in the World*. New York: The Viking Press, 1973.

Kahn, Roger. *The Boys of Summer*. New York: Harper and Row, 1971.

Kalinsky, George, and Bill Shannon. *The Ballparks*. New York: Hawthorn Books, 1975.

Leuchtenburg, William E. *The LIFE History of the United States*. New York: TIME-LIFE Books, 1976.

Lewine, Harris, and Daniel Okrent. *The Ultimate Baseball Book*. Boston: Houghton Mifflin, 1979.

Lipsyte, Robert. *SportsWorld*, New York: Quadrangle, 1975.

Major League Baseball Promotion Corporation. *Baseball: The First 100 Years*. New York: Poretz-Ross Publishers, 1969.

——. *The Game and the Glory*. Englewood Cliffs, N.J.: Prentice-Hall, 1976.

——. *The World Series: A 75th Anniversary*. New York: Simon and Schuster, 1978.

——. *This Great Game*. New York: Rutledge Books, 1971.

Manchester, William. *One Brief Shining Moment*. Boston: Little, Brown and Company, 1983.

Michener, James A. *Sports in America*. New York: Random House, 1976.

Morris, Willie. *North Toward Home*. Boston: Houghton Mifflin, 1967.

National League. *A Baseball Century*. New York: Rutledge Books, 1976.

Piersall, Jimmy, with Al Hirshberg. *Fear Strikes Out*. Boston: Little, Brown and Company, 1955.

Reichler, Joseph. *Baseball's Great Moments*. New York: Bonanza Books, 1983.

Reidenbaugh, Lowell. *Take Me Out to the Ball Park*. St. Louis: The Sporting News Publishing Company, 1983.

Riley, Dan, ed. *The Red Sox Reader*. Thousand Oaks, Calif.: Ventura Arts, 1978.

Rosenthal, Harold. *The 10 Best Years of Baseball*. New York: Van Nostrand Reinhold Company, 1980.

Seidel, Michael: *Ted Williams: A Baseball Life*. Chicago: Contemporary Books, 1991.

Shaughnessy, Dan. *The Curse of the Bambino*. New York: Penguin Books, 1991.

Smelser, Marshall. *The Life That Ruth Built*. New York: Quadrangle/ New York Times Books, 1975.

Smith, Robert. *Illustrated History of Baseball*. New York: Grosset and Dunlap, 1973.

Smithsonian Exposition Books. *Every Four Years*. New York: W.W. Norton and Company, 1980.

Stockton, J. Roy. *The Gas House Gang*. New York: A.S. Barnes and Company, 1945.

Sullivan, George. *Picture History of the Boston Red Sox*. Indianapolis: Bobbs-Merrill, 1981.

Vecsey, George, ed. *The Way It Was*. Mobil Oil and McGraw-Hill Book Company, 1974.

Walton, Ed. *Red Sox Triumphs and Tragedies*. New York: Stein & Day, 1980.

White, Theodore H. *In Search of History*. New York: Harper and Row, 1978.

Wood, Bob. *Dodger Dogs to Fenway Franks*. New York: McGraw-Hill Publishing Company, 1988.

APPENDIX A: BOSTON RED SOX

Franchise History: Boston Americans, Plymouth Rocks, Puritans, Speed Boys, Somersets (after original owner Charles W. Somers), or Pilgrims, 1901–07; Boston Red Sox, 1907–present. The name Red Sox stemmed from the National League Boston Red Stockings, who in 1907 deserted their red hosiery. Manager Fred Tenney believed that red dye in the socks could cause spike-wound infections. Said Sox owner John I. Taylor: "From now on *we'll* wear red stockings, and I'm grabbing the name Red Sox!" They, and he, did.

 Franchise Homes: Huntington Avenue Grounds (AL, 1901–11). First game: May 8, 1901. Boston 12, Philadelphia 4. Last game: October 7, 1911. Boston 8, Washington 1. *Fenway Park* (AL, 1912–present). First game: April 20, 1912. Boston 7, New York 6.

 World Series titles: 1903, 1912, 1915, 1916, and 1918.

 American League Pennants: 1903, 1904, 1912, 1915, 1916, 1918, 1946, 1967, 1975, and 1986.

 Division Titles: 1975, 1986, 1988, 1990, and 1995.

ALL-TIME FAMILY

Owners: 1901–02, Charles W. Somers; 1903–04, Henry J. Killilea; 1904–11, John I. Taylor; 1912–13, James R. McAleer; 1913-16, Joseph J. Lannin; 1917–23, Harry H. Frazee; 1923–1933, J. A. Robert Quinn; 1933–76, Thomas A. Yawkey; 1976–77, Jean R. Yawkey; 1978–86, JRY Corp. (Jean R. Yawkey, Haywood C. Sullivan, and Edward G. LeRoux Jr.); 1987–92, JRY Corp. (Jean R. Yawkey and Haywood C. Sullivan); 1992–93, JRY Corp. (Haywood C. Sullivan); 1994–present, Jean R. Yawkey Trust.

General Managers: 1933–47, Edward T. Collins; 1948–58, Joseph E. Cronin; 1959–60, Stanley R. (Bucky) Harris; 1961–62, Richard H. O'Connell; 1963–65, Michael F. (Mike) Higgins; 1965–77, Richard H. O'Connell; 1978–83, Haywood C. Sullivan; 1984–93, James (Lou) Gorman; 1994–present, Daniel F. Duquette.

Managers: 1901–06, Jimmy Collins; 1906, Chick Stahl; 1907, Cy Young, George Huff, Bob Unglaub, and Deacon McGuire; 1908, McGuire and Fred Lake; 1909, Lake; 1910–11, Patsy Donovan; 1912, Jake Stahl; 1913, Stahl and Bill Carrigan; 1914–16, Carrigan; 1917, Jack Barry; 1918–20, Ed Barrow; 1921–22, Hugh Duffy; 1923, Frank Chance; 1924–26, Lee Fohl; 1927–29, Carrigan; 1930, Heinie Wagner; 1931, Shano Collins; 1932, Collins and Marty McManus; 1933, McManus; 1934, Bucky Harris; 1935–47, Joe Cronin; 1948–49, Joe McCarthy; 1950, McCarthy and Steve O'Neill; 1951, O'Neill; 1952–54, Lou Boudreau; 1955–58, Mike Higgins; 1959, Higgins, Rudy York, and Billy Jurges; 1960, Jurges, Del Baker, and Higgins; 1961–62, Higgins; 1963, Johnny Pesky; 1964, Pesky and Billy Herman; 1965, Herman; 1966, Herman and Pete Runnels; 1967–68, Dick Williams; 1969, Williams and Eddie Popowski; 1970–73, Eddie Kasko; 1974–75, Darrell Johnson; 1976, Johnson and Don Zimmer; 1977–79, Zimmer; 1980, Zimmer and Pesky; 1981–84, Ralph Houk; 1985–87, John McNamara; 1988, McNamara and Joe Morgan; 1989–91, Morgan; 1992–94, Butch Hobson; 1995–96, Kevin Kennedy; 1997–98, Jimy Williams.

Overall Managerial Records: Del Baker, 2–5; Ed Barrow, 213–203; Jack Barry, 90–62; Lou Boudreau, 229–232; Bill Carrigan, 489–500; Frank Chance, 61–91; Jimmy Collins, 464–389; Shano Collins, 73–136; Joe Cronin, 1,071–916; Patsy Donovan, 159–147; Hugh Duffy, 136–172; Lee Fohl, 160–299; Bucky Harris, 76–76; Billy Herman, 128–182; Mike Higgins, 560–556; Butch Hobson, 207–232; Ralph Houk, 312–282; George Huff, 3–5; Darrell Johnson, 220–188; Billy Jurges, 59–63; Eddie Kasko, 345–295; Kevin Kennedy, 171–135; Fred Lake, 110–80; Joe McCarthy, 224–147; Deacon McGuire, 98–123; Marty McManus, 95–151; John McNamara, 297–273; Joe Morgan, 305–258; Steve O'Neill, 149–97; Johnny Pesky, 147–179; Eddie Popowski, 6–4; Pete Runnels, 8–8; Chick Stahl, 5–13; Jake Stahl, 144–88; Bob Unglaub, 8–20; Heinie Wagner, 52–102; Dick Williams, 260–217; Jimy Williams, 170–154; Rudy York, 0–1; Cy Young, 3–4; Don Zimmer, 411–304.

Coaches: Gary Allenson, 1992–94; Del Baker, 1945–48 and 1953–60; Dick Berardino, 1989–91; Moe Berg, 1939–41; Mace Brown, 1965; Don Bryant, 1974–76; Al Bumbry, 1988–93; Jimmy Burke, 1921–23; Rick Burleson, 1992–93; Jack Burns, 1955–59; Bill Burwell, 1944; Doug Camilli, 1970–73; Tom Carey, 1946–47; Dave Carlucci, 1996; Bob Coleman, 1928; Earle Combs, 1948–52; John Cumberland, 1995; Kiki Cuyler, 1949; Tom Daly,

1933–46; Bobby Doerr, 1967–69; Harry Dorish, 1963; Hugh Duffy, 1931 and 1939; Mike Easler, 1993–94; Sammy Ellis, 1996; Bibb Falk, 1934; Dave Ferriss, 1955–59; Bill Fischer, 1985–91; Rich Gale, 1992–93; Billy Gardner, 1965–66; Harvey Haddix, 1971; Tommy Harper, 1980–84; Richie Hebner, 1989–91; Billy Herman, 1960–64; Walt Hriniak, 1977–88; Rudy Hulwsitt, 1931–33; Al Jackson, 1977–79; Dave Jauss, 1997–98; Darrell Johnson, 1968–69; Tim Johnson, 1995–96; Joe Kerrigan, 1997–98; Wendell Kim, 1997–98; Rene Lachemann, 1985–86; Al Lakeman, 1963–64 and 1967–69; Lefty Leifield, 1924–26; Don Lenhardt, 1970–73; Grady Little, 1997–98; Sal Maglie, 1960–62 and 1966–67; Harry Malmberg, 1963–64; Eddie Mayo, 1951; Jack McCallister, 1930; Bill McKechnie, 1952–53; John McLaren, 1991; Jerry McNertney, 1988; Oscar Melillo, 1952–53; Bing Miller, 1937; Buster Mills, 1954; Joe Morgan, 1985–88; Al Nipper, 1995–96; Len Okrie, 1961–62 and 1965–66; Dave Oliver, 1995–96; Steve O'Neill, 1950; Jack Onslow, 1934; Mickey Owen, 1955–56; Herb Pennock, 1936–39; Johnny Pesky, 1975–84; Johnny Podres, 1980; Dick Pole, 1998; Eddie Popowski, 1967–74 and 1976; Jim Rice, 1995–98; Mike Roarke, 1994; Pete Runnels, 1965–66; John Ryan, 1923–27; Al Schacht, 1935–36; Paul Schreiber, 1947–58; John Schulte, 1949–50; Frank Shellenback, 1940–44; Rac Slider, 1987–90; Lee Stange, 1972–74 and 1981–84; Herm Starrette, 1995–97; George Susce, 1950–54; George Thomas, 1970; Tony Torchia, 1985; Bob Turley, 1964; Charlie Wagner, 1970; John Wathan, 1994; Heinie Wagner, 1927–29; Frank White, 1994–96; Stan Williams, 1975–76; Larry Woodall, 1942–48; Rudy York, 1959–62; Eddie Yost, 1977–84; Don Zimmer, 1974–76 and 1992.

Players: Below are the nearly fourteen hundred players who have appeared in at least one game for the Red Sox since the team was founded in 1901 through the 1998 season.

Don Aase, 1977; Jerry Adair, 1967–68; Bob Adams, 1925; Doc Adkins, 1902; Harry Agganis, 1954–55; Sam Agnew, 1916–18; Rick Aguilera, 1995; Dale Alexander, 1932–33; Luis Alicea, 1995; Gary Allenson, 1979–84; Mel Almada, 1933–37; Nick Altrock, 1902–03; Luis Alvarado, 1968–70; Brady Anderson, 1988; Larry Anderson, 1990; Fred Anderson, 1909 and 1913; Ernie Andres, 1946; Kim Andrew, 1975; Ivy Andrews, 1932–33; Mike Andrews, 1966–70; Luis Aparicio, 1971–73; Luis Aponte, 1980–83; Frank Arellanes, 1908–1910; Tony Armas, 1983–86; Charley Armbruster, 1905–07; Asby Asbjornson, 1928–29; Billy Ashley, 1998; Ken Aspromonte, 1957–58; Jim Atkins, 1950 and 1952; Eldon Auker, 1939; Doyle Aulds, 1947; Steve Avery, 1997–98; Bobby Avila, 1959; Ramon Aviles, 1977; Joe Azcue, 1969.

Loren Bader, 1917–18; Jim Bagby Jr., 1938–40 and 1946; Bob Bailey, 1977–78; Cory Bailey, 1993–94; Gene Bailey, 1920; Al Baker, 1938; Floyd Baker, 1953–54; Jack Baker, 1976–77; Tracy Baker, 1911; Neal Ball, 1912–13;

Scott Bankhead, 1993–94; Walter Barbare, 1918; Frank Barberich, 1910; Brian Bark, 1995; Brian Barkley, 1998; Babe Barna, 1943; Steve Barr, 1974–75; Bill Barrett, 1929–30; Bob Barrett, 1929; Frank Barrett, 1944–45; Jimmy Barrett, 1907–08; Marty Barrett, 1982–90; Tommy Barrett, 1992; Ed Barry, 1905–07; Jack Barry, 1915–17 and 1919; Matt Batts, 1947–51; Frank Baumann, 1955–59; Don Baylor, 1986–87; Bill Bayne, 1929–30; Hugh Bedient, 1912–14; Stan Belinda, 1995–96; Gary Bell, 1967–68; Juan Bell, 1995; Esteban Beltre, 1996; Juan Beniquez, 1971–72 and 1974–75; Mike Benjamin, 1997–98; Dennis Bennett, 1965–67; Frank Bennett, 1927–28; Al Benton, 1952; Todd Benzinger, 1987–88; Lou Berberet, 1958; Moe Berg, 1935–39; Boze Berger, 1939; Charley Berry, 1928–32; Damon Berryhill, 1994; Hal Bevan, 1952; Charley Beville, 1901; Elliott Bigelow, 1929; Jack Billingham, 1980; Doug Bird, 1983; John Bischoff, 1925–26; Max Bishop, 1934–35; Dave Black, 1923; Tim Blackwell, 1974–75; Greg Blosser, 1993–94; Clarence Blethen, 1923; Red Bluhm, 1918; Mike Boddicker, 1988–90; Larry Boerner, 1932; Wade Boggs, 1982–92; Bob Bolin, 1970–73; Milt Bolling, 1952–57; Tom Bolton, 1987–92; Ike Boone, 1923–25; Ray Boone, 1960; Toby Borland, 1997; Tom Borland, 1960–61; Lou Boudreau, 1951–52; Sam Bowen, 1977–78 and 1980; Stew Bowers, 1935–37; Joe Bowman, 1944–45; Ted Bowsfield, 1958–60; Dennis Boyd, 1982–89; Herb Bradley, 1927–29; Hugh Bradley, 1910–12; Cliff Brady, 1920; King Brady, 1908; Darren Bragg, 1996–98; Mark Brandenburg, 1996–97; Darrell Brandon, 1966–68; Fred Bratchi, 1926–27; Ed Bressoud, 1962–65; Ken Brett, 1967 and 1969–71; Tom Brewer, 1954–61; Ralph Brickner, 1952; Jim Brillheart, 1931; Dick Brodowski, 1952 and 1955; Jack Brohamer, 1978–80; Hal Brown, 1953–55; Lloyd Brown, 1933; Mace Brown, 1942–43 and 1946; Mike Brown, 1982–86; Mike Brumley, 1991–92; Tom Brunansky, 1990–92 and 1994; Jim Bucher, 1944–45; Bill Buckner, 1984–87 and 1990; Don Buddin, 1956 and 1958–61; Damon Buford, 1998; Fred Burchell, 1907–09; Bob Burda, 1972; Tom Burgmeier, 1978–82; Jesse Burkett, 1905; Ellis Burks, 1987–92; Rick Burleson, 1974–80; George Burns, 1922–23; Jim Burton, 1975 and 1977; Jim Busby, 1959–60; Joe Bush, 1918–21; Jack Bushelman, 1911–12; Frank Bushey, 1927 and 1930; Bill Butland, 1940, 1942, and 1946–47; Bud Byerly, 1958; Jim Byrd, 1993.

Hick Cady, 1912–17; Earl Caldwell, 1948; Ray Caldwell, 1919; Ivan Calderon, 1993; Dolf Camilli, 1945; Bill Campbell, 1977–81; Paul Campbell, 1941–42 and 1946; Jose Canseco, 1995–96; Bernie Carbo, 1974–78; Tom Carey, 1939–42 and 1946; Walter Carlisle, 1908; Swede Carlstrom, 1911; Cleo Carlyle, 1927; Roy Carlyle, 1925–26; Bill Carrigan, 1906 and 1908–16; Ed Carroll, 1929; Jerry Casale, 1958–60; Joe Cascarella, 1935–36; Danny Cater, 1972–74; Rex Cecil, 1944–45; Orlando Cepeda, 1973; Rick Cerone, 1988–89; Chet Chadbourne, 1906–07; Bob Chakales, 1957;

Wes Chamberlain, 1994–95; Esty Chaney, 1913; Ed Chapin, 1920–22; Ben Chapman, 1937–38; Pete Charton, 1964; Ken Chase, 1942–43; Charley Chech, 1909; Robinson Checo, 1997–98; Jack Chesbro, 1909; Nels Chittum, 1959–60; Jin Ho Cho, 1998; Joe Christopher, 1966; Lloyd Christopher, 1945; Joe Cicero, 1929–30; Ed Cicotte, 1908–12; Galen Cisco, 1961–62 and 1967; Bill Cissell, 1934; Danny Clark, 1924; Jack Clark, 1991–92; Otie Clark, 1945; Phil Clark, 1996; Mark Clear, 1981–85; Roger Clemens, 1984–96; Lance Clemons, 1974; Reggie Cleveland, 1974–78; Tex Clevenger, 1954; Lu Clinton, 1960–64; Bill Clowers, 1926; George Cochran, 1918; Jack Coffey, 1918; Alex Cole Jr., 1996; Dave Coleman, 1977; Michael Coleman, 1997; Jimmy Collins, 1901–07; Ray Collins, 1909–15; Rip Collins, 1922; Shano Collins, 1921–25; Merrill Combs, 1947 and 1949–50; Ralph Comstock, 1915; Bunk Congalton, 1907; Billy Conigliaro, 1969–71; Tony Conigliaro, 1964–67, 1969–70, and 1975; Gene Conley, 1961-63; Bud Connally, 1925; Ed Connolly Sr., 1929–32; Ed Connolly Jr., 1964; Joe Connolly, 1924; Bill Conroy, 1942–44; Billy Consolo, 1953–59; Dusty Cooke, 1933–36; Jimmy Cooney, 1917; Cecil Cooper, 1971–76; Guy Cooper, 1914–95; Scott Cooper, 1990–94; Wilfredo Cordero, 1996–97; Rheal Cormier, 1995; Vic Correll, 1972; Jim Corsi, 1997–98; Marlan Coughtry, 1960; Fritz Coumbe, 1914; Ted Cox, 1977; Doc Cramer, 1936–40; Gavvy Cravath, 1908; Steve Crawford, 1980–82 and 1984–87; Pat Creeden, 1931; Bob Cremins, 1927; Lou Criger, 1901–08; Joe Cronin, 1935–45; Zach Crouch, 1988; Leon Culberson, 1943–47; Ray Culp, 1968–73; Midre Cummings, 1998; Nig Cuppy, 1901; Steve Curry, 1988; John Curtis, 1970–73; Milt Cuyler, 1996.

Babe Dahlgren, 1935–36; Pete Daley, 1955–59; Dom Dallessandro, 1937; Babe Danzig, 1909; Bobby Darwin, 1976–77; Danny Darwin, 1991–94; Bob Daughters, 1937; Andre Dawson, 1993–94; Cot Deal, 1947–48; Rob Deer, 1993; Pep Deininger, 1902; Alex Delgado, 1996; Ike Delock, 1952–53 and 1955–63; Don Demeter, 1966–67; Brian Denman, 1982; Sam Dente, 1947; Mike Derrick, 1970; Gene Desautels, 1937–40; Mel Deutsch, 1946; Mickey Devine, 1920; Hal Deviney, 1920; Al De Vormer, 1923; Bo Diaz, 1977; George Dickey, 1935–36; Emerson Dickman, 1936 and 1938–41; Bob Didier, 1974; Steve Dillard, 1975–77; Dom DiMaggio, 1940–42 and 1946–53; Bill Dinneen, 1902–07; Bob DiPietro, 1951; Ray Dobens, 1929; Joe Dobson, 1941–43, 1946–50, and 1954; Sam Dodge, 1921–22; Pat Dodson, 1986–88; Bobby Doerr, 1937–44 and 1946–51; John Doherty, 1996; John Donahue, 1923; Pat Donahue, 1908–10; Chris Donnels, 1995; Pete Donohue, 1932; John Dopson, 1989–93; Tom Doran, 1904–06; Harry Dorish, 1947–49 and 1956; Jim Dorsey, 1984–85; Patsy Dougherty, 1902–04; Tommy Dowd, 1901; Danny Doyle, 1943; Denny Doyle, 1975–77; Dick Drago, 1974–75 and 1978–80;

Clem Dreisewerd, 1944–46; Walt Dropo, 1949–52; Jean Dubuc, 1918; Frank Duffy, 1978–79; Joe Dugan, 1922; Bob Duliba, 1965; George Dumont, 1919; Ed Durham, 1929–32; Cedric Durst, 1930; Jim Dwyer, 1979–80.

Arnold Earley, 1960–65; Mike Easler, 1984–85; Dennis Eckersley, 1978–84 and 1998; Elmer Eggert, 1927; Howard Ehmke, 1923–26; Hack Eibel, 1920; Dick Ellsworth, 1968–69; Steve Ellsworth, 1988; Clyde Engle, 1910–14; Nick Esasky, 1989; Vaughn Eshelman, 1995–97; Al Evans, 1951; Bill Evans, 1951; Dwight Evans, 1972–90; Hoot Evers, 1952–54; Homer Ezzell, 1924–25.

Carmen Fanzone, 1970; Steve Farr, 1994; Doc Farrell, 1935; Duke Farrell, 1903–05; Alex Ferguson, 1922–25; Rick Ferrell, 1933–37; Wes Ferrell, 1934–37; Hobe Ferris, 1901–07; Dave Ferriss, 1945–50; Chick Fewster, 1922–23; Joel Finch, 1979; Tom Fine, 1947; Lou Finney, 1939–42 and 1944–45; Gar Finnvold, 1994; Mike Fiore, 1970–71; Hank Fischer, 1966–67; Carlton Fisk, 1969 and 1971–80; Howie Fitzgerald, 1926; Ira Flagstead, 1923–29; John Flaherty, 1992–93; Al Flair, 1941; Bill Fleming, 1940–41; Scott Fletcher, 1993–94; Ben Flowers, 1951 and 1953; Frank Foreman, 1901; Happy Foreman, 1926; Mike Fornieles, 1957–63; Gary Fortune, 1920; Tony Fossas, 1991–94; Eddie Foster, 1920–22; Rube Foster, 1913–17; Bob Fothergill, 1933; Boob Fowler, 1926; Pete Fox, 1941–45; Jimmie Foxx, 1936–42; Joe Foy, 1966–68; Ray Francis, 1925; Buck Freeman, 1901–07; Hersh Freeman, 1952–53 and 1955; John Freeman, 1927; Charley French, 1909–10; Barney Friberg, 1933; Owen Friend, 1955; Todd Frohwirth, 1994; Jeff Frye, 1996–97; Oscar Fuhr, 1924–25; Frank Fuller, 1923; Curt Fullerton, 1921–25 and 1933.

Fabian Gaffke, 1936–39; Phil Gagliano, 1971–72; Del Gainor, 1914–17 and 1919; Rich Gale, 1984; Denny Galehouse, 1939–40 and 1947–49; Bob Gallagher, 1972; Ed Gallagher, 1932; Jim Galvin, 1930; Bob Garbark, 1945; Rich Garces, 1996–98; Nomar Garciaparra, 1996–98; Mike Gardiner, 1991–92; Billy Gardner, 1962–63; Larry Gardner, 1908–17; Wes Gardner, 1986–90; Mike Garman, 1969 and 1971–73; Cliff Garrison, 1928; Ford Garrison, 1943–44; Alex Gaston, 1926 and 1929; Milt Gaston, 1929–31; Rich Gedman, 1980–90; Gary Geiger, 1959–65; Charley Gelbert, 1940; Wally Gerber, 1928–29; Dick Gernert, 1952–59; Doc Gessler, 1908–09; Chappie Geygan, 1924–26; Joe Giannini, 1911; Norwood Gibson, 1903–06; Russ Gibson, 1967–69; Andy Gilbert, 1942 and 1946; Don Gile, 1959–62; Frank Gilhooley, 1919; Bob Gillespie, 1950; Grant Gillis, 1929; Joe Ginsberg, 1961; Ralph Glaze, 1906–08; Harry Gleason, 1901–03; Joe Glenn, 1940; John Godwin, 1905–06; Chuck Goggin, 1974; Eusebio Gonzales, 1918; Joe Gonzales, 1937; Johnny Gooch, 1933; Billy Goodman, 1947–57; Tom Gordon, 1996–98; Jim Gosger, 1963 and 1965–66; Charley Graham, 1906; Lee Graham, 1983; Skinny Graham, 1934–35; Dave Gray, 1964; Jeff Gray,

1990–91; Lenny Green, 1965–66; Pumpsie Green, 1959–62; Mike Greenwell, 1985–96; Vean Gregg, 1914–16; Doug Griffin, 1971–77; Marty Griffin, 1928; Guido Grilli, 1966; Ray Grimes, 1920; Moose Grimshaw, 1905–07; Marv Grissom, 1953; Turkey Gross, 1925; Lefty Grove, 1934–41; Ken Grundt, 1996–97; Mike Guerra, 1951; Mario Guerrero, 1973–74; Bob Guindon, 1964; Randy Gumpert, 1952; Eric Gunderson, 1995–96; Hy Gunning, 1911; Jackie Gutierrez, 1983–85; Don Gutteridge, 1946–47.

Casey Hageman, 1911–12; Odell Hale, 1941; Ray Haley, 1915–16; Charley Hall, 1909–13; Chris Hammond, 1997–98; Garry Hancock, 1978 and 1980–82; Fred Haney, 1926–27; Erik Hanson, 1995; Carroll Hardy, 1960–62; Harry Harper, 1920; Tommy Harper, 1972–74; Billy Harrell, 1961; Ken Harrelson, 1967–69; Bill Harris, 1938; Greg Harris, 1989–94; Joe Harris, 1905–07; Joe Harris, 1922–25; Mickey Harris, 1940–41 and 1946–49; Reggie Harris, 1996; Slim Harriss, 1926–28; Jack Harshman, 1959; Chuck Hartenstein, 1970; Grover Hartley, 1927; Mike Hartley, 1995; Charley Hartman, 1908; Bill Haselman, 1995–97; Herb Hash, 1940–41; Andy Hassler, 1978–79; Billy Hatcher, 1992–94; Fred Hatfield, 1950–52; Scott Hatteberg, 1995–98; Grady Hatton, 1954–56; Clem Hausmann, 1944–45; John Hayden, 1906; Frankie Hayes, 1947; Ed Hearn, 1910; Danny Heep, 1989–90; Bob Heffner, 1963–65; Randy Heflin, 1945–46; Fred Heimach, 1926; Bob Heise, 1975–76; Tommy Helms, 1977; Charley Hemphill, 1901; Dave Henderson, 1986–87; Tim Hendryx, 1920–21; Olaf Henriksen, 1911–17; Bill Henry, 1952–55; Butch Henry, 1997–98; Jim Henry, 1936–37; Ramon Hernandez, 1977; Mike Herrera, 1925–26; Tom Herrin, 1954; Joe Hesketh, 1990–94; Eric Hetzel, 1989–90; Joe Heving, 1938–40; Johnnie Heving, 1924–25 and 1928–30; Piano Legs Hickman, 1902; Mike Higgins, 1937–38 and 1946; Hob Hiller, 1920–21; Dave Hillman, 1960–61; Gordie Hinkle, 1934; Paul Hinrichs, 1951; Paul Hinson, 1928; Harley Hisner, 1951; Billy Hitchcock, 1948–49; Dick Hoblitzell, 1914–18; Butch Hobson, 1975–80; George Hockette, 1934–35; Johnny Hodapp, 1933; Mel Hoderlein, 1951; Billy Hoeft, 1959; John Hoey, 1906–08; Glenn Hoffman, 1980–87; Fred Hofmann, 1927–28; Ken Holcombe, 1953; Dave Hollins, 1995; Billy Holm, 1945; Harry Hooper, 1909–20; Sam Horn, 1987–89; Tony Horton, 1964–67; Dwayne Hosey, 1995–96; Tom House, 1976–77; Wayne Housie, 1991; Elston Howard, 1967–68; Chris Howard, 1994; Paul Howard, 1909; Les Howe, 1923–24; Peter Hoy, 1992; Waite Hoyt, 1919–20; Joe Hudson, 1995–97; Sid Hudson, 1952–54; Ed Hughes, 1905–06; Long Tom Hughes, 1902–03; Terry Hughes, 1974; Tex Hughson, 1941–44 and 1946–49; Bill Humphrey, 1938; Ben Hunt, 1910; Buddy Hunter, 1971, 1973, and 1975; Herb Hunter, 1920; Tom Hurd, 1954–56; Bruce Hurst, 1980–88; Bert Husting, 1902.

Daryl Irvine, 1990–92.

Pete Jablonowski (later known as Pete Appleton), 1932; Ron Jackson, 1960; Baby Doll Jacobson, 1926–27; Beany Jacobson, 1907; Charley Jamerson, 1924; Bill James, 1919; Chris James, 1995; Hal Janvrin, 1911 and 1913–17; Ray Jarvis, 1969–70; Reggie Jefferson, 1995–98; Ferguson Jenkins, 1976–77; Tom Jenkins, 1925–26; Jackie Jensen, 1954–59 and 1961; Keith Johns, 1998; Adam Johnson, 1914; Bob Johnson, 1944–45; Deron Johnson, 1974–76; Earl Johnson, 1940–41 and 1946–50; Hank Johnson, 1933–35; John Henry Johnson, 1983–84; Roy Johnson, 1932–35; Vic Johnson, 1944–45; Joel Johnston, 1995; Smead Jolley, 1932–33; Charley Jones, 1901; Dalton Jones, 1964–69; Jake Jones, 1947–48; Rick Jones, 1976; Sad Sam Jones, 1916–21; Eddie Joost, 1955; Duane Josephson, 1971–72; Oscar Judd, 1941–45; Joe Judge, 1933–34; Ed Jurak, 1982–85.

Rudy Kallio, 1925; Ed Karger, 1909–11; Andy Karl, 1943; Marty Karow, 1927; Benn Karr, 1920–22; Eddie Kasko, 1966; George Kell, 1952–54; Al Kellett, 1924; Red Kellett, 1934; Win Kellum, 1901; Ed Kelly, 1914; Ken Keltner, 1950; Russ Kemmerer, 1954–55 and 1957; Fred Kendall, 1978; Bill Kennedy, 1953; John Kennedy, 1970–74; Marty Keough, 1956–60; Dana Kiecker, 1990–91; Joe Kiefer, 1925–26; Leo Kiely, 1951, 1954–56, and 1958–59; Jack Killilay, 1911; Ellis Kinder, 1948–55; Walt Kinney, 1918; Bruce Kison, 1985; Billy Klaus, 1955–58; Red Kleinow, 1910–11; Bob Kline, 1930–33; Ron Kline, 1969; Bob Klinger, 1946–47; Brent Knackert, 1996; John Knight, 1907; Hal Kolstad, 1962–63; Cal Koonce, 1970–71; Andy Kosco, 1972; Jack Kramer, 1948–49; Lew Krausse, 1972; Rick Kreuger, 1975–77; Rube Kroh, 1906–07; John Kroner, 1935–36; Marty Krug, 1912; Randy Kutcher, 1988–90.

Candy LaChance, 1902–05; Kerry Lacy, 1996–97; Ty LaForest, 1945; Roger LaFrancois, 1982; Joe Lahoud, 1968–71; Eddie Lake, 1943–45; Jack Lamabe, 1963–65; Bill Lamar, 1919; Dennis Lamp, 1988–91; Rick Lancellotti, 1990; Bill Landis, 1967–69; Jim Landis, 1967; Sam Langford, 1926; Carney Lansford, 1981–82; Frank LaPorte, 1908; John LaRose, 1978; Lyn Lary, 1934; Johnny Lazor, 1943–46; Bill Lee, 1969–78; Dud Lee, 1924–26; Lefty LeFebvre, 1938–39; Lou Legett, 1933–35; Regis Leheny, 1932; Paul Lehner, 1952; Nemo Leibold, 1921–23; John Leister, 1987 and 1990; Mark Lemke, 1998; Don Lenhardt, 1952 and 1954; H. Dutch Leonard, 1913–18; Ted Lepcio, 1952–59; Dutch Lerchen, 1910; Louis LeRoy, 1910; Darren Lewis, 1998; Duffy Lewis, 1910–17; John Lewis, 1911; Ted Lewis, 1901; Jim Leyritz, 1998; John Lickert, 1981; Derek Lilliquist, 1995; Johnny Lipon, 1952–53; Hod Lisenbee, 1929–32; Dick Littlefield, 1950; Greg Litton, 1994; Don Lock, 1969; Skip Lockwood, 1980; George Loepp, 1928; Tim Lollar, 1985–86; Jim Lonborg, 1965–71; Walt Lonergan, 1911; Brian Looney, 1995; Harry Lord, 1907–10; Derek Lowe, 1997–98; Johnny Lucas, 1931–32;

Joe Lucey, 1925; Lou Lucier, 1943–44; Del Lundgren, 1926–27; Tony Lupien, 1940 and 1942–43; Sparky Lyle, 1967–71; Walt Lynch, 1922; Fred Lynn, 1974–80; Steve Lyons, 1985–86 and 1991–93.

Mike Macfarlane, 1995; Danny MacFayden, 1926–32; Shane Mack, 1997; Bill MacLeod, 1962; Keith MacWhorter, 1980; Tom Madden, 1909–11; Mike Maddux, 1995–96; Pete Magrini, 1966; Ron Mahay, 1995 and 1997–98; Pat Mahomes, 1996–97; Chris Mahoney, 1910; Jim Mahoney, 1959; Jose Malave, 1996–97; Jerry Mallett, 1959; Paul Maloy, 1913; Frank Malzone, 1955–65; Felix Mantilla, 1963–65; Jeff Manto, 1996; Heinie Manush, 1936; Josias Manzanillo, 1991; Phil Marchildon, 1950; Johnny Marcum, 1936–38; Juan Marichal, 1974; Ollie Marquardt, 1931; Bill Marshall, 1931; Mike Marshall, 1990–91; Babe Martin, 1948–49; Pedro Martinez, 1998; John Marzano, 1987–92; Walt Masterson, 1949–52; Tommy Matchick, 1970; Bill Mathews, 1909; Gene Mauch, 1956–57; Charley Maxwell, 1950–52 and 1954; Wally Mayer, 1917–18; Chick Maynard, 1922; Carl Mays, 1915–19; Dick McAuliffe, 1974–75; Tom McBride, 1943–47; Dick McCabe, 1918; Windy McCall, 1948–49; Emmett McCann, 1926; Tom McCarthy, 1985; Tim McCarver, 1974–75; Amby McConnell, 1908–10; Maurice McDermott, 1948–53; Jim McDonald, 1950; Ed McFarland, 1908; Ed McGah, 1946–47; Willie McGee, 1995; Lynn McGlothlen, 1972–73; Art McGovern, 1905; Bob McGraw, 1919; Deacon McGuire, 1907–08; Jim McHale, 1908; Marty McHale, 1910–11 and 1916; Stuffy McGinnis, 1918–21; Archie McKain, 1937–38; Walt McKeel, 1996–97; Jud McLaughlin, 1931–33; Larry McLean, 1901; Don McMahon, 1908; Don McMahon, 1966–67; Marty McManus, 1931–33; Norm McMillan, 1923; Eric McNair, 1936–38; Mike McNally, 1915–17 and 1919–20; Gordon McNaughton, 1932; Jeff McNeely, 1993; Norm McNeil, 1919; Bill McWilliams, 1931; Roman Mejias, 1963–64; Sam Mele, 1947–49 and 1954–55; Jose Melendez, 1993–94; Oscar Melillo, 1935–37; Bob Melvin, 1993; Mike Menosky, 1920–23; Mike Meola, 1933 and 1936; Orlando Mercedes, 1998; Andy Merchant, 1975–76; Spike Merena, 1934; Lou Merloni, 1998; Jack Merson, 1953; George Metkovich, 1943–46; Russ Meyer, 1957; John Michaels, 1932; Dick Midkiff, 1938; Dee Miles, 1943; Bing Miller, 1935–36; Elmer Miller, 1922; Hack Miller, 1918; Otto Miller, 1930–32; Rick Miller, 1971–77 and 1981–85; Buster Mills, 1937; Dick Mills, 1970; Rudy Minarcin, 1956–57; Nate Minchey, 1993–94 and 1996; Charlie Mitchell, 1984–85; Fred Mitchell, 1901–02; Johnny Mitchell, 1922–23; Keith Mitchell, 1998; Kevin Mitchell, 1996; Herb Moford, 1959; Vince Molyneaux, 1918; Bill Monbouquette, 1958–65; Freddie Moncewicz, 1928; Bob Montgomery, 1970–79; Bill Moore, 1926–27; Wilcy Moore, 1931–32; Dave Morehead, 1963–68; Roger Moret, 1970–75; Cy Morgan,

1907–09; Eddie Morgan, 1934; Red Morgan, 1906; Ed Morris, 1928–31; Deacon Morrissey, 1901; Guy Morton, 1954; Kevin Morton, 1991; Earl Moseley, 1913; Walter Moser, 1911; Jerry Moses, 1965 and 1968–70; Wally Moses, 1946–48; Doc Moskiman, 1910; Les Moss, 1951; Jamie Moyer, 1996; Gordy Mueller, 1950; Billy Muffett, 1960–62; Greg Mulleavy, 1933; Freddie Muller, 1933–34; Joe Mulligan, 1934; Frank Mulroney, 1930; Bull Mundy, 1913; Johnny Murphy, 1947; Rob Murphy, 1989–90; Tom Murphy, 1976–77; Walter Murphy, 1931; George Murray, 1923–24; Matt Murray, 1995; Tony Muser, 1969; Paul Musser, 1919; Alex Mustaikis, 1940; Buddy Myer, 1927–28; Elmer Myers, 1920–22; Hap Myers, 1910–11.

Chris Nabholz, 1994; Tim Naehring, 1990–97; Judge Nagle, 1911; Mike Nagy, 1969–72; Bill Narleski, 1929–30; Ernie Neitzke, 1921; Hal Neubauer, 1925; Don Newhauser, 1972–74; Jeff Newman, 1983–84; Bobo Newsom, 1937; Dick Newsome, 1941–43; Skeeter Newsome, 1941–45; Gus Niarhos, 1952–53; Chet Nichols, 1960–63; Reid Nichols, 1980–85; Al Niemiec, 1934; Harry Niles, 1908–10; Al Nipper, 1983–87; Merlin Nippert, 1962; Otis Nixon, 1994; Russ Nixon, 1960–65 and 1968; Trot Nixon, 1996 and 1998; Willard Nixon, 1950–58; Leo Nonnenkamp, 1938–40; Chet Nourse, 1909; Les Nunamaker, 1911–14.

Frank Oberlin, 1906–07; Mike O'Berry, 1979; Buck O'Brien, 1911–13; Jack O'Brien, 1903; Syd O'Brien, 1969; Tom O'Brien, 1949–50; Lefty O'Doul, 1923; Ben Oglivie, 1971–73; Bob Ojeda, 1980–85; Ken Okrie, 1952; Troy O'Leary, 1995–98; Gene Oliver, 1968; Tom Oliver, 1930–33; Hank Olmstead, 1905; Karl Olson, 1951 and 1953–55; Marv Olson, 1931–33; Ted Olson, 1936–38; Bill O'Neill, 1904; Emmett O'Neill, 1943–45; Steve O'Neill, 1924; George Orme, 1920; Frank O'Rourke, 1922; Luis Ortiz, 1993–94; Dan Osinski, 1966–67; Harry Ostdiek, 1908; Fritz Ostermueller, 1934–40; John Ostrowski, 1948; Marv Owen, 1940; Mickey Owen, 1954; Spike Owen, 1986–88; Frank Owens, 1905.

Jim Pagliaroni, 1955 and 1960–62; Mike Palm, 1948; Jim Pankovits, 1990; Al Papai, 1950; Larry Pape, 1909 and 1911–12; Stan Papi, 1979–80; Freddy Parent, 1901–07; Mel Parnell, 1947–56; Larry Parrish, 1988; Roy Partee, 1943–44 and 1946–47; Stan Partenheimer, 1944; Ben Paschal, 1920; Casey Patten, 1908; Hank Patterson, 1932; Marty Pattin, 1972–73; Don Pavletich, 1970–71; Mike Paxton, 1977; Johnny Peacock, 1937–44; Eddie Pellagrini, 1946–47; Rudy Pemberton, 1996–97; Alejandro Pena, 1995; Tony Pena, 1990–93; Brad Pennington, 1996; Herb Pennock, 1915–17, 1919–22, and 1934; Tony Perez, 1980–82; Jack Perrin, 1921; Bill Pertica, 1918; Johnny Pesky, 1942 and 1946–52; Gary Peters, 1970–72; Bob Peterson, 1906–07; Rico Petrocelli, 1963 and 1965–76; Dan Petry, 1991; Dave Philley, 1962; Ed

Phillips, 1970; Val Picinich, 1923–25; Urbane Pickering, 1931–32; Jeff Pierce, 1995; Bill Piercy, 1922–24; Jimmy Piersall, 1950 and 1952–58; George Pipgras, 1933–35; Greg Pirkl, 1906; Pinky Pittenger, 1921–23; Juan Pizarro, 1968–69; Phil Plantier, 1990–92; Herb Plews, 1959; Jeff Plympton, 1991; Jennings Poindexter, 1936; Dick Pole, 1973–76; Nick Polly, 1945; Ralph Pond, 1910; Tom Poquette, 1979 and 1981; Dick Porter, 1934; Bob Porterfield, 1956–58; Nelson Potter, 1941; Ken Poulsen, 1967; Arquimedez Pozo, 1996–97; Del Pratt, 1921–22; Larry Pratt, 1914; George Prentiss, 1901–02; Joe Price, 1989; Curtis Pride, 1997; Doc Prothro, 1925; Tex Pruiett, 1907–08; Billy Purtell, 1910–11; Frankie Pytlak, 1941 and 1945–46.

Paul Quantrill, 1992–94; Frank Quinn, 1949–50; Jack Quinn, 1922–25; Rey Quinones, 1986; Carlos Quintana, 1988–91 and 1993.

Dick Radatz, 1962–66; Dave Rader, 1980; Chuck Rainey, 1979–82; Jeff Reardon, 1990–92; Johnny Reder, 1932; Jerry Reed, 1990; Jody Reed, 1987–92; Bobby Reeves, 1929–31; Bill Regan, 1926–30; Wally Rehg, 1913–15; Dick Reichle, 1922–23; Win Remmerswaal, 1979–80; Jerry Remy, 1978–84; Steve Renko, 1979–80; Bill Renna, 1958–59; Rip Repulski, 1960–61; Carlos Reyes, 1998; Carl Reynolds, 1934–35; Gordon Rhodes, 1932–35; Tuffy Rhodes, 1995; Hal Rhyne, 1929–32; Jim Rice, 1974–89; Woody Rich, 1939–41; Jeff Richardson, 1993; Al Richter, 1951 and 1953; Joe Riggert, 1911; Topper Rigney, 1926–27; Ernest Riles, 1993; Allen Ripley, 1978–79; Walt Ripley, 1935; Pop Rising, 1905; Jay Ritchie, 1964–65; Luis Rivera, 1989–93; Billy Jo Robidoux, 1990; Aaron Robinson, 1951; Floyd Robinson, 1968; Jack Robinson, 1949; Mike Rochford, 1988–90; Bill Rodgers, 1915; Carlos Rodriguez, 1994–95; Frankie Rodriguez, 1995; Steve Rodriguez, 1995; Tony Rodriguez, 1996; Billy Rogell, 1925 and 1927–28; Lee Rogers, 1938; Garry Roggenburk, 1966 and 1968–69; Billy Rohr, 1967; Red Rollings, 1927–28; Ed Romero, 1986–89; Mandy Romero, 1998; Kevin Romine, 1985–91; Vicente Romo, 1969–70; Buddy Rosar, 1950–51; Brian Rose, 1997–98; Si Rosenthal, 1925–26; Braggo Roth, 1919; Jack Rothrock, 1925–32; Rich Rowland, 1994–95; Stan Royer, 1994; Joe Rudi, 1981; Muddy Ruel, 1921–22 and 1931; Red Ruffing, 1924–30; Pete Runnels, 1958–62; Allan Russell, 1919–22; Jack Russell, 1926–32 and 1936; Jeff Russell, 1993–94; Rip Russell, 1946–47; Babe Ruth, 1914–19; Jack Ryan, 1909; Jack Ryan, 1929; Ken Ryan, 1992–95; Mike Ryan, 1964–67; Mike Ryba, 1941–46; Gene Rye, 1931.

Bret Saberhagen, 1997–98; Donnie Sadler, 1998; Bob Sadowski, 1966; Ed Sadowski, 1960; Joe Sambito, 1986–87; Ken Sanders, 1966; Jose Santiago, 1966–70; Tom Satriano, 1969–70; Dave Sax, 1985–87; Bill Sayles, 1939; Ray Scarborough, 1951–52; Russ Scarritt, 1929–31; Wally Schang, 1918–20; Charley Schanz, 1950; Bob Scherbarth, 1950; Chuck Schilling, 1961–65;

Calvin Schiraldi, 1986–87; Rudy Schlesinger, 1965; Biff Schlitzer, 1909; George Schmees, 1952; Dave Schmidt, 1981; Johnny Schmitz, 1956; Dick Schofield, 1969–70; Pete Schourek, 1998; Ossee Schreckengost, 1901; Al Schroll, 1958–59; Don Schwall, 1961–62; Everett Scott, 1914–21; George Scott, 1966–71 and 1977–79; Tom Seaver, 1986; Bob Seeds, 1933–34; Diego Segui, 1974–75; Kip Selbach, 1904–06; Bill Selby, 1996; Aaron Sele, 1993–97; Jeff Sellers, 1985–88; Merle Settlemire, 1928; Wally Shaner, 1926–27; Howard Shanks, 1923–24; Red Shannon, 1919; Al Shaw, 1907; John Shea, 1928; Merv Shea, 1933; Danny Sheaffer, 1987; Dave Shean, 1918–19; Rollie Sheldon, 1966; Keith Shepherd, 1995; Neill Sheridan, 1948; Ben Shields, 1930; Strick Shofner, 1947; Ernie Shore, 1914–17; Bill Short, 1966; Chick Shorten, 1915–17; Brian Shouse, 1998; Terry Shumpert, 1995; Norm Siebern, 1967–68; Sonny Siebert, 1969–73; Al Simmons, 1943; Pat Simmons, 1928–29; Dave Sisler, 1956–59; Ted Sizemore, 1979–80; Camp Skinner, 1923; Craig Skok, 1973; Jack Slattery, 1901; Steve Slayton, 1928; Heathcliff Slocumb, 1996–97; Charley Small, 1930; Al Smith, 1964; Bob Smith, 1955; Broadway Aleck Smith, 1903; Charley Smith, 1909–11; Doug Smith, 1912; Eddie Smith, 1947; Elmer Smith, 1922; Frank Smith, 1910–11; George Smith, 1930; George Smith, 1966; John Smith, 1931; Lee Smith, 1988–90; Paddy Smith, 1920; Pete Smith, 1962–63; Reggie Smith, 1966–73; Riverboat Smith, 1958; Zane Smith, 1995; Mike Smithson, 1988–89; Wally Snell, 1913; Chris Snopek, 1998; Moose Solters, 1934–35; Rudy Sommers, 1926–27; Allen Sothoron, 1921; Bill Spanswick, 1964; Tully Sparks, 1902; Tris Speaker, 1907–15; Stan Spence, 1940–41 and 1948–49; Tubby Spencer, 1909; Andy Spognardi, 1932; Jack Spring, 1957; Bobby Sprowl, 1978; Chick Stahl, 1901–06; Jake Stahl, 1903, 1908–10, and 1912–13; Matt Stairs, 1995; Tracy Stallard, 1960–62; Jerry Standaert, 1929; Lee Stange, 1966–70; Bob Stanley, 1977–89; Mike Stanley, 1996–98; John Stansbury, 1918; Mike Stanton, 1995–96; Dave Stapleton, 1980–86; Jigger Statz, 1920; Elmer Steele, 1907–09; Ben Steiner, 1945–46; Red Steiner, 1945; Mike Stenhouse, 1986; Gene Stephens, 1952–53 and 1955–60; Vern Stephens, 1948–52; Jerry Stephenson, 1963 and 1965–68; Sammy Stewart, 1986; Dick Stigman, 1966; Carl Stimson, 1923; Chuck Stobbs, 1947–51; Al Stokes, 1925–26; Dean Stone, 1957; George Stone, 1903; Jeff Stone, 1989–90; Howie Storie, 1931–32; Lou Stringer, 1948–50; Amos Strunk, 1918–19; Dick Stuart, 1963–64; George Stumpf, 1931–33; Tom Sturdivant, 1960; Jim Suchecki, 1950; Denny Sullivan, 1907–08; Frank Sullivan, 1953–60; Haywood Sullivan, 1955, 1957, and 1959–60; Marc Sullivan, 1982 and 1984–87; Carl Sumner, 1928; Jeff Suppan, 1995–97; George D. Susce, 1955–58; Bill Swanson, 1914; Bill Sweeney, 1930–31; Greg Swindell, 1998; Len Swormstedt, 1906.

Jim Tabor, 1938–44; Doug Taitt, 1928–29; Frank Tanana, 1981; Jesse Tannehill, 1904–08; Arlie Tarbert, 1927–28; Jose Tartabull, 1966–68; LaSchelle Tarver, 1986; Willie Tasby, 1960; Bennie Tate, 1932; Jim Tatum, 1996; Ken Tatum, 1971–73; Jesus Tavares, 1997; Harry Taylor, 1950–52; Scott Taylor, 1992–93; Birdie Tebbetts, 1947–50; Yank Terry, 1940 and 1942–45; Jake Thielman, 1908; Blaine Thomas, 1911; Fred Thomas, 1918; George Thomas, 1966–71; Lee Thomas, 1964–65; Pinch Thomas, 1912–17; Tommy Thomas, 1937; Bobby Thomson, 1960; Jack Thoney, 1908–09 and 1911; Hank Thormahlen, 1921; Faye Throneberry, 1952 and 1955–57; Luis Tiant, 1971–78; Bob Tillman, 1962–67; Lee Tinsley, 1994–96; Jack Tobin, 1926–27; Jackie Tobin, 1945; Phil Todt, 1924–30; Andy Tomberlin, 1994; Tony Tonneman, 1911; Mike Torrez, 1978–82; John Trautwein, 1988; Joe Trimble, 1955; Ricky Trlicek, 1994 and 1997; Dizzy Trout, 1952; Frank Truesdale, 1918; Mike Trujillo, 1985–86; John Tudor, 1979–83; Bob Turley, 1963.

Tom Umphlett, 1953; Bob Unglaub, 1904–05 and 1907–08.

Tex Vache, 1925; Carlos Valdez, 1998; Julio Valdez, 1980–83; Sergio Valdez, 1994; John Valentin, 1992–98; Dave Valle, 1994; Al Van Camp, 1931–32; Hy Vandenburg, 1935; Ben Van Dyke, 1912; Tim VanEgmond, 1994–95; Jason Varitek, 1997–98; Mo Vaughn, 1991–98; Bobby Veach, 1924–25; Bob Veale, 1972–74; Dario Vegas, 1998; Mickey Vernon, 1956–57; Sammy Vick, 1921; Frank Viola, 1992–94; Oscar Vitt, 1919–21; Clyde Vollmer, 1950–53; Jake Volz, 1901; Joe Vosmik, 1938–39.

Jake Wade, 1939; Charlie Wagner, 1938–42 and 1946; Gary Wagner, 1969–70; Hal Wagner, 1944 and 1946–47; Heinie Wagner, 1906–13, 1915–16, and 1918; Tim Wakefield, 1995–98; Rube Walberg, 1934–37; Chico Walker, 1980–81 and 1983–84; Tilly Walker, 1916–17; Murray Wall, 1957–59; Jimmy Walsh, 1916–17; Bucky Walters, 1933–34; Fred Walters, 1945; Roxy Walters, 1919–23; Bill Wambsganss, 1924–25; Pee Wee Wanninger, 1927; John Warner, 1902; Rabbit Warstler, 1930–33; John Wasdin, 1997–98; Gary Waslewski, 1967–68; Bob Watson, 1979; Johnny Watwood, 1932–33; Monte Weaver, 1939; Earl Webb, 1930–32; Ray Webster, 1960; Eric Wedge, 1991–92 and 1994; Bob Weiland, 1932–34; Frank Welch, 1927; Herb Welch, 1925; Johnny Welch, 1932–36; Tony Welzer, 1926–27; Fred Wenz, 1968–69; Bill Werber, 1933–36; Bill Werle, 1953–54; Vic Wertz, 1959–61; David West, 1998; Sammy White, 1951–59; George Whiteman, 1907 and 1918; Mark Whiten, 1995; Ernie Whitt, 1976; Al Widmar, 1947; Bill Wight, 1951–52; Del Wilber, 1952–54; Joe Wilhoit, 1919; Dana Williams, 1989; Dave Williams, 1902; Denny Williams, 1924–25 and 1928; Dib Williams, 1935; Dick Williams, 1963–64; Ken Williams, 1928–29; Rip Williams, 1911; Stan Williams, 1972; Ted Williams, 1939–42 and 1946–60. Jim Willoughby, 1975–77; Ted Wills,

1959–62; Archie Wilson, 1952; Duane Wilson, 1958; Earl Wilson, 1959–60 and 1962–66; Gary Wilson, 1902; Jack Wilson, 1935–41; Jim Wilson, 1945–46; John Wilson, 1927–28; Les Wilson, 1911; Squanto Wilson, 1914; Hal Wiltse, 1926–28; Ted Wingfield, 1924–27; George Winn, 1919; Herm Winningham, 1992; Tom Winsett, 1930–31 and 1933; George Winter, 1901–08; Clarence Winters, 1924; Rick Wise, 1974–77; Johnny Wittig, 1949; Larry Wolfe, 1979–80; Harry Wolter, 1909; Smoky Joe Wood, 1908–15; Joe Wood, 1944; Ken Wood, 1952; Wilbur Wood, 1961–64; John Woods, 1924; Pinky Woods, 1943–45; Rob Woodward, 1985–88; Hoge Workman, 1924; Al Worthington, 1960; Jim Wright, 1978–79; Tom Wright, 1948–51; John Wyatt, 1966–68; John Wyckoff, 1916–18.

Carl Yastrzemski, 1961–83; Steve Yerkes, 1909 and 1911–14; Rudy York, 1946–47; Cy Young, 1901–08; Matt Young, 1991–92.

Paul Zahniser, 1925–26; Al Zarilla, 1949–50 and 1952–53; Norm Zauchin, 1951 and 1955–57; Matt Zeiser, 1914; Bill Zuber, 1946–47; Bob Zupcic, 1991–94.

FINISHES

Year	Position	W	L	Pct.	*GB	Attendance
1901	2nd	79	57	.581	4	289,448
1902	3rd	77	60	.562	6½	348,567
1903	1st	91	47	.659	+14½	379,338
1904	1st	95	59	.617	+ 1½	623,295
1905	4th	78	74	.513	16	466,828
1906	8th	49	105	.318	45½	410,209
1907	7th	59	90	.396	32½	436,777
1908	5th	75	79	.487	15½	473,048
1909	3rd	88	63	.583	9½	668,965
1910	4th	81	72	.529	22½	584,619
1911	5th	78	75	.510	24	503,961
1912	1st	105	47	.691	+14	597,096
1913	4th	79	71	.527	15½	437,194
1914	2nd	91	62	.595	8½	481,359
1915	1st	101	50	.669	+2½	539,885
1916	1st	91	63	.591	+2	496,397
1917	2nd	90	62	.592	9	387,856
1918	1st	75	51	.595	+2½	249,513
1919	6th	66	71	.482	20½	417,291
1920	5th	72	81	.471	25½	402,445
1921	5th	75	79	.487	23½	279,273

FINISHES (continued)

Year	Position	W	L	Pct.	*GB	Attendance
1922	8th	61	93	.396	33	259,184
1923	8th	61	91	.401	37	229,688
1924	7th	67	87	.435	25	448,556
1925	8th	47	105	.309	49½	267,782
1926	8th	46	107	.301	44½	285,155
1927	8th	51	103	.331	59	305,275
1928	8th	57	96	.373	43½	396,920
1929	8th	58	96	.377	48	394,620
1930	8th	52	102	.338	50	444,045
1931	6th	62	90	.408	45	350,975
1932	8th	43	111	.279	64	182,150
1933	7th	63	86	.423	34½	268,715
1934	4th	76	76	.500	24	610,640
1935	4th	78	75	.510	16	558,568
1936	6th	74	80	.481	28½	626,895
1937	5th	80	72	.526	21	559,659
1938	2nd	88	61	.591	9½	646,459
1939	2nd	89	62	.589	17	573,070
1940	4th (tie)	82	72	.532	8	716,234
1941	2nd	84	70	.545	17	718,497
1942	2nd	93	59	.612	9	730,340
1943	7th	68	84	.447	29	358,275
1944	4th	77	77	.500	12	506,975
1945	7th	71	83	.461	17½	603,794
1946	1st	104	50	.675	+12	1,416,944
1947	3rd	83	71	.539	14	1,427,315
1948	2nd**	96	59	.619	1	1,558,798
1949	2nd	96	58	.623	1	1,596,650
1950	3rd	94	60	.610	4	1,344,080
1951	3rd	87	67	.565	11	1,312,282
1952	6th	76	78	.494	19	1,115,750
1953	4th	84	69	.549	16	1,026,133
1954	4th	69	85	.448	42	931,127
1955	4th	84	70	.545	12	1,203,200
1956	4th	84	70	.545	13	1,137,158
1957	3rd	82	72	.532	16	1,181,087
1958	3rd	79	75	.513	13	1,077,047
1959	5th	75	79	.487	19	984,102
1960	7th	65	89	.422	32	1,129,866
1961	6th	76	86	.469	33	850,589
1962	8th	76	84	.475	19	733,080

FINISHES (continued)

Year	Position	W	L	Pct.	*GB	Attendance
1963	7th	76	85	.472	28	942,642
1964	8th	72	90	.444	27	883,276
1965	9th	62	100	.383	40	652,201
1966	9th	72	90	.444	26	811,172
1967	1st	92	70	.568	+1	1,727,832
1968	4th	86	76	.531	17	1,940,788
1969	3rd	87	75	.537	22	1,833,246
1970	3rd	87	75	.537	21	1,595,278
1971	3rd	85	77	.525	18	1,678,732
1972	2nd	85	70	.548	½	1,441,718
1973	2nd	89	73	.549	8	1,481,002
1974	3rd	84	78	.519	7	1,556,411
1975	1st ***	95	65	.594	+4½	1,748,587
1976	3rd	83	79	.512	15½	1,895,846
1977	2nd (tie)	97	64	.602	2½	2,074,549
1978	2nd †	99	64	.607	1	2,320,643
1979	3rd	91	69	.569	11½	2,353,114
1980	4th	83	77	.519	19	1,956,092
1981	5th/2nd (tie)††	59	49	.546	††	1,060,379
1982	3rd	89	73	.549	6	1,950,124
1983	6th	78	84	.481	20	1,782,285
1984	4th	86	76	.531	18	1,661,618
1985	5th	81	81	.500	18½	1,786,633
1986	1st †††	95	66	.590	+5½	2,147,641
1987	5th	78	84	.481	20	2,231,551
1988	1st ‡	89	73	.549	+1	2,464,851
1989	3rd	83	79	.512	6	2,510,012
1990	1st ‡‡	88	74	.543	+2	2,528,986
1991	2nd (tie)	84	78	.519	7	2,562,435
1992	7th	73	89	.451	23	2,468,574
1993	5th	80	82	.494	15	2,422,021
1994	4th	54	61	.470	17	1,775,818
1995	1st §	86	58	.597	+7	2,164,410
1996	3rd	85	77	.525	7	2,315,231
1997	4th	78	84	.481	20	2,226,136
1998	2nd §§	92	70	.568	22	2,343,947

*   Games behind winner.
**   1948, finished regular season tied for first; lost one-game playoff
     to Cleveland.
*** 1975, won Championship Series over Oakland.

† 1978, finished regular season tied for first; lost one-game playoff
   to New York.
†† 1981, first half, 30–26; second half, 29–23.
††† 1986, won Championship Series over California.
‡ 1988, lost Championship Series to Oakland.
‡‡ 1990, lost Championship Series to Oakland.
§ 1995, lost Division Series to Cleveland.
§§ 1998, lost Division Series to Cleveland.

CAREER BATTING LEADERS

Games. Carl Yastrzemski, 3,308; Dwight Evans, 2,505; Ted Williams, 2,292;
Jim Rice, 2,089; Bobby Doerr, 1,865; Harry Hooper, 1,646; Wade Boggs,
1,625; Rico Petrocelli, 1,553; Dom DiMaggio, 1,399; Frank Malzone, 1,359;
Mike Greenwell, 1,269; George Scott, 1,192; Duffy Lewis, 1,184; Billy
Goodman, 1,177; Joe Cronin, 1,134.

At Bats. Yastrzemski, 11,988; Evans, 8,726; Rice, 8,225; T. Williams,
7,706; Doerr, 7,093; Hooper, 6,269; Boggs, 6,213; DiMaggio, 5,640;
Petrocelli, 5,390; Malzone, 5,273; Greenwell, 4,623; Goodman, 4,399;
D. Lewis, 4,325; G. Scott, 4,234; Johnny Pesky, 4,085.

Runs. Yastrzemski, 1,816; T. Williams, 1,798; Evans, 1,435; Rice, 1,249;
Doerr, 1,094; Boggs, 1,067; DiMaggio, 1,046; Hooper, 988; Pesky, 776;
Jimmie Foxx, 721; Tris Speaker, 704; Goodman, 688; Greenwell, 657;
Petrocelli, 653; Cronin, 645; Mo Vaughn, 628.

Runs Batted In. Yastrzemski, 1,844; T. Williams, 1,839; Rice, 1,451;
Evans, 1,346; Doerr, 1,247; Foxx, 788; Petrocelli, 773; Vaughn, 752; Cronin,
737; Jackie Jensen, 733; Greenwell, 726; Malzone, 716; Boggs, 687; Lewis,
643; DiMaggio, 618; Speaker, 570; Carlton Fisk, 568; G. Scott, 562; Vern
Stephens, 562; Reggie Smith, 536.

Hits. Yastrzemski, 3,419; T. Williams, 2,654; Rice, 2,452; Evans, 2,373;
Boggs, 2,098; Doerr, 2,042; Hooper, 1,707; DiMaggio, 1,680; Malzone,
1,454; Greenwell, 1,400; Petrocelli, 1,352; Goodman, 1,344; Speaker, 1,327;
Pesky, 1,277.

Batting Average (1,500 at bats). T. Williams, .344; Boggs, .338; Speaker,
.337; Foxx, .320; Pete Runnels, .320; Bob Johnson, .313; Pesky, .313; Fred Lynn,
.308; Goodman, .306; Vaughn, .304; Greenwell, .303; Doc Cramer, .302; Rick
Ferrell, .302; Lou Finney, .301; Cronin, .300; DiMaggio, .298; Rice, .298;
Stuffy McGinnis, .296; Jimmy Collins, .295.

Doubles. Yastrzemski, 646; T. Williams, 525; Evans, 474; Boggs, 422;
Doerr, 381; Rice, 373; DiMaggio, 308; Greenwell, 275; Cronin, 270;

D. Lewis, 254; Goodman, 248; Hooper, 246; Speaker, 241; Petrocelli, 237; John Valentin, 236.

Triples. Hooper, 130; Speaker, 106; Buck Freeman, 91; Doerr, 89; Larry Gardner, 87; Rice, 79; Hobe Ferris, 77; Evans, 72; T. Williams, 71; J. Collins, 65; Chick Stahl, 64; Freddy Parent, 63; D. Lewis, 62, Yastrzemski, 59.

Home Runs. T. Williams, 521; Yastrzemski, 452; Rice, 382; Evans, 379; Vaughn, 230; Doerr, 223; Foxx, 222; Petrocelli, 210; Jensen, 170; Tony Conigliaro, 162; Fisk, 162; G. Scott, 154; R. Smith, 149; Malzone, 131; Greenwell, 130; Lynn, 124, V. Stephens, 122; Cronin, 119; Tony Armas, 113; Dick Gernert, 101.

Extra-Base Hits. Yastrzemski, 1,157; T. Williams, 1,117; Evans, 925; Rice, 834; Doerr, 693; Boggs, 554; Petrocelli, 469; DiMaggio, 452; Foxx, 448; Vaughn, 439; Greenwell, 433; Hooper, 408; Fisk, 402; Malzone, 386; R. Smith, 386; Speaker, 386.

Total Bases. Yastrzemski, 5,539; T. Williams, 4,884; Rice, 4,129; Evans, 4,128; Doerr, 3,270; Boggs, 2,869; DiMaggio, 2,363; Hooper, 2,303; Petrocelli, 2,263; Greenwell, 2,141; Malzone, 2,123; Vaughn, 2,074; Foxx, 1,988; Speaker, 1,898; Cronin, 1,883; Fisk, 1,856; Jensen, 1,842.

Slugging Percentage. T. Williams, .634; Foxx, .605; Nomar Garciaparra, .552; Vaughn, .542; Lynn, .520; Rice, .502; V. Stephens, .492; T. Conigliaro, .488; Cronin, .484; Speaker, .482; Fisk, .481; John Valentin, .472; Jensen, .478; Evans, .473; R. Smith, .471; Greenwell, .463; Boggs, .462; Yastrzemski, .462.

Stolen Bases. Hooper, 300; Speaker, 266; Yastrzemski, 168; Heinie Wagner, 141; L. Gardner, 134; Parent, 129; Tommy Harper, 107; Bill Werber, 107; C. Stahl, 105; J. Collins, 102; D. Lewis, 102; DiMaggio, 100; Jerry Remy, 98; Jensen, 95; Ellis Burks, 93; R. Smith, 84; Greenwell, 80.

Walks. T. Williams, 2,019; Yastrzemski, 1,845; Evans, 1,337; Boggs, 1,004; Hooper, 826; Doerr, 809; DiMaggio, 750; Rice, 670; Petrocelli, 661; Foxx, 624; Cronin, 585; Jensen, 585; Pesky, 581; Goodman, 561; Vaughn, 519; Greenwell, 460; Speaker, 459.

On-Base Percentage. T. Williams, .483; Foxx, .429; Boggs, .428; Speaker, .414; Runnels, .408; Pesky, .401; Vaughn, .394; Cronin, .394; B. Johnson, .387; Goodman, .386; DiMaggio, .383; Lynn, .382; Yastrzemski, .379; Jensen, .374; Evans, .370; Valentin, .369; Greenwell, .368.

TOP SINGLE-SEASON BATTING LEADERS

Games. Jim Rice, 163 (1978); Bill Buckner, 162 (1985); Dwight Evans, 162 (1984); Evans, 162 (1982); Carl Yastrzemski, 162 (1969); George Scott, 162 (1966); Mo Vaughn, 161 (1996); Yastrzemski, 161 (1970); Yastrzemski, 161

(1967); Rice, 160 (1977); Yastrzemski, 160 (1966); Yastrzemski, 160 (1962); Butch Hobson, 159 (1977); G. Scott, 159 (1967).

At Bats. Nomar Garciaparra, 684 (1997); Rice, 677 (1978); Buckner, 673 (1985); Rick Burleson, 663 (1977); Doc Cramer, 661 (1940); Cramer, 658 (1938); Rice, 657 (1984); Wade Boggs, 653 (1985); Dom DiMaggio, 648 (1948); Yastrzemski, 646 (1962); Chuck Schilling, 646 (1961); Tom Oliver, 646 (1930); Burleson, 644 (1980); Cramer, 643 (1936).

Runs. Ted Williams, 150 (1949); T. Williams, 142 (1946); T. Williams, 141 (1942); Jimmie Foxx, 139 (1938); Tris Speaker, 136 (1912); T. Williams, 135 (1941); T. Williams, 134 (1940); DiMaggio, 131 (1950); T. Williams, 131 (1939); Foxx, 130 (1939); Foxx, 130 (1936).

Runs Batted In. Foxx, 175 (1938); Vern Stephens, 159 (1949); T. Williams, 159 (1949); T. Williams, 145 (1939); Walt Dropo, 144 (1950); V. Stephens, 144 (1950); Vaughn, 143 (1996); Foxx, 143 (1936); Rice, 139 (1978); V. Stephens, 137 (1948); T. Williams, 137 (1942); Rice, 130 (1979).

Hits. Boggs, 240 (1985); Speaker, 222 (1912); Boggs, 214 (1988); Rice, 213 (1978); Boggs, 210 (1983); Garciaparra, 209 (1997); Johnny Pesky, 208 (1946); Vaughn, 207 (1996); Boggs, 207 (1986); Pesky, 207 (1947); Rice, 206 (1977); Vaughn, 205 (1998); Boggs, 205 (1989); Pesky, 205 (1942).

Batting Average (400 At Bats). T. Williams, .406 (1941); T. Williams, .388 (1957); Speaker, .383 (1912); Dale Alexander, .372 (1932); T. Williams, .369 (1948); Boggs, .368 (1985); Boggs, .366 (1988); Boggs, .363 (1987); Speaker, .363 (1913); Boggs, .361 (1983); Foxx, .360 (1939).

Singles. Boggs, 187 (1985); Pesky, 172 (1947); Pesky, 165 (1942); Boggs, 162 (1984); Cramer, 160 (1940); Patsy Dougherty, 160 (1903); Pesky, 159 (1946); Boggs, 158 (1988); Boggs, 154 (1983); Cramer, 154 (1938); Jerry Remy, 153 (1982); Oliver, 153 (1930).

Doubles. Earl Webb, 67 (1931); Speaker, 53 (1912); Boggs, 51 (1989); Joe Cronin, 51 (1938); John Valentin, 47 (1997); Boggs, 47 (1986); Fred Lynn, 47 (1975); George Burns, 47 (1923); Bill Buckner, 46 (1985); Speaker, 46 (1914); Jody Reed, 45 (1990); Boggs, 45 (1988); Yastrzemski, 45 (1965); Valentin, 44 (1998).

Triples. Speaker, 22 (1913); Chick Stahl, 22 (1904); Buck Freeman, 21 (1903); Freeman, 20 (1902); Larry Gardner, 19 (1914); Freeman, 19 (1904); Speaker, 18 (1914); L. Gardner, 18 (1912); Russ Scarritt, 17 (1929); Harry Hooper, 17 (1920); Jimmy Collins, 17 (1903); Freddy Parent, 17 (1903).

Home Runs. Foxx, 50 (1938); Rice, 46 (1978); Vaughn, 44 (1996); Yastrzemski, 44 (1967); Tony Armas, 43 (1984); T. Williams, 43 (1949); Dick Stuart, 42 (1963); Foxx, 41 (1936); Vaughn, 40 (1998); Yastrzemski, 40 (1970); Yastrzemski, 40 (1969).

Extra-Base Hits. Foxx, 92 (1938); Rice, 86 (1978); T. Williams, 86 (1939); Garciaparra, 85 (1997); T. Williams, 85 (1949); Rice, 84 (1979); Webb, 84 (1931); Rice, 83 (1977); T. Williams, 83 (1946); Lynn, 82 (1979); T. Williams, 81 (1947); Foxx, 81 (1936); Garciaparra, 80 (1998).

Total Bases. Rice, 406 (1978); Foxx, 398 (1938); Rice, 382 (1977); Vaughn, 370 (1996); Rice, 369 (1979); Foxx, 369 (1936); T. Williams, 368 (1949); Garciaparra, 365 (1997); Vaughn, 360 (1998); Yastrzemski, 360 (1967); Garciaparra, 353 (1998); Rice, 344 (1983); T. Williams, 344 (1939); T. Williams, 343 (1946).

Stolen Bases. Tommy Harper, 54 (1973); Speaker, 52 (1912); Speaker, 46 (1913); Otis Nixon, 42 (1994); Speaker, 42 (1914); Hooper, 40 (1910); Bill Werber, 40 (1934); Hooper, 38 (1911); Harry Lord, 36 (1909); Speaker, 35 (1910); Speaker, 35 (1909).

Walks. T. Williams, 162 (1949); T. Williams, 162 (1947); T. Williams, 156 (1946); T. Williams, 145 (1942); T. Williams, 144 (1951); T. Williams, 136 (1954); Yastrzemski, 128 (1970); T. Williams, 126 (1948); Boggs, 125 (1988); Yastrzemski, 119 (1968); T. Williams, 119 (1957); Foxx, 119 (1938).

Pinch Hits. Cronin, 18 (1943); Rick Miller, 16 (1983); Dick Williams, 16 (1963); R. Miller, 14 (1984); Lenny Green, 14 (1966); Dalton Jones, 13 (1967); D. Jones, 13 (1966); Lou Finney, 13 (1939); Bing Miller, 13 (1935); Herm Winningham, 12 (1992); Charley Maxwell, 12 (1954).

Multihomer Games. Foxx, 10 (1938); Rice, 7 (1977); Armas, 6 (1983); Rice, 6 (1983); Vaughn, 6 (1996); Carlton Fisk, 5 (1977); Fisk, 5 (1979); Yastrzemski, 5 (1967).

CAREER PITCHING LEADERS

Games. Bob Stanley, 637; Roger Clemens, 383; Ellis Kinder, 365; Cy Young, 327; Ike Delock, 322; Bill Lee, 321; Mel Parnell, 289; Greg Harris, 287; Mike Fornieles, 286; Dick Radatz, 286; Luis Tiant, 274; Sparky Lyle, 260; Joe Dobson, 259; Jack Wilson, 258; Bill Monbouquette, 254; Frank Sullivan, 252; Jack Russell, 242; Tom Brewer, 241.

Innings. Clemens, 2,776.0; C. Young, 2,728.1; Tiant, 1,774.0; Parnell, 1,752.2; Stanley, 1,707.0; Monbouquette, 1,622.0; George Winter, 1,599.2; Dobson 1,544.0; Lefty Grove, 1,539.2; Brewer, 1,509.1; F. Sullivan, 1,505.1; B. Lee, 1,504.0; Bill Dinneen, 1,501.0; Bruce Hurst, 1,459.0; Smoky Joe Wood, 1,418.0; Tex Hughson 1,375.2; Dutch Leonard, 1,359.1.

Games Started. Clemens, 382; C. Young, 297; Tiant, 238; Parnell, 232; Monbouquette, 228; Brewer, 217; Hurst, 217; Dobson, 202; F. Sullivan, 201; Dennis Eckersley, 191; Grove, 189; Willard Nixon, 177; Winter, 176; Dinneen, 174; Lee, 167; Jim Lonborg, 163.

Complete Games. C. Young, 275; Dinneen, 156; Winter, 141; J. Wood, 121; Grove, 119; Parnell, 113; Tiant, 113; Babe Ruth, 105; Clemens, 100; Hughson, 99; Leonard, 96; Ray Collins, 90; Dobson, 90; Carl Mays, 87; Howard Ehmke, 83; Wes Ferrell, 81; Brewer, 75; Red Ruffing, 73; Monbouquette, 72; F. Sullivan, 72.

Wins. Clemens, 192; C. Young, 192; Parnell, 123; Tiant, 122; J. Wood, 117; Stanley, 115; Dobson, 106; Grove, 105; Hughson, 96; Monbouquette, 96; B. Lee, 94; Brewer, 91; Leonard, 90; F. Sullivan, 90; Ruth, 89; Hurst, 88; Kinder, 86; Dinneen, 85.

Losses. C. Young, 112; Clemens, 111; Stanley, 97; Winter, 97; Ruffing, 96; Ja. Russell, 96; Monbouquette, 91; Dinneen, 85; Brewer, 82; Tiant, 81; F. Sullivan, 80; Danny MacFayden, 78; Parnell, 75; Hurst, 73; Dobson, 72; W. Nixon, 72; Delock, 70; Eckersley, 71.

Winning Percentage (100 Decisions). J. Wood (117–56), .676; Ruth (89–46), .659; Hughson (96–54), .640; Clemens (192–111), .634; C. Young (192–112), .632; Grove (105–62), .629; Kinder (86–52), .623; Parnell (123–75), .621; Jesse Tannehill (62–38), .620; W. Ferrell (62–40), .608; Tiant (122–81), .601; Dobson (106–72), .596; Mays (72–51), .585; Leonard (90–64), .584; B. Lee (94–68), .580; Ra. Collins (84–62), .575; Ray Culp (71–58), .550.

Earned Run Average (1,000 Innings). J. Wood, 1.99; C. Young, 2.00; Leonard, 2.11; Ruth, 2.19; Mays, 2.21; Ra. Collins, 2.51; Dinneen, 2.81; Winter, 2.91; Hughson, 2.94; Clemens, 3.06; Kinder, 3.28; Grove, 3.34; Tiant, 3.36; Sad Sam Jones, 3.39; F. Sullivan, 3.47; Culp, 3.50; Parnell, 3.50; Dobson, 3.57.

Strikeouts. Clemens, 2,590; C. Young, 1,341; Tiant, 1,075; Hurst, 1,043; J. Wood, 990; Monbouquette, 969; F. Sullivan, 821; Culp, 794; Lonborg, 784; Leonard, 771; Grove, 743; Brewer, 733; Parnell, 732; Eckersley, 738; Earl Wilson, 714; Hughson, 693; Stanley, 693; Dobson, 690.

Walks. Clemens, 856; Parnell, 758; Brewer, 669; Dobson, 604; W. Nixon, 530; Delock, 514; Maurice McDermott, 514; Tiant, 501; Fritz Ostermueller, 491; E. Wilson, 481; Hurst, 479; F. Sullivan, 475; Stanley, 471; Ruffing, 459; B. Lee, 448; Grove, 447.

Shutouts. Clemens, 38; C. Young, 38; J. Wood, 28; Tiant, 26; Leonard, 25; Parnell, 20; Ra. Collins, 19; Hughson, 19; S. Jones, 18; Dobson, 17; Ruth, 17; Dinneen, 16; Monbouquette, 16; George Foster, 15; Grove, 15; Mays, 14; F. Sullivan, 14; Tannehill, 14.

Ten-Strikeout Games. Clemens, 68; J. Wood, 18; Hurst, 13; Culp, 10; Lonborg, 10; Dave Morehead, 9; Tiant, 9; C. Young, 8; Monbouquette, 6; Dennis Boyd, 4; Leonard, 4; E. Wilson, 4.

Saves. Stanley, 132; Radatz, 104; Kinder, 91; Jeff Reardon, 88; Lyle, 69; Lee Smith, 58; Bill Campbell, 51; Fornieles, 48; Jeff Russell, 45; Dick

Drago, 41; Tom Burgmeier, 40; Mark Clear, 38; Delock, 31; Heathcliff
Slocumb, 31; Bob Bolin, 28; Leo Kiely, 28; John Wyatt, 28.

Relief Wins. Stanley, 85; Radatz, 49; Kinder, 39; Clear, 35; Delock, 34;
Fornieles, 31; Campbell, 28; Ja. Wilson, 26; Mike Ryba, 26; Charley Hall,
24; Earl Johnson, 24; Lyle, 22.

Relief Winning Percentage (20 Wins). Hall (24–4), .857; J. Wood
(20–8), .714; Delock (34–18), .694; E. Johnson (24–13), .649; Burgmeier
(21–12), .636; Ja. Wilson (26–17), .605; M. Ryba (26–17), .605; Clear (35–23),
.603; Campbell (28–19), .596; Radatz (49–34), .590; Stanley (85–61), .582;
Kinder (39–29), .574; Fornieles (31–23), .574.

TOP SINGLE-SEASON PITCHING LEADERS

Games. Greg Harris, 80 (1993); Dick Radatz, 79 (1964); Heathcliff
Slocumb, 75 (1996); Rob Murphy, 74 (1989); Tom Gordon, 73 (1998); Tony
Fossas, 71 (1993); Sparky Lyle, 71 (1969); Harris, 70 (1992); Mike Fornieles,
70 (1960); Bill Campbell, 69 (1977); Ellis Kinder, 69 (1953); Murphy, 68
(1990); Bob Stanley, 66 (1986); Radatz, 66 (1963).

Innings. Cy Young, 384.2 (1902); C. Young, 380 (1904); Bill Dinneen,
371.1 (1902); C. Young, 371.1 (1901); Smoky Joe Wood, 344 (1912); C. Young,
343.1 (1907); C. Young, 341.2 (1903); Dinneen, 335.2 (1904); Babe Ruth,
326.1 (1917); Ruth, 323.2 (1916).

Games Started. C. Young, 43 (1902); Dinneen, 42 (1902); C. Young, 41
(1904); C. Young, 41 (1901); Ruth, 40 (1916); Jim Lonborg, 39 (1967);
Howard Ehmke, 39 (1923); Luis Tiant, 38 (1976); Tiant, 38 (1974); Wes
Ferrell, 38 (1936); W. Ferrell, 38 (1935); Sad Sam Jones, 38 (1921); Ruth, 38
(1917); J. Wood, 38 (1912).

Complete Games. C. Young, 41 (1902); C. Young, 40 (1904); Dinneen,
39 (1902); C. Young, 38 (1901); Dinneen, 37 (1904); Ruth, 35 (1917); J. Wood,
35 (1912); C. Young, 34 (1903); C. Young, 33 (1907); Dinneen, 32 (1903);
W. Ferrell, 31 (1935); C. Young, 31 (1905); Ted Lewis, 31 (1901).

Wins. Wood, 34–5 (1912); C. Young, 33–10 (1901); C. Young, 32–11
(1902); C. Young, 28–9 (1903); C. Young, 26–16 (1904); Mel Parnell, 25–7
(1949); Dave Ferriss, 25–6 (1946); W. Ferrell, 25–14 (1935); Roger Clemens,
24–4 (1986); Ruth, 24–13 (1917).

Losses. Red Ruffing, 10–25 (1928); Ruffing, 9–22 (1929); Slim Harriss,
14–21 (1927); Joe Harris, 2–21 (1906); C. Young, 13–21 (1906); Dinneen, 21–21
(1902); Milt Gaston, 13–20 (1930); Jack Russell, 9–20 (1930); Ehmke, 9–20
(1925); S. Jones, 12–20 (1919).

Earned Run Average. Dutch Leonard, 1.00 (1914); C. Young, 1.26
(1908); J. Wood, 1.49 (1915); Ray Collins, 1.62 (1910); C. Young, 1.62 (1901);

Ernie Shore, 1.64 (1915); Rube Foster, 1.65 (1914); J. Wood, 1.68 (1910); Carl Mays, 1.74 (1917); Ruth, 1.75 (1916).

Strikeouts. Clemens, 291 (1988); J. Wood, 258 (1912); Clemens, 257 (1996); Clemens, 256 (1987); Pedro Martinez, 251 (1998); Lonborg, 246 (1967); Clemens, 241 (1991); Clemens, 238 (1986); J. Wood, 231 (1911); Clemens, 230 (1989); C. Young, 210 (1905); Clemens, 209 (1990).

Walks. Parnell, 134 (1949); Maurice McDermott, 124 (1950); Mike Torrez, 121 (1979); Don Schwall, 121 (1962); Bobo Newsom, 119 (1937); Jack Wilson, 119 (1937); W. Ferrell, 119 (1936); Ehmke, 119 (1923); Ruffing, 118 (1929); Ruth, 118 (1916).

Shutouts. J. Wood, 10 (1912); C. Young, 10 (1904); Ruth, 9 (1916); Clemens, 8 (1988); Mays, 8 (1918); Clemens, 7 (1987); Tiant, 7 (1974); Joe Bush, 7 (1918); Leonard, 7 (1914); C. Young, 7 (1903).

Ten-Strikeout Games. Clemens, 12 (1988); Clemens, 9 (1987); Martinez, 8 (1998); Clemens, 8 (1996); Clemens, 8 (1986); Lonborg, 8 (1967); Clemens, 7 (1991); J. Wood, 6 (1911); Clemens, 5 (1994); Clemens, 5 (1989); Bruce Hurst, 5 (1986); Hurst, 5 (1985); Ray Culp, 5 (1968); J. Wood, 5 (1913); J. Wood, 5 (1912); C. Young, 5 (1905).

Consecutive Complete-Game Wins. C. Young, 10 (1902); J. Wood, 9 (1912); Bush, 9 (1921); D. Ferriss, 9 (1946); C. Young, 8 (1901); Jesse Tannehill, 8 (1905); J. Wood, 8 (1912); Elmer Myers, 8 (1920); Lefty Grove, 8, (1939); Allan Russell, 7 (1919); D. Ferriss, 7 (1945); Tiant, 7 (1972); Dennis Eckersley, 7 (1979).

Saves. Gordon, 46 (1998); Jeff Reardon, 40 (1991); Jeff Russell, 33 (1993); Stanley, 33 (1983); Campbell, 31 (1977); Lee Smith, 29 (1988); Radatz, 29 (1964); Reardon, 27 (1992); Kinder, 27 (1953); L. Smith, 25 (1989); Radatz, 25 (1963).

Home Runs Allowed. Tim Wakefield, 38 (1996); Earl Wilson, 37 (1964); Hurst, 35 (1987); Rick Wise, 34 (1975); Bill Monbouquette, 34 (1964); Gene Conley, 33 (1961); John Tudor, 32 (1983); Tiant, 32 (1973); Monbouquette, 32 (1965); Danny Darwin, 31 (1993); Hurst, 31 (1985); Eckersley, 31 (1982); Marty Pattin, 31 (1973); Monbouquette, 31 (1963).

Relief Wins. Radatz, 16 (1964); Radatz, 15 (1963); Mark Clear, 14 (1982); Campbell, 13 (1977); Stanley, 12 (1982); Stanley, 12 (1978); Ike Delock, 11 (1956); Joe Heving, 11 (1939); Stanley, 10 (1981); Dick Drago, 10 (1979); John Wyatt, 10 (1967); Fornieles, 10 (1960); Ellis Kinder, 10 (1953); Kinder, 10 (1951).

TWENTY-GAME WINNERS

Cy Young—1901 (33–10), 1902 (32–11), 1903 (28–9), 1904 (26–16), 1907 (21–15), and 1908 (21–11). Bill Dinneen—1902 (21–21), 1903 (21–13), and 1904

(23–14). Tom Hughes—1903 (20–7). Jesse Tannehill—1904 (21–11) and 1905 (22–9). Joe Wood—1911 (23–17) and 1912 (34–5). Hugh Bedient—1912 (20–9). Buck O'Brien—1912 (20–13). Ray Collins—1914 (20–13). Babe Ruth—1916 (23–12) and 1917 (24–13). Carl Mays—1917 (22–9) and 1918 (21–13). Sam Jones—1921 (23–16). Howard Ehmke—1923 (20–17). Wes Ferrell—1935 (25–14) and 1936 (20–15). Lefty Grove—1935 (20–12). Tex Hughson—1942 (22–6) and 1946 (20–11). Dave Ferriss—1945 (21–10) and 1946 (25–6). Mel Parnell—1949 (25–7) and 1953 (21–8). Ellis Kinder—1949 (23–6). Bill Monbouquette—1963 (20–10). Jim Lonborg—1967 (22–9). Luis Tiant—1973 (20–13), 1974 (22–13), and 1976 (21–12). Dennis Eckersley— 1978 (20–8). Roger Clemens—1986 (24–4), 1987 (20–9), and 1990 (21–6).

MOST GAMES BY POSITION

Designated hitter—Jim Rice (1974–89), 530. First Base —George Scott (1966–71, '77–79), 988. Second Base—Bobby Doerr (1937–51), 1,853. Shortstop—Everett Scott (1914–21), 1,093. Third Base—Wade Boggs (1982–92), 1,521. Outfield—Ted Williams (1939–60), 2,151; Dwight Evans (1972–90), 2,079; Carl Yastrzemski (1961–83), 2,076. Catcher—Carlton Fisk (1969, 1971–80), 990. Pitcher—Bob Stanley (1977–89), 637 games. Roger Clemens (1984–96), 382 starts.

CONSECUTIVE-GAME STREAKS

Everett Scott, 832—6/20/16 to 10/2/21. Buck Freeman, 535—7/27/01 to 6/6/05. Frank Malzone, 475—5/21/57 to 6/7/60. Candy LaChance, 448— 4/19/02 to 4/28/05. Freddy Parent, 413—4/26/01 to 9/25/03—and 408, 5/23/04 to 9/4/06. Dwight Evans, 380—10/4/80 to 8/6/83. Vern Stephens, 360— 4/19/48 to 8/28/50. Bobby Doerr, 352—7/19/42 to 8/22/44. Carl Yastrzemski, 350—7/28/68 to 8/21/70.

TWO HUNDRED HITS IN A SEASON

Tris Speaker—1912 (222). Billy Werber—1934 (200). Joe Vosmik—1938 (201). Doc Cramer—1940 (200). Johnny Pesky—1942 (205), 1946 (208), and 1947 (207). Jim Rice—1977 (206), 1978 (213), 1979 (201), and 1986 (200). Wade Boggs—1983 (210), 1984 (203), 1985 (240), 1986 (207), 1987 (200), 1988 (214), and 1989 (205). Bill Buckner—1985 (201). Mo Vaughn—1996 (207). Nomar Garciaparra—1997 (209).

CONSECUTIVE-GAME HITTING STREAKS

Buck Freeman—1902 (26). Tris Speaker—1912 (30, 20, and 20) and 1913 (22).
Babe Ruth—1919 (20). George Burns—1922 (23). Del Pratt—1922 (23). Ike
Boone—1925 (20). Buddy Myer—1928 (23). Smead Jolley—1932 (20). Ted
Williams—1941 (23). Bobby Doerr—1943 (21). George Metkovich—1944 (25).
Johnny Pesky—1947 (26). Dom DiMaggio—1942 (22), 1949 (34), and 1951
(27). Eddie Bressoud—1964 (20). Denny Doyle—1975 (22). Fred Lynn—1975
(20) and 1979 (20). Jim Rice—1980 (21). Mike Easler—1984 (20). Wade
Boggs—1985 (28), 1986 (20), and 1987 (25). Mike Greenwell—1989 (21).
Nomar Garciaparra—1997 (30) and 1998 (24). Reggie Jefferson—1997 (22).

HITTING FOR THE CYCLE

Buck Freeman—6/21/03 at Cleveland. Pat Dougherty—7/29/03 versus New
York. Tris Speaker—6/9/12 at St. Louis. Roy Carlyle—7/21/25 at Chicago.
Moose Solters—8/19/34 at Detroit. Joe Cronin—8/2/40 at Detroit. Leon
Culberson—7/3/43 at Cleveland. Bobby Doerr—5/17/44 versus St. Louis
and 5/13/47 versus Chicago. Bob Johnson—7/6/44 versus Detroit. Ted
Williams—7/21/46 versus St. Louis. Lu Clinton—7/13/62 at Kansas City.
Carl Yastrzemski—5/14/65 versus Detroit. Bob Watson—9/15/79 at
Baltimore. Fred Lynn—5/13/80 versus Minnesota. Dwight Evans—6/28/84
versus Seattle. Rich Gedman—9/18/85 versus Toronto. Mike Greenwell—
9/14/88 versus Baltimore. Scott Cooper—4/12/94 at Kansas City. John
Valentin—6/6/96 versus Chicago.

MOST VALUABLE PLAYERS

Tris Speaker—1912 (.383 average, 10 home runs, and 98 runs batted in).
Jimmie Foxx—1938 (.349, 50, 175). Ted Williams—1946 (.342, 38, 123) and
1949 (.343, 43, 159). Jackie Jensen—1958 (.286, 35, 122). Carl Yastrzemski—
1967 (.326, 44, 121). Fred Lynn—1975 (.331, 21, 105). Jim Rice—1978 (.315,
46, 139). Roger Clemens—1986 (24–4, 2.48 earned run average). Mo
Vaughn—1995 (.300, 39, 126).

ROOKIES OF THE YEAR

Walt Dropo—1950 (.322, 34 home runs, and 144 runs batted in.) Don
Schwall—1961 (15–7, 3.22 earned run average). Carlton Fisk—1972 (.293, 22,
61). Fred Lynn—1975 (.331, 21, 105). Nomar Garciaparra—1997 (.306, 30, 98).

BATTING CHAMPIONS

Dale Alexander—1932 (.367, including 23 games with Detroit). Jimmie Foxx—1938 (.349). Ted Williams—1941 (.406), 1942 (.356), 1947 (.343), 1948 (.369), 1957 (.388), and 1958 (.328). Billy Goodman—1950 (.354). Pete Runnels—1960 (.320) and 1962 (.326). Carl Yastrzemski—1963 (.321), 1967 (.326), and 1968 (.301). Fred Lynn—1979 (.333). Carney Lansford—1981 (.336). Wade Boggs—1983 (.361), 1985 (.368), 1986 (.357), 1987 (.363), and 1988 (.366).

HOME RUN CHAMPIONS

Buck Freeman—1903 (13). Jake Stahl—1910 (10). Tris Speaker—1912 (12, tie with Frank Baker). Babe Ruth—1918 (11, tie with Tilly Walker) and 1919 (29). Jimmie Foxx—1939 (35). Ted Williams—1941 (37), 1942 (36), 1947 (32), and 1949 (43). Tony Conigliaro—1965 (32). Carl Yastrzemski—1967 (44, tie with Harmon Killebrew). Jim Rice—1977 (39), 1978 (46), and 1983 (39). Dwight Evans—1981 (22, tie with Tony Armas, Bobby Grich, and Eddie Murray). Tony Armas—1984 (43).

RUNS BATTED IN CHAMPIONS

Buck Freeman—1902 (121) and 1903 (104). Babe Ruth—1919 (112). Jimmie Foxx—1938 (175). Ted Williams—1939 (145), 1942 (137), 1947 (114), and 1949 (159, tie with Vern Stephens). Vern Stephens—1949 (159, tie with Ted Williams) and 1950 (144, tie with Walt Dropo). Walt Dropo—1950 (144, tie with Vern Stephens). Jackie Jensen—1955 (116, tie with Ray Boone), 1958 (122), and 1959 (112). Dick Stuart—1963 (118). Carl Yastrzemski—1967 (121). Ken Harrelson—1968 (109). Jim Rice—1978 (139) and 1983 (126, tie with Cecil Cooper). Tony Armas—1984 (123). Mo Vaughn—1995 (126, tie with Albert Belle).

EARNED RUN AVERAGE CHAMPIONS

Cy Young—1901 (1.62). H. Dutch Leonard—1914 (1.00). Joe Wood—1915 (1.49). Babe Ruth—1916 (1.75). Lefty Grove—1935 (2.70), 1936 (2.81), 1938 (3.07), and 1939 (2.54). Mel Parnell—1949 (2.78). Luis Tiant—1972 (1.91). Roger Clemens—1986 (2.48), 1990 (1.93), 1991 (2.62), and 1992 (2.41).

STRIKEOUT CHAMPIONS

Cy Young—1901 (158). Tex Hughson—1942 (113, tie with Bobo Newsom). Jim Lonborg—1967 (246). Roger Clemens—1988 (291), 1991 (241), and 1996 (257).

CY YOUNG AWARD WINNERS

Jim Lonborg—1967 (22–9, 3.16 earned run average). Roger Clemens—1986 (24–4, 2.84), 1987 (20–9, 2.97), and 1991 (18–10, 2.62).

LEAGUE-LEADING ATTENDANCE

At Huntington Avenue Grounds: 1904, 623,295. At Fenway Park: 1914, 481,359. 1915, 539,885. 1967, 1,727,832. 1969, 1,833,246. 1970, 1,595,278. 1971, 1,678,732. 1974, 1,566,411. 1975, 1,748,587.

NO-HIT GAMES BY RED SOX

1904—May 5, Cy Young versus Philadelphia, 3–0; August 17, Jesse Tannehill at Chicago, 6–0. 1905—September 27, Bill Dinneen versus Chicago, 2–0. 1908—June 30, Young at New York, 8–0. 1911—July 29, Joe Wood versus St. Louis, 5–0. 1916—June 21, George Foster versus New York, 2–0; August 30, Dutch Leonard versus St. Louis, 4–0. 1917—June 23, Ernie Shore versus Washington, 4–0. 1918—June 3, Leonard at Detroit, 5–0. 1923—September 7, Howard Ehmke at Philadelphia, 4–0. 1956—July 14, Mel Parnell versus Chicago, 4–0. 1962—June 26, Earl Wilson versus Los Angeles, 2–0; August 1, Bill Monbouquette at Chicago, 1–0. 1965— September 16, Dave Morehead versus Cleveland, 2–0. 1992—April 12, Matt Young at Cleveland, 1–2.

NO-HIT GAMES AGAINST RED SOX

1908—September 18, Bob "Dusty" Rhoads at Cleveland. Boston lost, 2–1. 1911—August 27, Ed Walsh at Chicago, 5–0. 1917—April 24, George Mogridge, New York (home), 2–1. 1920—July 1, Walter Johnson, Washington (home), 1–0. 1926—August 21, Ted Lyons, Chicago (home), 6–0. 1931—August 8, Bob Burke at Washington, 5–0. 1934—September 18, Bobo Newsom at St. Louis, pitched nine hitless innings, allowed a hit in the tenth inning. Boston won, 2–1. 1951—September 28, Allie Reynolds at New York, 8–0. 1958—July 20, Jim Bunning, Detroit (home), 3–0. 1967— August 6, Dean Chance at Minnesota, 2–0, five innings, rain. 1968—April 27, Tom Phoebus at Baltimore, 6–0. 1983—July 4, Dave Righetti at New York, 4–0. 1993—April 22, Chris Bosio at Seattle, 7–0.

GOLD GLOVE AWARD WINNERS

Frank Malzone—third base, 1957, '58, '59. Jim Piersall—center field, 1958.

Jackie Jensen—right field, 1959. Carl Yastrzemski—outfield, 1963, '65, '67, '68, '69, '71, '77. George Scott—first base, 1967, '68, '71. Reggie Smith—outfield, 1968. Carlton Fisk—catcher, 1972. Doug Griffin—second base, 1972. Fred Lynn—outfield, 1975, '78, '79, '80. Dwight Evans—outfield, 1976, '78, '79, '81, '82, '83, '84, '85. Rick Burleson—shortstop, 1979. Mike Boddicker—pitcher, 1990. Ellis Burks—outfield, 1990. Tony Pena—catcher, 1991.

ALL-TIME TEAMS

Voted by Fans in 1969

Catcher: Birdie Tebbetts. First base: Jimmie Foxx. Second base: Bobby Doerr. Shortstop: Joe Cronin. Third base: Frank Malzone. Outfield: Ted Williams, Carl Yastrzemski, and Tris Speaker. Right-handed pitcher: Cy Young. Left-handed pitcher: Lefty Grove. Greatest player: Ted Williams.

Voted by Fans in 1982

First Team. Catcher: Carlton Fisk. First base: Jimmie Foxx. Second base: Bobby Doerr. Shortstop: Rick Burleson. Third base: Rico Petrocelli. Outfield: Ted Williams, Carl Yastrzemski, and Dwight Evans. Right-handed pitcher: Cy Young. Left-handed pitcher: Babe Ruth. Relief pitcher: Dick Radatz. Manager: Dick Williams. Greatest player: Ted Williams.

Second team. Catcher: Birdie Tebbetts. First base: George Scott. Second base: Jerry Remy. Shortstop: Johnny Pesky. Third base: Frank Malzone. Outfield: Jim Rice, Dom DiMaggio, and Fred Lynn. Right-handed pitcher: Luis Tiant. Left-handed pitcher: Lefty Grove. Relief pitcher: Sparky Lyle. Manager: Joe Cronin.

RED SOX IN THE HALL OF FAME

Fourteen members of the Baseball Hall of Fame played a major part of their careers with the Red Sox. In order of their admission: Babe Ruth—pitcher, outfield, 1914–19, 391 games with the Red Sox (entered 1936). Tris Speaker—outfield, 1907–15, 1,065 games (1937). Cy Young—pitcher, 1901–08, 327 games (1937). Jimmy Collins—third base, 1901–07, 741 games (1945). Lefty Grove—pitcher, 1934–41, 214 games (1947). Herb Pennock—pitcher, 1915–22, 201 games (1948). Jimmie Foxx—first base, 1936–42, 887 games (1951). Joe Cronin—shortstop, 1935–45, 1,134 (1956). Ted Williams—outfield, 1939–60,

2,292 games (1966). Red Ruffing—pitcher, 1924–30, 237 games (1967). Harry Hooper—outfield, 1909–20, 1,646 games (1971). Rick Ferrell—catcher, 1933–37, 522 games (1984). Bobby Doerr—second base, 1937–51, 1,865 games (1986). Carl Yastrzemski—outfield, 1961–83, 3,308 games (1989).

The above are joined in Cooperstown by two longtime Red Sox executives: Eddie Collins, 1933–51 (entered 1939), and Thomas A. Yawkey, 1933–76 (1980). Numerous other Hall of Famers have worn a Red Sox uniform. In order of admission: Jesse Burkett—outfield, 1905, 149 games (entered 1946). Orlando Cepeda—designated hitter, 1973, 142 games (1999). Jack Chesbro—pitcher, 1909, 1 game (1946). Al Simmons—outfield, 1943, 40 games (1953). Heinie Manush—outfield, 1936, 82 games (1964). Waite Hoyt—pitcher, 1919–20, 35 games (1969). Lou Boudreau—shortstop, 1951–52, 86 games (1970). George Kell—second base, outfield, 1952–54, 235 games (1983). Juan Marichal—pitcher, 1974, 11 games (1983). Luis Aparicio—shortstop, 1971–73, 367 games (1984). Ferguson Jenkins—pitcher, 1976–77, 58 games (1992). Tom Seaver—pitcher, 1986, 16 games (1992).

Ten Hall of Famers have managed the Red Sox. In order of admission: Cy Young—1907, 7 games (entered 1937). Jimmy Collins—1901–06, 864 games (1945). Hugh Duffy—1921–22, 308 games (1945). Frank Chance—1923, 154 games (1946). Ed Barrow—1918–20, 418 games (1953). Joe Cronin—1935–47, 2,007 games (1956). Joe McCarthy—1948–50, 372 games (1957). Lou Boudreau—1952–54, 463 games (1970). Bucky Harris—1934, 153 games (1975). Billy Herman—1964–66, 310 games (1975).

ALL-STAR GAMES AT FENWAY PARK

In 1999, the Red Sox host the last All-Star Game of the American Century, and the third ever played at Fenway Park. The first was on July 9, 1946: the American League blanked the Nationals, 12–0, in a game recalled for the Splendid Splinter's two home runs, the latter off Rip Sewell's blooper pitch, two singles, a walk, four runs scored, and five batted in. Seven other Sox made the 1946 All-Star team: Johnny Pesky, Dom DiMaggio, Bobby Doerr, Rudy York, Hal Wagner, Dave Ferriss, and Mickey Harris.

From 1958 to 1962, the majors held two All-Star Games per year. In 1961, Fenway hosted the second set, which was stopped by rain after nine innings with the score tied, 1–1. Red Sox rookie pitcher Don Schwall allowed all five hits and the only National League run in three innings. Other Sox all-stars that year were pitcher Mike Fornieles and manager Mike Higgins, who served as a coach.

ALL-STAR GAME CHOICES

Mike Andrews, second base, 1969; Luis Aparicio, 1971, '72; Tony Armas, out-
fielder, 1984; Del Baker, coach, 1947; Gary Bell, pitcher, 1968; Wade Boggs,
third base, 1985, '86, '87, '88, '89, '90, '91, '92; Lou Boudreau, coach, 1953;
Eddie Bressoud, shortstop, 1964; Tom Brewer, pitcher, 1956; Don Bryant,
coach, 1976; Tom Burgmeier, pitcher, 1980; Ellis Burks, outfielder, 1990;
Rick Burleson, shortstop, 1977, '78, '79; Bill Campbell, pitcher, 1977; Mark
Clear, pitcher, 1982; Roger Clemens, pitcher, 1986, '88, '90, '91, '92; Eddie
Collins, coach, 1933; Tony Conigliaro, outfielder, 1967; Scott Cooper, third
base, 1993, '94; Roger Cramer, outfielder, 1937, '38, '39, '40; Joe Cronin,
manager, coach, shortstop, 1935, '36, '37, '38, '39, '40, '41, '44, '47 (honorary
AL captain, '83); Ray Culp, pitcher, 1969; Tom Daley, coach, 1940; Dom
DiMaggio, outfielder, 1941, '42, '46, '49, '50, '51, '52; Job Dobson, pitcher,
1948; Bobby Doerr, second base, 1941, '42, '43, '44, '46, '47, '48, '50, '51 (honorary AL captain, '88); Walt Dropo, first base, 1950; Dennis Eckersley,
pitcher, 1982; Dwight Evans, outfielder, 1978, '81, '87; Rick Ferrell, catcher,
1933, '34, '35, '36; Dave Ferriss, 1946; Lou Finney, outfielder, 1940; Bill
Fischer, coach, 1987; Carlton Fisk, catcher, 1972, '73, '74, '76, '77, '78, '80;
Mike Fornieles, pitcher, 1961; Pete Fox, outfielder, 1944; Jimmie Foxx, third
base, first base, outfielder, 1936, '37, '38, '39, '40, '41; Nomar Garciaparra,
shortstop, 1997, '98; Rich Gedman, catcher, 1985, '86; Billy Goodman, first
base, second base, 1949, '53; Tom Gordon, pitcher, 1998; Mike Greenwell,
outfielder, 1988, '89; Lefty Grove, pitcher, 1935, '36, '37, '38, '39; Erik
Hanson, pitcher, 1995; Ken Harrelson, outfielder, 1968; Mickey Harris,
pitcher, 1946; Mike Higgins, coach, 1961 second game; Tex Hughson,
pitcher, 1942, '43, '44; Bruce Hurst, pitcher, 1987; Jackie Jensen, outfielder,
1955, '58; Bob Johnson, outfielder, 1944; Darrell Johnson, manager, 1976;
Oscar Judd, pitcher, 1943; George Kell, third base, 1952, '53; Bill Lee,
pitcher, 1973; Jim Lonborg, pitcher, 1967; Fred Lynn, outfielder, 1975, '76,
'77, '78, '79, '80; Frank Malzone, third base, 1957, '58, '59, '59, '60, '60, '63,
'64; Felix Mantilla, second base, 1965; Pedro Martinez, pitcher, 1998; John
McNamara, manager, coach, 1986, '87; Bill Monbouquette, pitcher, 1960,
'60, '62, '63; Joe Morgan, coach, 1989; Jerry Moses, catcher, 1970; Mel
Parnell, pitcher, 1949, '51; Johnny Pesky, shortstop, coach, 1946, '63; Rico
Petrocelli, shortstop, 1967, '69; Jimmy Piersall, outfielder, 1954, '56; Dick
Radatz, pitcher, 1963, '64; Jeff Reardon, pitcher, 1991; Jerry Remy, second
base, 1978; Jim Rice, outfielder, 1977, '78, '79, '80, '83, '84, '85, '86; Pete
Runnels, first base, second base, 1959, '59, '60, '60, '62; Jose Santiago,
pitcher, 1968; Don Schwall, pitcher, 1961; George Scott, first base, 1966,
'77; Sonny Siebert, pitcher, 1971; Reggie Smith, outfielder, 1969, '72;

Bob Stanley, pitcher, 1979, '83; Vern Stephens, shortstop, third base, 1948, '49, '50, '51; Frank Sullivan, pitcher, 1955, '56; Birdie Tebbetts, catcher, 1948, '49; Luis Tiant, pitcher, 1974, '76; Mo Vaughn, first base, 1995, '96, '98; Mickey Vernon, first base, 1956; Hal Wagner, catcher, 1946; Sammy White, catcher, 1953; Dick Williams, manager, 1968; Ted Williams, outfielder, 1940, '41, '42, '46, '47, '48, '49, '50, '51, '54, '55, '56, '57, '58, '59, '59, '60, '60; Carl Yastrzemski, outfielder, first base, 1963, '65, '66, '67, '68, '69, '70, '71, '72, '73, '74, '75, '76, '77, '78, '79, '82, '83 (honorary captain, '89); Rudy York, first base, 1946; Don Zimmer, coach, 1978.

Italics indicates started game. From 1947 to 1957 and since 1970, teams were chosen by vote of fans. Two games were played each year from 1959 to 1962.

PLAYOFF RECORD

1948. History will little note—though Braves and Red Sox fans will long remember—how Lou Boudreau voided an all-Boston World Series. The Indians' player-manager clubbed two home runs against the Sox in the American League's first-ever playoff game.

Monday, October 4		R	H	E
Cleveland	100 410 011	8	13	1
Boston	100 002 000	3	5	1

Bearden (W) and Hegan. Galehouse (L), Kinder (4) and Tebbetts. HR: Boudreau (2), Keltner, Doerr. T: 2.24. A: 33,957.

1975. For three years, the champion Oakland A's had swaggered. Versus Boston, they encountered shock. The Red Sox wrote a new version of *The Twilight of the Gods* by sweeping the best-of-five Championship Series.

Game 1. Saturday, Oct. 4		R	H	E
Oakland	000 000 010	1	3	4
Boston	200 000 50x	7	8	3

Holtzman (L), Lindblad (7), Bosman (7), Abbott (8) and Tenace. Tiant (W) and Fisk. HR: None. T: 2.40 A: 35,578.

Game 2. Sunday, Oct. 5		R	H	E
Oakland	200 100 000	3	10	0
Boston	000 301 11x	6	12	0

Blue, Todd (4), Fingers (5-L) and Fosse, Tenace (7). Cleveland, Moret (6-W), Drago (7-SV) and Fisk. HR: Jackson, Yastrzemski, Petrocelli. T: 2.27. A: 35,578.

Game 3. Tuesday, Oct. 7		R	H	E
Boston	000 130 010	5	11	1
Oakland	000 001 020	3	6	2

Wise (W), Drago (8-sv) and Fisk. Holtzman (L), Todd (5), Lindblad (5) and Tenace. HR: None. T: 2.30 A: 49,358.

1978. Where were you when these ancient rivals dueled for the AL East pennant? Anyone who can't remember should go to jail, pay $200, then serve time in the Bobby Sprowl Fantasy Camp.

Monday, October 2		R	H	E
New York	000 000 410	5	8	0
Boston	010 001 020	4	11	0

Guidry (W), Gossage (7-sv) and Munson. Torrez (L), Stanley (7), Hassler (8), Drago (8) and Fisk. HR: Yastrzemski, Dent, Jackson. T: 2.52. A: 32,925.

1986. Dave Henderson's swing still stirs the memory. In a bizarre, schizophrenic classic, the Bosox rallied to beat California in the best-of-seven Championship Series and win their first pennant since 1975.

Game 1. Tuesday, Oct. 7		R	H	E
California	041 000 030	8	11	0
Boston	000 001 000	1	5	1

Witt (W) and Boone. Clemens (L), Sambito (8), Stanley (8) and Gedman. HR: None. T: 2.52. A: 32,993.

Game 2. Wednesday, Oct. 8		R	H	E
California	000 110 000	2	11	3
Boston	110 010 33x	9	13	2

McCaskill (L), Lucas (8), Corbett (8) and Boone. Hurst (W) and Gedman. HR: Joyner, Rice. T: 2.47. A: 32,786.

Game 3. Friday, Oct. 10		R	H	E
Boston	010 000 020	3	9	1
California	000 001 31x	5	8	0

Boyd (L), Sambito (7), Schiraldi (8) and Gedman. Candelaria (W), Moore (8-sv) and Boone. HR: Schofield, Pettis. T: 2.48. A: 64,206.

Game 4. Saturday, Oct. 11		R	H	E
Boston	000 001 020 00	3	6	1
California	000 000 003 01	4	11	2

Clemens, Schiraldi (9-L) and Gedman. Sutton, Lucas (7), Ruhle (7), Finley (8), Corbett (8-W) and Boone, Narron (10). HR: DeCinces. T: 3.50. A: 64,223.

Game 5. Sunday, Oct. 12		R	H	E
Boston	020 000 004 01	7	12	0
California	001 002 201 00	6	13	0

Hurst, Stanley (7), Sambito (9), Crawford (9-W), Schiraldi (11-sv) and Gedman. Witt, Lucas (9), Moore (9-L), Finley (11) and Boone. HR: Gedman, Boone, Grich, Henderson. T: 3.54. A: 64,223.

Game 6. Tuesday, Oct. 14		R	H	E
California	200 000 110	4	11	1
Boston	205 010 20x	10	16	1

McCaskill (L), Lucas (3), Corbett (4), Finley (7) and Boone, Narron (8). Boyd (W), Stanley (8) and Gedman. HR: Downing. T: 3.23. A: 32,998.

Game 7. Wednesday, Oct. 15		R	H	E
California	000 000 010	1	6	2
Boston	030 400 10x	8	8	1

Candelaria (L), Sutton (4), Moore (8) and Boone. Clemens (W), Schiraldi (8) and Gedman. HR: Rice, Evans. T: 2.39 A: 33,001.

1988. The Oakland A's had not won a pennant since 1974—that is, until they met the Red Sox in the Championship Series. The contest was no-contest: Oakland swept the Olde Towne Team.

Game 1. Wednesday, Oct. 5		R	H	E
Oakland	000 100 010	2	6	0
Boston	000 000 100	1	6	0

Stewart, Honeycutt (7-W), Eckersley (8-sv) and Steinbach, Hassey (8). Hurst (L) and Gedman. HR: Canseco. T: 2.44. A: 34,101.

Game 2. Thursday, Oct. 6		R	H	E
Oakland	000 000 301	4	10	1
Boston	000 002 100	3	4	1

Davis, Cadaret (7), Nelson (7-W), Eckersley (9-sv) and Hassey. Clemens, Stanley (8), Smith (8-L) and Gedman. HR: Canseco, Gedman. T: 3.14. A: 34,605.

Game 3. Saturday, Oct. 8

		R	H	E
Boston	320 000 100	6	12	0
Oakland	042 010 12x	10	15	1

Boddicker (L), Gardner (3), Stanley (8) and Gedman. Welch, Nelson (2-W), Young (6), Plunk (7), Honeycutt (7), Eckersley (8-sv) and Hassey. HR: Greenwell, McGwire, Lansford, Hassey, Henderson. T: 3.14. A: 49,261.

Game 4. Sunday, Oct. 9

		R	H	E
Boston	000 001 000	1	4	0
Oakland	101 000 02x	4	10	1

Hurst (L), Smithson (5) and Gedman. Stewart (W), Honeycutt (8), Eckersley (9-sv) and Steinbach, Hassey (9). HR: Canseco. T: 2.55. A: 49,406.

1990. For the second straight time, the defending champion A's swept the Sox in the Championship Series—their prize, a third consecutive pennant.

Game 1. Saturday, Oct. 6

		R	H	E
Oakland	000 000 117	9	13	0
Boston	000 100 000	1	5	1

Stewart (W), Eckersley (9) and Steinbach. Clemens, Anderson (7-L), Bolton (8), Gray (8), Lamp (9), Murphy (9) and Pena. HR: Boggs. T: 3.26. A: 35,192.

Game 2. Sunday, Oct. 7

		R	H	E
Oakland	000 100 102	4	13	1
Boston	001 000 000	1	6	0

Welch (W), Honeycutt (8), Eckersley (8-sv) and Hassey. Kiecker, Harris (6-L), Anderson (7), Reardon (8) and Pena. HR: None. T: 3.42. A: 35,070.

Game 3. Tuesday, Oct. 9

		R	H	E
Boston	010 000 000	1	8	3
Oakland	000 202 00x	4	6	0

Boddicker (L) and Pena. Moore (W), Nelson (7), Honeycutt (8), Eckersley (9-sv) and Steinbach. HR: None. T: 2.47. A: 49,026.

Game 4. Wednesday, Oct. 10

		R	H	E
Boston	000 000 001	1	4	1
Oakland	030 000 00x	3	6	0

Clemens (L), Bolton (2), Gray (5), Anderson (8) and Pena. Stewart (W), Honeycutt (9-sv) and Steinbach. HR: None. T: 3.02. A: 49,052.

1995. In baseball's first year of the wild card/expanded playoff format, Cleveland darned the Red Sox in three straight games in the inaugural best-of-five Division Series.

Game 1. Tuesday, Oct. 3		R	H	E
Boston	002 000 010 010 0	4	11	2
Cleveland	000 003 000 010 1	5	10	2

Clemens, Cormier (8), Belinda (8), Stanton (8), Aguilera (11), Maddux (11), Smith (12-L) and Macfarlane, Hasselman (9). D. Martinez, Tavarez (7), Assenmacher (8), Plunk (8), Mesa (10), Poole (11), Hill (12-W) and Alomar, Pena (11). HR: Valentin, Alicea, Naehring, Belle, Pena. T: 5.01. A: 44,218.

Game 2. Wednesday, Oct. 4		R	H	E
Boston	000 000 000	0	3	1
Cleveland	000 002 02x	4	4	2

Hanson (L) and Macfarlane. Hershiser (W), Tavarez (8), Assenmacher (8), Mesa (8) and Alomar. HR: Murray. T: 2.33. A: 44,264.

Game 3. Friday, Oct. 6		R	H	E
Cleveland	021 005 000	8	11	2
Boston	000 100 010	2	7	1

Nagy (W), Tavarez (8), Assenmacher (9) and Alomar, Pena (9). Wakefield (L), Cormier (6), Maddux (6), Hudson (9) and Macfarlane. HR: Thome. T: 3.18. A: 34,211.

1998. The Indians again won the Division Series to hail the golden anniversary of the AL's first playoff—like 1948, beating the Red Sox in October at Fenway Park.

Game 1. Tuesday, Sept. 29		R	H	E
Boston	300 032 030	11	12	0
Cleveland	000 002 100	3	7	0

Martinez (W), Corsi (8) and Hatteberg. Wright (L), Jones (5), Reed (8), Poole (8), Shuey (8), Assenmacher (9) and Alomar. HR: Vaughn (2), Garciaparra, Lofton, and Thome. T: 3.16. A: 45,185.

Game 2. Wednesday, Sept. 30		R	H	E
Boston	201 002 000	5	10	0
Cleveland	151 001 01x	9	9	1

Wakefield (L), Wasdin (2), Lowe (4), Swindell (6), Gordon (8) and Varitek. Gooden, Burba (1-W), Shuey (6), Assenmacher (8), Jackson (8-SV) and Alomar. HR: Justice. T: 3.25. A: 45,229.

Game 3. Friday, Oct. 2	R	H	E
Cleveland 000 011 101	4	5	0
Boston 000 100 002	3	6	0

Nagy (W), Jackson (S-9) and Alomar. Saberhagen (L), Corsi (8), and Eckersley (9). HR: Thome, Lofton, Ramirez (2), and Garciaparra. T: 2.27. A: 33,114.

Game 4. Saturday, Oct. 3	R	H	E
Cleveland 000 000 020	2	5	0
Boston 000 100 000	1	6	0

Colon, Poole (6), Reed (7), Assenmacher (8), Shuey (8), Jackson (S-9) and Alomar. Schourek, Lowe (6), Gordon (8-L) and Hatteberg. HR: Garciaparra. T: 3.00. A: 33,537.

WORLD SERIES RECORD

1903. Hallo to historic firsts. Baseball's inaugural American League versus National League collision paired the Boston then-Pilgrims and favored Pittsburgh Pirates. To heck with Honus Wagner. The upstarts triumphed, five games to three.

Game 1. Thursday, Oct. 1	R	H	E
Pittsburgh 401 100 100	7	12	2
Boston 000 000 201	3	6	4

Phillippe (W) and Phelps. Young (L) and Criger. HR: Sebring. T: 1.55 A: 16,242.

Game 2. Friday, Oct. 2	R	H	E
Pittsburgh 000 000 000	0	3	2
Boston 200 001 00X	3	9	0

Leever (L), Veil (2) and Smith. Dinneen (W) and Criger. HR: Dougherty (2). T: 1:47. A: 9,415.

Game 3. Saturday, Oct. 3	R	H	E
Pittsburgh 012 000 010	4	7	0
Boston 000 100 010	2	4	2

Phillippe (W) and Phelps. Hughes (L), Young (3) and Criger. HR: None. T: 1.50. A: 18,010.

Game 4. Tuesday, Oct. 6	R	H	E
Boston 000 010 003	4	9	1
Pittsburgh 100 010 30X	5	12	1

Dinneen (L) and Criger. Phillippe (W) and Phelps. HR: None. T: 1.30.
A: 7,600.

Game 5. Wednesday, Oct. 7		R	H	E
Boston	000 006 410	11	14	2
Pittsburgh	000 000 020	2	6	4

Young (W) and Criger. Kennedy (L), Thompson (8) and Phelps. HR: None.
T: 2.00. A: 12,322.

Game 6. Thursday, Oct. 8		R	H	E
Boston	003 020 100	6	10	1
Pittsburgh	000 000 300	3	10	3

Dinneen (W) and Criger. Leever (L) and Phelps. HR: None. T: 2.02.
A: 11,556.

Game 7. Saturday, Oct. 10		R	H	E
Boston	200 202 010	7	11	4
Pittsburgh	000 101 001	3	10	3

Young (W) and Criger. Phillippe (L) and Phelps. HR: None. T: 1.45.
A: 17,038.

Game 8. Tuesday, Oct. 13		R	H	E
Pittsburgh	000 000 000	0	4	3
Boston	000 201 00x	3	8	0

Phillippe (L) and Phelps. Dinneen (W) and Criger. HR: None. T: 1.35.
A: 7,455.

1904. Since 1918, The Big Sox Fan in the Sky has denied Boston access to
the World Series tabernacle. Talk about overdue; He clearly owes us one.
Pittsburgh blackballed the '04 Series. God willing, assume the Sox would
have won.

1912. "To err(or) is (Fred) Snodgrass," Red Sox fans still proclaim. New
York's center fielder dropped a Game Eight, tenth-inning fly ball to key a
Boston rally. The Sox scored twice to win the game, 3–2, and their second
world championship.

Game 1. Tuesday, Oct. 8		R	H	E
Boston	000 001 300	4	8	1
New York	002 000 001	3	8	1

Wood (W) and Cady. Tesreau (L), Crandall (8) and Meyers. HR: None.
T: 2:10. A: 35,730.

Game 2. Wednesday, Oct. 9		R	H	E
New York	010 100 030 10	6	11	5
Boston	300 010 010 10	6	10	1

Mathewson and Wilson. Collins, Hall (8) and Bedient. HR: None. T: 2.38. A: 30,148.

Game 3. Thursday, Oct. 10		R	H	E
New York	010 010 000	2	7	1
Boston	000 000 001	1	7	0

Marquard (W) and Meyers. O'Brien (L), Bedient (9) and Carrigan, Cady (7). HR: None. T: 2.16. A: 34,624.

Game 4. Friday, Oct. 11		R	H	E
Boston	010 100 001	3	8	1
New York	000 000 100	1	9	1

Wood (W) and Cady. Tesreau (L), Ames (8) and Meyers. HR: None. T: 2.06. A: 36,502.

Game 5. Saturday, Oct. 12		R	H	E
New York	000 000 100	1	3	1
Boston	002 000 00x	2	5	1

Mathewson (L) and Meyers. Bedient (W) and Cady. HR: None. T: 1.43. A: 34,683.

Game 6. Monday, Oct. 14		R	H	E
Boston	020 000 000	2	7	2
New York	500 000 000	5	11	2

O'Brien (L), Collins (2) and Cady. Marquard (W) and Meyers. HR: None. T: 1.59. A: 30,622.

Game 7. Tuesday, Oct. 15		R	H	E
New York	610 002 101	11	18	4
Boston	010 000 210	4	9	3

Tesreau (W) and Wilson. Wood (L), Hall (2) and Cady. HR: Doyle, Gardner. T: 2.21. A: 32,694.

Game 8. Wednesday, Oct. 16		R	H	E
New York	001 000 000 1	2	9	2
Boston	000 000 100 2	3	8	5

Mathewson (L) and Meyers. Bedient, Wood (8-W) and Cady. HR: None. T: 2.39. A: 17,034.

1915. A year earlier, Philadelphia and Boston staged the Autumn Occasion. In '15, the same cities met again, but this time the Red Sox and Phillies, not the A's versus Braves. Four one-run victories sired the Sox' third Series title in as many tries.

Game 1. Friday, Oct. 8	R	H	E
Boston 000 000 010	1	8	1
Philadelphia 000 100 02x	3	5	1

Shore (L) and Cady. Alexander (W) and Burns. HR: None. T: 1.58. A: 19,343.

Game 2. Saturday, Oct. 9	R	H	E
Boston 100 000 001	2	10	0
Philadelphia 000 010 000	1	3	1

Foster (W) and Barry. Mayer (L) and Burns. HR: None. T: 2.05. A: 20,306.

Game 3. Monday, Oct. 11	R	H	E
Philadelphia 001 000 000	1	3	0
Boston 000 100 001	2	6	1

Alexander (L) and Burns. Leonard (W) and Carrigan. HR: None. T: 1.48. A: 42,200.

Game 4. Tuesday, Oct. 12	R	H	E
Philadelphia 000 000 010	1	7	0
Boston 001 001 00x	2	8	1

Chalmers (L) and Burns. Shore (W) and Cady. HR: None. T: 2.05. A: 41,096.

Game 5. Wednesday, Oct. 13	R	H	E
Boston 011 000 021	5	10	1
Philadelphia 200 200 000	4	9	1

Foster (W) and Cady. Mayer, Rixey (3-L) and Burns. HR: Hooper (2), Lewis, Luderus. T: 2.15. A: 26,306.

1916. As 1949–60 Yankees manager, Casey Stengel tormented the Hub. He did the same as a 1916 Brooklyn outfielder, batting a Series-high .364. The then-Robins flaunted Zach Wheat and Rube Marquard. Boston settled for its third world championship in five years.

Game 1. Saturday, Oct. 7	R	H	E
Brooklyn 000 100 004	5	10	4
Boston 001 010 31x	6	8	1

Marquard (L), Pfeffer (8) and Meyers. Shore (W), Mays (9) and Scott. HR: None. T: 2.16. A: 36,117.

Game 2. Monday, Oct. 9		R	H	E
Brooklyn	100 000 000 000 00	1	6	2
Boston	001 000 000 000 01	2	7	1

Smith (L) and Miller. Ruth (W) and Thomas. HR: Myers. T: 2.32. A: 41,373.

Game 3. Tuesday, Oct. 10		R	H	E
Boston	000 002 100	3	7	1
Brooklyn	001 120 00x	4	10	0

Mays (L), Foster (6) and Thomas. Coombs (W), Pfeffer (7) and Miller.
HR: Gardner. T: 2.01. A: 21,087.

Game 4. Wednesday, Oct. 11		R	H	E
Boston	030 110 100	6	10	1
Brooklyn	200 000 000	2	5	4

Leonard (W) and Carrigan. Marquard (L), Cheney (5), Rucker (8) and
Meyers. HR: Gardner. T: 2.36. A: 21,682.

Game 5. Thursday, Oct. 12		R	H	E
Brooklyn	010 000 000	1	3	3
Boston	012 010 00x	4	7	2

Pfeffer (L), Dell (8) and Meyers. Shore (W) and Cady. HR: None. T: 1.43.
A: 42,820.

1918. In the last year of the War to end All Wars, the Red Sox won perhaps
their last World Series of the twentieth century. Ironically, they defeated
another endearing munchkin of a team, the Chicago Cubs, four games
to two.

Game 1. Thursday, Sept. 5		R	H	E
Boston	000 100 000	1	5	0
Chicago	000 000 000	0	6	0

Ruth (W) and Agnew. Vaughn (L) and Killefer. HR: None. T: 1.50 A: 19,274.

Game 2. Friday, Sept. 6		R	H	E
Boston	000 000 001	1	6	1
Chicago	030 000 00x	3	7	0

Bush (L) and Agnew, Schang (8). Tyler (W) and Killefer. HR: None. T: 1.58.
A: 20,040.

Game 3. Saturday, Sept. 7		R	H	E
Boston	000 200 000	2	7	0
Chicago	000 010 000	1	7	1

Mays (W) and Schang. Vaughn (L) and Killefer. HR: None. T: 1.57.
A: 27,054.

Game 4. Monday, Sept. 9		R	H	E
Chicago	000 000 020	2	7	1
Boston	000 200 01x	3	4	0

Tyler, Douglas (8-L) and Killefer. Ruth (W), Bush (9) and Agnew,
Schang (8). HR: None. T: 1.50. A: 22,183.

Game 5. Tuesday, Sept. 10		R	H	E
Chicago	001 000 020	3	7	0
Boston	000 000 000	0	5	0

Vaughn (W) and Killefer. Jones (L) and Agnew, Schang (9). HR: None.
T: 1.42. A: 24,694.

Game 6. Wednesday, Sept. 11		R	H	E
Chicago	000 100 000	1	3	2
Boston	002 000 00x	2	5	0

Tyler (L), Hendrix (8) and Killefer, O'Farrell (8). Mays (W) and Schang.
HR: None. 1.46. A: 15,238.

1946. Baseball's first post–World War II World Series pit its eastern and
westernmost settlements, who staged a rapt affair. The Cardinals beat the
Red Sox, four games to three—Boston's first loss in six World Series.

Game 1. Sunday, Oct. 6		R	H	E
Boston	010 000 001 1	3	9	2
St. Louis	000 001 010 0	2	7	0

Hughson, Johnson (9-W) and H. Wagner, Partee (9). Pollet (L) and
Garagiola. HR: York. T: 2.39. A: 36,218.

Game 2. Monday, Oct. 7		R	H	E
Boston	000 000 000	0	4	1
St. Louis	001 020 00x	3	6	0

Harris (L), Dobson (8) and Partee, H. Wagner (6). Brecheen (W) and Rice.
HR: None. T: 1.56. A: 35,815.

Game 3. Wednesday, Oct. 9		R	H	E
St. Louis	000 000 000	0	6	1
Boston	300 000 01x	4	8	0

Dickson (L), Wilks (8) and Garagiola. Ferriss (W) and H. Wagner. HR: York.
T: 1.54. A: 34,500.

Game 4. Thursday, Oct. 10	R	H	E
St. Louis 033 010 104	12	20	1
Boston 000 100 020	3	9	4

Munger (W) and Garagiola. Hughson (L), Bagby (3), Zuber (6), Brown (8), Ryba (9), Dreisewerd (9) and H. Wagner. HR: Slaughter, Doerr. T: 2.31. A: 35,645.

Game 5. Friday, Oct. 11	R	H	E
St. Louis 010 000 002	3	4	1
Boston 110 001 30x	6	11	3

Pollet, Brazle (1-L), Beazley (8) and Garagiola. Dobson (W) and Partee. HR: Culberson. T: 2.23. A: 35,982.

Game 6. Sunday, Oct. 13	R	H	E
Boston 000 000 100	1	7	0
St. Louis 003 000 01x	4	8	0

Harris (L), Hughson (3), Johnson (8) and Partee. Brecheen (W) and Rice. HR: None. T: 1.56. A: 35,768.

Game 7. Tuesday, Oct. 15	R	H	E
Boston 100 000 020	3	8	0
St. Louis 010 020 01x	4	9	1

Ferriss, Dobson (5), Klinger (8-L), Johnson (8) and H. Wagner, Partee (8). Dickson, Brecheen (8-W) and Garagiola, Rice (8). HR: None. T: 2.17. A: 36,143.

1967. Ask anyone who was born, say, before JFK became president. Gallant and almost mystical, the '67 Red Sox engrossed New England. The Cardiac Kids won the pennant on the final day and then lost a World Series no one expected them to get near.

Game 1. Wednesday, Oct. 4	R	H	E
St. Louis 001 000 100	2	10	0
Boston 001 000 000	1	6	0

B. Gibson (W) and McCarver. Santiago (L), Wyatt (8) and R. Gibson, Howard (9). HR: Santiago. T: 2.22. A: 34,796.

Game 2. Thursday, Oct. 5	R	H	E
St. Louis 000 000 000	0	1	1
Boston 000 101 30x	5	9	0

Hughes (L), Willis (6), Hoerner (7), Lamabe (7) and McCarver. Lonborg (W) and Howard. HR: Yastrzemski (2). T: 2.24. A: 35,188.

Game 3. Saturday, Oct. 7		R	H	E
Boston	000 001 100	2	7	1
St. Louis	120 001 01X	5	10	0

Bell (L), Waslewski (3), Stange (6), Osinski (8) and Howard. Briles (W) and McCarver. HR: Shannon, Smith. T: 2.15. A: 54,575.

Game 4. Sunday, Oct. 8		R	H	E
Boston	000 000 000	0	5	0
St. Louis	402 000 00X	6	9	0

Santiago (L), Bell (1), Stephenson (3), Morehead (5), Brett (8) and Howard, Ryan (5). B. Gibson (W) and McCarver. HR: None. T: 2.05. A: 54,575.

Game 5. Monday, Oct. 9		R	H	E
Boston	001 000 002	3	6	1
St. Louis	000 000 001	1	3	2

Lonborg (W) and Howard. Carlton (L), Washburn (7), Willis (9), Lamabe (9) and McCarver. HR: Maris. T: 2.20. A: 54,575.

Game 6. Wednesday, Oct. 11		R	H	E
St. Louis	002 000 200	4	8	0
Boston	010 300 40X	8	12	1

Hughes, Willis (4), Briles (5), Lamabe (7-L), Hoerner (7), Jaster (7), Washburn (7), Woodeshick (8) and McCarver. Waslewski, Wyatt (6-W), Bell (8) and Howard. HR: Petrocelli (2), Yastrzemski, Smith, Brock. T: 2.48. A: 35,188.

Game 7. Thursday, Oct. 12		R	H	E
St. Louis	002 023 000	7	10	1
Boston	000 010 010	2	3	1

B. Gibson (W) and McCarver. Lonborg (L), Santiago (7), Morehead (9), Osinski (9), Brett (9) and Howard, R. Gibson (9). HR: B. Gibson, Javier. T: 2.23. A: 35,188.

1975. "I may not have been the greatest pitcher ever, but I was amongst 'em," Dizzy Dean often said. The Reds–Red Sox classic of a Classic may or may not be the greatest World Series ever. But it is amongst 'em, then and now.

Game 1. Saturday, Oct. 11		R	H	E
Cincinnati	000 000 000	0	5	0
Boston	000 000 60X	6	12	0

Gullett (L), Carroll (7), McEnaney (7) and Bench. Tiant (W) and Fisk.
HR: None. T: 2.27. A: 35,205.

Game 2. Sunday, Oct. 12		R	H	E
Cincinnati	000 100 002	3	7	1
Boston	100 001 000	2	7	0

Billingham, Borbon (6), McEnaney (7), Eastwick (9-W) and Bench.
Lee, Drago (9-L) and Fisk. HR: None. T: 2.38. A: 35,205.

Game 3. Tuesday, Oct. 14		R	H	E
Boston	010 001 102 0	5	10	2
Cincinnati	000 230 000 1	6	7	0

Wise, Burton (5), Cleveland (5), Willoughby (7-L), Moret (10) and Fisk.
Nolan, Darcy (5), Carroll (7), McEnaney (7), Eastwick (9-W) and Bench.
HR: Fisk, Carbo, Evans, Bench, Concepcion, Geronimo. T: 3.03. A: 55,392.

Game 4. Wednesday, Oct. 15		R	H	E
Boston	000 500 000	5	11	1
Cincinnati	200 200 000	4	9	1

Tiant (W) and Fisk. Norman (L), Borbon (4), Carroll (5), Eastwick (7) and
Bench. HR: None. T: 2.52. A: 55,667.

Game 5. Thursday, Oct. 16		R	H	E
Boston	100 000 001	2	5	0
Cincinnati	000 113 01x	6	8	0

Cleveland (L), Willoughby (6), Pole (8), Segui (8) and Fisk. Gullett (W),
Eastwick (9-sv) and Bench. HR: Perez (2). T: 2.23. A: 56,393.

Game 6. Tuesday, Oct. 21		R	H	E
Cincinnati	000 030 210 000	6	14	0
Boston	300 000 030 001	7	10	1

Nolan, Norman (3), Billingham (3), Carroll (5), Borbon (6), Eastwick (8),
McEnaney (9), Darcy (10–L) and Bench. Tiant, Moret (8), Drago (9), Wise
(12-W) and Fisk. HR: Lynn, Geronimo, Carbo, Fisk. T: 4.01. A: 35,205.

Game 7. Wednesday, Oct. 22		R	H	E
Cincinnati	000 002 101	4	9	0
Boston	003 000 000	3	5	2

Gullett, Billingham (5), Carroll (7-W), McEnaney (9-sv) and Bench. Lee,
Moret (7), Willoughby (7), Burton (9-L), Cleveland (9) and Fisk. HR: Perez.
T: 2.52. A: 35,205.

1986. In *The Gathering Storm*, Winston Churchill wrote, "Without measureless and perpetual uncertainty, the drama of human life would be destroyed." Was he portending the upheaval of the Ground Ball Heard 'Round the World?

Game 1. Saturday, Oct. 18		R	H	E
Boston	000 000 100	1	5	0
New York	000 000 000	0	4	1

Hurst (W), Schiraldi (9-sv) and Gedman. Darling (L), McDowell (8) and Carter. HR: None. T: 2.59. A: 55,076.

Game 2. Sunday, Oct. 19		R	H	E
Boston	003 120 201	9	18	0
New York	002 010 000	3	8	1

Clemens, Crawford (5-W), Stanley (7-sv) and Gedman. Gooden (L), Aguilera (6), Orosco (7), Fernandez (9), Sisk (9) and Carter. HR: Henderson, Evans. T: 3.36. A: 55,063.

Game 3. Tuesday, Oct. 21		R	H	E
New York	400 000 210	7	13	0
Boston	001 000 000	1	5	1

Ojeda (W), McDowell (8) and Carter. Boyd (L), Sambito (8), Stanley (8) and Gedman. HR: Dykstra. T: 2.58. A: 33,595.

Game 4. Wednesday, Oct. 22		R	H	E
New York	000 300 210	6	12	0
Boston	000 000 020	2	7	1

Darling (W), McDowell (8), Orosco (8-sv) and Carter. Nipper (L), Crawford (7), Stanley (9) and Gedman. HR: Carter (2), Dykstra. T: 3.22. A: 33,920.

Game 5. Thursday, Oct. 23		R	H	E
New York	000 000 011	2	10	1
Boston	011 020 00X	4	12	0

Gooden (L), Fernandez (5) and Carter. Hurst (W) and Gedman. HR: Teufel. T: 3.09. A: 34,010.

Game 6. Saturday, Oct. 25		R	H	E
Boston	110 000 100 2	5	13	2
New York	000 020 010 3	6	8	0

Clemens, Schiraldi (8-L), Stanley (10) and Gedman. Ojeda, McDowell (7), Orosco (8), Aguilera (9-W) and Carter. HR: Henderson. T: 4.02. A: 55,078.

Game 7. Monday, Oct. 27		R	H	E
Boston	030 000 020	5	9	0
New York	000 003 320	8	10	0

Hurst, Schiraldi (7-L), Sambito (7), Stanley (7), Nipper (8), Crawford (8) and Gedman. Darling, Fernandez (4), McDowell (7-W), Orosco (8-sv) and Carter. HR: Evans, Gedman, Knight, Strawberry. T: 3.11. A: 55,032.

APPENDIX B: FENWAY PARK PASTICHE

Address: 4 Yawkey Way, Boston, Massachusetts 02215-3496. Phone: (617) 267-9440. For tour information: (617) 236-6666. Fax: (617) 236-6640. Website: http://www.redsox.com.

Constructed in 1912 and named Fenway Park by then–Sox owner John Taylor because "It's in the Fenway section [of Boston], isn't it? Then call it Fenway Park." Rebuilt in 1934 by new owner Thomas Yawkey. Opened on April 20, 1912, with a 7–6 Sox victory over the New York Highlanders.

Dimensions: Left-field line—310 feet. Left-center field—379. Center field—390. Deep center field—420. Right-center field—380. Right-field line—302. Heights of fences: Left-field wall—37 feet (screen extends 23 feet, 7 inches). Center-field wall—17 feet. Bull pens—5 feet. Right-field wall—3–5 feet. Turf: Grass.

Seating capacity: roof, 2,168; boxes, 13,121; reserved grandstand, 12,075; bleachers, 6,507. Daytime total: 33,455. Nighttime total: 33,871.

Ticket information: (617) 267-8661. Hours: Monday-Saturday, 9 A.M.– 5 P.M. Mail orders to Red Sox Tickets at address above. Prices—field box, $35; loge box and infield roof, $32; right-field box and right-field roof, $26; grandstand, $24; outfield grandstand, $18; lower bleacher, $14; upper bleacher, $12.

BEST FENWAY BATTING AVERAGE (200 AT BATS)

Ted Williams—.428 (1941) and .403 (1951 and 1957). Wade Boggs—.418 (1985), .411 (1987), and .397 (1983). Jimmie Foxx—.405 (1938). Dom DiMaggio—.397 (1950). Tris Speaker—.392 (1912).

LIFETIME FENWAY HOME RUNS

Ted Williams—248 Fenway homers (521 as member of Red Sox overall). Carl Yastrzemski—237 (452). Jim Rice—208 (382). Dwight Evans—199 (379). Bobby Doerr—145 (223). Rico Petrocelli—134 (210). Jimmie Foxx—126 (222). Mo Vaughn—118 (230). Carlton Fisk—90 (162). George Scott—90 (154). Tony Conigliaro—87 (162). Jackie Jensen—86 (170). Reggie Smith—76 (149). Joe Cronin—74 (119). Vern Stephens—70 (122). Fred Lynn—69 (124). Frank Malzone—68 (131). Dick Gernert—66 (101). Mike Greenwell—64 (130). John Valentin—56 (106). Tony Armas—54 (113).

OPPONENTS' LIFETIME FENWAY HOME RUNS

Babe Ruth—38, 1920–34. Mickey Mantle—38, 1951–68. Harmon Killebrew—37, 1954–75. Lou Gehrig—30, 1923–39. Al Kaline—30, 1953–74. Joe DiMaggio—29, 1936–51. Gus Zernial—28, 1949–59. Rocky Colavito—26, 1955–68. Willie Horton—26, 1963–80. Reggie Jackson—25, 1967–87. Roy Sievers—25, 1949–65. Vic Wertz—25, 1947–58 and 1961–63. (Ruth also hit 11 home runs at Fenway Park for the 1914–19 Red Sox. Wertz also hit 24 homers at Fenway for the 1959–61 Sox.)

SINGLE-SEASON RED SOX HOME RUNS

The Fenway Park single-season record for homers is Jimmie Foxx's 35 in 1938. Fred Lynn holds the record for left-handed batters with 28 in 1979. Mo Vaughn (1996), Lynn (1978), and Jim Rice (1978 and '79) are tied with 27 Fenway homers. The Sox road high for homers is 26 by Ted Williams in 1957. Close behind are Vaughn (24 in 1995), Rice (23, 1983), Tony Armas (22, 1984), and Don Baylor (22, 1986). Williams also smashed 20 away from Fenway in 1942-46-49. The only other Red Sox players to hit 20 away home runs were Babe Ruth (1919), Jimmie Foxx (1936), Dwight Evans (1987), and Vaughn (1997).

SINGLE-SEASON OPPONENTS' HOME RUNS AT FENWAY

Babe Ruth—8, 1927, Yankees. Joe Carter—7, 1987, Indians. Vic Wertz—7, 1957, Indians. Harmon Killebrew—6, 1963, Twins. Mickey Mantle—6, 1961, Yankees. Pat Seerey—6, 1944, Indians. Hank Greenberg—6, 1937, Tigers. Lou Gehrig—6, 1927, Yankees.

OPPONENTS' THREE HOMERS IN FENWAY GAME

Lou Gehrig—6/23/27, New York. Ken Keltner—5/25/39, Cleveland. Bobby Avila—6/20/51, Cleveland. Harmon Killebrew—9/21/63, Minnesota. Boog Powell—8/15/66, Baltimore. Bill Freehan—8/9/71, Detroit. Fred Patek—6/20/80, California. Joe Carter—8/29/86 and 5/82/87, Cleveland. Tim Raines—4/18/94, Chicago. Mark McGwire—6/11/95, Oakland. Frank Thomas—9/15/96, Chicago.

RED SOX' THREE HOMERS IN FENWAY GAME

Ted Williams—7/14/46, Cleveland. Bobby Doerr—6/8/50, St. Louis. Clyde Vollmer—7/26/51, Chicago. Norm Zauchin—5/27/55, Washington. Jim Rice—8/29/77, Oakland. Tom Brunansky—9/29/90, Toronto. Jack Clark—7/31/91, Oakland. John Valentin—6/2/95, Seattle. Mo Vaughn—9/24/96, Baltimore, and 5/30/97, New York Yankees.

RED SOX LEFT-HANDERS AT FENWAY

Lefty Grove—.764 (55–17), 1934–41. Roger Moret—.720 (18–7), 1970–75. Babe Ruth—.710 (49–20), 1914–19. Mel Parnell—.703 (71–30), 1947–56. Joe Hesketh—.643 (18–10), 1990–94. Sparky Lyle—.640 (16–9), 1967–71. John Tudor—.639 (23–13), 1979–83. Bruce Hurst—.629 (56–33), 1980–88. Bill Lee—.623 (48–29), 1969–78. Herb Pennock—.597 (37–25), 1916–22. Ray Collins—.585 (24–17), 1912–15. Dutch Leonard—.564 (44–34), 1913–18. Bob Ojeda—.541 (20–17), 1980–85.

FENWAY PARK ATTENDANCE

All-time record: 47,627 (New York, doubleheader, September 22, 1935); 46,995 (Detroit, doubleheader, August 19, 1934); 46,766 (New York, doubleheader, August 12, 1934). Postwar and single-game record: 36,388 (Cleveland, April 22, 1978). Opening Day record: 35,343 (Baltimore, April 14, 1969). Night game record: 36,228 (New York, June 28, 1949).

BEST FENWAY ATTENDANCE FOR THREE-DATE SERIES, 1967–98

1. 105,582 v. Toronto, September 28–30, 1990. 2. 105,271, Baltimore, August 20–22, 1990. 3. 105,168, Toronto, August 14–16, 1989. 4. 105,072, Kansas

City, July 28–30, 1978. 5. 105,037, Detroit, August 15–17, 1986. 6. 104,852, Oakland, August 23–25, 1974. 7. 104,752, New York, June 23–25, 1986. 8. 104,404, New York, August 31–September 2, 1990. 9. 104,349, Baltimore, June 20–22, 1986. 10. 104,339, Kansas City, August 1–3, 1986. 11. Chicago, 104,338, July 21–23, 1989. 12. 104,280, Baltimore, June 24–26, 1988. 13. 104,154, Chicago, July 30–August 1, 1990. 14. 104,151, Detroit, August 3–4, 1990. 15. 103,910, New York, June 17–19, 1977.

BEST FENWAY ATTENDANCE FOR FOUR-DATE SERIES, 1967–98

1. 140,743, New York, September 15–18, 1988. 2. 138,810, Baltimore, July 31–August 2, 1989. 3. 138,293, Oakland, July 16–19, 1987. 4. 137,560, Oakland, July 22–25, 1993. 5. 137,360, Detroit, August 25–28, 1989. 6. 136,364, Chicago, August 16–19, 1979. 7. 136,171, New York, June 26–29, 1975. 8. 136,165, New York, June 15–18, 1992. 9. 136,165, Cleveland, August 3–6, 1989. 10. 135,987, Oakland, June 20–23, 1991. 11. 135,696, Detroit, July 4–7, 1991. 12. 135,520, Baltimore, May 30–June 2, 1991. 13. 135,188, Texas, June 29–July 2, 1990. 14. 135,155, Chicago, July 9–12, 1992. 15. 135,106, Baltimore, August 10–13, 1995. 16. 134,252, Seattle, July 15–18, 1993. 17. 134,242, Minnesota, July 18–21, 1991. 18. 133,903, Cleveland, April 11–15, 1991. 19. 133,650, New York, September 7–10, 1978. 20. 133,437, New York, September 11–14, 1980. 21. 133,343, Toronto, June 26–28, 1990. 22. 133,289, Baltimore, July 18–21, 1996. 23. 133,251, Seattle, July 7–10, 1994. 24. 132,835, Baltimore, June 10–13, 1993. 25. 132,143, New York, June 27–30, 1994. 26. 132,109, California, June 14–17, 1991. 27. 132,087, Baltimore, September 7–10, 1979. 28. 132,085, New York, June 4–7, 1990. 29. 132,017, Detroit, June 18–21, 1979.

1967–98 BEST FENWAY ATTENDANCE

1. 36,388, Cleveland, April 22, 1978. 2. 36,296, Cleveland, April 23, 1978 (doubleheader). 3. 35,939, New York, May 31, 1976. 4. 35,869, New York, May 17, 1968. 5. 35,866, Baltimore, August 4, 1975. 6. 35,866, Oakland, August 23, 1974. 7. 35,853, Baltimore, August 5, 1975. 8. 35,852, Detroit, August 16, 1968. 9. 35,783, Minnesota, July 7, 1968 (doubleheader). 10. 35,748, Kansas City, August 16, 1977. 11. 35,735, Toronto, September 29, 1990. 12. 35,716, Kansas City, August 1, 1986. 13. 35,714, Oakland, May 28, 1971. 14. 35,710, Detroit, May 2, 1969. 15. 35,707, Baltimore, June 21, 1986.

16. 35,691, California, August 11, 1977. 17. 35,689, New York, September 11, 1979. 18. 35,664, Toronto, June 15, 1985. 19. 35,643, Baltimore, June 30, 1985. 20. 35,634, Minnesota, May 30, 1969. 21. 35,610, New York, May 19, 1968. 22. 35,599, Chicago, July 30, 1990. 23. 35,522, Chicago, August 1, 1990. 24. 35,478, Milwaukee, April 16, 1990. 25. 35,458, New York, September 2, 1990. 26. 35,444, Toronto, September 29, 1990. 27. 35,408, Oakland, September 4, 1990. 28. 35,310, Toronto, August 16, 1989.

ABOUT THE AUTHOR

Curt Smith is an author, radio/television commentator, TV documentarian, and former presidential speechwriter. *Our House* is his eighth book. Others include *Voices of the Game* ("monumental," said *Publisher's Weekly*), *Windows on the White House* ("elegantly written," hailed the *New York Daily News*), and *Long Time Gone* ("entrancing," said *Time* columnist Hugh Sidey).

Mr. Smith is the Senior Lecturer in English at the University of Rochester. In 1998, his regular commentary for Rochester's National Public Radio affiliate, WXXI, was voted best in New York State by the Associated Press and the New York State Broadcasters Association. He hosts a daily talk show on Rochester CNN Radio affiliate WYSL and contributes to ESPN-TV, the Empire Sports TV Network, and *Reader's Digest*.

From 1989 to 1993, Mr. Smith wrote more speeches than anyone for President George Bush. Among them were the "Just War" Persian Gulf address; Nixon and Reagan Library dedication speeches; and the emotional December 7, 1991, speech aboard the USS *Missouri* at Pearl Harbor, called by many the finest speech of the Bush presidency.

Prior to the White House, Mr. Smith served as senior editor of the *Saturday Evening Post* magazine and chief speechwriter in President Reagan's cabinet. Since leaving the Bush Administration, he has hosted series at the Smithsonian Institution, hosted a daily talk show over Milwaukee's 50,000-watt affiliate WISN, and created and written three prime-time ESPN documentaries based upon his book *Voices of the Game*. Most recently, he has helped to write the ABC/ESPN-TV documentaries *Greatest Games* and *Greatest Coaches* of the century.

Mr. Smith has written for the *Boston Globe*, *New York Times*, *Washington Post*, *Newsweek*, and *Sports Illustrated*. Raised in Caledonia, New York, the 1973 SUNY at Geneseo graduate has been named among the "one hundred Outstanding Alumni" of New York's State University System, is a member of the Judson Welliver Society of former White House speechwriters, and lives with his wife, Sarah, in Rochester.